GARDENS OF THE RIGHTEOUS

GARDENS OF THE RIGHTEOUS

Riyadh as-Salihin
of Imam Nawawi

Translated from the Arabic by
MUHAMMAD ZAFRULLA KHAN

With a Foreword by
C. E. BOSWORTH
Professor of Arabic Studies
in the University of Manchester

1996
ISLAM INTERNATIONAL PUBLICATIONS LTD.

Gardens of the Righteous
(Riadh as-Salihin)

Published with the Permission of Curzon Press by:
Islam International Publications Limited
'Islamabad', Sheephatch Lane
Tilford, Surrey GU10 2AQ U.K.

First Published 1975
Reprinted 1980
Reprinted 1989
Reprinted 1996

© Muhammad Zafrulla Khan

ISBN 1 85372 568 4
(Curzon Press edition ISBN 0 7007 0073 0)

Printed and bound by Unwin Brothers Ltd.,
The Gresham Press, Old Woking, Surrey GU22 9LH
A Member of the Martins Printing Group

CONTENTS

FOREWORD

It has long been recognised by western scholars how valuable is the vast corpus of *Hadith* (sc. the sayings of the Prophet, his companions, the early Caliphs and other leading Muslim scholars) for the study of early Islam. The pioneer efforts of the great Hungarian orientalist Ignaz Goldziher — now available in English as Volume II of his *Muslim Studies* (London 1971) — demonstrated how much light these traditions threw on the religious development of Islam and on the political and sectarian disputes of its first three, formative centuries. Subsequent scholars like the late Joseph Schacht have examined critically the body of *Hadith* and have corrected some of the misconceptions which had arisen over its historical interpretation; the results of these inquiries were embodied in his difficult but very significant book, *The Origins of Muhammadan Jurisprudence* (Oxford 1950).

Yet the average Muslim believer knows the *Hadith* not as a historical document, but as a fundamental element in the vital fabric of his faith, which has been second only to the direct revelation of God in the Qur'an itself. For the Muslim community, the *Hadith* has traditionally provided a norm of conduct and behaviour in the ethical sphere, and a source of legal prescriptions in the practical one, a means of following the *sunna* or example of the Prophet and of the generations of pious, early Muslims, *as-salaf as-salihun*. Where the Qur'an has not been explicit, the *Hadith* has often supplied guidance, providing an intermediate source of knowledge between the text of the Holy Book itself and the ratiocinations of the religious lawyers, the *fuqaha'*, who had recourse, when all else failed, to such principles as analogical reasoning and personal judgement.

However, it is not easy for the Muslim today, even if he be a native Arabic speaker, to read the *Hadith;* the language is archaic and at times difficult, and indeed, philologists and grammarians of the classical period came to regard the *Hadith* as a valuable quarry for rare words. Although many translations of *Hadith* collections, or of selections from it, have been made into the other great Islamic languages like Turkish, Persian and Urdu, there are few available in western European languages. The most important of these is the French translation by O. Houdas and W. Marçais of the *Sahih* of Bukhari, as *Les traditions islamiques* (Paris 1903-14, 4 vols.). Also, various of the anthologies of Islamic religious and devotional literature in translation devote some space to the *Hadith;* especially valuable here is the section on Tradition in the late Arthur Jeffery's *A Reader on Islam* (The Hague 1962), pp. 79-250.

The present book provides a translation by Muhammad Zafrulla Khan (who has already given us a translation of the Qur'an, *The Quran,* Curzon Press, London 1971) of the *Riyad as-Salihin,* literally "Gardens of the Righteous",

written by the Syrian Shafi'i scholar Muhyi ad-Din Abu Zakariyya' Yahya b.
Sharaf an-Nawawi (1233-78), who was the author of a large number of legal and
biographical works, including a celebrated collection of forty well-known
hadiths, the *Kitab al-Arba'in* (actually containing some forty-three traditions),
much commented upon in the Muslim countries and translated into several
European languages. His *Riyad as-Salihin* is a concise collection of traditions,
which has been printed on various occasions, e.g. at Mecca and Cairo, but never
before translated into a western language. Hence the present translation by
Muhammad Zafrulla Khan will make available to those unversed in Arabic one
of the most typical and widely-known collections of this type.

Manchester, 1974   C. E. BOSWORTH

INTRODUCTION

The Holy Quran is the one fundamental source of all Islamic values. These values were illustrated in the life of the Holy Prophet (on whom be peace): You have in the Messenger of Allah an excellent exemplar for him who hopes to meet Allah and the Last Day, and who remembers Allah much (33.22). O ye who believe, obey Allah and obey His Messenger and those who are in authority among you. Then if you differ in anything, refer it to Allah and His Messenger if you are believers in Allah and the Last Day. That is the best and most commendable in the end (4.60).

The object of human existence being the winning of Allah's pleasure, the means for the attainment thereof is obedience to Allah, and the visible illustration of that ideal is to be found in the Holy Prophet. Announce: If you love Allah, then follow me, Allah will then love you, and forgive you your faults. Allah is Most Forgiving, Ever Merciful. Call on them: Obey Allah and the Messenger, then if they turn away, let them remember that Allah loves not the disbelievers (3.32-33). Whatever the Messenger gives you, that take; and whatsoever he forbids you, from that abstain. Be mindful of your duty to Allah. Surely Allah is Severe in retribution (59.8).

The highest spiritual rewards are attainable only through obedience to Allah and the Messenger: Whoso obeys Allah and the Messenger shall be among those upon whom Allah has bestowed His favours — the Prophets, the Faithful ones, the Martyrs and the Righteous — and excellent companions these are. This is Allah's grace and Allah is All-Comprehending (7.70-71).

It thus became necessary that a group of people should be trained and disciplined in Islamic values by the Holy Prophet both by his precept and his example. In the discharge of this assignment all directions given by the Holy Prophet were binding and were revered and carried out as having the authority of the Divine in their support, for in carrying out his prophetic functions the Holy Prophet was an instrument of the Divine: He does not speak out of his own desire; it is revelation sent down to him (53.4-5).

It had to be so, for obvious reasons. The Holy Quran left many matters to be regulated by the Holy Prophet. The *Salat* was prescribed very early in the Meccan period but the content and the manner of the performance of the services was left to be prescribed and illustrated by the Holy Prophet. That is why through the centuries and throughout the House of Islam, the five daily services have followed the pattern set by the Holy Prophet. The same applies to the Fast of Ramadhan and indeed to all ordinances and prohibitions of Islam.

The warp and woof of the Islamic pattern of life is, therefore, furnished by the Holy Quran and the *Sunnah* (precept and example) of the Holy Prophet. The source of the Sunnah, the indispensable complement and illustration of the Quran, is the *Hadith*, that is to say, whatever the Holy Prophet said or did or abstained from in his capacity as the Excellent Exemplar, the following of whose example was the source of all blessing and the way of winning through to the pleasure and love of the Divine. It is understandable, therefore, how keenly the Companions of the Holy Prophet watched his every gesture and drank in and preserved the memory of every word that he uttered. It is due to this keen watchfulness on the part of his devoted followers that we have a complete picture available to us, in its minutest detail, of the life of the Holy Prophet.

The Quran is the code, the Sunnah of the Prophet is its illustration. The Holy Prophet cautioned his Companions to be extremely careful in watching, listening to, and reporting whatever he said or did or abstained from. To make assurance doubly sure, he laid down the criterion that if anything attributed to him was not in accord with the Quran it was to be rejected as not proceeding from him. This criterion prescribed by the Prophet himself is a wholesome safeguard in judging the weight and value of what might be ascribed to him.

With the early and rapid spread of the dominion of Islam, the need of an authentic record of the Sunnah of the Prophet began to be insistent, and it became meritorious to report from mouth to mouth whatever came to anyone's knowledge having a bearing upon the Sunnah. A large part of this related to the niceties of juristic definition and interpretation. With that we are not here primarily concerned. We are concerned here, mainly, with that part of the Sunnah which illustrates the carrying into effect of moral and spiritual values.

There began to emerge fairly early a Science of Tradition. It is not necessary for our purpose to describe it in detail; suffice it to say that it concentrated mainly on examining and checking on the chain of narrators of a hadith. If a single link in the chain was judged weak or defective, the whole was rejected. Despite great care taken in that regard, and the use of a wise discretion in other respects, an enormous store of Tradition began to be accumulated as time passed.

The first great Teacher of Tradition was the revered founder of the Maliki School of Jurisprudence, Imam Malik ibn Anas. His collection of hadith known as the Muwatta of Imam Malik ranks with the most authentic compilations of hadith which had become known as the *Sahih Sitta*, i.e. the Six Authentic Compilations. These were the *Sahih* of Bokhari, Muslim, Tirmidhi, Abu Daud, Nisai and Ibn Majah. The best known traditions are often found in two or more of these compilations. It is rare for a tradition to have been included only in one of them. It does not follow, however, that for that reason the authority of the particular hadith is in any way reduced. There are other criteria to be applied for judging the weight and value of a tradition included in the Sahih. This enormous collection of tradition, though freely available in Arabic, could not be easily mastered even by devout scholars, more particularly as a large number of comentaries on the Sahih began to be compiled and were circulated. The need thus arose of briefer compilations designed to serve limited purposes. Of these, one of the most useful and popular is that known as *Riyadh as-Salihin*, of which an English translation is, for the first time, here respectfully presented.

Riyadh as-Salihin is a selection of hadith made by Imam Muhyi ad-Din Abu Zakariyya Yahya ibn Sharaf an-Nawawi; for short, Imam Nawawi. Imam Nawawi was born in the village of Nawa in the vicinity of Damascus in 631 A.H. (= A.D. 1233). He grew up in Nawa and at the age of nineteen moved into Damascus where he completed his studies and later wrote on and taught all the subjects which were then current among religious scholars of that age. At one time he was attracted to the study of medicine but soon abandoned the attempt as he thought that it would distract his mind and wean it away from the study and pursuit of subjects in which he was more vitally interested. Imam Nawawi led a life of singular piety, righteousness, simplicity and concentration on the spiritual. He left behind a large number of valuable works on different topics, the best known of which is his Commentary on the Sahih of Muslim. He also wrote a Commentary on a part of the Sahih of Bokhari.

Ryadh as-Salihin is a selection from the Sahih and one or two other works on hadith, among them the Muwatta of Imam Malik. The greater part of the hadith included in the *Riyadh as-Salihin* is a selection from Bokhari and Muslim; most of these are to be found in both. Most sections of *Riyadh as-Salihin* set out the relevant verses from the Holy Quran at the outset of the section, as emphasising that the Sunnah of the Holy Prophet is an illustration of the values inculcated by the Quran. It was inescapable that some of the traditions relevant to more sections than one would be repeated. In such cases, repetition has been largely avoided in the translation by furnishing cross references.

Imam Nawawi, the saintly scholar, died at the early age of forty-six in 676 A.H. (= A.D. 1278) in the village of his birth, and was deeply mourned by all sections of Muslim society in Damascus.

We set out below in an English translation the preface written by Imam Nawawi to the *Riyadh as-Salihin:*

'In the name of Allah, Most Gracious, Ever Merciful.

'All praise belongs to God, the One, the Mighty, the Supreme, the Most Forgiving and Forbearing, Who makes the night follow the day so that it would be an admonition and warning for those who have been blessed with insight and should be a lesson for the wise and far-sighted. He it is Who chooses whom He wills and awakens them from the sleep of neglect and bestows upon them the bounty of piety and enables them to be occupied with reflection and observation, and equips them with the capacity to retrace their steps after a mistake and to accept and follow good advice. He enables them to worship Him, to prepare for the hereafter and to be constant in the pursuit of these objectives. I praise Him in the most eloquent, pure and comprehensive terms.

'I bear witness that there is no one worthy of worship save God alone Who is Holy, Noble, Gracious and Merciful. I bear witness that our lord and master is His Servant and Messenger and His friend and loved one, who points out the straight path and calls people to the true faith. May Allah have mercy on him and on all Prophets and the righteous and their descendants.

'After praise of Allah and calling down blessings on the Holy Prophet I proceed. Allah has affirmed: I have created men, high and low, so that they might worship Me. I desire no support from them, nor do I desire that they should feed Me (51.57-58). These verses clearly establish that the purpose of man's creation is that he should obey God. It is, therefore, imperative that he should keep this purpose constantly in mind and should pay no attention to worldly adornment and ornament, for this home is not eternal and this is not a place of permanent abode. This world is merely a means of conveyance to the hereafter. This is not a place of joy and happiness. The highway of this life will abandon one at a certain turn, it will not keep one company forever. Then those are awake who pass their life in worship and obedience, and those are wise and reasonable who make righteousness their rule of life.

'The Holy Quran describes the transitory character of the hither life in the following terms: The life of this world is like water that We send down from the clouds, then the vegetation of the earth, of which men and cattle eat, mingles with it and the earth is embellished and looks beautiful, and its owners believe that they are its complete masters; then by day or by night, Our command comes to it and We convert it into a mown-down field, as if nothing had existed there the day before. Thus do We expound the Signs for a people who reflect (10.25).

'There are numerous verses in the Quran to the same purpose. A poet has said in the same context: There are many wise servants of Allah who have withdrawn from the world being apprehensive of its trials and tribulations. When they looked deeply into the world they realized that it was not man's true home. They took it as a deep ocean and raised in it the anchors of vessels equipped with righteous deeds.

'Thus the world being transitory and the purpose of our creation being such as I have set out, it becomes the duty of every wise adult Muslim to follow the way of the chosen ones and adopt the methods of men of wisdom and understanding and to be occupied in preparing for the attainment of the purpose to which I have drawn attention, keeping in mind that which I have pointed out. The best and most correct way to be adopted for the attainment of this purpose is total obedience to the Holy Prophet.

'God has commanded: Assist one another in piety and rectitude (5.2); and the Holy Prophet has said: So long as a Muslim occupies himself with helping a brother, Allah, the Exalted, occupies himself with helping him (Muslim, Tirmidhi and Nisai). He has also said: He who directs another towards good will have such merit as the one who follows his direction; and has said: If a person calls another towards guidance he will have as much merit as the one who follows his direction, without there being the least diminution in the merit of either (Muslim and Abu Daud).

'It is reported that the Holy Prophet said to Ali: Should Allah guide one person along the right path through thee, that will be better for thee than many red camels (Bokhari and Muslim).

'Having in mind these verses of the Holy Quran and these directions of the Holy Prophet (on whom be peace and blessings of Allah) I was moved to prepare a compendium of such of the *ahadith* of the Holy Prophet which should help to render easy the journey of a reader to the hereafter and should serve him as a means of acquiring external and internal order in his life and which should comprise urgings and warnings and the discipline, piety and exercises towards the reform of conduct and the training of morals and the purification of hearts.

'I have taken care in this book to select from well-known sources only such *ahadith* as are clear and authoritative. In the beginning of each section attention will be drawn to relevant verses of the Holy Quran.

'I am hoping that if this book is completed it will help to guide the reader, by Allah's grace, towards virtue and goodness and will guard him against evil and ruin. I request everyone of my brethren who might draw some benefit from this book to pray for me, my parents, my teachers, my friends and for all Muslims. I depend entirely upon God, in Him I believe and in Him I put my trust. He is sufficient for me and He is the Best helper. There is no strength to resist evil, nor any power to do good except through Allah, the Mighty, the Wise.'

August, 1974   ZAFRULLA KHAN

NOTE

The salutation to the Holy Prophet in the words 'upon whom be the peace and blessings of Allah' after his name, and the invocation 'may Allah be pleased with him' after the names of his companions are expressly set out in the manuscript but are omitted in print in order to accommodate the text to the modern reader. They should, nevertheless, be understood as repeated in each case.

In this translation the form *ibn* has been used in both initial and medial positions in the names of persons, in order to conform with current usage, although *bin* occurs medially in the original text.

IN THE NAME OF ALLAH, MOST GRACIOUS, EVER MERCIFUL

1.

On Sincerity and the Importance of Motive in every type of Action

Allah, the Exalted, has said:

1. They had only been commanded to worship Allah, devoting themselves wholly to Him in full sincerity, and to observe Prayer and to pay the Zakat. This is the enduring faith (98.6).

2. Their flesh reaches not Allah, nor their blood, but it is your righteousness that reaches Him (22.37).

3. Warn them, O Prophet: Whether you keep hidden that which is in your minds, or disclose it, Allah knows it well (3.30).

1. Umar ibn Khattab has related that he heard the Holy Prophet say: Motive determines the value of all conduct, and a person attains that which he desires. If the motive of one who emigrates is to attain to Allah and His Messenger, then that is the purpose of his migration; and he who migrates seeking the world attains to it, and he who migrates for the sake of a woman, marries her and thus his migration is for the purpose he has in mind (Bokhari and Muslim).

2. Ayesha has related that the Holy Prophet said: A host will advance upon the Ka'aba and when it reaches the plain all of them, the first and the last, will be swallowed up by the earth. Whereupon she said: Messenger of Allah, why all of them? He replied: All of them will be swallowed up, but they will be raised up for judgment according to their motives (Bokhari and Muslim).

3. Ayesha has related that the Holy Prophet said: After the fall of Mecca emigration is no longer obligatory; but striving in the cause of Allah and yearning for it continue obligatory; when you are called you should go forth (Bokhari and Muslim).

4. Jabir ibn Abdullah has related: We were with the Holy Prophet in a campaign when he said: There are some people in Medina who are with you in spirit wherever you march and whatever valley you traverse. It is only illness that has kept them from being with you in person; and one version adds: They are your partners in reward (Muslim). Bokhari's version is: Anas has related: We were returning from the campaign of Tabuk with the Holy Prophet when he said: There are people left behind in Medina who were with us in spirit in every pass we crossed and every valley we traversed. They were kept back by some disability.

5. Ma'an ibn Yathid ibn Akhnas (all three Companions) has related: My father set aside some dinars for charity and gave them to a person in the

1

mosque. I went to that person and brought back the dinars to my father. He said: I had not intended these for you. So we went to the Holy Prophet and submitted the matter to him. He said to my father: Yathid, you have earned merit for what you intended; and to me he said: Ma'an, you are entitled to what you have taken (Bokhari).

6. Sa'ad ibn Abi Waqqas (one of the ten who had been given the glad tidings of admission into Paradise) has related: The Holy Prophet came to inquire after my health when I was seriously ill in the year of the Farewell Pilgrimage and I said to him: Messenger of Allah, you see how it is with me. I am a man of means and my sole heir is my daughter. May I, then, give away two-thirds of my property in charity? He said: No. Then one-half, O Messenger of Allah? Again he said: No. Well then, one-third, Messenger of Allah? On which he said: One-third, and one-third is ample. It is better that you should leave your heirs in easy circumstances rather than in want, reduced to soliciting alms from others. Whatever you spend seeking the pleasure of Allah, even a morsel of food that you put in the mouth of your wife, will bring its reward. Then I said: Messenger of Allah, shall I be left behind in Mecca, when you return to Medina with my fellow-companions? He said: You will certainly not be left behind. Whatever you do seeking the pleasure of Allah will raise your station and your high status. I am hoping that you will survive to be a source of benefit for some people and of trouble for others. Then he supplicated: Make perfect the emigration of my Companions, O Allah, and do not turn them back on their heels. But the one to be pitied was Sa'ad ibn Khaulah who died in Mecca, and the Messenger of Allah expressed mercy and compassion for him (Bokhari and Muslim).

7. Abu Hurairah has related that the Holy Prophet said: Allah does not regard your bodies and looks, but looks at your hearts (Muslim).

8. Abu Musa Asha'ri has related: The Holy Prophet was asked: Which of three strives in the cause of Allah, one who fights in order that he should display his bravery, or one who fights out of a feeling of indignation, or one who fights in order to show off? He replied: He who fights so that the word of Allah be exalted, is the one who strives in the cause of Allah (Bokhari and Muslim).

9. Abu Bakarah Thaqfi has related that the Holy Prophet said: When two Muslims confront each other with swords and one is killed, both end up in hell. I said: Messenger of Allah, as to the one who kills it is understandable; but why the other? He answered: The other was also eager to kill his opponent (Bokhari and Muslim).

10. Abu Hurairah has related that the Holy Prophet said: Prayer in congregation is more than twenty-five times greater in merit than Prayer at home or in the shop etc. Therefore, when a person makes his ablutions carefully and proceeds to the mosque with the sole purpose of joining in the service his station rises in grade at every step and one of his sins is wiped out. From the moment he enters the mosque he is accounted as a participant in the service while waiting for the service to begin, and, so long as he causes no inconvenience to anyone and his state of purity is maintained, the angels continue to pray for him: Allah, have mercy upon him; Allah, forgive him; Allah, turn to him with compassion (Bokhari and Muslim).

11.   Abdullah ibn Abbas has related that the Holy Prophet repeated Allah's affirmation that He has defined good and evil and has expounded their gradation. He, therefore, who makes up his mind to do a good deed, is rewarded by Allah for one full measure of it, and if he then proceeds to carry it out Allah rewards him from ten to seven hundred times and even many times more. He who is inclined towards an evil deed, but does not carry it out, is rewarded by Allah for one full measure of good deed. Should he carry it out, he is debited only one evil deed (Bokhari and Muslim).

12.   Abdullah ibn Umar has related that he heard the Holy Prophet recount the following: Three persons, of a people before you, were on a journey when they were overtaken by a storm and they took refuge in a cave. A rock slithered down from the mountain and blocked the exit from the cave. One of them said: The only way for deliverance left is to beseech God for it by virtue of some righteous deed. Thereupon one of them supplicated: Lord, my parents were very old and I used to offer them their nightly drink of milk before my children and the other members of the family. One day I was drawn far away in search of green trees and did not get back till after my parents had gone to sleep. When I had milked and brought their drink to them they were asleep, and I hated to disturb them, nor would I give any part of the milk to my children and others till after my parents had had their drink. Thus, with the vessel in hand, I awaited their wakening till the flush of dawn, while the children cried out of hunger at my feet. When they woke up they had their drink. Lord, if I did this seeking Thy pleasure, then do Thou relieve us of the distress imposed upon us by this rock. Thereupon the rock moved a little but not enough to let them pass out. Then one of the other two supplicated: Lord, I had a cousin whom I loved more passionately than any man loves a woman. I tried to seduce her but she would have none of me, till in a season of great hardship from famine she approached me and I gave her one hundred and twenty dinars on condition that she would yield herself to me. She agreed, and when we got together she pleaded: Fear God, and do not break the seal unlawfully; whereupon I moved away from her despite the fact that I desired her most passionately; and I let her keep the money I had given her. Lord, if I did this seeking Thy pleasure, do Thou move the distress in which we find ourselves. Again, the rock moved a little but not enough to let them pass out. Then the third supplicated: Lord, I hired some labourers and paid them their due, but one of them left leaving behind what was due to him. I invested it in business and the business prospered greatly. After a time the labourer came back and said: O servant of God, hand over to me my wages. I said to him: All that you see is yours; camels, cattle, goats and slaves. He said: Mock me not, O servant of Allah. I assured him: I am not mocking you. So he took all of it, sparing nothing. Lord, if I did this seeking Thy

pleasure, do Thou relieve us of our distress. The rock then moved away, and they emerged walking freely (Bokhari and Muslim).

2.
On Repentance

Allah, the Exalted, has said:

4.   *Turn ye to Allah, all together, O believers, that you may prosper (24.32).*

5.   *Seek forgiveness of your Lord and turn to Him in repentance (11.4).*

6.   *O ye who believe, turn to Allah in sincere repentance (66.9).*

13.   Abu Hurairah relates that he heard the Holy Prophet say: Allah is my witness, that I seek forgiveness of Allah and turn to Him more than seventy times a day (Bokhari).

14.   Aghirr ibn Yasar Muzanni relates that the Holy Prophet admonished: Turn to Allah, ye people, and seek forgiveness of Him. For myself, I turn to Allah a hundred times a day (Muslim).

15.   Anas ibn Malik, servant of the Holy Prophet, said: Allah is more pleased with the repentance of a servant of His than would be one of you who were to lose his camel in a barren desert and then find it suddenly (Bokhari and Muslim). The version in Muslim adds: Allah is more pleased with the repentance of a servant of His than would be one of you who were to lose his riding camel, which carries his food and drink, in a barren desert, and losing all hope of finding it he were to lie down in the shade of a tree, and then should suddenly find it standing near him and should seize its nose-string and in his excess of joy should blurt out: O Allah, Thou art my servant and I am Thy lord.

16.   Abu Musa Ash'ari relates that the Holy Prophet said: Allah will continue to hold out His hand at night so that he who has sinned during the day might repent, and to hold out His hand during the day so that he who has sinned at night might repent, till the sun should rise from the west (Muslim).

17.   Abu Hurairah relates that the Holy Prophet said: Allah will turn with mercy to whoever repents before the sun rises from the west (Muslim).

18.   Abdullah ibn Umar relates that the Holy Prophet said: Allah, the Lord of honour and glory, will accept the repentance of a servant of His till his death-rattle begins (Tirmidhi).

19.   Zirr ibn Jubaish relates: I went to Safwan ibn Assal to inquire about the symbolic passing of the hands over socks in the course of ablutions. He asked me: Zirr, what brings you? I replied: Search of knowledge. He said: Angels spread their wings for one who seeks knowledge out of pleasure at what he seeks. I told him: Some doubt has arisen in my mind concerning the symbolic passing of hands over socks in the course of ablutions after one has been to the privy or the urinal. Now, you are one of the Companions of the Holy Prophet and I have come to ask you: Did you hear him mention anything concerning it? He replied: Yes. He directed us that while we were on a journey we need not take off our socks for washing the feet in the course of ablutions during a period of three days and nights, except after consorting with our wives. In other cases, e.g. sleep, a visit to the privy or urinal etc., the symbolic passing of the hands over socks would suffice during that period. I then asked him: Did you hear him say anything concerning love and affection? He replied: We were with the Holy Prophet in the course of a journey when a desert Arab called out to him in a loud rough voice: O Muhammad! The Holy Prophet answered him in almost the same tone: Here I am. I said to the Arab: Fie on thee, lower thy voice in his presence; Allah has so commanded. To me he retorted: I will not lower my voice; and then addressing the Holy Prophet said: What about a person who loves a people but has not yet found himself in their company? The Holy Prophet made answer: On the day of Judgment a person will be in the company of those he loves. He then continued talking to us and in the course of his talk made mention of a gateway in the west, the width of which could be traversed by a rider in forty or seventy years. Sufyan, who is one of the narrators of this *hadith*, adds: This gateway is in the direction of Syria. Allah created it along with the creation of the heavens and the earth. It is open for repentance, and will not be closed till the sun rises from that direction (Tirmidhi and others).

20. Abu Sa'id Khudri relates that the Holy Prophet said: An individual from among a people before you having killed as many as ninety-nine persons inquired who was the most learned person on earth. He was directed to a monk. He went to the monk and said: I have killed ninety-nine persons. Is there any chance of repentance left for me? The monk answered: No. Forthwith he dispatched the monk also and completed a full century of victims. Then he inquired again: Who is the most learned person on earth? and was directed to a savant, to whom he said: I have killed a hundred persons. Is there a chance of repentance left for me? The savant said: Yes. What can stand between you and repentance? Proceed to such and such a land. In it there are people who worship God. Join them in the worship of God and do not return to thine own land, for it is an evil place. So he set out. He had traversed only half the distance when he was overtaken by death, and a contention arose over him between the angels of mercy and the angels of torment. The angels of mercy pleaded that he had come a penitent turning towards God; and the angels of torment contended that he had never done a good deed. Then there arrived an angel in human form and the contending angels agreed that he should be the arbiter between them. He directed them: Measure the distance between the two lands. To whichever he is closer to that one he belongs. So they carried out the measurement and he was found to be closer to the land whither he was bound. The angels of mercy thus took charge of him (Bokhari and Muslim). One version has it that he was found to be closer to the land of the righteous by the width of a hand and was thus accounted one of them. Another version is that God directed the space on one side to expand and the space on the other to shrink, and then said: Now carry out the measurement. It was found that he was nearer to his goal by the width of a hand and was forgiven. It is also related that he came closer by crawling on his chest.

21.   Abdullah ibn Ka'ab, who had become his father's guide when the latter became blind, relates that he had heard from his father, Ka'ab ibn Malik a full account of the incident of his remaining behind the Holy Prophet when he proceeded on the campaign of Tabuk. Ka'ab said: I had accompanied the Holy Prophet in every campaign except in that of Badr, and in that case there was no question of any penalty for the Holy Prophet and the Muslims had in view ostensibly the Quraish caravan, but Allah brought about a confrontation between them and their enemies unexpectedly. I was present with the Messenger of Allah the night of Aqabah, when we covenanted complete dedication to Islam. I would not exchange Aqabah with Badr, for all the fame of Badr as compared with Aqabah. My failure to accompany the Holy Prophet in the campaign of Tabuk fell out in this wise. I was stronger and more affluent at the time of this campaign than at any other time. I had then two riding camels, and never before did I have two. Whenever the Holy Prophet decided on a campaign he would not disclose his real objective till the last moment. In this case, as the season was one of intense heat, the journey was long across the desert and the enemy was in great strength; he warned the Muslims clearly and told them his objective so that they should make full preparation. The number of those ready to accompany the Messenger of Allah was also large. No register would have sufficed for setting down the particulars of all of them. Most of those who were minded to keep away imagined that they would get away with it, unless their defection was disclosed through divine revelation. Also the fruit on the trees had ripened and their shade was thick and this too operated on my mind.

The Messenger of Allah and the Muslims who were to accompany him occupied themselves with their preparations and I would go out in the morning meaning to do the same along with him but would return without settling anything, saying to myself: There is plenty of time. I can get ready whenever I wish. This went on and the Muslims completed their preparations, and one day the Messenger of Allah started with them on his march, and I had not yet done anything to prepare myself. I still continued in my state of indecision, without settling anything, while the Muslims continued on the march. I thought I would go forth alone and overtake them. How I wish I had done it, but it was not to be. Now when I went about in the town it grieved me to observe that among those who were still at home like me were only those who were either suspected of hypocrisy or were excused on account of age or such like.

The Holy Prophet made no mention of me till after he had arrived at Tabuk. There sitting among the people on that day he inquired what had happened to Ka'ab? Someone from among the Bani Salimah said: Messenger of Allah, he has been hindered by his two cloaks and his habit of admiring his finery. On this Mu'az ibn Jabal admonished him. The Holy Prophet said nothing. At this time he observed someone at a distance in the desert clad in white and exclaimed: May it be Abu Khaisamah; and so he proved to be. He was the one who was taunted by the hypocrites when he gave away a quantity of dates in charity.

When I learnt that the Messenger of Allah was on his way back from Tabuk I was much distressed and began to revolve false excuses in my mind that might serve to shield me from his anger. I also consulted such members of my family whose judgment I trusted. When I heard that the Holy Prophet was approaching I realized that no false excuse would avail me and I resolved to stick to the truth. He arrived the next morning. It was his wont that when he returned from a journey he first entered the mosque and offered two *raka'as* of Prayer and then sat facing the people. He did the same on this occasion and those who had remained behind from the campaign came up and began to put forward their excuses on oath. They were well over eighty in number. The Holy Prophet accepted their verbal declarations, renewed their covenants, prayed for forgiveness for them and committed to Allah whatever was in their minds. When it came to my turn and I saluted him, he smiled, but it was the smile of one angry and said: Come forward. So, I stepped forward and sat down before him. He asked: What kept you back? Had you not purchased your mount? I replied: Messenger of Allah, were I confronted by someone other than yourself, a man of the world, I could easily escape his displeasure by some excuse, for I am gifted with skill in argument, but I know that if I were to spin before you a false tale today, which might even convince you, most certainly will Allah soon rouse your anger against me over something. On the other hand, if I tell you the truth and you are wroth with me, I might still hope for a good end from Allah, the Exalted, the Glorious. I have no excuse. I was never stronger and more affluent than when I held back from accompanying you. The Holy Prophet said: This one has told the truth. Now withdraw, till Allah issues His decree concerning you. Some men of Bani Salimah followed me out of the mosque and said: We have not known you to commit a fault before this, then why did you not put forward an excuse before the Holy Prophet like the others who had held back from the campaign? Your fault would have found its forgiveness through the prayer of the Holy Prophet for your forgiveness. They kept on reproaching me so severely that I made up my mind to go back to the Holy Prophet and to retract my confession. Then I asked them: Is anyone else in similar case to mine? They said: Murarah ibn Rabi'a 'Amiri and Hilal ibn Umayyah Waqifi. When they mentioned two such persons who were righteous, had participated in the battle of Badr, and possessed many good qualities, I was confirmed in my original resolve.

The Holy Prophet directed the Muslims to stop speaking to the three of us. People kept away from us, as if they were strangers, and it seemed to me that I was in a strange land which I could not recognize. This continued for fifty days. My two companions in misery were resigned and took to keeping inside their homes. But I being the youngest of the three and the toughest used to go out and join the Muslims in Prayer and walked the streets but nobody would talk to me.

I would attend upon the Holy Prophet when he sat in the mosque after Prayer and would salute him and wonder whether he had moved his lips in returning my salutation. I would stand in Prayer near him and I noticed that he would look in my direction when I was occupied with the Prayer and would look away when I looked in his direction. Being oppressed by the hardness of the Muslims towards me I went one day and vaulted over the garden wall of my cousin Abu Qatadah of whom I was very fond, and saluted him, but he did not return my salutation. I said to him: Abu Qatadah, I adjure you in the name of Allah, do you not know that I love Allah and His Messenger? But he said nothing. I repeated my adjuration. Still no reply. I asked a third time and he said: Allah and His Messenger know best; on which I could not restrain my tears and beat a retreat the way I had come.

One day I was sauntering in the market-place of Medina when I heard a peasant from Syria, who had brought a quantity of corn for sale, say: Would someone direct me to Ka'ab ibn Malik? People pointed in my direction. He came to me and handed me a letter from the King of Ghassan. Being literate myself I read it. Its purport was: We have heard that your master has treated you harshly. God has not made you to be humiliated and maltreated. Come over to us and we shall receive you graciously. Having read it, I said to myself: This is another trial; and I committed it to the oven.

When forty days had elapsed without any indication in the revelation concerning us, a messenger of the Holy Prophet came to me and said: The Messenger of Allah directs you to keep away from your wife. I inquired: Shall I divorce her or what? He said: No. Only do not associate with her. I understood that my two companions had been directed likewise. So I told my wife: Go to your parents and remain with them till Allah determines this matter. Hilal ibn Umayyah's wife went to the Holy Prophet and said: Messenger of Allah, Hilal ibn Umayyah is old and is not able to look after himself, nor has he a servant. Would it displease you if I were to serve him? He said: No. But he should not associate with you. She said: He has no desire for me; since this incident he is occupied only with weeping. Some of my people said to me: You should also seek the permission of the Holy Prophet that your wife should look after you as the wife of Hilal ibn Umayyah looks after him. I told them: I shall not ask the Holy Prophet for permission for I do not know what he might say. Besides, I am young.

Ten more days passed like this and on the fifty-first morning, after communication with us had been interdicted, when, after the dawn Prayer at home, I was sitting in a melancholy state and the wide world, as Allah, the Exalted, has described it, seemed closing in on me, I suddenly heard someone shout at the top of his voice from the crest of Mount Sala'ah: O Ka'ab ibn Malik, good news! I immediately fell into prostration and realized that relief had come. It seems that the Holy Prophet had informed the people at the time of the dawn Prayer that Allah, the Lord of honour and glory, had turned to us in mercy, and several people had set out to convey the good news to us. Some went to my two companions. One spurred his horse in the direction of my home. One of the tribe of Aslam ran up to the mount and his voice reached me before the arrival of the cavalier. When the one whose voice I had heard arrived to felicitate me, I took off my garments and made him wear them. I had no other garments for my own wearing and borrowed a pair to put on and set out to present myself before the Holy Prophet. On the way I encountered crowds of people who congratulated me, saying: Blessed be the acceptance by Allah of thy repentance. When I entered the mosque I found the Holy Prophet seated surrounded by people. Of them, Talha ibn Ubaidullah got up and sprang towards me and, shaking my hand, congratulated me. He was the only one out of the Emigrants who got up and I have never forgotten this gesture of his.

When I saluted the Holy Prophet his face was aglow with joy and he said: Be happy with the best one of all thy days that have passed since thy mother gave thee birth. I said: Messenger of Allah, is this from you or from Allah? He answered: It is indeed from Allah. It was usual with him that his happy face glowed as if it were a segment of the moon, which we took as a signal that he was pleased. I then submitted to him: Messenger of Allah, to complete my repentance I would like to give up all my possessions as charity in the cause of Allah and His Messenger. He said: Hold back part of it; that would be better for you. On which I said: I shall hold back that portion which is in Khaibar. Then I submitted: Messenger of Allah, Allah, the Exalted, has delivered me only because I adhered to the truth, and it is part of my repentance that for the rest of my days I shall speak nothing but the truth. Ever since I declared this before the Holy Prophet, Allah, the Exalted, has not tried anyone so well in the matter of telling the truth as He has tried me. To this day, since my declaration, I have never had any inclination to tell a lie, and I hope that Allah will continue to safeguard me against it during the rest of my days.

Allah, the Exalted, revealed: Allah has assuredly turned with mercy to the Prophet and to the Emigrants and the Helpers who stood by him in the hour of distress when the hearts of a party of them had well-nigh swerved, and He has turned with mercy to these last also. He is Compassionate and Merciful to all of them. He has also turned with mercy to the three whose matter had been deferred and who felt as if the wide earth was closing in upon them and whose lives became a burden to them and who became convinced that there was no refuge against the wrath of Allah save in Himself. He turned to them with mercy that they might turn to Him in repentance. Surely, it is Allah Who is Oft-Returning with compassion and is Ever Merciful. O ye who believe, be mindful of your duty to Allah and keep company with the righteous (9.117-119).

Ka'ab continued: After Allah had guided me to Islam, His greatest bounty in my estimation, that He bestowed upon me, was my telling the truth to the Holy Prophet, and not lying to him and ruining myself as were ruined those who did tell lies to him. In His revelation Allah had said concerning those who told lies worse than He said concerning anyone: They will swear to you by Allah, when you return to them that you may leave them alone. So leave them alone. They are, indeed, an abomination, and their abode is hell, a recompense for that which they did. They will swear to you that you may be pleased with them but even if you are pleased with them, Allah will not be pleased with the rebellious people (9.95-96).

Our matter had been left pending, of the three of us, apart from the matter of those who had made excuses on oath before the Holy Prophet which he accepted, and whose convenants he renewed and for whom he prayed for forgiveness. The Holy Prophet kept our matter pending till Allah determined it with: He has also turned with mercy to the three whose matter was deferred. The reference here is not to our holding back from the campaign, but to his deferring our matter and keeping it pending beyond the matter of those who made their excuses on oath which he accepted. One version adds: The Holy Prophet set out for Tabuk on Thursday. He preferred setting out on a Thursday. Another version has it that he always returned from a journey in the early forenoon and went directly to the mosque where he offered two *raka'as* of Prayer, whereafter he sat down there receiving people (Bokhari and Muslim).

22.   Imran ibn Husain Khuza'ai relates that a woman of the Juhainah, who had become pregnant in consequence of adultery, came to the Holy Prophet and said: Messenger of Allah, I have committed a capital offence, so direct the execution of the sentence. The Holy Prophet sent for her guardian and said to him: Treat her kindly, and when she is delivered of the child bring her back. He did accordingly. Her clothes were secured around her and the sentence was directed to be carried out. She was accordingly stoned to death. The Holy Prophet led the funeral prayers for her. Umar submitted: Messenger of Allah, she had been guilty of adultery. He answered: She repented so that her repentance spread over seventy of the people of Medina would suffice them. Can there be any higher degree of repentance than that she laid down her life voluntarily to win the pleasure of Allah, the Lord of honour and glory (Muslim)?

23.   Ibn Abbas and Anas ibn Malik relate that the Holy Prophet said: If a son of man had a valley full of gold he would desire two of them. Only the earth of the grave can fill his mouth. Allah turns with mercy to him who turns to Him in repentance (Bokhari and Muslim).

24.   Abu Hurairah relates that the Holy Prophet said: Allah, the Exalted, will be greatly pleased with two, one of whom kills the other and both enter Paradise. The first one while fighting in the cause of Allah is slain by the second, and thereafter Allah turns in mercy to the second and he becomes a Muslim and in his turn becomes a martyr like the first (Bokhari and Muslim).

3.

On Steadfastness

Allah, the Exalted, has said:

7.   *O ye who believe, be steadfast and strive to excel in steadfastness (3.201).*

8.   We will surely try you with somewhat of fear and hunger, and loss of wealth and lives and fruits, then give glad tidings to the steadfast (2.156).

9.   Verily, the steadfast shall have their reward without measure (39.11).

10.   One who endures with fortitude and forgives achieves a matter of high resolve (42.44).

11.   O ye who believe, seek the help of Allah through steadfastness and Prayer; surely Allah is with the steadfast (2.154).

12.   We will surely try you until We make known those from among you who strive in the cause of Allah, and those who are steadfast (47.32).

There are many well-known verses of the Holy Quran inculcating steadfastness and extolling it.

25. Abu Malik Ash'ari relates that the Holy Prophet said: Cleanliness is half of faith; the utterance of: All praise belongs to Allah; fills the scales of good works; the utterance of: Holy is Allah and worthy of all praise; fills the space between the heavens and the earth; Prayer is light; charity is proof of faith: steadfastness is a glow and the Quran is a plea in your favour or against you. Everyone begins the morning ready to bargain with his soul as a stake and ransoms it or ruins it (Muslim).

26. Abu Sa'id Khudri relates that some people from among the Ansar asked the Holy Prophet to give them something, and he gave them; they asked again and he gave them till he exhausted all he had. Then he said to them: Whenever there is anything in hand I do not keep it back from you. Remember: he who seeks chastity, Allah makes him chaste; he who seeks self-sufficiency, Allah makes him self-sufficient; and he who seeks steadfastness Allah bestows steadfastness upon him. Upon no one has been bestowed a bounty better and more comprehensive than steadfastness (Bokhari and Muslim).

27. Suhaib ibn Sinan relates that the Holy Prophet said: Wondrous is the case of a believer; there is good for him in everything, and it is so for him alone. If he experiences something agreeable, he is grateful to God and that is good for him; and if he experiences adversity, he is steadfast and that is good for him (Muslim).

28. Anas relates that when the illness of the Holy Prophet became grave so that his suffering would make him unconscious, Fatimah exclaimed: Ah, the suffering of my dear father; and he reassured her: There is no more suffering for thy father after today. When he died she said: Ah, my father, he has responded to the call of his Lord; Ah, my father, the garden of Paradise has become his resort; Ah, my father, we apprise Gabriel of his death. When he was buried she said: How were your hearts reconciled to pouring earth over the Messenger of Allah? (Bokhari).

29.　Usamah ibn Zaid, loved by the Holy Prophet and the son of one loved by him, relates that a daughter of the Holy Prophet sent word to him that her son was at his last breath and begged him to go to her. He sent his salutation to her with the message: To Allah belongs that which He bestowed and to Him belongs that which He takes. Everything has its term fixed by Him. Let her be steadfast, therefore, and hope for His grace and mercy. She sent back word to him begging him for the sake of Allah to go to her. He stood up and proceeded to her accompanied by Sa'ad ibn Ubadah, Mu'az ibn Jabal, Ubayy ibn Ka'ab, Zaid ibn Thabit and others. When he arrived the child was presented to him and he took it in his lap. Observing its distress his tears began to run, whereupon Sa'ad said: Messenger of Allah, what is this? He made answer: This is compassion which Allah has placed in the hearts of His servants (and one version has it: in the hearts of such of His servants as He has willed) and Allah has compassion on such of His servants as are compassionate (Bokhari and Muslim).

30.　Suhaib relates that the Holy Prophet said: In earlier times there was a King who had a magician. When he grew old he said to the King: I am grown old, send me a young man whom I could instruct in magic. The King sent him a young man to be instructed. In the young man's way to the magician was a monk with whom he sat and to whom he listened. He was so pleased with the discourse of the monk that every time he went to the magician he would sit with the monk on the way. The magician would beat him and the young man complained to the monk of this. He told him: When you are afraid of the magician say to him: My people detained me; and when you are afraid of your people say to them: The monk detained me. This went on and one day the young man saw that a huge beast blocked the road so that people could not pass. The young man thought: Now I can find out whether the magician is superior or the monk. So he took up a stone and said: Lord, if the way of the monk is more to Thy liking than the way of the magician, then do Thou bring about the death of this beast so that the people can pass; and hit the beast with the stone and killed it thus letting the people pass; The young man told the monk of this who said to him: Son, you have become better than I, and I conceive that you have arrived at a stage when you will get into trouble. Should that happen, do not disclose my whereabouts.

The young man began to cure people of blindness and leprosy and all manner of diseases. His fame reached a courtier of the King who had become blind. He came to the young man with costly offerings and said: All this will be yours if you will heal me. The young man said to him: I cannot heal any one. It is God who bestows healing. If you will believe in God I will pray for you and He will heal you. So he believed in God and God cured him of his blindness. He went to the King and sat with him as he used to. The King asked him: Who has restored thy sight? The man answereu: My God. The King inquired; Have you a god beside me? He replied: Allah is your God and my God. The King ordered the man to be seized and he was tortured till he told about the young man who was summoned and the King said to him: Son, have you become so skilled in magic that you can heal the blind and the leprous and all manner of afflicted ones? He said: I do not heal anyone. It is God Who heals. Then he was seized and tortured till he disclosed the whereabouts of the monk who was summoned and directed: Retract thy faith. He refused. The King sent for a saw which was placed in the middle of the monk's head and he was sawn down in two. Then the King's courtier was sent for and was directed to abjure his faith. He too refused and was sawn down. Then the young man was brought and was told to retract his faith and refused. The King handed him over to a party of his men and told them: Take him to such and such a mountain and when you get to the top, if he still refuses to abjure his faith, drop him down from the top. They took him to the mountain and ascended to the top of it with him. There he supplicated: Lord, deliver me from them whatever way Thou wouldst. The mountain was shaken and they fell down. The young man walked back to the King who asked: What have thy companions done? He answered: God has delivered me from them. He was then handed over to another party and they were told to take him in a caique to deep water and in case of persistence in refusing to abjure his faith to drop him into the ocean. They took him along and he supplicated: Lord, deliver me from them whichever way Thou wouldst. The boat sank with them and they were drowned and the young man walked back to the King who asked him: What have thy companions done? he answered: God has delivered me from them; and added: You will not be able to kill me unless you do what I tell you. The King inquired: What is that? The young man made answer: Assemble the people in an open space and hang me from the trunk of a palm-tree. Then take an arrow from my quiver and placing it in the middle of a bow say: In the name of Allah, the Lord of this young man; and shoot the arrow at me. If you do thus you will kill me. The King proceeded accordingly. The people were assembled in an open space, the young man was hanged from the trunk of a palm-tree, the King took an arrow from his quiver and placing it in the middle of a bow said: In the name of Allah, the Lord of this young man; and shot it. The arrow struck the young man in the temple who raised his hand to his temple and died.

The people said: We believe in the Lord of this young man. The King was told: You see, that has happened which you had feared; the people have believed. The King ordered trenches to be dug along the roads; they were dug and fire was lighted in them. Then the command went forth that whoever should refuse to abjure his faith would be thrown in the trenches, or would be told to jump in. This went on. A woman came accompanied by a boy and shrank from being thrown in, whereupon the boy said to her: Be steadfast, mother, you are in the right (Muslim).

31. Anas relates that the Holy Prophet passed by a woman who was crying over a grave. He said to her: Be mindful of thy duty to Allah and be steadfast. She retorted: Leave me alone; you have not been afflicted as I have been. She had not known who he was. Someone told her: That was the Holy Prophet. She proceeded to the door of the Holy Prophet and not finding any doorman went in and said to him: I had not recognised you. He said: Steadfastness means to be resigned at the time of the first shock of grief (Bokhari and Muslim). Muslim's version adds: She had been crying over the grave of her son.

32.   Abu Hurairah relates that the Holy Prophet said: Allah, the Exalted, says: I have no reward other than Paradise for a believing servant of mine who is steadfast when I take away a beloved one of his from among the denizens of the world (Bokhari).

33.   Ayesha relates that she asked the Holy Prophet about the plague and he told her that the plague is a torment with which Allah afflicts those He determines; but that He has made it a source of mercy for the believers. If a servant of Allah is afflicted with the plague and stays in his town in a spirit of steadfastness hoping for his due from Allah, realising that only that will happen to him which Allah has determined for him, he will surely have a reward equal to that of a martyr (Bokhari).

34.   Anas relates that he heard the Holy Prophet say that Allah, the Lord of honour and glory, says: When I afflict a servant of Mine in respect of two of his beloved organs (meaning his eyes) and he proves steadfast under the affliction, I bestow Paradise on him in their stead (Bokhari).

35.   Ata ibn Abi Rabah relates that ibn Abbas said to him: Shall I show you a woman from among the dwellers of Paradise? He said: Certainly. Ibn Abbas then pointed to an ebony coloured woman and said: This woman came to the Holy Prophet and said: Messenger of Allah, I suffer from epilepsy and when I have a fit my body is exposed. Please pray to Allah for me. He said: If you choose to be steadfast under this affliction, you will gain Paradise, but if you so wish I shall pray that Allah may heal you. She said: I shall be steadfast, but please pray that my body may not be exposed. He prayed accordingly (Bokhari and Muslim).

36.   Abdullah ibn Mas'ud relates that he recalls as if he is looking at the Holy Prophet when he mentioned the case of a Prophet who was beaten and injured so severely by his people that he wiped away the blood from his face while supplicating: Allah, forgive my people, for they know not (Bokhari and Muslim).

37.   Abu Sa'id and Abu Hurairah relate that the Holy Prophet said: Whatever trouble, illness, anxiety, grief, hurt or sorrow afflicts a Muslim, even the pricking of a thorn, but Allah removes in its stead some of his defaults (Bokhari and Muslim).

38.   Abdullah ibn Mas'ud relates: I visited the Holy Prophet and he had fever. I said to him: Messenger of Allah, you have very high fever. He said: Indeed. My fever is as high as that of two of you. I said: That is because you have twice the reward. He said: That is so. No Muslim suffers anything, the prick of a thorn or more, but Allah wipes out in its stead some of his defaults and his sins fall away from him as leaves fall away from a tree.

39. Abu Hurairah relates that the Holy Prophet said: When Allah decrees good for a person He afflicts him (Bokhari).

40. Anas relates that the Holy Prophet said: No one of you should wish for death because of any misfortune that befalls him. Should anyone be sore afflicted, he should say: Allah, keep me alive so long as life is the better for me, and cause me to die when death is the better for me (Bokhari and Muslim).

41. Khubaib ibn Arat relates: We complained to the Holy Prophet of the increasing persecution inflicted upon us by the disbelievers of Mecca. He was reclining in the shade of the Ka'aba, having made a pillow of his cloak. We submitted: Why do you not supplicate for help for us? Why do you not pray for us? He made answer: From among those who have gone before you a man would be caught and held in a pit dug for him in the earth and he would then be sawn in two with a saw placed over his head, or his flesh would be combed away from his bones with iron combs but none of this would wean him away from his faith. Allah will surely bring this matter to its consummation till a rider will proceed from Sana'a to Hadhramaut fearing nothing save Allah and the hazard of the wolf concerning his sheep. But you are in too much of a hurry (Bokhari).

42. Abdullah ibn Mas'ud relates: On the day of Hunian the Holy Prophet favoured some people in the division of spoils. He gave Aqra' ibn Habis and Uyainah ibn Hisn a hundred camels each and showed favour also to some of those honoured among the Arabs. Someone said: This is not a just division designed to win the pleasure of Allah. I decided to apprise the Holy Prophet of this and went and told him of it. His face became deep red and he said: Who will then do justice if Allah and His Messenger do not? and added: May Allah have mercy on Moses, he was caused more distress than this and was patient. Hearing this I said to myself: I shall never communicate anything of this kind to him again (Bokhari and Muslim).

43. Anas relates that the Holy Prophet said: When Allah decrees good for a servant of His He afflicts him quickly in this world, and if He decrees evil for him He does not hasten to call him to account for his sins in this world but takes him to task on the Day of Judgment. He also said: High reward is for high endeavour; and when Allah, the Exalted, loves a people, he puts them to trial. Then for him who accepts the affliction cheerfully is His pleasure, and for him who evades or shirks it is His wrath (Tirmidhi).

44. Anas relates: Abu Talha had a son who was ailing. He went out and the boy died in his absence. When he came back he inquired: How is the boy? Umm Sulaim, the mother of the boy, answered: Better than he was. Then she placed his evening meal before him and he ate and thereafter slept with her. At last she said to him: Arrange for the burial of the boy. In the morning Abu Talha went to the Holy Prophet and informed him of the event. He inquired: Were you together last night? Abu Talha replied in the affirmative, on which the Holy Prophet supplicated: Allah, bless them both. Thereafter she gave birth to a boy. Abu Talha said to her: Take up the boy so that we may carry him to the Holy Prophet; and he took some dates with him. The Holy Prophet inquired: Is there anything with him? Abu Talha said: Yes, some dates. The Holy Prophet took a date and having chewed it put it in the mouth of the baby and blessed it and named it Abdullah (Bokhari and Muslim).

Bokhari's version adds: Ibn Uyainah relates that a man of the Ansar told him that he saw nine sons of this Abdullah every one of whom had read the Quran. Muslim's version runs: Abu Talha's son from Umm Sulaim died and she said to the other members of the family: Do not tell Abu Talha about the boy; I shall tell him myself. When he came she put the evening meal before him and he ate. Then she made herself up well as she used to and they were together. Thereafter she said to him: Abu Talha, tell me, if someone lends something to another and thereafter demands it back, would the borrower be in the right to hold back the borrowed article? He answered: No. On which she said: Then hope for thy reward from Allah in respect of that which has befallen thy son. Abu Talha was upset and said: You left me in ignorance about my son's condition till after we had been together. So he left her and went to the Holy Prophet and told him what had happened. He said: May Allah bless your night. She conceived. Thereafter the Holy Prophet was on a journey and they were with him. It was his custom that when he returned from a journey he would not enter Medina by night. When they approached Medina her pains started. So Abu Talha stayed with her and the Holy Prophet went forward. Then Abu Talha prayed: Thou knowest, Lord, that I am eager that I should issue forth with the Holy Prophet when he issues forth and that I should return with him when he returns, and now I am detained here by what Thou seest. On this Umm Sulaim said: Abu Talha, I no longer feel pain. Let us proceed. So they proceeded and she gave birth to a boy after they arrived in Medina. My mother (Umm Sulaim) said to me: Anas, no one should suckle the baby till after we have taken it to the Holy Prophet tomorrow. Next morning I carried it to the Holy Prophet.

45.   Abu Hurairah relates that the Holy Prophet said: The strong one is not he who knocks out others in wrestling, the strong one is he who keeps control over himself when he is roused (Bokhari and Muslim).

46.   Sulaiman ibn Surad relates that he was sitting with the Holy Prophet when two men began to quarrel and one of them went red in the face and the veins of his neck stood out. The Holy Prophet said: If he were to repeat a phrase I know he would be rid of the condition in which he finds himself. The phrase is: I seek refuge with Allah against Satan, the rejected one. So they said to him: The Holy Prophet says: Seek refuge with Allah against Satan, the rejected one (Bokhari and Muslim).

47.   Mu'az ibn Anas relates that the Holy Prophet said: One who despite possessing the power to give effect to his anger suppresses it will be singled out and called by Allah, the Holy, the Exalted, above the multitude on the Day of Judgment and given his choice of black-eyed houris (Abu Daud and Tirmidhi).

48.   Abu Hurairah relates that someone asked the Holy Prophet to advise him. He said: Do not yield to anger. The man repeated his request several times. Every time the Holy Prophet said: Do not yield to anger (Bokhari).

49. Abu Hurairah relates that the Holy Prophet said: A believer male or female continues to be tried in respect of self, children and property till he or she faces Allah, the Exalted, in a state in which all his or her sins have been wiped out (Tirmidhi).

50. Ibn Abbas relates: Uyainah ibn Hisn came to Medina and put up with his nephew Hurr ibn Qais who was one of those who had access to Umar and who were consulted by him. Uyainah said to Hurr: Son of my brother, you enjoy the favour of the Commander of the Faithful, will you obtain permission for me to wait on him? Hurr asked for permission and Umar granted him leave. When Uyainah came into the presence of Umar, he addressed him thus: Son of Khattab, you do not bestow much upon us nor do you deal fairly with us. Umar was incensed and would have chastised him when Hurr said: Commander of the Faithful, Allah said to His Prophet: Make forbearance thy rule, and enjoin equity and turn away from the ignorant (7.200). This one is one of the ignorant. When Hurr recited this Umar became motionless in his seat. He always adhered strictly to the Book of Allah (Bokhari).

51. Ibn Mas'ud relates that the Holy Prophet said: After I am gone you will experience discrimination and will observe things that you will disapprove. Someone asked: Messenger of Allah, what do you command us we should do in such case? He said: Discharge your obligations and supplicate Allah for your rights (Bokhari and Muslim).

52. Usyad ibn Huzair relates that a person from among the Helpers said to the Holy Prophet: Will you not appoint me to public office as you have appointed So and So? He replied: You will experience discrimination after I am gone, but be steadfast till you meet me in Paradise (Bokhari and Muslim).

53. Abdullah ibn Abi Aufa relates that the Holy Prophet was on a campaign and while waiting for the sun to decline he stood up and addressed his companions: Do not desire fighting and keep supplicating Allah for security. But when you are confronted with the enemy be steadfast and remember that Paradise is under the shade of the swords. Then he supplicated: Allah, Revealer of the Book, Driver of the Clouds, Vanquisher of Hosts, vanquish them and help us overcome them (Bokhari and Muslim).

4.

On Truthfulness

Allah, the Exalted, has said:

13. O ye who believe, be mindful of your duty to Allah and keep company with the righteous (9.119).

14. Men who are truthful and women who are truthful (33.36).

15. Had they been true to their duty to Allah, it would have been the better for them (47.22).

54. Abdullah ibn Mas'ud relates that the Holy Prophet said: Truth guides to virtue and virtue guides to Paradise. A person persists in telling the truth till in the sight of Allah he is named Truthful. Lying leads to vice and vice leads to the Fire; and a person goes on lying till in the sight of Allah he is named a liar (Bokhari and Muslim).

55. Hasan ibn Ali relates that he learnt the following from the Holy Prophet: Leave alone that which involves thee in doubt and adhere to that which is free from doubt, for truth is comforting, falsehood is disturbing (Tirmidhi).

56. Abu Sufyan relates as part of his statement about Hiraclius that the latter asked him what does he (i.e. the Holy Prophet) teach you and Abu Sufyan said: He tells us: Worship Allah alone and do not associate anything with Him, and discard all that your ancestors said; and he commands us to observe Prayer, to tell the truth, to be chaste and to strengthen the ties of kinship (Bokhari and Muslim).

57. Sahl ibn Hunaif relates that the Holy Prophet said: He who supplicates Allah sincerely for martyrdom is raised by Him to the station of a martyr even if he should die in his bed (Muslim).

58. Abu Hurairah relates that the Holy Prophet said: One of the earlier Prophets went to war and proclaimed among his people that no one should accompany him who had made a contract of marriage with a woman whom he intends to bring home but has not yet brought her, nor anyone who has constructed the walls of a house but has not yet put a roof on them, nor anyone who has purchased ewes or she-camels carrying their young and is awaiting the season of lambing. Then he set out and approached the town that was his objective an hour or so before sunset and said to the sun: Thou art commissioned and I am also commissioned, and supplicated: Lord, hold it back for us; and it was held back till God gave him the victory. Then the spoils were collected to be burnt as an offering but the fire would not consume them. Then he announced: Someone among you has embezzled a portion of the spoils, so now let one man from each tribe renew the covenant at my hands. In this process the hand of one man stuck to the hand of the Prophet and he announced: Some one of your tribe has been guilty of embezzlement; so now let each man of your tribe renew the covenant at my hands. In doing this the hands of two or three men stuck to the hand of the Prophet and he announced that one of them had been guilty of embezzlement. Upon this they produced a mass of gold like the head of a cow which was placed among the spoils and the fire consumed them. The Holy Prophet added: Spoils of war were not lawful for anyone before us. Allah made them lawful for us in view of our weakness and lack of means (Bokhari and Muslim).

59. Hakim ibn Hizam relates that the Holy Prophet said: A sale agreement is revocable till the buyer and seller part company. If they tell the truth and disclose everything relevant to the transaction, it becomes full of blessings for both of them; but if they speak falsely and conceal that which should be disclosed, the blessing of the transaction is wiped out (Bokhari and Muslim).

5.
On Self-Examination

Allah, the Exalted, has said:

16. Who sees thee when thou standest alone for prayer, and also sees thy movements in the company of those who prostrate themselves in Prayer along with thee (26.219-22).

17. He is with you wheresoever you may be (57.5).

18. Nothing is hidden from Allah, in the earth or in the heaven (3.6).

19. Surely, thy Lord is on the watch (89.15).

20. He knows the treachery of the eyes and that which the minds conceal (40.20).

60.   Umar ibn Khattab relates: We were sitting one day with the Holy Prophet when a man appeared among us whose clothes were of an intense whiteness, whose hair was very black, who bore no mark of travel and who was not known to any of us. He sat down in front of the Holy Prophet, their knees touching, and placing his hands on his thighs he said: Muhammad, tell me about Islam. The Holy Prophet said: Islam is that you should bear witness that there is no one worthy of worship save Allah alone and that Muhammad is His Messenger, and that you should observe Prayer, pay the *Zakat*, observe the fast during Ramadhan, and perform the Pilgrimage to the House if you can afford the journey thither. The man said: That is right. We were surprised that he inquired and also confirmed the correctness of the answer. He then said: Tell me about faith. The Holy Prophet said: That you should believe in Allah, His Angels, His Books, His Messengers, the Last Day, and that you should believe that He determines the measure of good and evil. The man said: That is right. Now tell me about the due performance of obligations. The Holy Prophet said: That you should worship Allah as if you are beholding Him, and if not then in the consciousness that He is watching you. The man said: Now tell me about the Hour of Judgment. The Holy Prophet said: He who is being asked knows no more about it than the one who asks. The man then said: Well, tell me some of the signs of its approach. The Holy Prophet made answer: That the hand-maiden should give birth to her master and that barefooted, barebodied, penurious goatherds should be seen lording it in great mansions. Then the man departed, and I remained a while. The Holy Prophet said to me: Umar, do you know who the questioner was? I said: Allah and His Messenger know best. He said: It was Gabriel who came to instruct you in your faith (Muslim).

61. Abu Dharr and Mu'az ibn Jabal relate that the Holy Prophet said: Mind your duty to Allah, wherever you are; and follow up evil with good, the latter will wipe out the former; and behave well towards people (Tirmidhi).

62. Ibn Abbas relates: I was riding behind the Holy Prophet one day when he said: Boy, I would instruct thee in some matters. Be watchful of Allah, He will be watchful of thee. Safeguard His commandments, He will be ever with thee. When thou must ask, ask of Allah alone; and when thou must seek help, implore Allah alone for help. Remember that if all the people were to combine to bestow some benefit upon thee, they would not be able to bestow anything upon thee except that which Allah has appointed for thee, and that if all of them were to combine to do thee harm, they would not be able to afflict thee with anything except that which Allah has decreed against thee. The pens have been lifted and the ink of the books has become dry (Tirmidhi). Another version has it: Safeguard the commandments of Allah, you will find Him before you; remember Him in prosperity, He will remember you in adversity. Be sure that that which has led you into error will not lead you aright, and that which has guided you to good will not lead you astray. Remember that help comes with steadfastness, there is prosperity after adversity and that hardship is followed by ease.

63. Anas has said: You indulge in things which you account as less than a hair whereas in the time of the Holy Prophet we shunned them as fatal (Bokhari).

64. Abu Hurairah relates that the Holy Prophet said: Allah is jealous, and His jealousy is roused by a person indulging in that which He has forbidden (Bokhari and Muslim).

65. Abu Hurairah relates that he heard the Holy Prophet narrate the following: Allah having determined to try a leper, a bald one and a blind one from among the Bani Israel sent an angel to them. The angel came to the leper and asked him: What is it that you would like best? He said: A good complexion and a clear skin and removal of my affliction on account of which people shun me. The angel passed his hands over him and his affliction left him and he acquired a good complexion. Then the angel asked him: What property would you like best? The man said: Camels. He was given a she-camel ten months pregnant; and the angel said: May Allah bless it for thee. Then the angel came to the bald one and asked him: What is it that you would like best? He said: Lovely hair and removal of the affliction on account of which people avoid me. The angel passed his hands over him and his affliction was removed and he acquired lovely hair. Then the angel asked him: What property would you like best? The man said: Cattle. He was given a cow which was carrying a calf; and the angel said: May Allah bless it for thee. Then the angel came to the blind one and asked him: What is it that you would like best? He said: That Allah may restore my sight so that I may see people. The angel passed his hands over his eyes and Allah restored his sight. Then the angel asked him: What property would you like best? The man said: Goats. He was given a she-goat which was carrying a kid. The animals multiplied greatly, so that one had a valley full of camels, the other a valley full of cattle and the third a valley full of goats.

Thereafter the angel came in his old guise to the leper and said: I am a poor man bereft of all resources in the course of my journey, and I have no means left for the completion of my journey save Allah. I beg you in the name of Allah Who has given you a good complexion and a clear skin and great wealth to furnish me with a camel that might help me to reach the end of my journey. The man said: I have many obligations. The angel said: I seem to recognise you. Were you not a leper, shunned by people and indigent, enriched by Allah? The man said: My wealth is inherited through generations. The angel said: If you are lying, may Allah restore you to the condition in which you were. Then he came to the bald one in his old guise and said to him the same as he had said to the leper and received a reply similar to the one he had received from the leper. To this one also he said: If you are lying, may Allah restore you to the condition in which you were.

Then the angel came to the blind one in his old guise and said to him: I am a poor man on a journey. My resources have all given out and I cannot reach the end of my journey save with the help of Allah. I beg you in the name of Him Who has restored your sight to you to give me a goat that might prove of help to me in reaching the end of my journey. The man said: Indeed I was blind and Allah restored my sight to me. Then take what you will and leave what you will, I shall not constrain you in any way in respect of whatever you may wish to take in the name of Allah, the Lord of honour and glory. The angel said: Keep all you have. All three of you were being tried. Allah is, indeed, pleased with thee and is wroth with thy companions (Bokhari and Muslim).

66. Shaddad ibn Aus relates that the Holy Prophet said: A wise person is one who watches over himself and restrains himself from that which is harmful and strives for that which will confront him after death; and a foolish one is he who gives rein to his cravings and seeks from Allah the fulfilment of his vain desires (Tirmidhi).

67. Abu Hurairah relates that the Holy Prophet said: It is part of the excellence of a person's Islam that he should eschew that which is of no benefit to him (Tirmidhi).

68. Omitted.

6.

On Righteousness

Allah, the Exalted, has said:

21. O ye who believe, be mindful of your duty to Allah in all respects (3.103).

22. Be mindful of your duty to Allah as best you can (64.17).

23. O ye who believe, be mindful of your duty to Allah and say the straightforward thing (33.71).

24. Allah will prepare a way out of his difficulties for him who is mindful of his duty to Him and will provide for him whence he expects not (65.3-4).

25. If you are mindful of your duty to Allah, He will bestow upon you a mark of distinction, and will remove from you your ills, and will forgive you. Allah is Lord of great bounty (8.30).

69. Abu Hurairah relates: The Holy Prophet was asked: Who is the most honoured of men? He said: He who is most righteous. The questioners said: That is not what we meant. He said: Then, Joseph, Prophet of Allah, son of a Prophet of Allah, son of a Prophet of Allah, son of Abraham, Friend of Allah. They said: This too is not what we meant. The Holy Prophet said: Then do you ask me concerning the Arab hierarchy? Those who were worthy of honour before Islam are worthy of honour in Islam once they are fully instructed in it (Bokhari and Muslim).

70. Abu Sa'id Khudri relates that the Holy Prophet said: The world is green and pleasant. Allah made you His vicegerents in it, so that He might show you how to react to it. So beware of the beguilement of the world and the women. The first trial of the Bani Israel was through women (Muslim).

71. Abdullah ibn Mas'ud relates that the Holy Prophet used to supplicate: Allah, I beg of Thee guidance, and righteousness and chastity and self-sufficiency (Muslim).

72. 'Adi ibn Hatim relates: I heard the Holy Prophet say: If a person takes an oath to do a certain thing and then discovers something that is closer to righteousness than the first, he should do the second (Muslim).

73. Abu Umamah Bahili relates that he heard the address of the Holy Prophet on the occasion of the Farewell Pilgrimage in the course of which he said: Be mindful of your duty to Allah, observe the five Prayers and the fast of Ramadhan, pay the *Zakat* duly and obey those in authority among you; you will enter the Garden of your Lord (Tirmidhi).

7.

On Certainty and Trust

Allah, the Exalted, has said:

26. When the true believers saw the Confederate hosts, they said: Here is that which Allah and His Messenger had promised us; Allah and His Messenger have been proved right. It only added to their faith and submission (33.23).

27. *Those who were told: People have mustered against you, so fear them; but this only added to their faith and they affirmed: Sufficient for us is Allah and an excellent Guardian is He. So they returned with a mighty favour from Allah and a great bounty, having suffered no harm; they followed the pleasure of Allah, and Allah is the Lord of great bounty (3.174-175).*

28. *Put thy trust in the One Who is Ever Living and is the Source of Life, Who dies not (25.59).*

29. *In Allah alone should the believers put their trust (14.12).*

30. *Then when thou has made up thy mind concerning a matter, put thy trust in Allah (3.160).*

31. *Allah is sufficient for him who puts his trust in him (65.4).*

32. *Believers are only those whose hearts are smitten with awe when Allah's name is mentioned and whose faith is strengthened when His Signs are recited to them, and who put their trust in their Lord (8.3-5).*

74. Ibn Abbas relates that the Holy Prophet said: I was shown many peoples. I saw a Prophet who had only a small party with him, some Prophets had only one or two persons with them and some did not have even one. Then suddenly I sighted a huge assemblage and I imagined that they were my people, but I was told: This is Moses and his people, but lift your eyes to the horizon. I looked and beheld a great multitude. Then I was told: Now look to the other horizon; and there was a great multitude. I was told: These are your people and of them there are seventy thousand who shall enter Paradise without any accounting or suffering. Then the Holy Prophet stood up and went into his chamber and the company began to speculate about those who would enter Paradise without any accounting or suffering. Some said: It may be they are the ones who kept company with the Holy Prophet; others said: It may be they are the ones who have been born Muslims and have never associated anyone with Allah; and so forth. Then the Holy Prophet came out and asked: What are you discussing? So they told him. He said: They are those who do not make charms or amulets nor seek them, nor seek omens but trust in their Lord. On this Ukasha ibn Muhsin stood up and begged: Supplicate Allah that He makes me one of them. The Holy Prophet said: You are one of them. Then another stood up and begged the same. The Holy Prophet answered: Ukasha has forestalled you (Bukhari and Muslim).

75. Ibn Abbas relates that the Holy Prophet used to supplicate: Allah, to Thee I have submitted, in Thee do I believe and in Thee I put my trust, to Thee do I turn and from Thee do I seek judgment. Allah, I seek refuge with Thee through Thy honour, there being no one worthy of worship save Thee alone, that

Thou safeguard me against going astray. Thou art the Ever-Living Who dies not, whereas men, high and low, will all die (Bokhari and Muslim).

76. Ibn Abbas relates that when Abraham was thrown into the fire his last words were: Sufficient for me is Allah and an excellent Guardian is He. So did the Holy Prophet when he was told: People have mustered against you, so fear them; this only added to the faith of the Muslims and he and the Muslims said: Sufficient for us is Allah and an excellent Guardian is He (Bokhari).

77. Abu Hurairah relates that the Holy Prophet said: Many people will enter Paradise whose hearts will be like the hearts of birds (Muslim).

78. Jabir relates that he accompanied the Holy Prophet in a campaign towards Nejd and returned with him. At noontime the party reached a valley of thorny trees where the Holy Prophet made a halt and his companions scattered in search of shade. He hung up his sword from the branch of a tree and lay down in its shade. We also took a siesta and suddenly we heard the Holy Prophet calling us. We hastened to him and saw that a desert Arab was sitting near him. The Holy Prophet said to us: This one drew my sword against me while I was asleep. I woke up and saw that he had the drawn sword in his hand. He said to me: Who will deliver you from me? I told him: Allah; and repeated it three times. The Holy Prophet sat up and imposed no penalty on the man (Bokhari and Muslim).

Another version runs: We were with the Holy Prophet in the campaign of Dhat-ir-Riqu'a. We came to a shady tree and we left it for him to rest under. A pagan came and seeing the sword of the Holy Prophet which was hanging from the tree, drew it, and said to him: Do you fear me? He answered: No. Then the man asked: Now who will deliver you from me? The Holy Prophet answered: Allah. Abu Bakr Ismaili has added in his book that thereupon the sword fell from the man's hand and the Holy Prophet having secured it asked him: Who will now deliver you from me? The man said: Be a good captor. The Holy Prophet asked him: Will you affirm that there is no one worthy of worship save Allah and that I am His Messenger? The man said: No. But I promise you that I will not fight against you, nor will I join those who do so. The Holy Prophet let him go free. He went back to his people and told them: I have come back to you from one who is the best of mankind.

79. Umar relates that he heard the Holy Prophet say: Were you to put your complete trust in Allah, He would provide for you as He provides for the birds. They issue forth hungry in the morning and return filled in the evening (Tirmidhi).

80. Bra'a ibn 'Ahili relates: The Holy Prophet said to me: When you lie down at night you should supplicate: Allah, I submit myself to Thee, and concentrate my mind on Thee, and commit my affairs to Thee, and make Thee my support out of love and fear of Thee. There is no escape from Thee, nor security against Thee save in Thyself. I believe in the Book that Thou hast sent down and in the Prophet Thou hast raised. Then if you die that night you will die in purity and if you survive you will encounter more good (Bokhari and Muslim). Another version has it: The Holy Prophet said to me: When you are ready for bed wash as you would wash for *salat*, then lie down on your right side and supplicate (as above) and let these be your last words.

81. Abu Bakr Siddique relates: When the Holy Prophet and I were in the cave and we were tracked by the Meccans I saw their feet above us outside the cave and I said: Messenger of Allah, if one of them were to look down below his feet he would see us. He said: Abu Bakr, what would you think of two with whom Allah is the third? (Bokhari and Muslim).

82. Umm Salamah (mother of the faithful) relates that when the Holy Prophet went out of the house he supplicated: I issue forth in the name of Allah, putting my trust in Him. Allah, I seek Thy protection against going astray or being led astray, or against slipping or being caused to slip, or against trespassing or being trespassed against, or against behaving ill towards any or that anyone should behave ill towards me. (Abu Daud and Tirmidhi).

83. Anas relates that the Holy Prophet said: He who on emerging from his house supplicates: I issue forth in the name of Allah, putting my trust in Him; there is no strength to resist evil and no power to do good save through Him; is greeted with: He is guided, is sufficed and is saved, and Satan withdraws from him (Abu Daud, Tirmidhi and Nisai). Abu Daud adds: One Satan says to another: How can you subdue one who is guided, is sufficed and is saved?

84. Anas relates that there were two brothers one of whom used to attend upon the Holy Prophet and the other used to occupy himself with his profession. On one occasion the latter complained to the Holy Prophet against the former that he paid no attention to earning his keep, who made answer: It may be that you are being provided because of him (Tirmidhi).

8.

On Perseverence

Allah, the Exalted, has said:

33.   Do thou continue to stand upright as thou hast been commanded (11.113).

34.   On them who affirm: Our Lord is Allah; and then remain steadfast, angels descend, reassuring them: Fear not, nor grieve, and rejoice in the Garden that you were promised. We are your friends in this life and in the hereafter. Therein you will have all that you desire, and therein you will be given all that you ask for; an entertainment from the Most Forgiving, the Ever Merciful (41.31-32).

35.   Those who say: Allah is our Lord, and then remain steadfast, will be subject to no fear, nor will they grieve. These are the dwellers of the Garden; they shall abide therein; a recompense for that which they did (46.14-15).

85.   Sufyan ibn Abdullah relates: I asked the Messenger of Allah: Tell me something about Islam which should enable me to dispense with having to ask anyone else. He said: Affirm: I believe in Allah; and then be steadfast (Muslim).

86.   Abu Hurairah relates that the Holy Prophet said: Follow the faith strictly and be steadfast; and remember that no one can achieve salvation through his conduct. Someone asked: Not even you, Messenger of Allah? He said: Nor I, save that Allah should cover me with His mercy and grace (Muslim).

9.
On Pondering over the Creation of Allah, etc.

Allah, the Exalted, has said:

36.   Say to them: I exhort you to do one thing: and that is that you stand before Allah two and two or singly and reflect (34.47).

37.   In the creation of the heavens and the earth and in the alternation of the night and the day there are indeed Signs for people of understanding, who remember Allah standing, sitting and lying on their sides and ponder over the creation of the heavens and the earth, which impels them to supplicate: Lord, Thou hast not created all this without purpose, Holy art Thou (3.191-192).

38.   Do they not observe the clouds how they have been created, and the heaven how it has been raised high, and the mountains how they are set up, and the earth how it is spread out? Then continue to admonish for thou art but an admonisher (88.18-22).

39.   Do they not travel in the earth so that they could observe what was the end of those who were before them? (47.11).

10.
On Vying with One Another in Doing Good

Allah, the Exalted, has said:

40.   Vie with one another in good works (2.149).

41.   Hasten towards forgiveness from your Lord and a Paradise whose price is the heavens and the earth, prepared for the righteous (3.134).

87. Abu Hurairah relates that the Holy Prophet said: Hasten to do good for soon there will be a succession of disorders like the chasing darknesses of night; a person will start the day believing and will end it disbelieving, or go to bed believing and get up in the morning disbelieving. He will be ready to sell his faith for a worldly advantage (Muslim).

88. Utbah ibn Harith relates: I joined the afternoon Prayer led by the Holy Prophet in Medina. The moment he concluded the service he stood up quickly and proceeded to one of his chambers stepping across the shoulders of the worshippers. People were perplexed by such haste. When he came back he perceived that people were wondering what had called him away so urgently. So he said: I recalled that there was left with me a piece of silver (or gold) and this disturbed me. I have now arranged for its distribution (Bokhari). Another version is: There was left with me a piece of silver (or gold) which was meant for charity. I was disturbed that it should remain with me overnight.

89. Jabir relates that one man asked the Holy Prophet on the day of Uhud: Tell me, where shall I be if I am killed in battle today? He answered: In Paradise. The man threw away the few dates he held in his hand, plunged into battle and fought on till he was killed (Muslim).

90. Abu Hurairah relates that a man came and asked the Holy Prophet: Which giving away in charity is most acceptable to God? He answered: That which you give away while you are in good health, seeking wealth, fearing adversity and hoping for prosperity. Do not delay spending in charity till you are in extremity and say: To So and So this, and to So and So that; for by then they already belong to So and So (Bokhari and Muslim).

91. Anas relates that the Holy Prophet took up a sword on the day of the battle of Uhud and said: Who will take this sword from me? Everyone stretched forth his hand saying: I, I. The Holy Prophet said: Who will take its full responsibility? The people hesitated. Then Abu Dujanah said: I shall take it; and with it he cracked the skulls of the pagans (Muslim).

92. Zubair ibn Adiyy relates: We went to Anas ibn Malik and complained to him of the inconvenience caused to us by the pilgrims. He counselled us to be patient and said: Each period will be followed by a worse, till you meet your Lord. I heard this from the Holy Prophet (Bokhari).

93. Abu Hurairah relates that the Holy Prophet said: Hasten to do good before you are overtaken by one of seven misfortunes: perplexing adversity, corrupting prosperity, disabling disease, babbling dotage, sudden death, the worst apprehended Anti-Christ, the Hour, and the Hour will be most grievous and most bitter (Tirmidhi).

94. Abu Hurairah relates that on the day of the battle of Khaibar the Holy Prophet said: I shall offer this standard to one who loves Allah and His Messenger, may Allah bestow victory through him. Umar relates: I had never desired a command but that day I hoped that I might be called. However, the Holy Prophet called Ali and handed the standard to him and said: Go forth and pay no heed to anything else till Allah bestows victory upon you. Ali proceeded a little way and stopped and without turning inquired in a loud voice: Messenger of Allah, for what shall I fight them? He answered: Fight on till they affirm that there is none worthy of worship save Allah and that Muhammad is Messenger of Allah. If they do that their lives and their properties will be secure against you, subject to their obligations under Islam, and they will be accountable to Allah (Muslim).

11.
On Striving

Allah, the Exalted, has said:

42.   *We will surely guide in Our ways those who strive after Us. Verily Allah is with those who do their duty to the utmost (29.70).*

43.   *Carry on the worship of thy Lord till death comes to thee (15.100).*

44.   *Remind thyself of the attributes of thy Lord and dedicate thyself wholly to His service (73.9).*

45.   *Then whoso will have done the smallest particle of good will see it (99.8).*

46.   *Whatever of good you send on for yourselves, you will find it with Allah. He is the Best and Greatest in bestowing reward (73.21).*

47.   *Whatever of your pure wealth you spend, Allah has full knowledge thereof (2.274).*

95.   Abu Hurairah relates that the Holy Prophet said: Allah says: Whoever is at enmity with one whom I befriend should beware of having to do battle with Me. When a servant of Mine seeks to approach Me through that which I like best out of what I have made obligatory upon him, and continues to advance towards Me by dint of voluntary effort beyond that prescribed then I begin to love him. When I love him I become his ears by which he hears, and his eyes with which he sees, and his hands with which he grasps, and his feet with which he walks. When he asks Me I bestow upon him and when he seeks My protection I protect him (Bokhari).

96.   Anas relates that the Holy Prophet said: Allah says: When a servant of Mine advances towards Me a foot, I advance towards him a yard, and when he advances towards Me a yard, I advance towards him the length of his arms spread out. When he comes to Me walking, I go to him running (Bokhari).

97.   Ibn Abbas relates that the Holy Prophet said: Most people incur loss in respect of two divine bounties, good health and leisure (Bokhari).

98. Ayesha relates: the Holy Prophet stood so long during his voluntary Prayer at night that the skin of his feet would crack; so I said to him: Messenger of Allah, why do you stand so long in Prayer when Allah has suppressed in you in the past and for the the future all inclination towards sin? He answered: Then should I not wish to be a grateful servant of Allah? (Bokhari and Muslim).

99. Ayesha relates: During the last ten days of Ramadhan the Holy Prophet would keep awake the whole night and would urge the members of his family to do the same, all occupying themselves with the worship of Allah. He girded up his loins and devoted himself entirely to prayer and supplication (Bokhari and Muslim).

100. Abu Hurairah relates that the Holy Prophet said: A strong believer is better and more loved by Allah than a weak one. Out of all good things desire that which is most beneficial for you. Keep imploring Allah for help and do not give up. Should you be afflicted in any way, do not say: Had I only done this and that things would have turned out so and so; but say only: Allah so determined and did as He willed. The phrase: Had I only; opens the gates of evil conduct (Muslim).

101. Abu Hurairah relates that the Holy Prophet said: Hell lies hidden behind evil desires and Paradise is screened by hard striving (Bokhari).

102. Huzaifah ibn Yaman relates: One night I joined the Holy Prophet in his voluntary Prayer. He began the recitation of *sura* Al-Baqarah. I thought he would go into *ruku'* after reciting a hundred verses but he continued the recitation. Then I thought he would complete its recitation in one *raka'a* but he continued his recitation and then began to recite *sura* Al-Nisa and thereafter *sura* Al-'Imran. His recitation was unhurried. When he recited a verse which mentioned glorification of God, he glorified Him, where supplication was mentioned he supplicated, and where seeking protection was mentioned he sought protection. Then he went into *ruku'* and began repeating: Holy is my Lord, the Great; and his *ruku'* was almost as long as his *qiyam*. Then he recited: Allah hears him who praises Him. Thine is the praise O Lord. He then stood up and his *qiyam* was as long as his *ruku'*. He then went into prostration and recited: Holy is my Lord, the High; and his prostration was like his *qiyam* (Muslim).

103. Ibn Mas'ud relates: One night I joined the Holy Prophet in his voluntary Prayer. He prolonged the *qiyam* so much that I made up my mind to commit an impertinence. He was asked: What had you made up your mind to? He answered: To sit down and stop following him (Bokhari and Muslim).

104. Anas relates that the Holy Prophet said: Three accompany a dead body: members of his family, his belongings and his deeds. Two of them come away and one remains. The members of his family and his belongings come away, his deeds remain (Bokhari and Muslim).

105. Ibn Mas'ud relates that the Holy Prophet said: Paradise is closer to you than your shoe-lace, and the same is the case with hell (Bokhari).

106. Rabi'ah ibn Ka'ab Aslami relates: I used to pass my night in the proximity of the Holy Prophet and used to put up water for his ablutions. One day he said to to me: Would you like to ask me for something? I said: I ask for your companionship in Paradise. He inquired: Is there anything else? I said: That is all. He said: Then help me with respect to yourself by multiplying your prostrations (Muslim).

107.   Thauban relates that he heard the Holy Prophet say: Multiply your prostrations. Every prostration before Allah will raise your status one degree and will remove one of your sins (Muslim).

108.   Abdullah ibn Busril Aslami relates that the Holy Prophet said: The best person is he who has a long life and is of good conduct (Tirmidhi).

109.   Anas relates: My uncle Anas ibn Nadhr was not present in the battle of Badr. He said to the Holy Prophet: Messenger of Allah, I was absent from your first battle with the pagans. If Allah will bring me to face the pagans in another battle Allah will demonstrate my performance. On the day of the battle of Uhud the Muslims were exposed. He said: Allah, I plead with Thee concerning that which the Muslims have done, and dissociate myself from that which the pagans have perpetrated. Then he went forward and encountered Sa'ad ibn Mu'az and said to him: Paradise! By the Lord of the Ka'aba, I perceive the fragrance of Paradise from beyond Uhud. Sa'ad said later: Messenger of Allah, I have not the power to describe what he did. Anas (the nephew) relates: We found on his body more than eighty injuries inflicted by swords, spears and arrows. Thus was he killed and the pagans had cut off his nose and ears. No one could identify him except his sister who recognised the tips of his fingers. We imagined that the following verse had reference to him and those like him: Among the believers are men who have been true to the covenant they made with Allah. Some have fulfilled their vow and laid down their lives in battle, and there are others who wait. They have not weakened in their resolve in the least (8.24) (Bokhari and Muslim).

110.   Abu Mas'ud Uqbah ibn Amr Ansari relates that when the verse enjoining charity was revealed we would carry loads on our backs to earn something that we could give away in charity. One person presented a substantial amount for charity and the hypocrites said he had done it to show off. Another gave away a few pounds of dates and they said: Allah is not in need of his dates. Thereupon was revealed: It is these hypocrites who find fault with such of the believers as give alms freely and decide those who have nothing to give save that which they earn through their toil. Allah shall requite them for their derision and for them there is a painful chastisement (9.79).

111.   Abu Dharr relates that the Holy Prophet said: Allah admonishes you: O My servants, I have charged Myself to wrong no one and have forbidden it between you, so wrong not anyone; O My servants, all of you are astray save those whom I should guide; O My servants, all of you are hungry save those whom I should feed, then supplicate Me for food, I shall feed you; O My servants, all of you are naked save those whom I should clothe, then supplicate Me for clothes, I shall clothe you; O My servants, you misbehave night and day and I forgive all sins, then supplicate Me for forgiveness, I shall forgive you; O

My servants, you can have no power to do Me harm, nor can you have power to confer any benefit upon Me; O My servants, if the first of you and the last of you, and the whole lot of you, high and low, were to become like one who has the most righteous soul among you, that would not add a whit to My Kingdom; O My servants, if the first of you and the last of you, and the whole lot of you, high and low, were to become like the one who has the most vicious soul among you, that would not detract a whit from My Kingdom; O My servants, if the first of you and the last of you, and the whole lot of you, high and low, were to assemble in one large plain and were to beg Me for whatever they desire and I were to bestow upon each of you all that he had asked for, that would not detract from My treasures any more than a needle would detract from the ocean by being immersed in it. O My servants, I compass your deeds and shall make a full requital for them to you. Then he who encounters good should praise Allah for it; and he who encounters something else should blame only himself (Muslim).

12.

On Urging Oneself towards Increasing Good in Later Life

Allah, the Exalted, has said:

48. Did we not grant you a long enough span of life to enable those to reflect who might desire to reflect; and did not a Warner come to you (35.38)?

112. Abu Hurairah relates that the Holy Prophet said: Allah continues to excuse a person till he reaches the age of sixty years (Bokhari).

113. Ibn Abbas relates: Umar used to call me to his council along with the elders who had fought in the battle of Badr. It seems some of them resented this and said: Why does he include him among us? Our sons are of his age. Umar told them: He belongs to the source of your knowledge. He called me one day among them and I felt that he had called me to demonstrate this to them. He said to them: What is the meaning of: When the succour of Allah comes and victory is achieved (110.2)? Some of them said: In this verse we have been commanded that we should praise Allah and supplicate for His forgiveness when He helps us and gives us victory. Some remained quiet and said nothing. Umar said to me: Do you say the same, Ibn Abbas? I said: No. Then what do you say? I said: This was an intimation of the approach of the death of the Holy Prophet which Allah conveyed to him. Allah said: The succour of Allah and victory having come (and this is an intimation of the approach of your death) then glorify your Lord, with His praise and seek forgiveness of Him; surely He is Oft-Returning with compassion. Umar said: No one knows better than that which you have said (Bokhari).

114. Ayesha relates that after the revelation of: The succour of Allah having come and the victory; the Holy Prophet used to recite in every *salat:* Holy art Thou, our Lord, and all praise is Thine; Forgive me, O Allah (Bokhari and Muslim).

Another version is: The Holy Prophet recited repeatedly in his *ruku'* and *sajdah:* Holy art Thou, O Allah, our Lord, and all praise is Thine; forgive me, O Allah; following the direction in the Quran.

Still another version is: Before his death the Holy Prophet often recited: Holy art Thou and all praise is Thine, I seek forgiveness of Thee and turn to Thee. I (Ayesha) asked him: Messenger of Allah, what are these new phrases I hear you repeat? He said: A sign has been appointed for me concerning my people that when I should see that sign I should repeat these phrases. Then he recited *sura* Al-Nasr.

A fourth version is: The Holy Prophet often recited: Holy is Allah and His is all praise: I seek forgiveness of Allah and turn to Him. I said to him: Messenger of Allah, I hear you recite often: Holy is Allah and His is all praise; I seek forgiveness of Allah and turn to Him. He said: My Lord told me that I would soon see a sign concerning my people and that when I see it I should often proclaim His holiness and praise and ask His forgiveness and turn to Him. Now I have seen that sign. The coming of the succour of Allah and victory was the fall of Mecca, and the sign was seeing people join the religion of Allah in large numbers. The command is: Proclaim the holiness of Allah with His praise and ask forgiveness of Him. He is Oft-Returning with compassion.

115. Anas relates: Allah, the Lord of honour and glory, sent revelation to the Holy Prophet much oftener before his death than at any other time (Bokhari and Muslim).

116. Jabir relates that the Holy Prophet said: Everyone will be raised in the condition in which he dies (Muslim).

13.
On the Variety of Ways of Goodness

Allah, the Exalted has said:

49. Whatever good you do, surely Allah knows it well (2.216).

50. Whatever good you do, Allah will recognise its value (2.198).

51. Then whoso will have done the smallest particle of good will see it (99.8).

52. Whoso does good, does it to his own benefit (45.16).

117. Abu Dharr relates: I asked the Holy Prophet: What is most meritorious? He said: Faith in Allah and striving in His cause. I asked: The freeing of which slave is best? He said: Of that one whom the master likes best and whose value is highest. I asked: If one is not able to do that? He said: Then help someone with his work, or make something for someone who is not able to make it himself. I asked: If one should not have the strength? He said: Restrain thyself from doing harm to anyone for that also is charity towards thyself (Bokhari and Muslim).

118. Abu Dharr relates that the Holy Prophet said: When you get up in the morning charity is due from every one of your limbs. All glorification of Allah is charity, all praise of Allah is charity; enjoining good is charity, forbidding evil is charity. Two *raka'as* of Prayer in the forenoon equal all this (Muslim).

119. Abu Dharr relates that the Holy Prophet said: I have been shown the deeds of my people, the good and the bad. Among the good I found the removal from a path of that which occasions inconvenience to people, and among the bad, spittal lying unburied in the mosque (Muslim).

120. Abu Dharr relates that some people said to the Holy Prophet: The wealthy walk away with a great deal of merit. They pray as we pray and fast as we fast, but then they are able to give away in charity of their spare wealth. He said: Has not Allah endowed you with that which you can employ for charity? All glorification of Allah is charity, all praise of Allah is charity, all affirmation of Allah's Unity is charity, all affirmation of Allah's Greatness is charity, enjoining good is charity, forbidding evil is charity, consorting with your wives is charity. They asked: Messenger of Allah, is it that one of us should satisfy his urge and he would be rewarded? He said: If he satisfied his urge unlawfully would it not be sinful? Thus when he satisfies it lawfully it is meritorious (Muslim).

121. Abu Dharr relates that the Holy Prophet said: Do not disdain doing the least good, even greeting your brother with a cheerful face (Muslim).

122. Abu Hurairah relates that the Holy Prophet said: Charity is due from every limb of a person on every day on which the sun rises. Doing justice between two persons is charity, to help a person ride his mount or to place his baggage on it is charity, a good word is charity, every step taken to participate in the *salat* is charity, removing anything from a path which occasions inconvenience is charity (Bokhari and Muslim). Muslim has also reported on the authority of Ayesha that the Holy Prophet said: Everyone has been created with three hundred and sixty joints. Then whoever affirms Allah's greatness, praises Allah, affirms His Unity, proclaims His holiness, asks His forgiveness, removes a stone or thorn or bone from a path frequented by people, enjoins good, or forbids evil to the number of three hundred and sixty, goes about having rescued himself from the Fire.

123. Abu Hurairah relates that the Holy Prophet said: Whoever walks to the mosque in the morning or the evening, Allah prepares an entertainment for him in Paradise every time he so walks (Bokhari and Muslim).

124. Abu Hurairah relates that the Holy Prophet said: O Muslim women, let not a neighbour refrain from sending her neighbour even a goat's shank (Bokhari and Muslim).

125. Abu Hurairah relates that the Holy Prophet said: Faith has more

than sixty or seventy factors, the highest of which is the affirmation: There is
none worthy of worship save Allah alone; and the least of which is to remove
from a path that which occasions inconvenience. Modesty is also a factor of faith
(Bokhari and Muslim).

126. Abu Hurairah relates that the Holy Prophet said: A man proceeding
along a track became very thirsty. Arriving at a well he descended into it and
came out after taking a drink and saw a dog with its tongue lolling out trying to
lick up mud from extreme thirst. The man thought this dog is suffering from
thirst as I was suffering. So he descended once more into the well, filled his
leather sock with water and came up holding it by his teeth and gave the dog a
drink. Allah appreciated his action and forgave his sins. The Holy Prophet was
asked: Messenger of Allah, are we rewarded for kindness to animals also? He
answered: There is a reward for kindness to every living thing (Bokhari and
Muslim). Bokhari's version concludes with: Allah appreciated his action,
forgave his sins and admitted him to Paradise. Another version is: A dog was
going round the brink of a well in an extremity of thirst, when a loose woman of
the Bani Israel espied it. She lowered her leather sock into the well, drew up
some water and gave the dog to drink. She was forgiven on account of this.

127. Abu Hurairah relates that the Holy Prophet said: I saw a man going
about in Paradise because he had cut down a tree from the side of a road which
occasioned inconvenience to the Muslims (Muslim). Another version is: A man
passed by a branch of a tree leaning over a road. He said: I must cut it down so
that it should not occasion inconvenience to the Muslims. He was admitted to
Paradise on account of it. Still another version is: A man passing along a road
found a thorny branch leaning over the road and pushed it away. Allah
appreciated his action and forgave him his sins (Bokhari and Muslim).

128. Abu Hurairah relates that the Holy Prophet said: He who makes his
ablutions carefully and comes to the Friday service and listens to the sermon in
silence is forgiven his sins since the previous Friday and three days more. He
who occupies himself with pebbles during the sermon behaves ill (Muslim).

129. Abu Hurairah relates that the Holy Prophet said: When a Muslim
makes his ablutions and washes his face the water carries away all sins
committed by his eyes, and when he washes his hands the water carries away all
sins committed by his hands and when he washes his feet the water carries away
all sins towards which he had walked, and he emerges cleansed of all his sins
(Muslim).

130. Abu Hurairah relates that the Holy Prophet said: The five daily
services, two Friday services and observing the fast during two Ramadhans
atone for whatever may be between them so long as major sins are guarded
against (Muslim).

131. Abu Hurairah relates that the Holy Prophet said: Shall I tell you
something whereby Allah would wipe out your sins and raise your status? Those
present said: Certainly, Messenger of Allah. He said: Performing the ablution
carefully even in difficulty, frequent walking to the mosque, and waiting eagerly

for the next *salat* after one is finished. This is your striving in the cause of Allah (Muslim).

132. Abu Musa Ash'ari relates that the Holy Prophet said: He who observes the *salats* of *Fajr* and *Asr* with diligence will enter Paradise (Bokhari and Muslim).

133. Abu Musa Ash'ari relates that the Holy Prophet said: When a servant of Allah falls ill or goes on a journey he is credited with the equal of whatever he used to do in his state of health or when he was at home (Bokhari).

134. Jabir relates that the Holy Prophet said: Every good deed is charity (Bokhari). Muslim has reported the same on the authority of Huzaifah.

135. Jabir relates that the Holy Prophet said: If a Muslim plants a tree, then whatever is eaten from it is charity on his part and whatever is stolen is charity and whatever is subtracted from it is charity (Muslim). Another version is: If a Muslim plants a tree or sows a field and men and beasts and birds eat from it, all of it is charity on his part.

136. Jabir relates that the Bani Salimah decided to move nearer to the mosque. On learning this the Holy Prophet said to them: I have heard that you intend to move nearer to the mosque. They said: That is so, Messenger of Allah, we intend to do that. He said: Bani Salimah, keep to your homes, your footprints are recorded; Bani Salimah, keeps to your homes, your footprints are recorded (Muslim). Another version adds; Every step you take towards the mosque enhances your rank.

137. Ubayy ibn Ka'ab relates: There was a person whose house was farthest from the mosque than that of anyone I knew and he never missed a Prayer service. I said to him: Why do you not purchase a donkey that you could ride in the dark and in the heat? He said: I would not like that my residence should be close to the mosque. I desire that my walking to the mosque and my return home therefrom should be recorded to my credit. The Holy Prophet said to him: Allah has credited all that to your account (Muslim) Another version adds: All that you do with a good motive is credited to you.

138. Abdullah ibn Amr ibn 'As relates that the Holy Prophet said: There are forty types of virtue (the highest of them being the loan of a she-camel yielding milk) whichever of them is practised in the hope of its reward and relying on its promise would lead its practitioner to Paradise (Bokhari).

139. Adiyy ibn Hatim relates that he heard the Holy Prophet say: Shield yourselves against the Fire, even if it be by giving away half a date in charity (Bokhari and Muslim). Another version is that the Holy Prophet said: There is not one of you but that his Lord will speak to him without the intervention of an interpreter. He will look to his right and will behold only his deeds and will look to his left and see only his deeds. He will look in front and will only see the Fire close to his face. Then shield yourselves against the Fire, even if it be by giving away half a date in charity, and if even that should be lacking, by saying a good word.

140. Anas relates that the Holy Prophet said: It pleases Allah that a

servant of His should praise Him when he eats and should praise Him when he drinks (Muslim).

141. Abu Musa Ash'ari relates that the Holy Prophet said: Charity is incumbent upon every Muslim. He was asked: If a person should have nothing? He answered: He should work with his hands to his own benefit and also give alms. If he is not able to work? He should help a needy helpless one. If he cannot do even that? He should urge others to goodness. If he lacks that also? He should restrain himself from doing evil. That too is charity (Bokhari and Muslim).

14.
On Moderation in Worship

Allah, the Exalted, has said:

53. We have not sent down the Quran to thee that thou may be distressed (20.3).

54. Allah desires ease for you and desires not hardship for you (2.186).

142. Ayesha relates that the Holy Prophet came in when there was a woman with her. He asked: Who is she? I said: She is the one whose *salat* is much talked about. Addressing her he said: Now wait a moment. You are required to do only that much which you can carry out easily. Allah does not tire of you until you tire of Him. Allah likes that spiritual exercise best which a worshipper can carry out diligently (Bokhari and Muslim).

143. Anas relates: Three persons inquired from the wives of the Holy Prophet about his practice in the matter of worship. When they were told they felt this would not be enough in their case and said: There is no comparison between the Holy Prophet and us. He has been forgiven in advance. One of them declared: I shall always spend the whole night in voluntary Prayer. The second announced: I shall observe a fast every day without interruption. The third said: I shall keep away from women and shall never marry. The Holy Prophet arrived and asked them: Did you say this and this? Now, I fear God more than you do and am more mindful of my duty to Him than you are, but I observe a fast and also abstain from fasting, and I perform voluntary Prayer at night and also sleep, and I consort with my wives. He who turns away from my practice is not of me (Bokhari and Muslim).

144. Ibn Mas'ud relates that the Holy Prophet said: Ruined are those who insist on hardship in matters of the faith. He repeated it three times (Muslim).

145. Abu Hurairah relates that the Holy Prophet said: The commandments of the faith are easy. Whoever imports hardship into them is vanquished by them. So be moderate, and perform in proportion to your strength and cheerfully, and seek Allah's help morn and eve and during a portion of the night (Bokhari). Another version adds: Be moderate, be moderate.

146. Anas relates: The Holy Prophet came into the mosque and noticed a rope stretched between two columns. He inquired: What is this rope for? He was told: This is Zainab's rope. When during her voluntary Prayer she begins to feel tired she grasps it for support. The Holy Prophet said: Undo it. You should pray so long as you feel alert. When you feel tired you should go to sleep (Bokhari and Muslim).

147. Ayesha relates that the Holy Prophet said: If any of you should be drowsy in the course of the *salat,* he should sleep till his drowsiness departs, for if he prays while he is drowsy he cannot be sure that while meaning to seek forgiveness he might be reviling himself (Bokhari and Muslim).

148. Jabir ibn Samurah relates: I had the opportunity of joining the Prayer services led by the Holy Prophet on many occasions. His prayer was moderate and his sermon was moderate (Muslim).

149. Abu Juhaifah Wahb ibn Abdullah relates that the Holy Prophet had established a bond of brotherhood between Salman and Abu Darda'. Salman went to see Abu Darda' and found his wife untidy. He asked her: What is the matter with you? She said: Your brother, Abu Darda' has no worldly desires. Then Abu Darda' arrived and prepared some food for Salman and said: Go ahead and eat, for I am fasting. Salman said: I shall not eat unless you eat with me. So Abu Darda' ate with him. At night Abu Darda' got up for voluntary Prayer. Salman told him to go to sleep and he slept. This happened again. In the latter part of the night Salman said to him: Now get up; and both performed the *salat* together. Then Salman said: It is true you owe your duty to your Lord, but you also owe a duty to yourself and you owe a duty to your wife. So you should render to everyone their due. Then they went to the Holy Prophet and related all this to him. He said: Salman was right (Bokhari).

150. Abdullah ibn Amr ibn 'As relates that the Holy Prophet was told that I had said: I shall observe the fast every day and shall spend the whole night in voluntary Prayer as long as I live. The Holy Prophet asked me: Are you the one who has said this? I replied: Indeed, I have said it, Messenger of Allah, may my father and mother be thy ransom. He said: You will not be able to sustain this. You may fast but with breaks, and you may get up for voluntary Prayer, but you should also sleep. Observe the fast for three days in a month, and as the value of a good deed is tenfold this would be equal to a full month's fast. I said: I am strong enough to do better than this. He said: Then fast one day and leave out two days. I said: I am strong enough enough to do better than that. He said: Well, then, fast one day and leave off one day. This was the fast of David and it is the best fast. I said: I am strong enough to do better than that. The Holy Prophet said: There is nothing better than this. I now wish I had agreed to the suggestion of the Holy Prophet that I should fast on three days in a month. This would be dearer to me than my property and my children (Bokhari and Muslim).

Another version is: The Holy Prophet said: Have I not been told that you observe the fast every day and stand for voluntary Prayer throughout the night? I said: That is so, Messenger of Allah. He said: Do not do so. Observe the fast and leave off, sleep and stand in Prayer. Your body has a right, your eyes have a right, your wife has a right, your guest has a right. It would be enough if you were to fast on three days in a month; for as every good deed has a tenfold value this would be equal to a whole month of fasting. But I was hard on myself and thus was hardship imposed upon me. I said: Messenger of Allah, I feel strong. He said: Then observe the fast of David, the Prophet of Allah, and do not add to it. I asked: What was the fast of David? He said: Half the time. Alas, how I wish I had accepted the first suggestion of the Holy Prophet!

Another version is: Have I not been told that you observe the fast every day and recite the entire Quran during one night? I said: That is so, Messenger of Allah, and I intend only good in doing so. He said: Observe the fast of David, the Prophet of Allah, for he performed more worship than any other man, and completed the recitation of the Quran in one month. I said: Prophet of Allah, I am strong enough to do better than this. He said: Then complete it in twenty days. I said: Prophet of Allah, I feel strong enough to do better than that. He said: Then recite it in ten days. I said: Prophet of Allah, I have strength for better than that. He said: Well, then, recite it in seven days and do not add to this recitation. Thus I was hard on myself and hardship was imposed upon me. The Holy Prophet said to me: You do not know, you may live quite long. Then I arrived at that which the Holy Prophet had said. When I became old I wished I had accepted the original suggestion of the Holy Prophet.

One version adds: Your son has a right.

One version is: The Holy Prophet said: He who fasts everyday, does not fast at all, and repeated it three times.

One version adds: The fast most acceptable to Allah is the fast of David, and the *salat* most acceptable to Allah is the *salat* of David. He slept through half the night, then stood in Prayer one third of it and then slept through one sixth; and he used to fast one day and leave off one. He did not retreat in the face of the enemy.

Another version is: My father had married me to a woman of good family and he used to inquire from his daughter-in-law about her husband. She would say: A fine man indeed. Since I have come to him he has not lain down with me nor has he looked at my face. When this continued for some time my father mentioned the matter to the Holy Prophet. He said to my father: Send him to me. So I went to him. He asked me: How often do you fast? I said: Every day. He asked me: How long do you take in reciting the entire Quran? I said: Once every night. Then followed that which has been related already. When Abdullah became old he would recite one seventh of his nightly recitation to some member of his family during the day to lighten his task at night. When he desired relief from his fasting on alternate days he would leave off fasting for a few days and make up later the number of fasts he had missed. He would not give up the number altogether as he disliked going back on what he had settled with the Holy Prophet in the latter's lifetime.

151. Hanzala ibn Rabi' Usaidi relates: Abu Bakr Siddique met me and greeted me with: How are you, Hanzala? I replied: Hanzala has become a hypocrite. Abu Bakr said: Holy is Allah! What are you saying, Hanzala? I said: When we are in the company of the Holy Prophet he reminds us of Paradise and the Fire and we feel as if we are looking at them. But when we depart from him we are beguiled by our wives and children and livelihoods and we forget the greater part. Abu Bakr said: We too are in the same state. Then Abu Bakr and I went along till we came to the Holy Prophet and I said: Messenger of Allah, Hanzala has become a hypocrite. He said: What is that? I said: Messenger of Allah, when we are in your company you talk to us of Paradise and the Fire and we feel as if we are looking at them. But when we depart from you we are beguiled by our wives and children and livelihoods and we forget the greater part. The Holy Prophet said: By Him in Whose hands is my life, if you were to continue as you are when you are with me occupied with the remembrance of Allah, angels would shake hands with you in your beds and your streets. But Hanzala, there are moments and moments, and he repeated this last phrase three times (Muslim).

152. Ibn Abbas relates: While the Holy Prophet was delivering his address he noticed a man who was standing and he inquired about him. He was told that his name was Abu Israel and he had made a vow that he would keep standing in the sun, would not sit down, would not move into the shade, would not talk to anyone and would observe a fast. The Holy Prophet said: Tell him to talk, to move into the shade and sit down. But let him complete his fast (Bokhari).

15.
On Constancy in Righteous Conduct

Allah, the Exalted, has said:

55. Is it not time that the hearts of those who believe should feel humbled at the remembrance of Allah and of that which has come down to them of the truth? Let them not be like those who were given the Book before them and the term of Allah's favour was prolonged for them, so that their hearts were hardened (57.17).

56. And We caused Jesus son of Mary to follow them, and We gave him the Gospel. We put compassion and mercy in the hearts of those who followed him. They took up monasticism for the seeking of Allah's pleasure. We did not prescribe it for them, but then they did not observe it duly (57.28).

*57. Be not like the woman who having made strong yarn
breaks it into pieces (16.93).*

*58. Carry on the worship of thy Lord till death comes to thee
(15.100).*

153.   Ayesha relates that the Holy Prophet liked that act of worship best in
the performance of which a person was regular and constant.

154.   Umar ibn Khattab relates that the Holy Prophet said: A person who
misses his voluntary Prayer or a portion of it at night because of sleep will be
credited with the same merit if he performs it at any time between *Fajr* and
Zohar (Muslim).

155.   Abdullah ibn Amr ibn 'As relates: The Holy Prophet directed me:
Abdullah, do not be like So and So. He used to get up at night for voluntary
Prayer but gave it up later (Bokhari and Muslim).

156.   Ayesha relates that when the Holy Prophet missed his voluntary
Prayer at night on account of indisposition or some such cause he would offer
twelve *raka'as* during the day (Muslim).

16.

On the Obligation of Obedience to the Holy Prophet

Allah, the Exalted, has said:

*59. Whatever the Messenger gives you, that take; and
whatsoever he forbids you, from that abstain (59.8).*

*60. He does not speak out of his own desire; the Quran is
pure revelation sent to him (53.4-5).*

*61. Announce: If you love Allah, then follow me; Allah will
then love you and forgive you your sins (3.32).*

*62. You have in the Messenger of Allah an excellent
exemplar, for him who hopes to meet with Allah and the Last
Day (33.22).*

*63. By thy Lord, they will not truly believe until they make
thee judge in all that is in dispute between them and then
find not any demur in their hearts concerning that which
thou decidest and submit with complete submission (4.65).*

*64.   Then if you differ in anything refer it to Allah and His
Messenger if you are believers in Allah and the Last Day
(4.60).*

*65.   Whoso obeys the Messenger has indeed obeyed Allah
(4.81).*

*66.   Truly, thou dost guide mankind to the right path; the
path of Allah (42.53).*

67. Let those who oppose the command of the Messenger beware lest a trial afflict them or a grievous punishment overtake them (24.64).

68.   Remember that which is rehearsed in your homes of the Signs of Allah and of wisdom (33.34).

157.   Abu Hurairah relates that the Holy Prophet said: Leave me alone in respect of that which I do not mention to you. Those who were before you were ruined by their habit of asking too many questions and their differences concerning their Prophets. When I forbid you anything keep away from it altogether, and when I prescribe anything for you carry it out as far as you can (Bokhari and Muslim).

158.   Irbah ibn Sariah relates: The Holy Prophet made us a moving address and we said: Messenger of Allah, this sounds like a farewell admonition, then tell us some more; whereupon he said: I adjure you to be mindful of your duty to Allah, and to hear and obey even if a negro slave is put in authority over you. Those of you who survive me will observe much contention. At such time hold fast to my practice and the practice of my rightly guided successors. Hold on to it by your hind teeth, and beware of innovations, for every innovation is error (Abu Daud and Tirmidhi).

159.   Abu Hurairah relates that the Holy Prophet said: All my people will enter Paradise, except those who deny me. He was asked: Who will be the deniers, Messenger of Allah? He said: He who obeys me will enter Paradise and he who disobeys me denies me (Bokhari).

160.   Salamah ibn Amr ibn Akwa' relates that a man ate with his left hand in the presence of the Holy Prophet, who said to him: Eat with your right hand. He said: I am not able to. The Holy Prophet said: May you not be able to. It was pure arrogance that had stopped him. Thereafter he could not raise his hand to his mouth (Muslim).

161.   Nu'man ibn Bashir relates that he heard the Holy Prophet direct: Do keep your rows straight during Prayer services, else Allah will create dissensions among you (Bokhari and Muslim).

Muslim also has a version: The Holy Prophet insisted on our keeping our rows straight, so much so as if he should be able to determine the straightness of arrows by them. He continued to emphasise this till he felt that we had recognised its importance. One day he came into the mosque to lead the Prayer and the *takbir* was about to be called when he noticed the chest of one of the worshippers sticking out of the line, on which he said: Servants of Allah, keep you rows straight, else Allah will create dissensions among you.

162.   Abu Musa relates that a house in Medina caught fire at night and the roof and walls fell down upon the occupants. When this was related to the Holy Prophet, he said: Fire is your enemy; when you go to sleep put it out (Bokhari and Muslim).

163. Abu Musa relates that the Holy Prophet observed: The case of the guidance and knowledge with which I have seen sent is that of rain which falls on land part of which is good and fertile and dry grass thereon turns green and a quantity of new and fresh grass is produced; and part of it is dry and it stores up the water and God makes it beneficial for people, they drink from it and use it for cultivation; and part of it is a barren plain which neither retains the water nor produces fresh grass. This is the case of those who understand the faith revealed by Allah and benefit from that with which Allah has sent me and learn it and teach it; and of those who do not stir their heads to gain knowledge of the faith and do not accept the guidance with which I have been sent (Bokhari and Muslim).

164. Jabir relates that the Holy Prophet said: You and I are as if a person kindles a fire and moths and such-like rush to fall into it and he strives to screen them from it. I hold you by your waists and you struggle to fall out of my hands (Muslim).

165. Jabir relates that the Holy Prophet urged the licking of fingers and the gleaning of vessels. He said: You do not know which part of the food is more richly blest (Muslim). Another version adds: If any of you should happen to drop a morsel, he should pick it up, cleanse it of dust etc. and eat it and not leave it for Satan. Nor should you wipe your hands with a napkin without licking the food off your fingers, for you know not which part of the food is more richly blest. Another version is: Satan is present with you on all occasions, even when you are eating. Then if a morsel should fall from your hand, you should pick it up, cleanse it of dust etc. and eat it and not leave it for Satan.

166. Ibn Abbas relates: The Holy Prophet admonished us: O ye people, you will be assembled before Allah bare-footed, naked and uncircumcised. As We began the first creation, so shall We repeat it. We have charged Ourself with it, and so shall We do (21.105). Hearken, the first creature to be clothed will be Abraham. Some of my people will be brought who will be led to the left. I shall call out: Lord, these are my companions. I will be told: You do not know what did they perpetrate after you. Then I shall say what another righteous servant of Allah said: I watched over them as long as I was present among them, but since Thou didst cause me to die, Thou hast been the One to watch over them. Indeed Thou dost watch over all things. If Thou decide to punish them they are Thy servants; and if Thou forgive them, Thou surely art the Mighty, the Wise (5.118-119). I shall be told: They continued to turn away on their heels since you parted from them (Bokhari and Muslim).

167. Abdullah ibn Mughaffal relates that the Holy Prophet forbade shooting pebbles by manipulating the thumb and forefinger as a sling, and said: Such a shot does not kill game, nor put the enemy out of action, but it gouges out an eye or breaks a tooth (Bokhari and Muslim). A close relative of Ibn Mughaffal shot a pebble in this manner and he rebuked him saying: The Holy Prophet forbade it and said that it does not kill game. But the man did not desist and repeated his act whereupon Ibn Mughaffal said to him: I told you that the Holy Prophet had forbidden such a shot and yet you repeated it. I shall never speak to you again.

168. 'Abis ibn Rabi'a relates: I saw Umar ibn Khattab kissing the Black Stone and I heard him say: I know well thou art but a piece of rock and hast no power to confer a benefit or to do harm. Had I not seen the Holy Prophet kiss thee I would never have kissed thee (Bokhari and Muslim).

17.

On the Obligation to obey the Commands of Allah

Allah, the Exalted, has said:

69. By thy Lord, they will not truly believe until they make thee judge in all that is in dispute between them and then find not in their hearts any demur concerning that which thou dost decide and submit with full submission (4.66).

70. The response of the believers, when they are called to Allah and His Messenger that he may judge between them is: We have heard and we obey. It is they who will prosper (24.52).

169. Abu Hurairah relates that when the following verse was revealed to the Holy Prophet: To Allah belongs whatever is in the heavens and whatever is in the earth. Whether you disclose that which is in your minds or keep it hidden, Allah will call you to account for it (2.285); his companions were distressed and went to him and, falling down on their knees, said to him: Messenger of Allah, we have been charged with that which is within our capacity, *salat*, striving, fasting and charity. Now this verse has been revealed to you and what it charges us with is beyond our capacity. He said: Do you wish to say, as said the People of the two Books: We have heard, but we shall disobey? Rather should you say: We have heard and we shall obey; we implore Thy forgiveness, Lord, and unto Thee is our return. When they had recited this and their tongues had adapted themselves to it, Allah revealed: The Messenger has full faith in that which has been sent down to him from his Lord and so have the believers; all of them believe in Allah, and in His angels, and in His Books and in His Messengers, affirming: We make no distinction between any of His Messengers. They say: We have heard and we shall obey. We implore They forgiveness, Lord, and to Thee is our return (2.286). When they had carried this out, Allah, the Lord of honour and glory, revealed: Allah requires not of anyone that which is beyond his capacity; each shall have the benefit of the good he does and shall suffer the consequences of the ill he works. Supplicate, therefore: Lord, take us not to task if we forget or fall into error; Lord, place us not under responsibility in the manner of those whom Thou didst place under responsibility before us; Lord, burden us not with that which we have not the strength to bear; overlook our defaults and grant us forgiveness and have mercy on us; Thou art our Master, so grant us succour against those who reject Thee (2.287) (Muslim).

18.
On Prohibition of Innovations in the Faith

Allah, the Exalted, has said:

71.   So what is there after discarding the truth but error (10.32)?

72.   We have not left out anything in the Book (6.39).

73.   Then if you differ in anything, refer it to Allah and His Messenger (4.60).

74.   This is My straight path, so follow it; and follow not diverse ways lest they lead you away from His way (6.154).

75.   Announce: If you love Allah, then follow me, Allah will then love you and forgive you your faults (3.32).

170.   Ayesha relates that the Holy Prophet said: If anyone seeks to introduce into this faith of ours something that does not belong to it, that is to be rejected (Bokhari and Muslim). Muslim adds: A practice that is not enjoined by us is to be rejected.

171.   Jabir relates: When the Holy Prophet delivered a sermon his eyes would become red, his voice would rise and he would be in a passion as if he was alerting us against an enemy host. He would say: The enemy is advancing against you in the morning; he is advancing against you in the evening. He would say: My advent and the advent of the Judgment are juxtaposed as my two fingers; and he would hold up his forefinger and middle finger held close together. He would point out: The best discourse is the Book of Allah and the best example is the example of Muhammad; the worst practice is the injection of new elements in the faith, and every innovation is misguidance. He would say: I am closer to every believer than his own self. If a believer leaves assets they would accrue to his heirs. If he dies an insolvent, survived by dependants, the responsibility for the payment of his debts and looking after his dependants is mine (Muslim).

172.   See No. 158 related by Irbah ibn Sariah.

19.
On New Ways of Doing Good or the Reverse

Allah, the Exalted, has said:

76.   Those who implore: Lord, grant us of our spouses and our offspring the delight of your eyes, and make us a model for the righteous (21.74).

77. *We made them leaders who guided people by Our command (21.74).*

173. Jarir ibn Abdullah relates: We were with the Holy Prophet in the forenoon when some people came to him who had pieces of woollen matting slung from their necks, some of them wore sleeveless garments and their swords were hanging from their sides. They were all of the Mudhar tribe. The Holy Prophet was deeply affected on observing their famished faces. He got up and entered his chamber, then came out and asked Bilal to make the call for Prayer, led the Prayer and addressed those present: O mankind, be mindful of your duty to your Lord Who created you from a single soul and from it created its mate and from the two created and spread many men and women; and be mindful of your duty to Allah in Whose name you appeal to one another, and of your obligations in respect of your ties of kinship. Verily, Allah watches over you (4.2). O ye who believe, be mindful of your duty to Allah, and let everyone look to that which he lays up for the morrow (59.19). He urged everyone to make a charitable contribution out of his dinars and dirhems, clothes, wheat and dates, even if it was only half a date. One of the Ansars came with a bag the weight of which became unsupportable for his wrist, and others followed one after the other, and soon there were two piled-up heaps of food and clothes. I noticed that the Holy Prophet's face shone like burnished gold. He said: Whoever initiates in Islam a way of doing good will have his reward for it and also a reward for everyone who acts in that way, without diminishing in any way the reward of the latter; and whoever initiates in Islam an evil practice will carry its burden and the burden of everyone who acts in that way, without diminishing in any way the burden of the latter (Muslim).

174. Ibn Mas'ud relates that the Holy Prophet said: The first son of Adam bears a portion of the guilt of everyone who kills another wrongfully because he was the first who committed murder (Bokhari and Muslim).

20.

On Pointing out the Way of Good and Urging towards Guidance or Error

Allah, the Exalted, has said:

78. *Call people to thy Lord (28.88).*

79. *Call unto the way of thy Lord with wisdom and goodly exhortation (16.126).*

80. *Assist one another in piety and rectitude (5.3).*

81. *Let there be from among you a party whose business it should be to call to goodness (3.105).*

175. Uqbah ibn Amr Ansari relates that the Holy Prophet said: The reward of one who guides another towards good is equal to the reward of the latter (Muslim).

176. Abu Hurairah relates that the Holy Prophet said: He who calls people to guidance has the same reward as those who follow him without any diminution of the reward of the latter, and he who calls people to error carries the same burden of sin as those who follow him without any diminution in the burdens of the latter (Muslim).

177. Sahl ibn Sa'ad relates that before the battle of Khaibar the Holy Prophet announced: Tomorrow I shall give the standard to a man at whose hands Allah will bestow victory upon us, he loves Allah and His Messenger, and Allah and His Messenger love him. The people spent the night guessing and discussing who would receive the standard. Next morning they went to the Holy Prophet, everyone hoping to receive it. The Holy Prophet inquired: Where is Ali ibn Abu Talib? He was told Ali had sore eyes. He said: Send for him. When he came, the Holy Prophet put his saliva in his eyes and prayed for him. He recovered as if he had never had any trouble at all. Then the Holy Prophet gave him the standard. Ali asked: Messenger of Allah, shall I fight them till they become like us? He answered: Continue till you arrive opposite to them. Then invite them to Islam and explain to them what are their obligations to Allah. Should a single person be guided by Allah through you that would be better for you than a whole lot of red camels (Bokhari and Muslim).

178. Anas relates that a young man of Bani Aslam came to the Holy Prophet and said to him: Messenger of Allah, I desire to join in the campaign but I have nothing with which I can procure equipment. He said: Go to So and So. He had procured his equipment but he has fallen ill. The young man went to him and said: The Messenger of Allah sends you greetings and says that you should hand over to me the equipment that you have procured. He called out to his wife and said: Give him all that I have procured and do not hold back anything from it. Do not hold back anything. Allah will make it a source of blessings for us (Muslim).

21.

On Assistance towards Piety and Rectitude

Allah, the Exalted, has said:

82. Assist one another in piety and rectitude (5.3).

83. We call to witness the passing time that surely man suffers continuous loss, except those who believe and work righteousness, and exhort one another to hold fast to the Truth, and exhort one another to be steadfast (103.2-4).

179. Zaid ibn Khalid Juhni relates that the Holy Prophet said: He who equips a fighter in the cause of Allah is as if he fights himself and he who looks after the dependants of a fighter in his absence is as if he fights himself (Bokhari and Muslim).

180. Abu Sa'id Khudri relates that the Holy Prophet sent a detachment of to Bani Lahyan and directed: Let one of every two men get ready to proceed, and both will earn the same reward (Muslim).

181. Ibn Abbas relates that the Holy Prophet encountered a party of mounted men at Rauha and asked them: Who are you? They answered: Muslims; and who are you? He said: Messenger of Allah. A woman from among them lifted a boy up to him and asked: Can this one go on Pilgrimage? He said: Yes, and you will have the reward (Muslim).

182. Abu Musa Ash'ari relates that the Holy Prophet said: A trusty Muslim treasurer is one who issues what he is ordered and makes it over cheerfully and in full to the person designated. Such a one has the same reward as if he was himself the donor (Bokhari and Muslim).

22.
On Goodwill

Allah, the Exalted, has said:

84. All believers are brothers (49.11).

85. Noah said: I wish you well (7.69); and Hud said: I am your sincere and faithful counsellor (7.69).

183. Tamim Dari relates that the Holy Prophet said: Faith is goodwill. We asked: Towards whom? He answered: Towards Allah, His Book, His Messenger, leading Muslims and the general public (Muslim).

184. Jarir ibn Abdullah relates: I made my covenant with the Holy Prophet that I would observe Prayer, pay the *Zakat* and have goodwill towards every Muslim (Bokhari and Muslim).

185. Anas relates that the Holy Prophet said: A person is not a believer unless he desires for his brother that which he desires for himself (Bokhari and Muslim).

23.
On Enjoining Good and Forbidding Evil

Allah, the Exalted, has said:

86. Let there be from among you a party whose business it should be to invite to goodness, to enjoin equity and to forbid evil. It is they who shall prosper (3.105).

87. You are the best people for you have been raised for the benefit of mankind; you enjoin good and forbid evil (3.111).

*88. Make forbearance thy rule, enjoin equity and turn away
from the ignorant (7.200).*

*89. The believers, men and women, are friends, one of
another; they enjoin good and forbid evil (9.71).*

*90. Those of the children of Israel who disbelieved were
cursed by David and by Jesus son of Mary. That was because
they disobeyed and were given to transgression. They did not
try to restrain one another from the iniquity which they
committed. Evil indeed was that which they used to do
(5.79-80).*

*91. Proclaim: This is the truth from your Lord; then let him
who will, believe; and let him who will, disbelieve (18.30).*

*92. Declare openly that which thou art commanded to
proclaim (15.95).*

*93. We delivered those who had admonished them, and We
afflicted the transgressors with a grievous chastisement
because they were rebellious (7.166).*

186. Abu Sa'id Khudri relates that he heard the Holy Prophet say: He who from among you observes something evil should reverse it with his hand; if he is unable to do that he should condemn it with his tongue; if he is unable to do that he should at least resent it in his heart; this is the lowest degree of faith (Muslim).

187. Ibn Mas'ud relates that the Holy Prophet said: Every one of the Prophets raised before me had devoted disciples and companions who followed his practice and obeyed his directions. These were followed by those who said that which they did not do, and did that which they were not commanded. He who challenges them with his hands is a believer, so also he who challenges them with his tongue, and so also he who challenges them with his heart. Beyond this there is not a grain of faith (Muslim).

188. Ubadah ibn Samat relates: We made a covenant with the Holy Prophet to hear and to obey in adversity and in prosperity, in hardship and in ease; to endure being discriminated against, and not to dispute the assumption of authority by others, except in a case of open repudiation of faith such as is condemned by clear authority; to tell the truth in every contingency and not to mind in that behalf any reproach or rebuke (Bokhari and Muslim).

189. Nu'man ibn Bashir relates that the Holy Prophet said: The case of those who observe the limits set by Allah and those who are careless about them is like passengers on a ship who cast lots to determine who should occupy the upper deck and who should be on the lower deck and disposed of themselves accordingly. Those who were on the lower deck passed through those of the upper deck whenever they had to fetch water. So they said to the occupants of the upper deck: If we were to bore a hole through our part, we would not then have to trouble you. Now, if the occupants of the upper deck were to leave the others to carry out their design they would all perish together; but if they were to stop them from carrying it out they would all be saved (Bokhari).

190. Umm Salamah (wife of the Holy Prophet) relates that the Holy Prophet said: There will be appointed in authority over you some in whose case you will recognise some of their actions as being in conformity with the law and others in conflict with it. Then he who refrains from following their example will be secure, and he who resents it will be guiltless; but he who is pleased and follows them will be accountable. He was asked: Messenger of Allah, shall we not fight them? He said: Not so long as they maintain the Prayer services among you (Muslim).

191. Zainab relates: The Holy Prophet came in one day in great perturbation saying: There is no one worthy of worship save Allah. Woe unto the Arabs from the evil that is approaching. A breach has been made in the wall holding back Gog and Magog of this size; and he made a circle of his thumb and forefinger. I said to him: Messenger of Allah, shall we be destroyed while there are a number of the righteous among us? He said: Yes; when evil becomes widespread (Bokhari and Muslim).

192. Abu Sa'id Khudri relates that the Holy Prophet directed: Refrain from sitting in the streets. It was said to him: Messenger of Allah, we cannot help sitting in the streets. There is no other place where we can sit and discuss matters. He said: In that case fulful the obligations due to the street. He was asked: What is due to the street? He said: Restraining of looks, removal of obstructions, reciprocation of greetings, enjoining good and forbidding evil (Bokhari and Muslim).

193. Ibn Abbas relates that the Holy Prophet noticed a gold ring on the finger of a man, took it off it and threw it away saying: One of you inclines towards a brand of fire and places it on his hand. After the Holy Prophet left, someone said to the man: Pick up the ring and make use of it in some other way. He said: The Holy Prophet has thrown it away, I shall never pick it up (Muslim).

194. Abu Sa'id Hasan Basri relates that A'aih ibn Amr visited Ubaidullah ibn Ziad and said to him: Son, I heard the Prophet say: The worst functionary is one who deals harshly with people. Beware, lest you should be one such. Ubaidullah said to him: Do sit down, you are but dry fodder from among the companions of the Holy Prophet. He retorted: And was there fodder among them? Surely, fodder came later among others (Muslim).

195. Huzaifah relates that the Holy Prophet said: By Him in Whose hands is my life, you will continue to enjoin good and forbid evil, or else Allah will certainly afflict you with torment from Him. Thereafter your supplications will not be heard (Tirmidhi).

196. Abu Sa'id Khudri relates that the Holy Prophet said: The highest striving is saying that which is just to a tyrant (Abu Daud and Tirmidhi).

197. Tariq ibn Shihab relates that a person asked the Holy Prophet when he had just put his foot in the stirrup: What is the highest form of striving? He said: Speaking truth to a tyrant (Nisai).

198. Abdullah ibn Mas'ud relates that the Holy Prophet said: The first weakness crept in among the children of Israel in this wise. One of them would meet another and say to him: Fear God and give up what you are doing, for this is not permissible for you. Then he would meet him the next day and find no change in him, but this would not prevent him from eating, drinking and associating with him. When it came to this Allah perverted the hearts of some on account of their association with others. Then he recited: Those of the children of Israel who disbelieved were cursed by David and by Jesus son of Mary. That was because they disobeyed and were given to transgression. They did not try to restrain one another from the iniquity that they committed. Evil indeed was that which they used to do. Thou shalt see many of them taking the disbelievers as their helpers. Evil indeed is that which they have chosen to send on ahead for themselves, which is that Allah is displeased with them and in this torment shall they abide. Had they believed in Allah and this Prophet, and in that which has been sent down to him, they would not have taken the disbelievers as their helpers, but most of them are disobedient (5.79-82). Then he continued: Indeed, by Allah, you must enjoin good and forbid evil and seize the hand of the wrongdoer and persuade him to act justly and establish him firmly on the right, else Allah will involve the hearts of some of you with the hearts of others and will curse you as he cursed them (Abu Daud and Tirmidhi).

The version of Tirmidhi has it: The Holy Prophet said: When the children of Israel became sinful their divines forbade them, but they would not desist. Yet the divines associated with them and ate and drank with them. So they were cursed by the mouths of David and Jesus son of Mary because they were disobedient and were given to transgression. At this stage the Holy Prophet who had been leaning back on a pillow sat up and said: No, No. By Him in Whose hands is my life, there is no escape for you but that you persuade them to act justly.

199. Abu Bakr Siddique relates: O ye people who read this verse: O ye who believe, be heedful of your own selves. If you make sure of being rightly guided yourselves, the going astray of another will not harm you (5.106); I have heard the Holy Prophet say: When the people see a wrongdoer committing a wrong and do not seize his hand to restrain him, it is most likely that Allah would afflict them with His chastisement (Abu Daud, Tirmidhi and Nisai).

24.
On Chastisement of One who enjoins Good and forbids Evil but his Conduct belies him

Allah, the Exalted, has said:

94. Do you, then, admonish others to do good and forget

your own selves while you read the Book? Will you not then understand (2.45)?

95. *O ye who believe, why do you say that which you do not? Most odious is it in the sight of Allah that you should say that which you do not (61.3-4).*

96. *Shuaib said: I do not desire to act contrary to that with which I admonish you (11.89).*

200. Usamah ibn Zaid relates that he heard the Holy Prophet say: A man will be brought on the Day of Judgment and will be thrown into the Fire, whereby his arteries will protrude out of his belly and he will go round and round holding them as does a donkey working a mill. The denizens of the Fire will gather round him and say: What is this? Did you not enjoin good and forbid evil? He will say: That is so. I enjoined good, but did not do it; and I forbade evil but did it (Bokhari and Muslim).

25.
On Discharging Trusts

Allah, the Exalted, has said:

97. *Allah commands you to render back the trusts to those entitled to them (4.59).*

98. *We offered the Trust to the heavens, and the earth and the mountains, but they refused to undertake it and were afraid of it. But man undertook it. Indeed he is capable of forcing himself to obey, disregardful of consequences (33.73).*

201. Abu Hurairah relates that the Holy Prophet said: A hypocrite has three characteristics: when he talks he lies, when he makes a promise he acts contrary to it, and when something is entrusted to him he embezzles it (Bokhari and Muslim). Another version adds: Even if he joins in Prayer, observes the fast and esteems himself a Muslim.

202. Huzaifah ibn Yaman relates: The Holy Prophet told us two things, one of which I have seen fulfilled, and of the other I am awaiting fulfillment. He told us that integrity was impregnated into the hearts of mankind. Then the Quran was revealed and they realised it from the Quran and learnt it from my practice. Then he told us about the disappearance of integrity and he said: A man will go to sleep and integrity will be lifted from his heart leaving only a mark on his heart like a boil which a spark of fire might leave on the skin of your foot, which arches out but is empty inside. Then he took up a pebble and started shooting it at his foot and continued: People will go on with their buying and selling, but not one of them will be a man of integrity, so much so that it will be said: There is among such and such a tribe a man who is trustworthy. It will be said of a man: How clever he is, how handsome and how intelligent; yet he will not have in his heart faith even as much as a mustard seed. Huzaifah added: Time was when I did not mind with whom I did business, for if he was a Muslim his faith was a sufficient guarantee, and if he was a Jew or a Christian his guardian was a sufficient guarantee. But today I do not do business except with So and So (Bokhari and Muslim).

203. Huzaifah and Abu Hurairah relate that the Holy Prophet said: On the Day of Judgment Allah, the Blessed and Exalted, will assemble mankind and the believers will be standing close to Paradise. They will approach Adam and ask him: Father, have Paradise opened for us. He will answer them: Was it not the default of your father which brought about your expulsion from the garden? I am not qualified for this. Go to my son Abraham, the Friend of Allah. Then they will approach Abraham, and he will say to them: I am not qualified for this. I was the Friend of Allah from long ago. Address yourselves to Moses with whom Allah talked at great length. They will go to Moses and he will say to them: I am not qualified for this; go to Jesus, word of Allah and a spirit from Him. He will also say: I am not qualified for this. Then they will come to Muhammad. He will stand forth and will be granted permission to intercede. The spirit of integrity and of kinship will be released and will stand on either side of me at the right and left of the Bridge; and the first group from among you will pass over the Bridge with the speed of lightning. At this we inquired: May our fathers and mothers be your ransom, what is the speed of lightning? He said: Have you not observed how the lightning flashes forth and back in the twinkling of an eye? Those following them will pass over with the speed of the wind, and then with the speed of flying birds, and with the speed of running men, according to the quality of their deeds. Your Prophet will continue standing at the Bridge, supplicating: Lord, keep them safe, keep them safe. When the quality of people's deeds declines the speed will slow down till a man will come who will not be able to walk but will creep along. On both sides of the Bridge will be hanging hooks which will attach themselves to those they are commanded to seize. He who is merely scratched will be saved, but those who are heaped up will fall into the Fire. Abu Hurairah adds: By Him in Whose hands is the life of Abu Hurairah, the depth of hell is equal to seventy years' travel (Muslim).

204. Abdullah ibn Zubair relates: When Zubair stood up ready to fight on the day of the battle of Jamal, he called me and I went and stood by his side. He said: My son, whoever is killed today will be a wrongdoer or one wronged. I am sure I shall be one of the wronged ones killed today. My greatest worry is my debt. Do you think that anything will be left over from our property after the discharge of my debt? My son, sell our property and discharge my debt. Should anything be left over after the discharge of my debts one ninth of it will be for thy sons. He kept on instructing me about his debts and then said: My son, should you find yourself unable to discharge any portion of my debt then have recourse to my Master and implore His help. I did not understand what he meant and asked: Father, who is your Master? He said: Allah. Whenever I faced a difficulty in discharging any portion of his debt, I would supplicate: O Master of Zubair, discharge his debt; and He discharged it. Zubair was killed. He left no cash, but he left certain lands, one of them in Ghabah, eleven houses in Medina, two in Basra, one in Kufa and one in Egypt. The cause of his indebtedness was that a person would come to him asking him to keep something of his in trust for him. Zubair would not agree to accept it as a trust, apprehending it might be lost, but would take it as a loan. He never accepted a governorship, or revenue office, or any public office. He fought along with the Holy Prophet, and Abu Bakr, Umar and Uthman.

I prepared a statement of his debts and they amounted to two million and two hundred thousand. Hakim ibn Hizam met me and asked me: Nephew, how much is due from my brother as debt? I concealed the real state of affairs and said: A hundred thousand. Hakim said: I do not think your assets will cover that much. I said: What would you think if the amount were two million and two hundred thousand? He said: I would not think that this would be within your capacity. Should you be unable to discharge any portion of it call upon me for help.

Zubair had purchased the land in Ghabah for a hundred and seventy thousand. Abdullah sold it for a million and six hundred thousand, and announced that whoso had a claim against Zubair should meet him in Ghabah. Abdullah ibn Ja'far came to him and said: Zubair owed me four hundred thousand, but I would release the debt if you wish. Abdullah said: No. Ibn Ja'far said: If you would wish for postponement I would postpone recovery of it. Abdullah said: No. Ibn Ja'far then said: In that case measure out a plot for me. Abdullah marked out a plot. Thus he sold the land and discharged his father's debt. There remained out of the land four and a half sahms (i.e. sixteenths). He then visited Mu'awiah who had with him at the time Amr ibn Uthman, Munzir ibn Zubair and Ibn Zam'ah. Mu'awiah asked Abdullah: What price did you put on the land in Ghabah? He said: One hundred thousand for a *sahm* (one sixteenth). Mu'awiah inquired: How much of it is left? Abdullah said: Four and a half *sahms*. Munzir ibn Zubair said: I take one *sahm* for a hundred thousand. Amr ibn Uthman said: I take one *sahm* for a hundred thousand. Ibn Zam'ah said: I take one *sahm* for a hundred thousand. Then Mu'awiah asked: How much of it is now left? Abdullah said: One and a half *sahms*. Mu'awiah said: I take it for one hundred and fifty thousand. Later, Abdullah ibn Ja'far sold to Mu'awiah his share for six hundred thousand.

When Abdullah ibn Zubair had completed the administration of the whole affair the heirs of Zubair said to him: Now distribute the inheritance among us. He said: I will not do that till after I have announced during four successive Pilgrimage seasons: Let him who has a claim against Zubair come forward and we shall discharge it. He made this announcement during four seasons and then distributed the inheritance among the heirs of Zubair according to his directions. Zubair had four wives. Each of them received a million and two hundred thousand. Thus Zubair's total estate came to fifty million and two hundred thousand (Bokhari).

26.
On Forbidding Wrong and Repelling it

Allah, the Exalted, has said:

99.   The wrongdoers will have neither friend nor any effective intercessor (40.19).

100.   The wrongdoers will have no helpers (22.72).

205.   Jabir relates that the Holy Prophet said: Eschew wrong, for on the Day of Judgment wrong will become manifold darknesses; and safeguard yourselves against miserliness, for miserliness ruined those who were before you. It incited them to murder and to treating the unlawful as lawful (Muslim).

206.   Abu Hurairah relates that the Holy Prophet said: Allah will enforce the discharge of all obligations on the Day of Judgment, even the obligation of a horned goat to make amends to a hornless goat (Muslim).

207.   Ibn Umar relates: We were talking about the Farewell Pilgrimage, not knowing what the expression meant, as the Holy Prophet was among us. Then he stood up and recited Allah's praise and discoursed at length about the Anti-Christ and said: Every Prophet raised by Allah has warned his people against his mischief. Noah did it and so did all the Prophets after him. If he appears among you his condition will not remain hidden from you. It is well known to you that your Lord is not one-eyed, while the Anti-Christ is one-eyed. His right eye is like a swollen grape. Hearken, Allah has sanctified for you your blood and your belongings, like the sanctity of this day and this month. Listen. Have I conveyed Allah's message to you? The people responded: Yes. On which he said: Bear witness, O Allah; and repeated it three times. He concluded: Woe unto you, take heed and do not revert to disbelief after I am gone, some of you slaying others (Bokhari, and as to certain portions Muslim also).

208.   Ayesha relates that the Holy Prophet said: He who acquires a hand's breadth of land wrongfully will have seven earths suspended from his neck. (Bokhari and Muslim).

209.   Abu Musa Ash'ari relates that the Holy Prophet said: Allah grants respite to a wrongdoer but when He seizes him, He does not let go. Then he recited: Such is the chastisement of the Lord which He inflicts upon corrupt cities. Surely, His chastisement is grievously painful (11.103) (Bokhari and Muslim).

210.   Mu'az relates: The Holy Prophet appointed me to a governorship and said: A group of the people of the Book will come to you. So invite them to bear witness that there is no one worthy of worship save Allah and that I am His

Messenger. When they have accepted this, inform them that Allah has appointed for them five Prayer services in twenty four hours. When they have submitted to this, tell them that Allah has made obligatory upon them alms which will be collected from those who are well-to-do among them and will be restored to the poor. When they submit to this, be mindful not to take their best belongings for this purpose. Guard yourself against the plaint of a wronged one, for between that and Allah there is no barrier (Bokhari and Muslim).

211. Abu Hamid Sa'idi relates that the Holy Prophet appointed a man of the Azd called Ibn al-Lutbiyyah as collector of *Zakat*. When he returned from his assignment he reported: This and this I have collected as *Zakat* and that and that are gifts presented to me. Thereupon the Holy Prophet ascended the pulpit, praised and glorified Allah and said: I appoint a man from among you to carry out some duty in connection with that which Allah has committed to me and he comes back and says: This is yours and that has been presented to me as a gift. If he is telling the truth why did he not sit in the house of his father or mother so that his gifts should have come to him? By Allah, if any one of you should take' anything to which he has no right, he will meet Allah on the Day of Judgment carrying that thing. So let me not see any of you meet Allah carrying a grunting camel or a mooing cow or a bleating goat. Then he raised his arms so high that the white of his armpits became visible and his supplication went up: Allah, I have conveyed Thy command (Bokhari and Muslim).

212. Abu Hurairah relates that the Holy Prophet said: Should a Muslim owe an obligation to his brother in respect of his honour or anything else, let him obtain a release of it today before the time comes when he will have neither dinars nor dirhems. Else, if he should have good deeds they will be taken away from him in proportion to his obligation, and if he should not have good deeds he would be burdened with the evil deeds of the one he wronged in the same proportion (Bokhari).

213. Abdullah ibn Amr ibn 'As relates that the Holy Prophet said: A Muslim is one against whose tongue and hands the Muslims are secure; and an Emigrant is one who departs from that which Allah has forbidden (Bokhari and Muslim).

214. Abdullah ibn Amr ibn 'As relates: A man named Kirkira who was in charge of the personal effects of the Holy Prophet died and the latter said: He is in the Fire. Some people went to his house looking for its cause and found therein a cloak that he had embezzled (Bokhari).

215. Nufai' ibn Harith relates that the Holy Prophet said: Time is running in the same manner as it was on the day Allah created the heavens and the earth. A year has twelve months, four of which are sacred, three in a row Zul Qa'ad, Zul Hajj and Muharram, and Rajab between Jumadi and Sha'aban. Which month is this? We said: Allah and His Messenger know best. He remained silent and we thought he would give it a new name. Then he said: Is it not Zul Hajj? We said: Indeed. Then he asked: Which city is this? We said: Allah and His Messenger know best. He remained silent and we thought he would give it a new name. Then he said: Is it not the Sacred City? We said: Indeed. Then he asked: Which day is this? We said: Allah and His Messenger know best. He remained silent and we thought he would give it a new name. Then he said: Is this not the Day of Sacrifice? We said: Indeed. Then he said: Your blood, your belongings and your honour are sacred as the sanctity of this day, this city and this month. Soon you will meet your Lord and He will call you to account for your deeds. So do not revert to disbelief after I am gone, slaying each other. Let him who is present convey this to him who is absent. Perchance, he who is told may remember it better than one who hears it today. Then he asked: Have I conveyed Allah's command; have I conveyed Allah's command? We said: Yes. He supplicated: Allah, bear Thou witness (Bokhari and Muslim).

216.   Abu Umamah Iyas ibn Harithi relates that the Holy Prophet said: Allah decrees the Fire and debars Paradise for one who takes away the right of a Muslim by a false oath. One man asked: Messenger of Allah, even if it should be an inconsiderable thing? He said: Even if it should be the twig of a wildberry bush (Muslim).

217.   Adiyy ibn Umairah relates that he heard the Holy Prophet say: When I appoint someone from among you to public office and he puts away by stealth a needle or even something less, that is embezzlement, and he will be called upon to produce it on the Day of Judgment. Thereupon one of the Ansar who had a dark complexion stood up (I can recall him as if I can see him before me) and said: Messenger of Allah, take back from me your assignment. He asked: What is the matter? The man said: I have just heard you say this and this. The Holy Prophet said: I say it again that one whom I appoint to public office must render an account of everything big and small. What he is given out of it he may take, and what he is forbidden he should abstain from (Muslim).

218.   Umar ibn Khattab relates that on the day of the battle of Khaibar a group of the companions of the Holy Prophet came and began to recount: So and So has become a martyr, So and So has become a martyr. Presently they passed by a dead body and exclaimed: He is also a martyr. The Holy Prophet thereupon said: Surely not. I have seen him in the Fire in a cloak which he had embezzled (Muslim).

219.   Abu Qatadah Harith ibn Ribi' relates that the Holy Prophet stood among them and mentioned that believing in Allah and striving in His cause were the highest category of deeds. A man stood up and said: Messenger of Allah, tell me, if I were killed in the cause of Allah, would all my sins be removed from me? He answered: Yes, if you were to be killed in the cause of Allah and you are steadfast, looking forward to your reward, marching forth and not turning away. Presently, the Holy Prophet said to him: Repeat what you had said: The man repeated: Tell me, if I were to be killed in the cause of Allah would all my sins be removed from me? He answered: Yes, if you are killed while you are steadfast, looking forward to your reward, marching forth and not turning away. But if you owe any debt that will not be remitted. Gabriel has just told me this (Muslim).

220. Abu Hurairah relates that the Holy Prophet asked: Do you know who is a pauper? He was told: Among us a pauper is one who has nothing, cash or property. He said: A pauper from among my people would be one who faces the Day of Judgment with a record of *salat* and fasts and *Zakat*, but who will have abused this one, and calumniated that one, and devoured the substance of a third, and shed the blood of a fourth and beaten a fifth. Then each of them will be allotted a portion of his good deeds. Should they not suffice, then their sins and defaults will be transferred from them to him and he will be thrown into the Fire (Muslim).

221. Umm Salamah relates that the Holy Prophet said: I am but a human being. You bring your disputes to me for decision. It might happen that one party might be better versed in presenting his case than the other and I might decide in his favour according to what I hear. But if I decide in favour of one contrary to the right of the other, I merely allot a brand of fire to him (Bokhari and Muslim).

222. Ibn Umar relates that the Holy Prophet said: A believer continues in the security of his faith so long as he does not shed blood unjustly (Bokhari).

223. Khaulah bint 'Amir relates that she heard the Holy Prophet say: Many people deal unjustly with Allah's property. For them is the Fire on the Day of Judgment (Bokhari).

27.

On Honouring that which is Sacred

Allah, the Exalted has said:

101.   Whoso honours that which is declared sacred by Allah, may be sure that it counts for good with his Lord (22.31).

102.   Whoso venerates the sacred signs of Allah may be sure that it counts as righteousness of the heart for him (22.33).

103.   Continue to be kindly gracious towards the believers (15.89).

104.   Whoso kills a person, except for killing another or for creating disorder in the land, it shall be as if he had killed all mankind; and whoso helps one to live, it shall be as if he had given life to all mankind (5.33).

224. Abu Musa Ash'ari relates that the Holy Prophet said: The relationship between one believer and another is like that between different parts of a building, one part strengthens another. Then he gripped the fingers of one hand between those of the other by way of illustration (Bokhari and Muslim).

225. Abu Musa Ash'ari relates that the Holy Prophet said: Whoever passes through our mosques or streets carrying something and he has an arrow he should muffle it or cover its point with his hand lest it should cause some hurt to a Muslim (Bokhari and Muslim).

226. Nu'man ibn Bashir relates that the Holy Prophet said: The believers in their love, kindness and compassion towards each other are like the human body; when one of its limbs is afflicted the whole of it is involved both in waking and in fever (Bokhari and Muslim).

227. Abu Hurairah relates that the Holy Prophet kissed his grandson Hasan ibn Ali Aqr'a ibn Habis, who was with him at the time, and he said: I have ten sons and have never kissed any of them. The Holy Prophet looked at him and said: He who has no compassion will receive none (Bokhari and Muslim).

228. Ayesha relates that some desert Arabs came to the Holy Prophet and asked: Do you kiss your children? He answered: Yes. They said: We never kiss them. He said: Can I help it if Allah has stripped your hearts of compassion (Bokhari and Muslim)?

229. Jarir ibn Abdullah relates that the Holy Prophet said: Allah has no mercy for him who has no mercy for his fellows (Bokhari and Muslim).

230. Abu Hurairah relates that the Holy Prophet said: When any of you leads the Prayer he should not make it long, for among the congregation are those who are weak, ill or old. When praying alone you can pray as long as you like (Bokhari and Muslim). One version adds: and those who have to attend to something.

231. Ayesha relates that the Holy Prophet would sometimes abstain from doing something he wished to do fearing lest others might follow him and it might become obligatory for them (Bokhari and Muslim).

232. Ayesha relates that the Holy Prophet forbade his companions continuous fasting without a break out of compassion for them. They said: But you fast continuously. He answered: I am not situated as you are. I pass the night while my Lord furnishes me with food and drink (Bokhari and Muslim). His meaning was that God had bestowed upon him the power of endurance like that of a person who eats and drinks.

233. Abu Qatadah Harith ibn Ribi' relates that the Holy Prophet said: I stand up to lead the Prayer having it in mind to lengthen it. Then I hear the cry of an infant and I shorten the Prayer fearing lest I should make it burdensome for its mother (Bokhari).

234. Jundub ibn Abdullah relates that the Holy Prophet said: He who performs the *salat* of *Fajr* places himself under the guardianship of Allah. So let him carry on during the day in such manner that Allah should not call upon him to account for that which is due from him under that guardianship; for if he is called upon and is found wanting he would be hurled down into hell (Muslim).

235. Ibn Umar relates that the Holy Prophet said: A Muslim is the brother of a Muslim; he does not wrong him nor does he hand him over to his enemy. He who occupies himself in relieving the need of a brother will find that Allah occupies Himself in relieving his need. He who removes the trouble of a Muslim will have one of his troubles removed by Allah on the Day of Judgment. He who covers up the fault of a Muslim will have his faults covered up by Allah on the Day of Judgment (Bokhari and Muslim).

236.   Abu Hurairah relates that the Holy Prophet said: A Muslim is the brother of a Muslim. He should not cheat him, nor tell him a lie, nor humiliate him. Everything of a Muslim is forbidden to a Muslim; his property and his blood. Righteousness is a quality of the heart. It is enough evil for a person to look down upon his brother Muslim (Tirmidhi).

237.   Abu Hurairah relates that the Holy Prophet said: Be not envious of each other, do not make fictitious bids at auctions, bear no grudge, do not turn away from each other, do not make an offer during a pending transaction and become servants of Allah, brothers to each other. A Muslim is the brother of a Muslim; he does not wrong him, or look down upon him or humiliate him. Righteousness is a matter of the heart. (He repeated it three times.) It is enough evil for a person that he should look down upon his Muslim brother. Everything of a Muslim is forbidden to a Muslim; his blood, his property, his honour (Muslim).

238.   Anas relates that the Holy Prophet said: No one believes truly until he desires for his brother that which he desires for himself (Bokhari and Muslim).

239.   Anas relates that the Holy Prophet said: Go to the help of your brother whether he commits a wrong or is wronged. Someone asked: Messenger of Allah, I would help him if he is wronged, but tell me how shall I help him if he is committing a wrong? He answered: Stop him from committing the wrong; that is helping him (Bokhari).

240.   Abu Hurairah relates that the Holy Prophet said: A Muslim owes a Muslim five obligations: returning his greeting, visiting him in sickness, following his funeral, accepting his invitation, and saying: Allah have mercy on you; when he says: All praise is to Allah; on sneezing (Bokhari and Muslim). Muslim's version is: A Muslim owes a Muslim six obligations: When you meet him say: Peace be on you; when he invites you accept his invitation; when he seeks your advice, advise him; when he sneezes and praises Allah, say to him: Allah have mercy on you; when he is sick visit him; and when he dies follow his funeral.

241.   Bra'a ibn 'Azib relates: The Messenger of Allah enjoined seven things upon us and forbade us seven. He commanded us to visit the sick; to follow funerals, to call down Allah's mercy on one who sneezes, to fulfil vows, to help the wronged, to accept an invitation and to multiply the greeting of peace. He forbade us wearing gold rings, drinking from silver vessels, sitting on red silk cushions, and wearing stuff made from silk and cotton mixed, pure silk, heavy silk and brocade (Bokhari and Muslim). One version substitutes in the first seven recovery of that which is lost in place of fulfillment of vows.

28.
On Covering up the Defaults of Muslims

Allah, the Exalted, has said:

105. Those who desire that indecencies should spread among the believers will have a painful chastisement in this world and the hereafter (24.20).

242. Abu Hurairah relates that the Holy Prophet said: Allah will cover up the faults on the Day of Judgment of him who covers up the faults of another in this world (Muslim).

243. Abu Hurairah relates that he heard the Holy Prophet say: Everyone of my people will be forgiven except those who expose faults. Exposure includes a person proclaiming his own fault which he commits during the night and which Allah had covered up. He says in the morning: So and So, listen I did this and this last night. During the night Allah had covered it up and in the morning he tears away Allah's cover (Bokhari and Muslim).

244. Abu Hurairah relates that the Holy Prophet said: If a slave-girl commits adultery and her offence is established she should suffer the penalty but should not be rebuked; the same if she offends a second time; but if she offends a third time she should be sold even if she fetches no more than a rope woven from hair (Bokhari and Muslim).

245. Abu Hurairah relates: A drunkard was brought to the Holy Prophet and he said: Give him a beating. Then some of us beat him with our hands, some with our shoes, and some with pieces of cloth. When he retired, someone said: May Allah disgrace you. The Holy Prophet said: Do not help Satan against him by uttering such words (Bokhari).

29.
On Relieving the Needs of Muslims

Allah, the Exalted, has said:

106. Do good that you may prosper (22.78).

246. This *hadith* is the same as No. 235.

247. Abu Hurairah relates that the Holy Prophet said: He who removes from a believer his distress in this world will have his distress of the Day of Judgment removed by Allah. He who eases the hardship of another, will have ease bestowed upon him by Allah in this world and the next. He who covers up the faults of a Muslim will have his faults covered up in this world and the next. Allah goes on helping a servant so long as he goes on helping his brother. He who treads a path in search of knowledge, has his path to Paradise made easy by Allah thereby. Whenever people gather in a house of Allah for the purpose of reading the Book of Allah and share its reading between them, serenity descends upon them, and mercy covers them and angels spread their wings over them and Allah discourses about them to those around Him. He who is slow in his conduct will not make it proceed faster by the nobility of his birth (Muslim).

30.
On Intercession

Allah, the Exalted, has said:

107. Whoso makes a righteous intercession shall partake of the good that ensues therefrom (4.86).

248. Abu Musa Ash'ari relates that whenever a needy person came to the Holy Prophet he would turn to those present and say: Intercede for him, you will have your reward and Allah causes that which He likes to issue from the tongue of His Prophet (Bokhari and Muslim). One version has: that which He wills.

249. Ibn Abbas relates, in the course of the case of Burairah and her husband, that the Holy Prophet said to her: Would that you went back to him. She said: Messenger of Allah, do you command me? He replied: I only recommend. She said: I have no use for him (Bokhari).

31.
On Making Peace between People

Allah, the Exalted, has said:

108. Most of their conferrings together are devoid of good, except such as enjoin charity, or the promotion of public welfare or of public peace (4.115).

109. Reconciliation is best (4.129).

110. Be mindful of your duty to Allah and try to promote accord between yourselves (8.2).

111. All believers are brothers; so make peace between your brothers (49.11).

250. Abu Hurairah relates that the Holy Prophet said: Charity is incumbent upon every human limb every day on which the sun rises. To bring about just reconciliation between two contestants is charity. Helping a person to mount his animal, or to load his baggage on to it is charity. A good word is charity. Every step taken towards the mosque for *salat* is charity. To remove anything from the street that causes inconvenience is charity (Bokhari and Muslim).

251. Umm Kulthum relates that she heard the Holy Prophet say: He who brings about peace between people and attains good or says that which is good is not a liar (Bokhari and Muslim). Muslim's version adds: I did not hear him let people have a latitude in what they said except in three situations: war, making peace, and talk between husband and wife.

252. Ayesha relates that the Holy Prophet heard two men contending with one another in loud voices outside his door. One of them begged the other to agree to reduce the amount of the debt he owed him and to deal kindly with him. The other said: By Allah, I shall not do it. The Holy Prophet went out to them and asked: Which is the one who swears by Allah he will not act kindly? The man said: It is I, Messenger of Allah, and for him is whatever he prefers (Bokhari and Muslim).

253. Sahl ibn Sa'ad Sa'idi relates that the Holy Prophet learnt that a contention had arisen between members of the Bani Amr ibn Auf. He went with some of his companions to make peace between them and was hospitably detained. The time for Prayer arrived and Bilal went to Abu Bakr and said to him: The Messenger of Allah has been detained and it is time for Prayer. Will you lead the people in Prayer? He said: Yes, if you wish. Bilal called the *iqamah* and Abu Bakr stepped forth and the service commenced. At this stage the Messenger of Allah arrived and walking through the rows took his stand in the first row. Thereupon the worshippers began to clap. Abu Bakr was intent upon the Prayer and paid no heed. When the clapping increased he noticed the Holy Prophet who indicated to him by a sign to remain in his place and continue the service. But Abu Bakr raised his hands, gave praise to Allah, retreated backwards and took his stand in the row. The Holy Prophet went forward and led the Prayer. When it was over he faced towards the congregation and said: Why is it that when something is encountered in the course of the *salat* you start clapping? Clapping is only for women. When any of you is faced with anything in the course of the *salat* he should say: Holy is Allah. This is bound to draw attention. And Abu Bakr, what stopped you from continuing to lead the Prayer after I had made a sign to you? He said: It did not behove the son of Abu Qahafah to lead the Prayer in front of the Messenger of Allah (Bokhari and Muslim).

32.

On the Superiority of the Poor and Weak among Muslims

Allah, the Exalted, has said:

112. Continue thy companionship with those who call on their Lord, morning and evening, seeking His pleasure, and look not beyond them (18.29).

254. Haritha ibn Wahb relates that he heard the Holy Prophet say: Shall I tell you who are the dwellers of Paradise? It is every weak one who is accounted weak and is looked down upon, who if he takes an oath relying upon Allah He would fulfil it. Now shall I tell you who are the denizens of the Fire? It is every ignorant, impertinent, prideful and arrogant one (Bokhari and Muslim).

255. Sahl ibn Sa'ad Sa'idi relates that a person passed near the Holy Prophet and he asked one sitting with him: What do you think of this one? He said: He is one of the noblest. He is worthy that if he should propose marriage his proposal should be accepted and if he should intercede for any his intercession should prove effective. The Holy Prophet said nothing on this. Presently another man passed and he asked: How do you esteem this one? He answered: Messenger of Allah, he is one of the poor Muslims. If he were to propose his proposal would not be accepted, if he were to intercede on behalf of any his intercession would be rejected, and if he were to speak he would not be listened to. The Holy Prophet said: This one is better than an earthful like the former one (Bokhari and Muslim).

256. Abu Sa'id Khudri relates that the Holy Prophet said: There was a contest between Paradise and the Fire. The Fire said: I shall compass the tyrants and the arrogant ones; and Paradise said: My dwellers will be the weak and the lowly. Allah decided between them, saying: Thou art Paradise, My mercy, through thee I shall have mercy on whomsoever I determine; and thou art the Fire, My torment, through thee I shall chastise whomsoever I determine. It is for Me to fill both of you (Muslim).

257. Abu Hurairah relates that the Holy Prophet said: On the Day of Judgment will be brought forward a great fat man whose value in the sight of Allah will be no more than the wing of a mosquito (Bokhari and Muslim).

258. Abu Hurairah relates that a dark-skinned woman (or perhaps young man) used to take care of the mosque. The Holy Prophet missed her (or him) and inquired about her (or him) and was told that she (or he) had died. He said: Why did you not let me know? as if they had not considered the matter of any importance. He then said: Show me the grave, and on being shown it he prayed over it and said: These graves cov_. those in them with darkness and Allah illumines them for the denizens in consequence of my prayers for them (Bokhari and Muslim).

259. Abu Hurairah relates that the Holy Prophet said: Many there are with ruffled hair and dusty faces who are pushed away from people's doors, but if they were to say in the name of Allah it will be thus and thus Allah would fulfil it (Muslim).

260. Usamah relates that the Holy Prophet said: I stood at the gate of Paradise and observed that the generality of those who entered it were the lowly. The wealthy had been held back from it. Then those condemned to the Fire were ordered to it and I stood at the gate of the Fire and observed that the generality of those who entered it were women (Bokhari and Muslim).

261. Abu Hurairah relates that the Holy Prophet said: Only three persons talked in their cradles. One was Jesus son of Mary. Another was the case of Juraij. He was a pious man given to worship who had built a retreat for himself. One day when he was engaged in worship his mother came and called him, and he supplicated: Lord, my mother and my devotion. He continued in worship and she went away. Next day she came again and called him and he supplicated: Lord, my mother and my worship. Again he continued in his worship. She came the third day and called him and he supplicated: Lord, my mother and my worship; and continued with his worship. She said: Allah, do not let him die till he has confronted the harlots. Juraij and his devotion became topics of conversation among the Bani Israel. There was among them a harlot whose beauty was proverbial. She said: If you would like I could involve Juraij in trouble. She tried to seduce him but Juraij paid no attention to her. Then she went to a shepherd who lived near the retreat of Juraij and offered herself to him and conceived from him. When she gave birth to the child she said it was from Juraij. The Bani Israel came to him, brought him down from his retreat, demolished it and started beating him up. He asked: Why all this? They said: You have committed adultery with this harlot and she has borne your child. He said: Where is the child? They brought it to him. He said: Now leave me alone so that I might pray. Then he prayed, and when he finished he came to the child, seated it in his lap and asked it: Who is thy father? The child replied: So and So, the shepherd. Then they all turned to Juraij, kissing him and seeking his blessing and said: We shall build thy retreat of gold. He said: Build it of clay as it was. So they did.

The third was the case of a boy who was being suckled by his mother when a man passed by riding a fast and good mount and clad in fine garments. The mother supplicated: Allah, do Thou make my son like this one. The infant released his mother's breast, and turning looked at the man and said: Allah, do not make me like him. Then he turned to his mother's breast and resumed the suckling. Here the Holy Prophet illustrated the suckling of the child by putting his forefinger into his mouth and sucking it. Then he continued: Then some people passed by with a young woman who was being beaten and those who beat her said: You committed adultery and theft; and she kept on saying: Sufficient for me is Allah and an excellent Guardian is He. The mother supplicated: Allah, do not make my son like her. Thereupon he left the suckling and looked upon the young woman and said: Allah, make me like her. On this the mother and son began to converse. She said: A man of good presence passed and I supplicated: Allah, make my son like him, and you said: Allah, do not make me like him. Then they passed with the slave-girl. They were beating her and were saying: You committed adultery and theft. I supplicated: Allah, do not make my son like her; and you said: Allah, make me like her. The boy replied: That man was a tyrant, so I said: Allah, do not make me like him. As to the girl, they said: You committed adultery; and she had not. They said: You stole; and she had not stolen. So I said: Allah, make me like her (Bokhari and Muslim).

33.
On Kind Treatment of Orphans, Girls, the Weak, the Poor, and the Lowly

Allah, the Exalted, has said:

113. Continue to be kindly gracious towards the believers (15.89).

114. Continue thy companionship with those who call on their Lord, morning and evening, seeking His pleasure, and look not beyond them, for if thou dost that thou wouldst be seeking the values of this life (18.29).

115. Oppress not the orphan and chide not him who asks (93.10-11).

116. Knowest thou him who rejects the faith? That is the one who drives away the orphan and urges not the feeding of the poor (107.2-4).

262. Sa'ad ibn Abi Waqqas relates: Six of us were with the Holy Prophet when the pagans said to him: Drive these ones away, lest they should begin to venture against us. The six were Ibn Mas'ud, a man of the Huzail, Bilal, two men whose names I do not know, and myself. The Holy Prophet thought what Allah wished him to think, and Allah sent down: Drive not away those who call upon their Lord morning and evening seeking His countenance (6.53) (Muslim).

263. Abu Hurairah 'Aiz ibn Amr Muzani relates that Abu Sufyan came with a party of people to Salman, Suhaib and Bilal and these latter said to him: Did not the swords of Allah exact their due from the enemy of Allah? Abu Bakr said to them: Do you speak like this to the chief of the Quraish and their master? Then he went to the Holy Prophet and related this to him. He said: Abu Bakr, perchance you have offended them. If so, you have offended your Lord. Abu Bakr went back to them and said: Brothers, did I offend you? They replied: No. May Allah forgive you, brother (Muslim).

264. Sahl ibn Sa'ad relates that the Holy Prophet said: He who takes care of an orphan and me will be like this in Paradise; and he raised his forefinger and middle finger by way of illustration (Bokhari).

265. Abu Hurairah relates that the Holy Prophet said: He who takes care of an orphan, whether related to him or a stranger, will be like these two in Paradise; and the narrator raised his forefinger and middle finger by way of illustration (Muslim).

266. Abu Hurairah relates that the Holy Prophet said: A poor one is not he who can be turned away with a date or two or a morsel or two: the truly poor one is he who despite his poverty refrains from asking (Bokhari and Muslim). Another version is: A poor one is not he who goes round asking people and who can be turned away with a morsel or two or a date or two. A truly poor one is he who does not find enough to suffice him, does not disclose his poverty so that he might be given alms, and does not stand up to ask.

267. Abu Hurairah relates that the Holy Prophet said: He who exerts himself on behalf of widows and the indigent is like one who strives in the cause of Allah; and the narrator thinks he added: and like the guardian who never retreats, and like one who observes the fast and does not break it (Bokhari and Muslim).

268. Abu Hurairah relates that the Holy Prophet said: The worst food is the food served at a *walima* from which those are excluded who would like to come and to which those are invited who refuse to come and he who declines an invitation disobeys Allah and His Messenger (Muslim). Another version is: The worst food is the food served at a *walima* to which the rich are invited and from which the poor are excluded.

269. Anas relates that the Holy Prophet said: He who brings up two girls through their childhood will appear on the Day of Judgment attached to me like two fingers of a hand (Muslim).

270. Ayesha relates: A woman came to me begging with her two daughters; I could not find anything except a single date which I gave to her. She divided it between her daughters and did not herself eat any of it. Then she got up and left. When the Holy Prophet came, I told him of it. He said: One who is tried with daughters and treats them well will find that they will become his shield from the Fire (Bokhari and Muslim).

271. Ayesha relates: A poor woman came to me with her two daughters. I gave her three dates. She gave one to each girl and raised the third to her own mouth to eat. The girls asked her for it. So she broke it into two parts and gave one to each of the girls. I was much struck by her action and mentioned what she had done to the Holy Prophet. He said: Allah appointed Paradise for her in consequence of it; or he said: Allah freed her from the Fire on account of it.

272. Abu Shuraih Khuwailad ibn Amr Khuza'i relates that the Holy Prophet said: Allah, I declare sinful any failure to safeguard the rights of two weak ones; orphans and women (Nisai).

273. Mus'ab ibn Sa'ad ibn Abi Waqqas relates: Sa'ad had a notion that he had a superiority over those who were not so well off as he was. The Holy Prophet said: You are helped and are provided for because of the weak and poor ones among you (Bokhari).

274. Abu Darda' relates that he heard the Holy Prophet say: Look for me among the weak ones, for you are helped and provided for on account of the weak ones among you (Abu Daud).

34.
On Kindness towards Women

Allah, the Exalted, has said:

117. Consort with them in kindness (4.20).

118. You cannot keep perfect balance emotionally between your wives, however much you might desire it, but incline not wholly towards one leaving the other in suspense. If you will maintain accord and are mindful of your duty to Allah, surely Allah is Most Forgiving, Ever Merciful (4.130).

275. Abu Hurairah relates that the Holy Prophet said: Treat women kindly. Woman has been created from a rib and the most crooked part of the rib is the uppermost. If you try to straighten it you will break it and if you leave it alone it will remain crooked. So treat women kindly (Bokhari and Muslim). Another version is: A woman is like a rib; if you try to straighten it you will break it and if you wish to draw benefit from it you can do so despite its crookedness. Muslim's version is: Woman has been created from a rib and you cannot straighten her. If you wish to draw benefit from her do so despite her crookedness. If you try to straighten her you will break her, and breaking her means divorcing her.

276. Abdullah ibn Zam'a relates that he heard the Holy Prophet delivering an address. He mentioned the she-camel of Saleh, the Prophet, and the one who hamstrung her. He said: When the most wretched of them stood up (91.13), means that a distinguished, wicked and most powerful chief of the people jumped up. Then he mentioned women and said: Some of you beat your wives as if they were slaves, and then consort with them at the end of the day. Then he admonished people against laughing at another's passing the wind, saying: Why does any of you laugh at another doing what he does himself (Bokhari and Muslim)?

277. Abu Hurairah relates that the Holy Prophet said: Let no Muslim man entertain any rancour against a Muslim woman. Should he dislike one quality in her, he would find another which is pleasing (Muslim).

278. Amr ibn Ahwas Jashmi relates that he heard the Holy Prophet say in his address on the occasion of the Farewell Pilgrimage, after he had praised Allah and glorified Him and admonished people: Treat women kindly, they are like prisoners in your hands. You are not owed anything more by them. Should they be guilty of open indecency you may leave them alone in their beds and inflict slight chastisement. Then if they obey you do not have recourse to anything else against them. You have your rights concerning your wives and they have their rights concerning you. Your right is that they shall not permit anyone you dislike to enter your home, and their right is that you should treat them well in the matter of food and clothing (Tirmidhi).

279. Mu'awiah ibn Haidah relates: I asked the Holy Prophet: What is the right of a wife against her husband? He said: Feed her when you feed yourself; clothe her when you clothe yourself, do not strike her on her face, do not revile her and do not separate yourself from her except inside the house (Abu Daud).

280. Abu Hurairah relates that the Holy Prophet said: The most perfect of believers in the matter of faith is he whose behaviour is best; and the best of you are those who behave best towards their wives (Tirmidhi).

281. Iyas ibn Abdullah relates that the Holy Prophet admonished: Do not strike the handmaidens of Allah. Some time later Umar came to him and said: Women have become very daring *vis-a-vis* their husbands. So he permitted their chastisement. Thereafter a large number of women came to the wives of the Holy Prophet and complained against their husbands. The Holy Prophet announced: Many women have come to my wives complaining against their husbands. These men are not well-behaved (Abu Daud).

282. Abdullah ibn Amr ibn 'As relates that the Holy Prophet said: The world is but a provision and the best provision of the world is a good woman (Muslim).

35.
On a Husband's Right concerning his Wife

Allah, the Exalted, has said:

119. Men are appointed guardians over women, because of that in respect of which Allah has made some of them excel others, and because the men spend their wealth. So virtuous women are obedient and safeguard, with Allah's help, matters the knowledge of which is shared by them with their husbands (4.35).

283. Abu Hurairah relates that the Holy Prophet said: When the husband calls his wife to his bed and she does not come and he spends the night offended with her, the angels keep cursing her through the night (Bokhari and Muslim). Another version is: When a woman spends the night away from her husband's bed, the angels keep cursing her through the night. Still another version runs: The Holy Prophet said: By Him in Whose hands is my life, when a husband calls his wife to his bed and she refuses him, He Who is in heaven is offended with her till her husband is pleased with her.

284. Abu Hurairah relates that the Holy Prophet said: It is not permissible for a woman to observe a voluntary fast when her husband is at home, except with his permission. Nor should she permit anyone to enter his house without his leave (Bokhari and Muslim).

285. Ibn Umar relates that the Holy Prophet said: Every one of you is a steward and is accountable for that which is committed to his charge. The ruler is a steward and is accountable for his charge, a man is a steward in respect of his household, a woman is a steward in respect of her husband's house and his children. Thus everyone of you is a steward and is accountable for that which is committed to his charge (Bokhari and Muslim).

286. Abu Ali Talq ibn Ali relates that the Holy Prophet said: When a man calls his wife for his need, she should go to him even if she is occupied in baking bread (Tirmidhi and Nisai).

287. Abu Hurairah relates that the Holy Prophet said: Had I ordained that a person should prostrate himself before another, I would have commanded that a wife should prostrate herself before her husband (Tirmidhi).

288. Umm Salamah relates that the Holy Prophet said: If a woman dies and her husband is pleased with her she will enter Paradise (Tirmidhi).

289. Mu'az ibn Jabal relates that the Holy Prophet said: Whenever a woman distresses her husband his mate from among the *houris* of Paradise says to her: Allah ruin thee, do not cause him distress for he is only thy guest and will soon part from thee to come to us (Tirmidhi).

290. Usamah ibn Zaid relates that the Holy Prophet said: I am not leaving a more harmful trial for men than women (Bokhari and Muslim).

36.
On Spending for Family and Children

Allah, the Exalted, has said:

120. The father of the child shall be responsible for the maintenance of the mother, during that period, according to usage (2.34).

121. Let one who is in easy circumstances spend according to his means, and let him whose means of subsistence are straitened spend out of that which Allah has given him. Allah does not require of anyone beyond that which He has bestowed upon him (65.8).

122. Whatever you spend, He will foster it (34.40).

291. Abu Hurairah relates that the Holy Prophet said: Of the dinar you spend in the cause of Allah; the dinar you spend in procuring the freedom of a slave; the dinar you give away in charity to the poor and the dinar you spend on your wife and children, the highest in respect of reward is the one you spend on your wife and children (Muslim).

292. Thauban ibn Buhdud relates that the Holy Prophet said: The best dinar is that which a person spends on his wife and children, and the dinar he spends on his horse in the cause of Allah, and the dinar he spends on his companions in the cause of Allah (Muslim).

293. Umm Salamah relates: I asked the Holy Prophet: Shall I deserve a reward if I spend on my children from my first husband? I cannot leave them running about here and there in search of a living. He answered: Yes, you will have a reward for whatever you spend on them (Bokhari and Muslim).

294. Sa'ad ibn Abi Waqqas relates in the course of a long *hadith* that the Holy Prophet said to him: Whatever you might spend seeking thereby the pleasure of Allah will have its reward, even that which you put in the mouth of your wife (Bokhari and Muslim).

295. Abu Mas'ud Badri relates that the Holy Prophet said: When a person spends on his wife and children hoping for a reward, it is counted as charity on his part (Bokhari and Muslim).

296. Abdullah ibn Amr ibn 'As relates that the Holy Prophet said: It is enough sin for a person to deny the right of one whose living he controls (Abu Daud). Muslim's version is: It is enough sin for a person to hold back the due of one whose living he controls.

297. Abu Hurairah relates that the Holy Prophet said: Everyday that rises two angels descend, one of them saying: Allah, bestow increase upon the spender; and the other saying: Allah, ruin the miser (Bokhari and Muslim).

298. Abu Hurairah relates that the Holy Prophet said: The upper hand is better than the lower; and begin with your dependants; and the best charity is out of surplus; and he who desires to abstain from asking will be shielded by Allah; and he who seeks self-sufficiency will be made self-sufficient by Allah (Bokhari).

37.
On Spending out of that which is Good.

Allah, the Exalted has said:

123.   Never will you attain to the highest degree of virtue unless you spend out of that which you love (3.93).

124.   O ye who believe, spend out of the good things that you have earned and of that which We produce for you from the earth; and do not select out of it for charity that which is useless (2.268).

299. Anas relates that Abu Talha was the wealthiest of the Ansar in Medina in date gardens and of all his properties he loved Bairaha best. It was right opposite the Mosque and the Holy Prophet used to go there and drink of its pure water. When this verse was revealed: Never will you attain to the highest degree of virtue unless you spend out of that which you love; Abu Talha came to the Holy Prophet and said: Messenger of Allah, Allah has sent down to you: Never will you attain to the highest degree of virtue unless you spend out of that which you love; and the property I love most is Bairaha. I offer it in charity for the sake of Allah, hoping for its reward from Allah. So dispose of it Messenger of Allah, as Allah might direct you. The Holy Prophet said: Well, well, this is a very good property, this is a very good property. I have heard what you have said, and I think you should divide it among your relatives. Abu Talha said: So shall I do, Messenger of Allah; and he divided it among his cousins and relatives (Bokhari and Muslim).

38.

On Obedience to Allah and Abstention from that which Forbidden

Allah, the Exalted, has said:

125. Enjoin Prayer on thy people and be constant therein (20.133).

126. O ye who believe, safeguard yourselves and your families against the Fire (66.7).

300. Abu Hurairah relates that Hasan ibn Ali picked up a date from among dates offered for charity and put it in his mouth. On observing this the Holy Prophet chided him and said: Throw it out. Know you not that we do not eat alms (Bokhari and Muslim).

301. Umar ibn Abi Salamah relates: I was a boy under the care of the Holy Prophet, and my hand would wander around the bowl when eating. He directed me: Pronounce the name of Allah, eat with thy right hand and from whatever is in front of thee. This became my way of eating thereafter (Bokhari and Muslim).

302. This *hadith* is the same as No. 285.

303. Amr ibn Shuaib relates from his grandfather through his father that the Holy Prophet directed: Order your children to perform the *salat* when they are seven years old, and chastise them in respect of any fault in this behalf when they are ten, and at that age put them in separate beds (Abu Daud).

304. Sabrah ibn Ma'abad Juhni relates that the Holy Prophet said: Teach a boy the *salat* at seven years and chastise him if he commits a default at ten years (Abu Daud and Tirmidhi). Abu Daud's version is: Order a boy to perform the *salat* when he reaches seven years of age.

39.

On Obligation due to a Neighbour and Kind Treatment of him

Allah, the exalted, has said:

127. Worship Allah and associate naught with Him and be benevolent towards parents, and kindred, and orphans, and the needy, and the neighbour who is a kinsman, and the neighbour who is not related to you, and your associates and the wayfarer, and those who are under your control (4.37).

305. Ibn Umar and Ayesha relate that the Holy Prophet said: Gabriel kept exhorting me about the neighbour till I imagined he would include him in the category of heirs (Bokhari and Muslim).

306. Abu Dharr relates that the Holy Prophet said: Abu Dharr, when you prepare broth put plenty of water in it and take care of your neighbours (Muslim). Another version is: My friend advised me: When you prepare broth put plenty of water in it, then find out about the families of your neighbours and share it with them as may be suitable.

307. Abu Hurairah relates that the Holy Prophet called out: By Allah he does not believe, by Allah he does not believe, by Allah he does not believe. He was asked: Who does not believe, Messenger of Allah? He said: He whose neighbour is not secure against his mischief (Bokhari and Muslim). Muslim's version is: That one will not enter Paradise whose neighbour is not secure against his mischief.

308. Abu Hurairah relates that the Holy Prophet said: O Muslim women, disdain not doing a kindness to a neighbour, even if it were sending her a lamb's shank (Bokhari and Muslim).

309. Abu Hurairah relates that the Holy Prophet said: Let no one forbid his neighbour placing his rafter on his wall. Abu Hurairah added: Now I see you turning away from this, but I shall continue to proclaim it (Bokhari and Muslim).

310. Abu Hurairah relates that the Holy Prophet said: He who believes in Allah and the Last Day must not put his neighbour to inconvenience; he who believes in Allah and the Last Day must honour his guest; and he who believes in Allah and the Last Day must speak beneficently or keep quiet (Bokhari and Muslim).

311. Abu Shuraih Khuza'i relates that the Holy Prophet said: He who believes in Allah and the Last Day should be benevolent towards his neighbour; he who believes in Allah and the Last Day should honour his guest; he who believes in Allah and the Last Day should speak beneficently or should keep quiet (Muslim).

312. Ayesha relates that she asked the Holy Prophet: I have two neighbours; to which of them shall I send a present? He said: To the one whose door is nearer to yours (Bokhari).

313. Abdullah ibn Umar relates that the Holy Prophet said: The best companion in the sight of Allah is he who behaves best towards his companions, and the best neighbour is he who behaves best towards his neighbours. (Tirmidhi).

40.
On Benevolence towards Parents and Strengthening the Ties of Kinship

Allah, the Exalted, has said:

128. Worship Allah and associate naught with Him, and be benevolent towards parents, and kindred, and orphans, and the needy, and the neighbour who is near and the neighbour who is far, and your associates, and the wayfarer, and those who are under your control (4.37).

129. Be mindful of your duty to Allah in Whose name you appeal to one another, and of your obligations in respect of ties of kinship (4.2).

130. Those who join together the ties of kinship that Allah has bidden to be joined (13.22).

131. We have enjoined on man benevolence towards his parents (29.9).

132. Thy Lord has commanded that ye worship none but Him and has enjoined benevolence towards parents. Should either or both of them attain old age in thy lifetime, never say: Ugh! to them nor chide them, but always speak gently to them. Be humbly tender with them and pray: Lord, have mercy on them, even as they nurtured me when I was little (17.24-25).

133. We have enjoined upon man concerning his parents, Be grateful to Me and to thy parents. His mother bears him in travail after travail, and his weaning takes two years (31.15).

314. Abdullah ibn Mas'ud relates that he asked the Holy Prophet: Which action is most acceptable to Allah? He answered: Performing the *salat* at its due time. I asked: Which next? He said: Benevolence towards parents. I asked: Which next? He said: Striving in the cause of Allah (Bokhari and Muslim).

315. Abu Hurairah relates that the Holy Prophet said: No son can repay his father, unless he should find him a slave and purchase him and set him free (Muslim).

316. Abu Hurairah relates that the Holy Prophet said: He who believes in Allah and the Last Day should honour his guest; he who believes in Allah and the Last Day should join the ties of kinship and he who believes in Allah and the Last Day should speak beneficently or keep quiet (Muslim).

317. Abu Hurairah relates that the Holy Prophet said: Allah created the universe and when He had finished, the womb stood up and said: Is this the place of that which seeks thy protection against being cut? Allah said: Yes, Would you be content that I should hold with him who holds with thee and should cut off from him who cuts thee off? It said: I am content. Allah said: Then this is thy station. The Holy Prophet said: Read if you will the verse: Is it not likely that if you turn away, you will by your conduct create disorder in the land and sever the ties of kinship? It is these whom Allah has cast away and has made them deaf and blinded their eyes (Bokhari and Muslim) Bokhari's version is: Allah said: He who holds with thee shall I hold with, and he who cuts thee off shall I cut off.

318. Abu Hurairah relates that a man came to the Holy Prophet and asked: Messenger of Allah, which of all the people is best entitled to kind treatment and the good companionship from me? He answered: Your mother. The man asked: And after her? He said: Your mother. And after her? He said: Your mother. and after her? Your father (Bokhari and Muslim). Another version is: The man asked: Messenger of Allah, who is best entitled to my good companionship? He answered: Your mother, and then your mother, and then your mother, and then your father, and then your near relations, your near relations.

319. Abu Hurairah relates that the Holy Prophet said: May his nose be rubbed in dust, may his nose be rubbed in dust, may his nose be rubbed in dust who found his parents, one or both, approaching old age and did not enter Paradise through serving them (Muslim).

320. Abu Hurairah relates that a man said to the Holy Prophet: Messenger of Allah, my relatives are such that I join the ties of kinship with them and they cut them asunder, and I am benevolent towards them and they illtreat me, and I forbear and they are churlish. He said: If you are as you have said, you are feeding them hot ash; and so long as you continue as you are you will always have a helper from Allah against them (Muslim).

321. Anas relates that the Holy Prophet said: He who desires that his provision be expanded and that his days be lengthened should join the ties of kinship (Bokhari and Muslim).

322. This *hadith* is the same as No. 299.

323. Abdullah ibn Amr ibn 'As relates that a man came to the Holy Prophet and said: I wish to make a covenant with you to emigrate and fight in the cause of Allah, seeking my reward from Him. He inquired: Is either of your parents alive? The man said: Indeed, both of them. The Holy Prophet asked him: Do you seek reward from Allah? The man said: Yes. The Holy Prophet said: Then return to your parents and serve them well (Bokhari and Muslim). Another version is: A man came and asked permission to join in the fighting. The Holy Prophet asked him: Are your parents alive? The man said: Yes. He said: Then find your fighting in serving them.

324. Abdullah ibn Amr relates that the Holy Prophet said: One who reciprocates in doing good is not the one who upholds the ties of kinship. It is the one who upholds them when the other party sunders them (Bokhari).

325. Ayesha relates that the Holy Prophet said: The womb is suspended from the Throne of Allah and proclaims: Allah will hold by him who holds by me, and Allah will cut asunder from him who cuts asunder from me (Bokhari and Muslim).

326. Maimunah bint Harith, wife of the Holy Prophet, relates that she freed her bondwoman without asking the Holy Prophet. When he came to her in her turn she said to him: Messenger of Allah, do you know I have freed my bondwoman? He said: Indeed? She said: Yes. He said: Had you given her to your uncles it would have been more meritorious (Bokhari and Muslim).

327. Asma'a bint Abu Bakr relates: My mother came to visit me while she was a pagan and I inquired from the Holy Prophet: My mother has come to see me and she is hoping for something from me. Shall I gratify her? He said: Yes. Be benevolent towards your mother (Bokhari and Muslim).

328. Zainab, wife of Abdullah ibn Mas'ud, relates: The Holy Prophet addressed us and said: Spend in charity, ye women, even out of your ornaments. So I went to my husband and said to him: You are not well off and the Holy Prophet has ordered us to spend in charity. So do you go to him and ask him if my giving you something will count as charity, for if not I should give to someone else. Abdullah said: You had better go yourself. So I went and I found a woman from the Ansar also at the door of the Holy Prophet who was bent on the same errand as myself. But we were afraid to venture in on account of awe of the Holy Prophet. Presently Bilal came out and we said to him: Go to the Holy Prophet and tell him two women at the door want to know whether it would be charity if they were to spend on their husbands and on the orphans under their care, but do not tell him our names. Bilal went to the Holy Prophet and asked him: He inquired: Who are they? Bilal said: A woman of the Ansar and Zainab. He asked: Which of the Zainabs is she? Bilal said: The wife of Abdullah. The Holy Prophet said: They will have a double reward, for benevolence towards relatives and for charity (Bokhari and Muslim).

329. Abu Sufyan relates that in the course of his meeting with Hiraclius the latter asked him: What does this Prophet teach you? I said: He tells us to worship Allah, the One, and not to associate anything with Him, to discard what our ancestors said, and to perform the *salat*, tell the truth, keep chaste and exercise benevolence towards kindred (Bokhari and Muslim).

330. Abu Dharr relates that the Holy Prophet said: You will soon conquer the land of Egypt. Then treat its people kindly, for there are ties of guarantee and kinship with them (Muslim).

331. Abu Hurairah relates that when this verse was revealed: Warn thy nearest kinsmen (26.215); the Holy Prophet summoned the Quraish and they all came. He said to them: O Bani Abd Shams, O Bani Ka'ab ibn Lu'ayy safeguard yourselves against the Fire; O Bani Murrah ibn Ka'ab, safeguard yourselves against the Fire; O Bani Abd Manaf, safeguard yourselves against the Fire; O Bani Hashim, safeguard yourselves against the Fire; O Bani Abdul Muttalib, safeguard yourselves against the Fire; O Fatimah, safeguard thyself against the Fire, for I can avail you nothing against Allah. I have ties of kinship with you, and these I shall continue to honour (Muslim).

332. Amr ibn 'As relates that he heard the Holy Prophet say openly without any attempt at concealment: Bani So and So are not my friends, my friends are Allah and the Muslims. But I have ties of kinship which I shall continue to nourish (Bokhari and Muslim).

333. Abu Ayub Khalid ibn Zaid Ansari relates that a man said: Messenger of Allah, tell me that which will cause me to be admitted to Paradise and will keep me away from the Fire. He answered: Worship Allah and do not associate anything with Him: observe Prayer; pay the *Zakat* and join the ties of kinship (Bokhari and Muslim).

334. Salman ibn 'Amir relates that the Holy Prophet said: When you break the fast, do it with a date, for there is blessing in it, and if you cannot find a date with water for it is pure. He added: Charity towards a poor one is charity, and towards a relation is both charity and benevolence (Tirmidhi).

335. Ibn Umar relates: I had a wife whom I loved and my father disliked her. He asked me to divorce her which I refused. Umar mentioned the matter to the Holy Prophet and he said to me: You had better divorce her (Abu Daud and Tirmidhi).

336. Abu Darda' relates that a man came to him and said: I have a wife and my mother directs me to divorce her. Abu Darda' said to him that he had heard the Holy Prophet say: A father is one of the highest doors of Paradise. If you wish you may demolish it, and if you wish you might safeguard it (Tirmidhi).

337. Bra'a ibn 'Azib relates that the Holy Prophet said: A mother's sister has the same standing as a mother (Tirmidhi).

41.

On Prohibition of Disobedience of Parents and Repudiation of Ties of Kinship

Allah, the Exalted, has said:

134. Is it not likely that if you turn away, you will by your conduct create disorder in the land and sever the ties of kinship? It is these whom Allah has cast away and has made them deaf and blinded their eyes (47.23.24).

135. Those who break the covenant of Allah after having made it firm, and cut asunder that which Allah has commanded to be joined together, and act corruptly in the land are under a curse and for them is an evil abode (13.26).

136. Thy Lord has commanded that ye worship none but Him and has enjoined benevolence towards parents. Should either or both of them attain old age in thy lifetime, never say: Ugh! to them, nor chide them, but always speak gently to them. Be humbly tender with them and pray: Lord, have mercy on them, even as they nurtured me when I was little (17.24-25).

338. Abu Bakarah Nufai' ibn Harith relates that the Holy Prophet said: Shall I tell you what are major sins? (He repeated this three times). We said: Certainly, Messenger of Allah. He said: Association of others with Allah; disobedience of parents (he had been leaning on a pillow, suddenly he sat up) and telling a lie or giving false evidence. He repeated this last so many times that we wished he should stop (Bokhari and Muslim).

339. Abdullah ibn Amr ibn 'As relates that the Holy Prophet said: Major sins are: Association of anything with Allah, disobedience of parents, murder and making a false oath (Bokhari).

340. Abdullah ibn Amr ibn 'As relates that the Holy Prophet said: Abusing one's parents is a major sin. He was asked: Messenger of Allah, does a person abuse his parents? He answered: Yes, if he abuses a person's father, the latter would in turn abuse his father; if he abuses another person's mother, the latter would in turn abuse his mother (Bokhari and Muslim). Another version is: One of the most heinous sins is that a person should curse his parents. He was asked: Messenger of Allah, how does a person curse his parents? He said: He abuses another's father who in turn abuses his father; and he abuses another's mother who in turn abuses his mother.

341. Jubair ibn Muti'm relates that the Holy Prophet said: He who cuts asunder the ties of kinship will not enter Paradise (Bokhari and Muslim).

342. Mughirah ibn Shu'bah relates that the Holy Prophet said: Allah has forbidden you disobedience of parents, miserliness, false claims, and the burying alive of female infants and has disapproved for you idle talk, too much asking and waste (Bokhari and Muslim).

42.

On Doing Good to Friends of Parents, and Relations and Wives and Others

343. Ibn Umar relates that the Holy Prophet said: The highest virtue is that a person should be benevolent towards his father's friends (Muslim).

344. Abdullah ibn Dinar relates about Abdullah ibn Umar that a desert Arab chanced to meet him on the way to Mecca; Abdullah ibn Umar greeted him, asked him to ride with him on the donkey he was riding and gave him the turban he was wearing. Abdullah ibn Dinar relates: We said to him: May Allah be good to you, these rustics are pleased with little. Abdullah ibn Umar said: This man's father was my father's friend and I have heard the Holy Prophet say: The highest virtue is that a person should be benevolent towards his father's friends and the members of their families (Muslim).

345. Ibn Dinar relates about Abdullah ibn Umar that when the latter travelled to Mecca and got tired riding a camel, he would take it easy riding on a donkey of his, and would wind a turban round his head. When one day he was riding on his donkey a desert Arab passed by him and he said to him: Are you not So and So son of So and So? The man said: Indeed. Abdullah gave him the donkey and said: Ride it; and gave him his turban and said: Wind it round your head. Some of his companions said to him. May Allah forgive you, you have given this rustic the donkey on which you took your ease and the turban that you wound round your head. He said: I have heard the Holy Prophet say: It is of the highest virtue that a person should be benevolent towards the members of the families of the friends of his father after his death. This man's father was a friend of my father (Muslim).

346. Malik ibn Rabi'a Sa'idi relates that they were sitting with the Holy Prophet when a man of the Bani Salamah came and asked: Messenger of Allah, is there anything by means of which I can exercise benevolence towards my parents after their death? He answered: Yes; by praying for them and asking forgiveness for them, fulfilling their promises, exercising benevolence towards those related through them and honouring their friends (Abu Daud).

347. Ayesha relates: I did not envy any of the wives of the Holy Prophet so much as I envied Khadijah, though I had never seen her. The Holy Prophet mentioned her often. When a goat was slaughtered, he would cut it into pieces and send them to Khadijah's friends. Sometimes I would say to him: You talk of her as if there never was any woman in the world beside Khadijah; and he would say: She was such and such, and I had children from her (Bokhari and Muslim). One version is: He would slaughter a goat and send the meat to her friends as a present as much as was available. Another version is: When a goat was slaughtered he would say: Send out of it to Khadijah's friends. On one occasion, Halah bint Khuwailad, sister of Khadijah, asked permission of the Holy Prophet to come in. He recognised and recalled the manner of Khadijah and was deeply moved. He exclaimed, O Allah, let it be Halah bint Khuwailad.

348. Anas ibn Malik relates that he went on a journey with Jarir ibn Abdullah Bujali and the latter served him though he was older than Anas. So Anas said to him: Do not do so. He replied: I saw the Ansar serve the Holy Prophet with such devotion that I made a vow that whenever I am in the company of any of them I must serve him (Bokhari and Muslim).

43.

On Honouring the Members of the Family of the Holy Prophet

Allah, the Exalted, has said:

137. Allah desires to remove from you all uncleanness, members of the Household, and to purify you completely (33.34).

138. Whoso venerates the sacred signs of Allah may be sure that it counts as righteousness of the heart for him (22.33).

349. Yazid ibn Hayyan relates that Husain ibn Sabrah, Amr ibn Muslim and he went to Zaid ibn Arqam and when they had sat down with him Husain said to him: Zaid, you have gathered a great amount of good. You saw the Holy Prophet, you heard him talk, you fought along with him, you performed the *salat* behind him. You have indeed garnered a great amount of good, Zaid. Now relate to us what you heard from the Holy Prophet. He said: Nephew, I have arrived at old age and have become ancient, and some of the things that I used to remember from the Holy Prophet I have forgotten. So what I might relate that accept, and do not force me to recall that which I leave out. The Holy Prophet addressed us at Khumma, a spring between Mecca and Medina. He rendered praise to Allah and glorified Him and admonished and exhorted us and then said: O ye people, I am but a man and soon the messenger of my Lord will come and I shall respond to him. I am leaving with you two weighty things. The first is the Book of Allah, in it there is guidance and light. Take fast hold of the Book of Allah and adhere to it. He emphasised this and urged recourse to the Book of Allah. Then he said: The second are the members of my family. I admonish you in the name of Allah concerning members of my family, I admonish you in the name of Allah concerning members of my family. Husain said: Zaid, who are the members of his family? Are not his wives the members of his family? Zaid said: His wives are members of his family and also those who are forbidden to accept alms after him. Husain asked: Who are they? Zaid said: They are the descendants of Ali, Aqil, Ja'far and Abbas. They have all been forbidden to accept alms? Zaid said: Yes (Muslim). Another version is: Hearken, I am leaving with you two weighty things. One is the Book of Allah; it is the rope of Allah. He who follows it will be rightly guided; and he who discards it will be astray.

350. Ibn Umar relates that Abu Bakr said: Honour Muhammad by honouring the members of his family (Bokhari).

44.

On Honouring the Learned and the Great

Allah, the Exalted, has said:

139.   Can those who know be like those who know not? It is
only those endowed with understanding that take heed
(39.10).

351. Uqbah ibn Amr relates that the Holy Prophet said: When people
are gathered for Prayer, the one who is best versed of them in the recitation of
the Quran should lead the Prayer; should they be all equal in that respect,
then the one who is best versed of them in the *sunnah;* should they be all equal
in that respect, then the one of them who migrated earliest; and should they be
all equal in that respect then the oldest of them in age. No one should lead the
Prayer in place of another without his permission, nor occupy another's seat in
his house without his permission (Muslim). In one version there occurs: the
seniormost of them in accepting Islam; in place of the oldest of them in age.
Another version is: The leader in Prayer should be the best versed from among
the congregation in the Book of Allah; should they be all equal in that respect
then the seniormost of them in migration; and should they be all equal in that
respect, the oldest of them in age.

352. Uqbah ibn Amr relates that the Holy Prophet would place his
hands upon our shoulders when we were lining up for Prayer and would say:
Stand in straight rows and do not differ among yourselves, else your hearts will
be in disaccord. Let those be nearest to me who are of age and possess
understanding, then those who are closest to them in these respects and then
those who are closest to them (Muslim).

353. Abdullah ibn Mas'ud relates that the Holy Prophet said: Let those
be nearest to me in Prayer who are of age and possessed of understanding,
then those who are closest to them in these respects (he repeated this three
times) and added: Beware of indulging in the nonsense of the streets when you
are in the mosque (Muslim).

354. Sahl ibn Abi Hathmah relates that Abdullah ibn Sahl and
Muhayysah ibn Mas'ud went to Khaibar, when there was no fighting there,
and separated in pursuit of their respective errands. Then Muhayysah came
back to Abdullah and found him dead, bathed in his blood. He arranged his
burial and came along to Medina. Then Abdur Rahman ibn Sahl and
Muhayysah and Huwayysah, sons of Mas'ud, proceeded to tne Holy Prophet
and Abdur Rahman began to speak; whereupon the Holy Prophet said: The
eldest, the eldest. Abdur Rahman being the youngest of the three then fell
silent and the other two addressed the Holy Prophet, who said: Do you swear
to this and demahd justice against the murderer (Bokhari and Muslim)?

355. Jabir relates that after the battle of Uhud the Holy Prophet
arranged the burial of two of the slain in every grave. In each case he would

inquire: Which of these had more of the Quran by heart? Whichever was thus pointed out to him was placed by him first in the grave (Bokhari).

356. Ibn Umar relates that the Holy Prophet said: I saw in my dream that I was brushing my teeth and two men came to me, one being older than the other. I gave the tooth-brush to the younger of the two, but I was told to give it to the older, and I did accordingly (Bokhari and Muslim).

357. Abu Musa relates that the Holy Prophet said: It is part of the glorification of Allah to do honour to an aged Muslim; to one who has the Quran by heart, provided he makes no interpolations in it and does not contradict it by his conduct; and to a just ruler (Abu Daud).

358. Amr ibn Shuaib relates on the authority of his father who heard it from his father, that the Holy Prophet said: He who has no compassion for our little ones and does not acknowledge the honour due to our older ones, is not of us (Abu Daud and Tirmidhi).

359. Maimun ibn Abi Shabib relates that a person asked Ayesha for charity and she gave him a piece of bread. Thereafter one better clothed asked her for charity and she invited him to sit down and served him food. When asked the reason for the difference, she said: The Holy Prophet directed us: Entertain people according to their standing (Abu Daud).

360. This *hadith* is the same as No. 50.

361. Abu Sa'id Samurah ibn Jundub relates: I was only a boy during the time of the Holy Prophet and used to preserve in my memory what he said, but I do not relate what I preserved because we have among us people older than myself (Bokhari and Muslim).

362. Anas relates that the Holy Prophet said: If a youth honours an older person on account of his age, Allah appoints someone who would honour him in his old age (Tirmidhi).

45.

On Visiting the Righteous and Keeping Company with them

Allah, the Exalted, has said:

140. Moses said to his young man: I will not quit until I arrive at the junction of the two seas . . . . . . Moses said to him: May I follow thee that thou mayest teach me part of the guidance that thou hast been taught (18.61-67).

141. Continue thy companionship with those who call on their Lord, morning and evening, seeking His pleasure (18.29).

363. Anas relates that after the death of the Holy Prophet, Abu Bakr said to Umar: Come, let us go visit Umm Aiman as the Holy Prophet used to visit her. When they came to her she started weeping, and they said to her: What makes you cry? Know you not that what Allah has is better for the Holy Prophet? She answered: Indeed I know that what Allah has is better for the Holy Prophet. I cry because revelation has stopped coming down from heaven. This moved the two and they too began to cry with her (Muslim).

364. Abu Hurairah relates that the Holy Prophet said: A man set out to visit a brother in another town. Allah appointed an angel to safeguard him on his way. When the man approached the angel he was asked: Whither are you bent? He answered: I intend to visit a brother of mine in yonder town. The angel asked: Have you committed some valuable to him which you desire to take care of? The man answered: No. I have no desire except to visit him because I love him for the sake of Allah. The angel said to him: I am a messenger of Allah sent to you to tell you that Allah loves you as you love your brother for His sake (Muslim).

365. Abu Hurairah relates that the Holy Prophet said: If a person visits an invalid or a brother of his for the sake of Allah, he is called by a caller, saying: May you be happy, may your progress be blessed, and may you be awarded a pleasant abode in Paradise (Tirmidhi).

366. Abu Musa Ash'ari relates that the Holy Prophet said: The case of a righteous companion and that of an evil companion is like that of one who carries perfume and of one who blows into a furnace. The carrier of perfume might give you some as a gift, or you might buy some from him, or at least you might smell its fragrance. As for the other, he might set your clothes on fire, and at the very least you will breathe the foul air issuing from the furnace (Bokhari and Muslim).

367. Abu Hurairah relates that the Holy Prophet said: A woman is sought in marriage on account of four things: her property, her family, her beauty and her piety. Seek to win one for the sake of her piety, may your hands be covered by dust (Bokhari and Muslim).

368. Ibn Abbas relates that the Holy Prophet said to Gabriel: What stops you from visiting us oftener than you do? Whereupon was revealed the verse: We descend not save by the command of thy Lord; to Him belongs all that is before us and all that is behind us and all that is between (19-65) (Bokhari).

369. Abu Sa'id Khudri relates that the Holy Prophet said: Keep company only with a believer, and let your food be eaten only by the righteous (Abu Daud and Tirmidhi).

370. Abu Hurairah relates that the Holy Prophet said: A person is apt to follow the faith of his friend, so be careful who you make friends with (Abu Daud and Tirmidhi).

371. Abu Musa Ash'ari relates that the Holy Prophet said: A person will be with him whom he loves (Bokhari and Muslim). Another version is: The Holy Prophet was asked: What about a person who loves a people but cannot be with them? He answered: A person will be with those he loves.

372. Anas relates that a rustic asked the Holy Prophet: When will the Judgment be? He countered with: What preparation have you made for it? The man said: The love of Allah and His Messenger. The Holy Prophet said: You will be with those you love (Bokhari and Muslim). Another version is: I have not prepared for it with many Prayers and fasts and much alms-giving; but I love Allah and His Messenger.

373. Ibn Mas'ud relates that a man came to the Holy Prophet and said: Messenger of Allah, what would you say about one who loves a people but is unable to emulate them? He said: A person will be with those he loves (Bokhari and Muslim).

374. Abu Hurairah relates that the Holy Prophet said: People are mines like mines of gold and silver. Those of them who were best before Islam are best in Islam, if they have understanding; and souls are like assembled hosts, those who have affinity with each other become attached and those who lack affinity drift away from each other (Bokhari and Muslim).

375. Usair ibn Amr relates that whenever a delegation came from the Yemen to Umar ibn Khattab he would inquire from them: Is Uwais ibn 'Amir among you? In the end, when he did meet Uwais he interrogated him: Are you Uwais ibn 'Amir? Answer: Yes. Of the Murad and out of them of the Qarn? Yes. Did you suffer from leucoderma and recover from it, except in respect of a space the size of a coin? Yes. Have you a mother? Yes. Umar said: I heard the Holy Prophet say: Uwais Ibn 'Amir will come to you among a delegation from the Yemen. He is of the Murad and out of them from the Qarn. He had leucoderma but he recovered from it, except for a space the size of a coin: He has a mother to whom he is devoted. If he were to swear, relying upon Allah, for something, Allah would fulfil his oath. If you can persuade him to supplicate for forgiveness for you, do so. So I ask you to pray for forgiveness for me. Uwais prayed for forgiveness for him. Umar then asked him: Whither are you bent? He said: Towards Kufa. Umar asked him: Shall I write to the Governor of Kufa in your behalf? Uwais said: I prefer to be among the lowly. The following year one of the nobles of Kufa came on Pilgrimage and met Umar. The latter inquired of him about Uwais. He said: I left him in a dilapidated house sparsely furnished. Umar said to him: I heard the Holy Prophet say: Uwais ibn 'Amir of the Murad and out of them from the Qarn will come to you with a delegation from the Yemen. He will have suffered from leucoderma but will have recovered except for a space the size of a coin. He will have a mother to whom he will be devoted. Were he to swear, relying upon Allah, for something, Allah would fulfil his oath. If you can persuade him to supplicate for forgiveness for you, do so. This man went to Uwais and asked him to pray for forgiveness for him. Uwais said to him: You have just returned from a blessed journey, it is you who should pray for forgiveness for me; and did you meet Umar? The man said: Yes. Uwais then prayed for forgiveness for him. People became aware of the standing of Uwais and he departed following his whim (Muslim).

Another version is: A deputation from Kufa waited upon Umar. Among them was őne who used to deride Uwais. Umar inquired: Is there anyone among you who is of the Qarn? So this man stepped forward. Then Umar said: The Holy Prophet had said: A man will come to you from the Yemen named Uwais. He will have left in the Yemen only his mother. He was suffering from leucoderma and prayed to Allah to be cured of it. So he was cured except for a space the size of a coin. Whoever of you should meet him should ask him to pray for forgiveness for him. Another version is: Umar said: I have heard the Holy Prophet say: The best one of the next generation is a man called Uwais, he has a mother and suffers from leucoderma. Go to him and ask him to pray for forgiveness for you.

376.   Umar ibn Khattab relates: I asked leave of the Holy Prophet to perform the Umra. He gave me leave and said: Brother of mine, do not forget us in your supplications. This is something I would not exchange for the whole world (Abu Daud and Tirmidhi). Another version is: He said: Include us, my brother, in your supplications.

377.   Ibn Umar relates: The Holy Prophet used to visit Quba, riding or walking, and perform two *raka'as* of Prayer in the mosque there (Bokhari and Muslim). Another version is: The Holy Prophet visited the mosque at Quba every week, riding or walking, and Ibn Umar did the same.

46.
On the Excellence of Love for the Sake of Allah

Allah, the Exalted, has said:

142.   Muhammad is the Messenger of Allah. Those who are with him are unyielding towards the disbelievers, com-passsionate towards one another . . . . Allah has promised forgiveness and a great reward to those of them who believe and work righteousness (48.30).

143.   Those who had established their homes in Medina and had accepted the faith before the coming of the Refugees, love those who come to them for refuge (59.10).

378.   Anas relates that the Holy Prophet said: Whoever possesses three qualities tastes through them the sweetness of faith: one, that he should love Allah and His Messenger above all else; two, that he should love someone solely for the sake of Allah; and three, that he should abhor reverting to disbelief, after Allah has rescued him from it, as he would abhor being thrown into the Fire (Bokhari and Muslim).

379.   Abu Hurairah relates that the Holy Prophet said: Seven will be sheltered under the safeguarding shade of Allah's mercy on the Day on which there will be no other shade beside the shade of His mercy: a just ruler; a youth who occupies himself with the worship of Allah, the Lord of honour and glory; one whose heart is ever suspended in the mosque; two who love each other for the sake of Allah, they come together for His sake and part for His sake: one who is called by a woman possessed of beauty and charm and declines, saying: I fear Allah; one who spends secretly in charity, so that his left hand does not know what his right hand spends; and one who remembers Allah in solitude so that his eyes brim over (Bokhari and Muslim).

380. Abu Hurairah relates that the Holy Prophet said: On the Day of Judgment Allah, the Exalted, will call: Where are those who loved each other to My glory? Today I shall give them shelter in the shade of My mercy. Today there is no shade beside My shade (Muslim).

381. Abu Hurairah relates that the Holy Prophet said: By Him in Whose hands is my life, you will not enter Paradise unless you believe, and you will not truly believe unless you love one another. Shall I tell you something whereby you will love one another? Multiply the greeting of peace among yourselves (Muslim).

382. This *hadith* is the same as No. 364.

383. Bra'a ibn 'Azib relates that the Holy Prophet said of the Ansar: Only a believer loves them and only a hypocrite dislikes them. Allah loves him who loves them and Allah dislikes him who dislikes them (Bokhari and Muslim).

384. Mu'az relates that he heard the Holy Prophet say: Allah, the Lord of honour and glory, says: For those who love one another to My glory, there will be columns of light that will be the envy of the Prophets and Martyrs (Tirmidhi).

385. Abu Idris Khaulani relates: I entered the mosque in Damascus and beheld a youth who had brilliant teeth in the company of a number of people. When they differed over anything they referred it to him and followed his view. I asked who he was and was told he was Mu'az ibn Jabal. The next day I hastened to the mosque, but found that he had arrived before me and was engaged in Prayer. I waited till he had finished and then approached him from the front, offered him the greeting of peace and said: Allah is witness that I love you. He asked: For the sake of Allah? I answered: For the sake of Allah. Then he took hold of the fold of my cloak, drew me to himself and said: Rejoice, for I heard the Holy Prophet say: Allah has announced: It becomes incumbent upon Me to bestow My love on those who love one another for My sake, meet one another for My sake, visit one another for My sake and spend for My sake (Malik).

386. Miqdad ibn Ma'dikarib relates that the Holy Prophet said: If a person loves his brother, he should tell him that he loves him (Abu Daud and Tirmidhi).

387. Mu'az relates that the Holy Prophet took his hand and said: Mu'az, I do love you and counsel you that you should not miss supplicating after every *salat:* Allah, help me in remembering You, and being grateful to You and worshipping You in the best manner (Abu Daud and Nisai).

388. Anas relates that a man was with the Holy Prophet when another man passed and the former said: Messenger of Allah, I love that one. The Holy Prophet asked: Have you told him? He said: No. The Holy Prophet said: Tell him. So he went up to the man and said to him: I love you for the sake of Allah; and the other replied: May Allah, for Whose sake you love me, love you (Abu Daud).

47.
On the Signs of Allah's Love for His Servants

Allah, the Exalted, has said:

144.   Announce: If you love Allah, then follow me, Allah will then love you and forgive you your faults. Allah is Most Forgiving, Ever Merciful (3.32).

145.   O ye who believe, whoso from among you turns back from his religion, let him remember that in his stead Allah will soon bring a people whom He will love and who will love Him, who will be kind and considerate towards the believers and firm and unyielding towards the disbelievers. They will strive hard in the cause of Allah and will not at all take to heart the reproaches of the fault-finders. That is Allah's grace; He bestows it upon whomsoever He pleases. Allah is the Lord of Vast bounty, All-knowing (5.55).

389. Abu Hurairah relates that the Holy Prophet said: Allah, the Exalted, says: I challenge to battle him who bears enmity towards a friend of Mine. When a servant of Mine seeks nearness to Me, with that which I love, out of whatever I have prescribed, I begin to love him and when I love him, I become his ear with which he hears and his eyes with which he sees and his hand with which he grasps and his foot with which he walks, and when he begs Me for anything I bestow it upon him and when he seeks shelter with Me, I give him shelter (Bokhari).

390. Abu Hurairah relates that the Holy Prophet said: When Allah loves a servant, a call goes out to Gabriel: Allah, the Exalted, loves So and So, do thou love him also. Then Gabriel also loves him and sends a call through to the dwellers of the heavens: Allah loves So and So, do you also love him. Then the dwellers of the heavens love him also, and then he is accepted in the earth (Bokhari and Muslim). Muslim adds: When Allah is offended with a servant, He calls Gabriel and says to him: I am offended with So and So; and Gabriel is offended with him also. Then he sends a call through to the dwellers of the heavens: Allah is offended with So and So, do you be offended with him also. Thereafter aversion towards him is spread in the earth.

391. Ayesha relates that the Holy Prophet appointed a man in charge of a scouting party who led the Prayers for the party and always concluded his recitation with *sura* Al-Ikhlas (Chapter 112): Proclaim: He is Allah, the One. When the party returned to Medina they mentioned this to the Holy Prophet who said: Ask him why he does this? He was asked and said: This chapter sets out the attributes of the Rahman and I love to recite it. The Holy Prophet, on being told this, said: Tell him Allah loves him (Bokhari and Muslim).

48.
On Warning against Persecution of the Righteous, the Weak and the Lowly

Allah, the Exalted, has said:

146. Those who malign believing men and believing women for that which they have not done shall bear the guilt of a calumny and a manifest sin (33.59).

147. Oppress not the orphan and chide not him who asks (93.10-11).

392. Jundub ibn Abdullah relates that the Holy Prophet said: He who performs the *salat* at *Fajr* comes under the guarantee of Allah, so beware lest Allah should call you to account in respect of anything concerning His guarantee, for should He call any of you to account in respect of anything concerning His guarantee and find him wanting, that one would be hurled down to the fire of hell (Muslim).

49.
On Judging People in respect of their Overt Conduct

Allah, the Exalted, has said:

148. Then if they repent and observe Prayer and pay the Zakat, leave them alone (9.5)

393. Ibn Umar relates that the Holy Prophet said: I have been commanded that I should continue to fight till the enemy bear witness that there is none worthy of worship save Allah and that Muhammad is His Messenger, and observe Prayer and pay the *Zakat*. When they do that they will have secured their lives and their properties against me, subject to their obligations under Islam, and they will be accountable to Allah (Bokhari and Muslim).

394. Tariq ibn Ushaim relates that he heard the Holy Prophet say: He who affirms that there is none worthy of worship save Allah and rejects all that is worshipped beside him secures his life and property and is accountable only to Allah (Muslim).

395. Miqdad ibn Aswad relates: I asked the Messenger of Allah: Tell me, if I am fighting a pagan and he cuts off one of my hands with his sword and then takes shelter behind a tree and says: I submit to Allah; shall I kill him after he has said this? He said: No. Do not kill him. I expostulated: Messenger of Allah, even after he cuts off one of my hands and thereafter says this? He said: Do not kill him, for if you kill him, he will be in the position in which you were before you killed him, and you will be in the position in which he was before he uttered the words that he did utter (Bokhari and Muslim).

396. Usamah ibn Zaid relates: The Holy Prophet sent us on a scouting expedition to Huraqah, a valley of the Juhnah, and we arrived at its springs in the morning. A man of the Ansar and I came upon one of their men and when we had covered him he called out: There is none worthy of worship save Allah. On this the Ansari held back, but I finished him off with my spear. When we returned to Medina, this incident came to the knowledge of the Holy Prophet. He asked me: Usamah, did you kill him after he had affirmed: There is none worthy of worship save Allah? I said: Messenger of Allah, he made the affirmation only to save himself. He said again: Did you kill him after he had affirmed: There is none worthy of worship save Allah? He went on repeating it till I wished I had not accepted Islam before that day (Bokhari and Muslim). Another version is: The Holy Prophet said: Did he affirm: There is none worthy of worship save Allah; and yet you killed him? I said: Messenger of Allah, he said it out of fear of our arms. He said: Why did you not cleave his heart to discover whether he had said it from his heart or not? He kept repeating it till I wished I had accepted Islam only that day.

397. Jundub ibn Abdullah relates that the Holy Prophet despatched a Muslim force against a pagan community and the two forces met in combat. One of the pagans would decide to go for a Muslim and advancing upon him would kill him. One of the Muslims, and it was said among us that it was Usamah ibn Zaid, was on the look out to take him at a disadvantage. When he raised his sword over him, the man called out: There is none worthy of worship save Allah. But the Muslim killed him. When the news of the combat reached the Holy Prophet he was also informed of this incident. He sent for the Muslim and inquired from him: Why did you kill him? He said: Messenger of Allah, he created confusion among the Muslims and killed several of them, So and So, So and So, etc. I advanced upon him and when he saw my sword he exclaimed: There is none worthy of worship save Allah. The Holy Prophet asked: Did you kill him? He said: Yes. The Holy Prophet said: When the Day of Judgment comes, what will you do to his: There is none worthy of worship save Allah? He said: Messenger of Allah, pray for forgiveness for me. The Holy Prophet kept on repeating without any change:

What will you do to his: There is none worthy of worship save Allah, when the Day of Judgment comes?

398. Abdullah ibn Utbah ibn Mas'ud relates that he heard Umar ibn Khattab say: In the time of the Holy Prophet people were called to account through revelation. Now revelation has been cut off and we shall call you to account on the basis of your overt acts. So that whoever displays to us good we shall confirm it and accept it and we shall not inquire into his secret conduct; Allah will call him to account for that; but whoever displays to us evil we shall not uphold it and shall not accept it, even if he protests that there was good in his heart (Bokhari).

50.
On Fear of Allah

Allah, the Exalted, has said:

149.   Fear Me alone (2.41).

150.   Surely, the vengeance of thy Lord is severe (85.13).

151.   Such is the chastisement of thy Lord which He inflicts upon corrupt cities. Surely, His chastisement is grievously painful. In that is a sign for him who fears the chastisement of the hereafter. That is a day for which mankind shall be gathered together, a day which shall be witnessed by all. We hold it back for a computed term. When it arrives no one shall speak except by Allah's leave, then some of them will prove unfortunate and some fortunate. Those who prove unfortunate shall be in the Fire, given to sighing and sobbing (11.103-107).

152.   Allah warns you against His chastisement (3.29).

153.   On the day when a man flees from his brother, his mother, his father, his wife and his sons; on that day everyone of them will be preoccupied with himself alone (80.35-38).

154. O mankind, be mindful of your duty to your Lord; verily the earthquake of the Judgment is a tremendous thing. On that day every woman giving suck will forget her suckling and every pregnant woman will cast her burden; and everyone will appear intoxicated, while they will not be intoxicated, but the chastisement of Allah will be severe indeed (22.2-3).

155. But for him who fears to stand before his Lord are two Gardens (55.47).

156. They will turn one to another asking questions. They will say: Before this among our people we were apprehensive; but Allah has been gracious unto us, and has saved us from the torment of the burning blast. We used to pray to Him aforetime. Surely, He is the Beneficent, the Ever Merciful (52.26-29).

399. Ibn Mas'ud relates that the Holy Prophet said: Everyone of you gets ready for his birth in the womb of his mother in the condition of a sperm-drop for forty days and then as a clot for forty days and then as a lump of flesh for forty days and then an angel is sent who breathes the soul into it and is commanded to record four things about it: its provision, its term of life, its conduct and whether it will be unfortunate or fortunate. Then by Him beside Whom there is none worthy of worship one of you behaves like the dwellers of Paradise till there is left between him and it but the space of a hand and then that which is recorded overtakes him and he begins to behave like the denizens of the Fire and eventually enters it. On the other hand, one of you behaves like the denizens of the Fire till there is left between him and it only the space of a hand then what is recorded overtakes him and he begins to behave like the dwellers of Paradise and eventually enters it (Bokhari and Muslim).

400. Ibn Mas'ud relates that the Holy Prophet said: On the Day of Judgment hell will be brought and it will have seventy thousand bridles, each bridle being pulled by seventy thousand angels (Muslim).

401. Nu'man ibn Bashir relates that he heard the Holy Prophet say that the least tormented of the denizens of the Fire will be a person who will have two brands of fire under his feet whereby his brain will be on the boil. He will imagine himself the worst tormented person and yet he will be the least tormented of them (Bokhari and Muslim).

402. Samurah ibn Jundub relates that the Holy Prophet said: Some will be caught in the Fire up to their ankles, some up to their knees, some up to their waists and some up to their necks (Muslim).

403. Ibn Umar relates that the Holy Prophet said: Mankind will face the Lord of the worlds while some of them will be sunk in their perspiration up to the middle of their ears (Bokhari and Muslim).

404. Anas relates: The Holy Prophet delivered an address to us the like of which I had never heard from him before, in the course of which he said: If you knew what I know, you would laugh little and weep much. Thereupon those present covered their faces and fell to sobbing (Bokhari and Muslim). Another version is: Some tidings reached the Holy Prophet concerning his companions upon which he addressed them and said: Paradise and the Fire were presented to my view, so that I have never seen the like of this day in good and in evil. If you were to know what I know you would laugh little and weep much. His companions then passed through an experience of suffering that had not an equal. They covered their faces and fell into a paroxysm of sobbing.

405. Miqdad relates that he heard the Holy Prophet say: On the Day of Judgment the sun will be as close to people as if it were only a mile away from them, and people will perspire according to the quality of their deeds. The perspiration of some will rise to their ankles, of others to their knees, of others to their waists and some will be bridled by their perspiration. The Holy Prophet pointed to his mouth by way of illustration (Muslim).

406. Abu Hurairah relates that the Holy Prophet said: People will perspire so much on the Day of Judgment that the earth will be soaked with it to a depth of seventy yards and people will be bridled with it after it has come up to their ears (Bokhari and Muslim).

407. Abu Hurairah relates: We were with the Holy Prophet when he heard the sound of something heavy falling, and he asked us: Do you know what that was? We said: Allah and His Messenger know best. He said: This was a stone that had been thrown into hell seventy years before; it kept falling into it up to this moment. It has now reached its bottom and you have heard the sound of its touching bottom (Muslim).

408. This *hadith* is the same as No. 139.

409. Abu Dharr relates that the Holy Prophet said: I see that which you do not. The heaven creaks and is justified in doing so. There is not in it a hand's breadth of space but is occupied by an angel whose forehead is in prostration before Allah. If you knew what I know you would laugh little and weep much, you would not enjoy consorting with your wives and you would issue forth into the streets and open spaces seeking shelter with Allah (Tirmidhi).

410. Abu Barzah relates that the Holy Prophet said: A servant of Allah will remain standing on the Day of Judgment till he is questioned about his age and how he spent it; and about his knowledge and what he did with it; and about his wealth, how he acquired it and in what did he spend it; and about his body and how he wore it out (Tirmidhi).

411. Abu Hurairah relates that the Holy Prophet recited: On that day the earth will narrate its account (95.5); and inquired: Do you know what its account is? He was told: Allah and His Messenger know best. He said: Its account is that it shall bear witness against every servant and handmaiden of Allah concerning that which they did on its back. It will say: You did this and this on such and such a day. This will be its account (Tirmidhi).

412. Abu Sa'id Khudri relates that the Holy Prophet said: How can I feel at rest when the Angel of the Trumpet has put his lips to the Trumpet so that he might blow it forthwith? He perceived as if this had distressed his companions, so he told them to seek comfort through repeating: Sufficient for us is Allah, and an excellent Guardian is He (Tirmidhi).

413. Abu Hurairah relates that the Holy Prophet said: He who is afraid sets out in the early part of the night and he who sets out early arrives at the goal. Be warned that the equipment of Allah is precious. Beware the equipment of Allah is Paradise (Tirmidhi).

414. Ayesha relates that she heard the Holy Prophet say: On the Day of Judgment people will be assembled barefooted, naked, uncircumcised. I said: Messenger of Allah, will men and women be together looking at one another? He said: Ayesha, the occasion will be too terrifying for them to be concerned with looking at one another (Bokhari and Muslim).

51:
On Hope and Good Expectation

Allah, the Exalted has said:

157.   Convey to them: My servants, who have committed excesses against your own selves, despair not of the mercy of Allah, surely Allah forgives all sins; He is Most Forgiving, Ever Merciful (39.54).

158.   None do We requite in that way but the ungrateful (34.18).

159.   It has been revealed to us that punishment shall overtake him who rejects the truth and turns away from it (20.49).

160.   My mercy encompasses all things (7.157).

415. Ubadah ibn Samit relates that the Holy Prophet said: He who bears witness that there is none worthy of worship save Allah, the One, without associate, and that Muhammad is His servant and Messenger, that Jesus is Allah's servant and Messenger and His word that He conveyed to Mary and a spirit from Him, that Paradise is true and that the Fire is true will be admitted by Allah to Paradise (Bokhari and Muslim). Muslim's version is: He who bears witness that there is none worthy of worship save Allah and that Muhammad is the Messenger of Allah will be safeguarded against the Fire.

416. Abu Dharr relates that the Holy Prophet said: Allah, the Lord of honour and glory, says: He who does one good deed shall be rewarded ten times or I shall give him more, and he who does an evil deed shall be chastised in proportion thereto, or I shall forgive him; and he who approaches Me a hand's breadth I shall approach him an arm's length, and he who approaches Me an arm's length I shall approach him the length of two arms; and he who comes to Me walking, I shall come to him running; and him who meets Me with an earthful of faults shall I meet with an equal degree of forgiveness (Muslim).

417. Jabir relates that a rustic came to the Holy Prophet and asked:

Messenger of Allah, what are the two imperatives? He answered: He who dies associating naught with Allah will enter Paradise, and he who dies associating aught with Allah will enter the Fire (Muslim).

418. Anas relates that Mu'az was riding pillion with the Holy Prophet when the latter called him by name and he responded: At your service, Messenger of Allah, may you be happy. This was repeated three times and thereafter the Holy Prophet said: Of the servants of Allah whoever affirms with perfect sincerity of heart that there is none worthy of worship save Allah and that Muhammad is His servant and His Messenger will be safeguarded by Allah against the Fire. Mu'az said: Messenger of Allah, shall I proclaim this among the people so that they may be cheered? He said; No, lest they should depend entirely upon this. Mu'az disclosed this only at the approach of death, fearing lest he should be held guilty of holding back something that was within his ken (Bokhari and Muslim).

419. Abu Hurairah (or Abu Sa'id Khudri) relates that on the day of the battle of Tabuk the Muslims were sore pressed by hunger and they asked the Holy Prophet: Messenger of Allah, if you would permit us, we would slaughter our camels and eat of their flesh and use their fat. He gave them permission. On this Umar came and said: Messenger of Allah, if this were done we would suffer from lack of transportation. But you might ask everyone to bring whatever they have left over and if you pray over it and supplicate Allah to bless it, He would bestow His blessing upon it. The Holy Prophet agreed and called for his leather table cover and had it spread out and asked people to bring their left-overs. They started doing it. One brought a handful of beans, another brought a handful of dates, a third brought a piece of bread and thus some provisions were collected on the table cover. The Holy Prophet prayed for blessings, and then said: Now take it up in your vessels. Everyone filled his vessel with food, so that there was not left a single empty vessel in the whole camp. All of them ate their fill and there was still some left over. The Holy Prophet said: I bear witness that there is none worthy of worship save Allah, and that I am His Messenger. No servant of Allah who meets Him with these two affirmations, believing sincerely in them, would be held back from Paradise (Muslim).

420. Itban ibn Malik relates: I used to join in the Prayer services with my people the Bani Salim, but there was a valley between them and me, and during the rains when it was flooded I found it difficult to cross over to their mosque. So I went to the Holy Prophet and said to him: My eyesight is affected and I find it difficult to cross over the valley which separates me from my people when it gets flooded during the rains. I wish very much that you would come to my house and say your prayers therein so that I might appoint that spot as my place of Prayer. He said: I shall do that. Next day, when the sun had risen high the Holy Prophet came to my house with Abu Bakr and asked for leave to enter, which I granted, and he said: Where do you wish me to say my Prayer? I pointed out the spot to him. He stood for Prayer and called out the *Takbir* and we arranged ourselves behind him. He led the Prayer for two *raka'as* and we prayed with him. When he had finished I detained him over pancakes that had been prepared for him. When the neighbours heard that the Holy Prophet was in my house they came and gathered in the house in large numbers. Someone said: What has happened to Malik? Another one said: He is a hypocrite. He does not love Allah and His Messenger. On this the Holy Prophet said: Do not say that. Do you not know that he says: There is none worthy of worship save Allah; seeking only the pleasure of Allah? The man said: Allah and His Messenger know best, but as for us we see that his friendship and conversation are confined to the hypocrites. The Holy Prophet said: Allah will safeguard against the Fire one who affirms: There is none worthy of worship save Allah; seeking thereby only the pleasure of Allah (Bokhari and Muslim).

421. Umar ibn Khattab relates: Some prisoners were brought to the Holy Prophet. There was a woman among them who ran about hither and yon. When she found a child she took it up, drew it close and suckled it. The Holy Prophet said to his companions: Can you imagine this woman throwing her child into the fire? We said: Surely not. On which he said: Allah is more compassionate towards His servants than she is towards her child (Bokhari and Muslim).

422. Abu Hurairah relates that the Holy Prophet said: When Allah created mankind He wrote in a book which is with Him on His Throne: My mercy shall overcome My wrath (Bokhari and Muslim).

423. Abu Hurairah relates that he heard the Holy Prophet say: Allah divided compassion into a hundred parts out of which He retained ninety-nine parts and sent down one part to the earth. From this one part proceeds all the compassion that one part of creation exercises towards another, so that an animal lifts its foot above its young lest they should receive a hurt. Another version is: Allah has a hundred parts of mercy of which He has sent down one part for jinn and men and animals and insects by virtue of which they deal kindly with one another and love one another and have compassion for one another and wild animals care for their young. Allah has retained the remaining ninety-nine parts to deal mercifully with His servants on the Day of Judgment (Bokhari and Muslim). Another version is: Allah has a hundred parts of mercy. One part of them is used by all creatures for kindness between them and ninety-nine parts are for use on the Day of Judgment. Still another version is: Allah created one hundred parts of mercy on the day on which He created the heavens and the earth, each part equal to the space between heaven and earth. Of them He put one part in the earth, by virtue of which a mother has compassion for her children and animals and birds have compassion for one another. On the Day of Judgment He will perfect and complete His mercy.

424. Abu Hurairah relates that the Holy Prophet said: A servant of Allah committed a sin and then supplicated: Allah, forgive me my sin. On

which Allah, the Blessed and the High, said: My servant committed a sin and then realised that he has a Lord Who forgives sin and also calls to account for it. The servant reverted to it and sinned again and supplicated: Lord, forgive me my sin. The Blessed and the High said: My servant committed a sin and then realised that he has a Lord Who forgives sin and also calls to account for it. The servant again reverted to it and sinned and supplicated: Lord, forgive me my sin. The Blessed and the High said: My servant committed a sin and then realised that he has a Lord Who forgives sin and also calls to account for it. I have forgiven My servant; so let him do what he wishes (meaning, so long as he goes on repenting) (Bokhari and Muslim).

425.   Abu Hurairah relates that the Holy Prophet said: By Him in Whose hands is my life, if you had not sinned, Allah would have removed you and put in your place a people who would have sinned and then asked for forgiveness, so that He would have forgiven them (Muslim).

426.   Abu Ayub Khalid ibn Zaid relates that he heard the Holy Prophet say: If you had not sinned, Allah would have created a creation that would have sinned and asked for forgiveness, so that He would have forgiven them (Muslim).

427.   Abu Hurairah relates: We were sitting with the Holy Prophet, Abu Bakr and Umar being also among us, when the Holy Prophet got up and left us. As time passed we became anxious lest he should come to harm while we were not with him. Being afraid, we got up: I was the first to do so and I set out in search of him, till I came to a garden belonging to the Ansar (here follows a long account, concluding with) and the Holy Prophet said: Go and whomsoever you encounter outside this garden who affirms out of the sincerity of his heart that there is none worthy of worship save Allah, give him the glad assurance that he will enter Paradise (Muslim).

428.   Abdullah ibn Amr ibn 'As relates that the Holy Prophet recited the words of Allah concerning Abraham that he prayed: Lord, they have indeed led astray large numbers of people. So whoever follows me, he is certainly of me; and whoever disobeys me in his case also Thou art surely Most Forgiving, Ever Merciful (14.37); and the words of Jesus: If Thou decide to punish them, they are Thy servants; and if Thou forgive them, Thou surely art the Mighty, the Wise (5.119); and then raised his hands and said: O Allah, my people, my people; and wept. Allah commanded Gabriel: Go to Muhammad (thy Lord knows all) and ask him: What makes you weep? So Gabriel came to him and the Holy Prophet told him what he had said. (Allah knew it). He commanded Gabriel: Go to Muhammad and tell him: We shall cause thee to be pleased in the matter of thy people, and shall not make thee sorrowful (Muslim).

429.   Mu'az ibn Jabal relates: I was riding a donkey pillion with the Holy Prophet when he asked me: Mu'az, do you know what is due to Allah from His servants and what is due to His servants from Allah? I said: Allah and His Messenger know best. He said: Allah's due from His servants is that they should worship Him and should not associate aught with Him; and the due of

His servants from Allah is that He should not chastise those who do not associate aught with Him. On this I said: Messenger of Allah, shall I give people this good news? He said: Do not do so, lest they should depend wholly on it (Bokhari and Muslim).

430. Bra'a ibn 'Azib relates that the Holy Prophet said: When a Muslim is questioned in his grave he testifies that there is none worthy of worship save Allah and that Muhammad is His Messenger. This is affirmed in the verse: Allah strengthens the believers with the Word that is firmly established both in this life and the hereafter (14.28). (Bokhari and Muslim).

431. Anas relates that the Holy Prophet said: When a disbeliever does good he is fed out of it in this world, and in the case of the Muslim Allah stores up his good works for him in the hereafter and provides for him in this life on account of his obedience. Another version is: Allah does not wrong anyone. A believer is rewarded for his good works both here and hereafter. A disbeliever is rewarded in this world for his good works done for the sake of Allah; so that when he proceeds to the hereafter there is no good work of his for which he can be rewarded there (Muslim).

432. Jabir relates that the Holy Prophet said: The five Prayer services are like a great canal running at your door in which you bathe five times a day (Muslim).

433. Ibn Abbas relates that he heard the Holy Prophet say: If a Muslim dies and forty people who do not associate aught with Allah, join in the funeral prayers over him, Allah accepts their intercession on his behalf (Muslim).

434. Ibn Mas'ud relates: About forty of us were with the Holy Prophet in a tent, when he asked us: Would it please you if you were to be a quarter of the dwellers of Paradise? We answered: Yes. Then he asked: Would you be pleased if you were to be a third of the dwellers of Paradise? We answered: Yes. He said: By Him in Whose hands is the life of Muhammad, I hope that you will be one half of the dwellers of Paradise. This is because none will enter Paradise except a soul that is in full submission to Allah, and your proportion among the pagans is like that of white hair on the skin of a black ox, or that of black hair on the skin of a red ox. (Bokhari and Muslim).

435. Abu Musa Ash'ari relates that the Holy Prophet said: On the Day of Judgment Allah will bestow upon every Muslim a Jew or a Christian and will say: He is your ransom for your deliverance from the Fire. Another version is: On the Day of Judgment some Muslims will come with sins piled up like mountains and Allah will forgive them (Muslim).

436. Ibn Umar relates that he heard the Holy Prophet say: A believer will approach his Lord on the Day of Judgment and enveloping him in His mercy He will question him concerning his sins: Do you recognise this sin and this sin? He will answer: Lord, I recognise. Then He will say: I covered it up for you in the world, and I forgive it you today. Then will the record of his good works be handed to him (Bokhari and Muslim).

437. Ibn Mas'ud relates that a man kissed a woman and came and told the Holy Prophet. At that time Allah revealed the following verse: Observe Prayer at the two ends of the day, and in the hours of the night in the proximity of the day. Surely good wipes out evil (11.115). The man asked: Messenger of Allah, is this for me? He answered: For all my people, everyone of them (Bokhari and Muslim).

438. Anas relates: A man came to the Holy Prophet and said: Messenger of Allah, I have committed a punishable offence. Please impose the penalty on me. At the same time the Prayer service was held and the man joined in it. When the service was over he again urged the Holy Prophet: Messenger of Allah, I have offended; please impose the penalty. The Holy Prophet asked him: Were you present in the *salat* with us? He answered: Yes. The Holy Prophet said: Then you have been forgiven (Bokhari and Muslim).

439. Anas relates that the Holy Prophet said: Allah is pleased with His servant who eats a morsel and praises Allah for it and drinks a mouthful and praises Allah for it (Muslim).

440. This *hadith* is the same as No. 16.

441. Abu Naji Amr ibn Abasah relates: In the days of Ignorance I used to think that people were astray and did not adhere to any truth. They worshipped idols. Then I heard of a man in Mecca that he puts forth new ideas. So I mounted my camel and went to him. I found that the Holy Prophet kept out of sight and was persecuted by his people. Through polite inquiries I found my way to him in Mecca. I asked him: What are you? He said: I am a Prophet. I asked: What is a Prophet? He said: Allah has sent me. I asked: With what has He sent you? He said: He has sent me to strengthen the ties of kinship, to break up idols and to establish that God is One and naught may be associated with Him. I asked: Who is with you in this? He said: A freeman and a slave. (At that time only Abu Bakr and Bilal were with him). I said: I shall follow you. He said: You are not able to do it just now. Do you not see my situation and the attitude of the people? Return to your people and when you hear about me that my cause has triumphed, then come to me. I went back to my people, and while I was with my people the Holy Prophet migrated to Medina. I continued to ask people about him till some of my people visited Medina. On their return I asked them: How goes it with the man who has arrived in Medina? They said: People are hastening to him. His own people had designed to kill him but did not succeed. Then I proceeded to Medina and came to him and said: Messenger of Allah, do you recognise me? He said: Yes, you are the one who met me in Mecca. I said: Messenger of Allah, tell me of that which Allah has taught you and which I do not know. Tell me of *salat*. He said: Say the morning Prayer and then refrain from Prayer till the sun has risen the length of a spear, for it rises between the two horns of Satan and at that time the pagans prostrate themselves before it. You may pray then, for *salat* is attended and testified to by angels, till the shadow of a spear equals the length of a spear. Restrain yourself from Prayer then, for hell is stoked up at that time. When the shadow lengthens you may pray, for *salat* is attended and testified to by angels till the time of *Asr* Prayer. After *Asr* Prayer refrain from Prayer till the sun has set, for it sets between the two horns of Satan and the pagans prostrate themselves before it at that time.

Then I said: Prophet of Allah, tell me about ablutions. He said: When a person begins the ablutions and washes out his mouth and nose the sins of his mouth and nose are washed out. Then as he washes his face as Allah has commanded, the sins of his face are washed out from the sides of his beard with the water. Then he washes his hands up to his elbows and the sins of his hands are washed out through his digits with the water. Then he passes his wet hands over his head and the sins of the head are washed out through the ends of his hair with the water. Then he washes his feet up to the ankles and the sins of his feet are washed out through his toes with the water. Then if he stands up for Prayer and praises Allah and glorifies Him and proclaims His greatness according to His worthiness and devotes his heart wholly to Allah, he emerges from his sins in a condition of purity as the one in which his mother bore him.

When Amr ibn Abasah related this to Abu Umamah, companion of the Holy Prophet, the latter said to him: Have a care, Amr ibn Abasah, about what you relate at one place about all that is bestowed upon such a person. Amr answered him: Abu Umamah, I have reached old age, my bones have become dry, my death is approaching and there is no need for me to tell lies concerning Allah and His Messenger. Had I not heard this from the Holy Prophet once, twice, three times (and he counted up to seven) I would never have related it. Indeed I have heard this even oftener (Muslim).

442. Abu Musa Ash'ari has related that the Holy Prophet said: When Allah determines upon mercy for a people He takes custody of the soul of its Prophet before it and makes him a herald for it and a storehouse for it in the hereafter, and when He determines upon the ruin of a people He chastises it while its Prophet is alive and destroys it while he is alive and watches it and delights in its destruction because they rejected him and disobeyed his directions (Muslim).

52.

On Exaltation of Hope

Allah, the Exalted, has said:

161. I commit my cause to Allah, surely Allah is watchful of His servants. So Allah safeguarded him against the mischief of that which they contrived (40.45-46).

443. Abu Hurairah relates that the Holy Prophet said: Allah says: I am towards every servant of Mine as he conceives Me to be. I am with him wherever he remembers Me. (Allah is more pleased with the repentance of a servant of His than one of you who recovers something of his in the desert after he has lost it). He who approaches Me over a distance of a hand's breadth, I approach him an arm's length, and he who approaches Me an arm's length, I approach him two arms' length. If a servant of Mine comes to Me walking, I go to him running (Bokhari and Muslim).

444. Jabir ibn Abdullah relates that he heard the Holy Prophet say, three days before his death: Let no one of you die except in a state of mind hoping for the best from Allah, the Lord of honour and glory (Muslim).

445. Anas relates that he heard the Holy Prophet say: Allah, the Exalted, has said: Son of Adam, I shall continue to forgive thee so long as thou callest on Me and hopest for My forgiveness, whatever may be thy defaults. I care not, son of Adam, even if thy sins should pile up to the sky and thou shouldst supplicate Me for forgiveness I would forgive thee. Son of Adam, if thou camest to Me with an earthful of sins and meetest Me, not associating aught with Me, I would come to thee with an earthful of forgiveness (Tirmidhi).

53.
On Combining Hope and Fear

Allah, the Exalted, has said:

162. None feels secure against the design of Allah, except those that are losers (7.100).

163. None despairs of Allah's mercy, save the unbelieving people (12.88).

164. On the day when some faces will be bright and some faces will be gloomy (3.107).

165. Thy Lord is swift in exacting retribution, and He is also Most Forgiving, Ever Merciful (7.168).

166. Verily, the virtuous will be in bliss and the wicked shall be in hell (82.14-15).

167. He whose scales will be heavy with good deeds will have a pleasant life; but he whose scales are light for want of good deeds will have hell as a resort (101.7-10).

446. Abu Hurairah relates that the Holy Prophet said: If a believer realised the full extent of the chastisement of Allah, none would desire His Paradise; and if a disbeliever realised the full extent of Allah's mercy, none would despair of His Paradise (Muslim).

447. Abu Sa'id Khudri relates that the Holy Prophet said: When the bier is lifted above the shoulders of the pall-bearers, if the corpse is that of a righteous man it urges: Go forward with me, go forward with me; if it is that of an unrighteous person, it says: Woe to it, where are you taking it? Its voice is heard by everything except man, and if man heard it he would be struck dead (Bokhari).

448. This *hadith* is the same as No. 105.

54.

On the Excellence of Weeping for Fear of Allah

Allah, the Exalted, has said:

168. They weep while prostrating and this adds to their humility (17.110).

169. Do you, then, wonder at this announcement, and laugh at it and do not weep (53.60-61)?

449. Ibn Mas'ud relates: The Holy Prophet asked me to recite the Quran to him. I said: Messenger of Allah, shall I recite the Quran to you, whereas it is you to whom it has been revealed? He said: I like to hear it recited by another. So I recited to him a portion from the fourth Chapter till I came to the verse: How will it be when We shall bring a witness from every people, and shall bring thee as a witness against these (4.42)? when he said: That is enough for now. I looked at him and saw that his eyes were running (Bokhari and Muslim).

450. This *hadith* is the same as the first part of No. 404.

451. Abu Hurairah relates that the Holy Prophet said: One who weeps out of fear of Allah will not enter the Fire till the milk recedes into the breasts and the dust endured in striving in the cause of Allah and the steam of hell will never subsist together (Tirmidhi).

452. This *hadith* is the same as No. 379.

453. Abdullah ibn Shikhir relates: I came to the Holy Prophet at a time when he was engaged in Prayer. The sound of his sobbing was like the sound of a boiling kettle (Abu Daud and Tirmidhi).

454. Anas relates that the Holy Prophet said to Ubayy ibn Ka'ab: Allah, the Lord of honour and glory, has commanded me to recite to you *sura* Al-Bayyinah (Chapter 98) of the Quran. He asked: Did He name me? The Holy Prophet said: Yes; whereupon Ubayy fell to sobbing (Bokhari and Muslim).

455. This *hadith* is the same as No. 363.

456. Ibn Umar relates that when the illness of the Holy Prophet became severe he was asked about the *salat* and he said: Tell Abu Bakr to lead the Prayer. On this, Ayesha said: Abu Bakr is very tender-hearted, he is bound to be overcome when he recites the Quran. The Holy Prophet repeated: Tell him to lead the Prayer. Another version is: Ayesha said: When Abu Bakr stands in your place people will not be able to hear him for his sobbing (Bokhari and Muslim).

457.   Ibrahim ibn Abdur Rahman ibn Auf relates that food was brought to Abdur Rahman ibn Auf when he had been fasting and he said: Mus'ab ibn Umair was killed, and he was a better man than I, and there was nothing that could serve as a shroud for him except a sheet so small that if his head was covered his feet remained uncovered and if his feet were covered his head remained uncovered. Then we have been endowed generously with the bounties of this world, so that I am afraid lest the reward of our good works might have been hastened for us. On this he began to sob and left off eating (Bokhari).

458.   Abu Umamah Sudayy ibn Ajalan Bahili relates that the Holy Prophet said: There is nothing dearer to Allah than two drops and two marks. The drops are: a tear shed out of fear of Allah, and a drop of blood shed in the cause of Allah. The marks are: a mark received in the cause of Allah, and a mark acquired in discharging an obligation imposed by Allah (Tirmidhi).

459.   This is only a reference to *hadith* No. 158.

55.
On the Excellence of Indifference to the World and of Poverty

Allah, the Exalted, has said:

170.   The life of this world is like water that We send down from the clouds, then the vegetation of the earth, of which men and cattle eat, mingles with it and the earth is embellished and looks beautiful, and its owners believe that they are its complete masters; then by day or by night, Our Command comes to it and We convert it into a mown-down field, as if nothing had existed there the day before. Thus We expound the Signs for a people who reflect (10.25).

171.   Expound to them the case of the life of this world. It is like water that We send down from the sky, and the vegetation of the earth grows and mingles with it and all becomes stubble which is scattered about by the winds. Allah has full power over everything. Wealth and children are an ornament of the life of this world; then of these that which is converted into a source of permanent beneficence is best in the sight of thy Lord, both in respect of immediate reward and in respect of expected benefits (18.46-47).

172.   Keep in mind that the life of this world is only sport and pastime, and a display, and a subject of boasting among yourselves, and rivalry in multiplying riches and children. It is like vegetation produced by the rain which rejoices the tiller. Then it dries up and takes on a yellow colour, then it becomes broken particles of stubble. In the hereafter there is severe chastisement and forgiveness from Allah and His pleasure. The life of this world is but illusory enjoyment (57.21).

173.   The love of desired objects like women and children and stored-up reserves of gold and silver, and pastured horses and cattle and crops, appears attractive to people. All this is the provision of the hither life; and it is Allah with Whom is an excellent abode (3.15).

174.   O ye people, assuredly the promise of Allah is true, so let not the hither life beguile you, nor let any deceiver deceive you concerning Allah (35.6).

175.   The desire of increase in worldly possessions beguiles you till you reach the graves. You will soon realise the vanity of your pursuits; again, you will soon realise how mistaken you are. If you only knew with the certainty of knowledge (102.2-6).

176.   The hither life is nothing but sport and pastime, and the home of the hereafter is the only true life, if they but knew (29.65).

460.   Amr ibn Auf Ansari relates that the Holy Prophet sent Abu Ubaidah ibn Jarrah to Bahrain to collect the poll tax and he returned from Bahrain with the money. The Ansar heard of this and came up to join in the morning Prayer service with the Holy Prophet. When the service was finished and he was about to leave, they presented themselves before him. When he saw them, he smiled and said: I imagine you have heard that Abu Ubaidah has come from Bahrain with something. They said: It is true, Messenger of Allah. He said: Rejoice, and hope for that which will please you. It is not poverty that I apprehend for you. What I apprehend for you is that you might begin to desire the would as they desired it and that it might destroy you as it destroyed them (Bokhari and Muslim).

461.   Abu Sa'id Khudri relates that the Holy Prophet sat in the pulpit and we sat around him and he said: What I am afraid of concerning you after I am gone is the ornament and embellishment of the world that might be thrown open to you (Bokhari and Muslim).

462.   Abu Sa'id Khudri relates that the Holy Prophet said: The world is green and pleasant and Allah will appoint you vicegerents in it and will see how you conduct yourselves. Then safeguard yourselves against the world and safeguard yourselves against women (Muslim).

463. Anas relates that the Holy Prophet said: Allah, there is no life but the life of the hereafter (Bokhari and Muslim).

464. This *hadith* is the same as No. 104.

465. Anas relates that the Holy Prophet said: The most prosperous person in the world who had been adjudged to hell will be brought up on the Day of Judgment and will be dipped once in the Fire and will be asked: Son of Adam, did you ever enjoy any good, did you ever experience any bliss? He will say: Never, O Lord. Then the one who had experienced the extreme of adversity in the world and was adjudged worthy of Paradise will be brought up and given one experience of Paradise and will be asked: Son of Adam, did you ever experience adversity, did you ever pass through hardship? He will say: No, I never experienced adversity, I never passed through hardship (Muslim).

466. Mustaurid ibn Shaddad relates that the Holy Prophet said: The value of the world in comparison with the hereafter is as if one of you dipped a finger in the ocean and then observed how much moisture sticks to it when he pulls it back (Muslim).

467. Jabir relates that the Holy Prophet was passing through the street with his companions on both sides of him when he noticed a short-eared lamb lying dead. He caught it by its ear and said: Which of you would like to have it for a dirhem? They said: We would not like to have it in return for anything, and what would we do with it? He then asked: Would you like to have it for nothing? They answered: Had it been alive it would have been defective being short-eared, and of what use is it dead? The Holy Prophet said: Truly, the world is even more useless in the sight of Allah than this is in your eyes (Muslim).

468. Abu Dharr relates: I was walking along with the Holy Prophet in the rocky plain of Medina when we saw Uhud in front of us. He called me and I said: At your service, Messenger of Allah. He said: If I had as much gold as Uhud yonder, it would not please me to have a single dinar out of it by me after the passage of three days, unless I were to retain something for the repayment of a debt. I would distribute it among the servants of Allah like this and this and this to the right and left and rear. He then walked on and said: Those who have much will be the ones who will have the least on the Day of Judgment, except those who spend their wealth like this and this and this, to the right and left and rear, and they are few. Then he said to me: Remain where you are and do not move till I come back to you: and he walked into the dark and disappeared. Presently I heard a loud voice and was afraid lest he should have encountered something untoward. I wanted to go to him but recalled his admonition: Do not move till I come back to you. So I did not move till he came back to me, and I said to him: I heard a voice which made me afraid but I remembered your direction to me. He asked: Did you hear him? I said: Yes. He said: It was Gabriel who came to me and said: He who dies from among your followers, not having associated aught with Allah, will enter Paradise; and I inquired: Even if he should have been guilty of adultery or of theft? He said: Even if he was guilty of adultery, or of theft (Bokhari and Muslim).

469. Abu Hurairah relates that the Holy Prophet said: If I had gold the equal of Uhud, it would please me that I should have nothing left of it with me after the passage of three nights except something that I might retain for the repayment of a debt (Bokhari and Muslim).

470. Abu Hurairah relates that the Holy Prophet said: Look at one who is below you and do not look at one who is above you. This would enable you to appreciate better the bounties that Allah has bestowed upon you (Bokhari and Muslim). The version of Muslim is: When any of you looks at one who is richer and handsomer than him, he should also look at one who is lower than him.

471. Abu Hurairah relates that the Holy Prophet said: Ruined are those devoted to dinars and dirhems and black cloaks and striped cloaks. If they are given they are pleased and if they are not given they are displeased (Bokhari).

472. Abu Hurairah relates: I have known seventy of the Company of the Lounge not one of whom possessed a cloak, only a loin cloth or a blanket which they suspended from their necks and which reached down half way to their shanks or to their ankles. They managed to keep it in place with their hands lest their private parts might be exposed (Bokhari).

473. Abu Hurairah relates that the Holy Prophet said: The world is the prison of the believer and the paradise of the disbeliever (Muslim).

474. Ibn Umar relates that the Holy Prophet took hold of his shoulders and said: Be in the world as if you are a stranger or a traveller. Ibn Umar used to say: When you arrive at the evening do not look forward to the morning and when you arrive at the morning do not look forward to the evening. During health prepare for illness and while you are alive prepare for death (Bokhari).

475. Abu Abbas Sahl ibn Sa'ad Sa'idi relates that a man came to the Holy Prophet and said to him: Messenger of Allah, instruct me in something by acting on which I should win the love of Allah and the love of people. He told him: Do not desire the world, and Allah will love you; and do not desire that which people have and they will love you (Ibn-i-Majah).

476. Nu'man ibn Bashir relates that Umar ibn Khattab expatiated upon the worldly prosperity that people had achieved and said: I have known the Holy Prophet pass his day in hunger depending upon a few cheap dates to assuage it (Muslim).

477. Ayesha relates: When the Holy Prophet died there was nothing eatable in my house except a small quantity of barley in a bin upon which I subsisted for a long time. Then I measured what was left of it and it was soon finished (Bokhari and Muslim).

478. Amr ibn Harith relates that on his death the Holy Prophet left no dinar or dirhem or slave or bondwoman, or anything except his white riding mule, his arms and his land which he had given in charity for travellers (Bokhari).

479. Khubaib ibn Arat relates: We migrated with the Holy Prophet seeking the pleasure of Allah and looking only to Him for our reward. Some of us died without enjoying anything of it. Of such was Mus'ab ibn Umair who was killed in the battle of Uhud, leaving only a small sheet. If we covered his head with it his feet were exposed, and if we covered his feet his head was left uncovered. So the Holy Prophet told us to cover his head and to put some fragrant grass over his feet. Others of us are reaping the ripe fruits of our reward (Bokhari and Muslim).

480 Sahl ibn Sa'ad Sa'idi relates that the Holy Prophet said: If in the sight of Allah the world had the value equal to that of the wing of a mosquito, He would not have allowed a disbeliever to drink a mouthful of water out of it (Tirmidhi).

481. Abu Hurairah relates that he heard the Holy Prophet say: The world is accursed and so is all that is in it save only the remembrance of Allah and that which pleases Allah, and the learned and the scholars (Tirmidhi).

482. Abdullah ibn Mas'ud relates that the Holy Prophet said: Do not run too much after property lest you should be absorbed by the world (Tirmidhi).

483. Abdullah ibn Amr ibn 'As relates: We were repairing our thatched cottage when the Holy Prophet passed by and asked us: What are you engaged in? We said: The thatch had become feeble and we are repairing it. He said: I see the matter approaching sooner than this (Abu Daud and Tirmidhi).

484. Ka'ab ibn Iyaz relates that he heard the Holy Prophet say: Every people is subjected to a trial; the trial of my people will be through wealth (Tirmidhi).

485. Uthman ibn Affan relates that the Holy Prophet said: A son of Adam is entitled only to three things: a dwelling to live in, a garment to cover his nakedness and a piece of bread and water (Tirmidhi).

486. Abdullah ibn Shikir relates: I came to the Holy Prophet while he was reciting *sura* Al-Takathur (Chapter 102) of the Quran. He said: Man says: My property, my property; while out of his property only that is his which he eats and consumes, and wears and wears out and spends in charity and sends ahead (Muslim).

487. Abdullah ibn Mughaffal relates: A man said to the Holy Prophet: Messenger of Allah, I do love you. He said: Watch what you are saying! The man said: Indeed, I love you; and repeated it three times. The Holy Prophet said: If you do love me prepare for poverty, for poverty advances more rapidly towards one who loves me than does flood water towards its objective (Tirmidhi).

488. Ka'ab ibn Malik relates that the Holy Prophet said: Two hungry wolves let loose among a flock of sheep do not do more damage than is caused by a man's greed for wealth and standing to his faith (Tirmidhi).

489. Abdullah ibn Mas'ud relates that the Holy Prophet slept on a mat and when he got up the impression of the mat was visible on his body. We said: Messenger of Allah, shall we prepare a mattress for you? He said: What have I to do with the world? I am in the world like a rider who stops in the shade of a tree awhile, then passes on and leaves it (Tirmidhi).

490.   Abu Hurairah relates that the Holy Prophet said: The poor will enter Paradise half a millennium sooner than the rich (Tirmidhi).

491.   Ibn Abbas and Imran ibn Husain relate that the Holy Prophet said: I had a view of Paradise and saw that most of its dwellers were the poor; and I had a view of the Fire and saw that most of its denizens were women (Bokhari and Muslim).

492.   Usamah ibn Zaid relates that the Holy Prophet said: I stood at the gate of Paradise and saw that most of those who entered it were the poor, while the rich were held back from it. But those destined for the Fire were commanded to be driven into it (Bokhari and Muslim).

493.   Abu Hurairah relates that the Holy Prophet said: The truest thing a poet said is the saying of Labid: Everything beside Allah is vain (Bokhari and Muslim).

56.
On the Excellence of Hunger etc.

Allah, the Exalted, has said:

177.   Then they were followed by a people who laid aside Prayer and pursued evil desires; they will be seized with ruin, except those of them who repent and believe and act righteously. Such will enter Paradise, not being wronged in the least (19.60-61).

178.   One day he went forth before his people in his panoply, and those who were eager for the life of this world exclaimed: Would that we had the like of that which Korah has been given. Indeed, he is the master of a great fortune. But those who had true knowledge rebuked them: Ruin seize you, Allah's reward is best for those who believe and act righteously (28.90-81).

179. Then you shall be called to account on that day in respect of the worldly favours conferred upon you (102.9).

180. Whoso desires only the hither life, We bestow upon those of them we please such immediate advantage as We determine; thereafter We appoint hell for them which they enter condemned and rejected (17.19).

494.   Ayesha relates: The family of the Holy Prophet never ate their fill of barley bread two days running till he died (Bokhari and Muslim). Another version is: Ever since he came to Medina, the family of the Holy Prophet never ate their fill of wheaten bread three nights running till he died.

495. Urwah relates of Ayesha that she used to say: Nephew, we would witness three crescents in two months without a fire being lit in the homes of the Holy Prophet. I asked: Aunt, how did you manage? She said: On dates and water, except that the Holy Prophet had some Ansars as neighbours who had she-camels yielding milk. They would send some of their milk to the Holy Prophet which we drank (Bokhari and Muslim).

496. Abu Sa'id Maqburi relates of Abu Hurairah that he passed some people who had a roast lamb before them. They invited him to join them, but he refused, saying: The Holy Prophet passed out of the world without having eaten his fill of barley bread (Bokhari).

497. Anas relates that the Holy Prophet never ate off a table-cloth, nor did he ever eat bread made of fine flour throughout his life (Bokhari). One version adds: He never even saw a whole roast lamb.

498. Nu'man ibn Bashir relates: I have seen your Prophet when he did not have enough of the poorest quality dates to eat his fill (Muslim).

499. Sahl ibn Sa'ad relates that the Holy Prophet never even saw bread made out of fine flour throughout his life. He was asked: Did you not have sieves in the time of the Holy Prophet? He said: The Holy Prophet never saw a sieve. He was asked: How did you manage to eat barley bread made of unsieved flour? He said: We ground it and then blew over it; the husk was thus blown off and that which remained we kneaded into dough (Bokhari).

500. Abu Hurairah relates: The Holy Prophet came out one day and found Abu Bakr and Umar. He asked them: What has brought you out of your houses at this time? They said: Hunger, O Messenger of Allah. He affirmed: By Him in Whose hands is my life, the same cause has brought me out that has brought both of you out; so come along. They stood up and all three went to the house of one of the Ansar, but he was not at home. When his wife saw the Holy Prophet she said: Welcome and blessings. He asked her: Where is So and So? She said: He has gone to fetch fresh sweet water for us. When the Ansari came and saw the Holy Prophet and his two companions, he said: Praise be to Allah. There is no one who has more honoured guests today than I have. He then went out and brought a branch of a date tree bearing ripe and semi-ripe dates and invited them to eat. He then took up a knife and the Holy Prophet said to him: Do not slaughter a goat that is yielding milk. So he slaughtered for them and they ate and drank. When they had had their fill and were refreshed, the Holy Prophet said to his two companions: By Him in Whose hands is my life you will be called to account for these bounties on the Day of Judgment. Hunger drove you out of your homes and you did not return till you had enjoyed these bounties (Muslim).

501. Khalid ibn Umar Adavi relates: We were addressed by Utbah ibn Ghazwan, Governor of Basrah. After praising Allah and glorifying Him, he said: The world is announcing its departure and is running swiftly, turning

away its face. All that is left of it is like the few drops left at the bottom of a
vessel after the water in it has been drunk. That is what the worldly ones are
drinking. You will surely be transferred from it to a home which will not be
subject to decline. Then make sure that you proceed thither with the best you
have. We have been told that a stone dropped from the edge of hell will
continue to fall for seventy years without reaching bottom. Yet it will be filled.
Then do you wonder at it? We have also been told that the distance between
the two leaves of the gate of Paradise is equal to a journey extending over forty
years, yet a day will come when it will be choked with people. I recall being
one of seven people with the Holy Prophet when our only food was leaves of
trees whereby the sides of our mouths had been cut open. I had procured a sheet
which I cut in two and shared it with Sa'ad ibn Malik. Each of us converted our
piece into a loin-cloth. Today every one of us is governor of a city. I seek the
protection of Allah against counting myself great and being small in the sight of
Allah (Muslim).

502. Abu Musa Ash'ari relates: Ayesha showed us a sheet and a thick
loin-cloth and told us that the Holy Prophet was wearing them when he died
(Bokhari and Muslim).

503. Sa'ad ibn Abi Waqqas relates: I am the first Arab who shot an arrow
in the cause of Allah. We fought along with the Holy Prophet when our only food
was the leaves of wild trees. The stools of some of us were like the droppings of
goats (Bokhari and Muslim).

504. Abu Hurairah relates that the Holy Prophet used to supplicate: Allah,
make the provision of the family of Muhammad that which suffices (Bokhari
and Muslim).

505. Abu Hurairah relates: By Him save Whom there is none worthy of
worship, I used to press my stomach against the earth out of hunger, or I would tie
a stone over it. One day I was sitting along the common path when the Holy
Prophet passed by me. He smiled when he saw me and recognised from my face
the condition I was in. Then he called me and I responded: At your service,
Messenger of Allah. He said: Keep by me: and walked on, and I followed him.
Arrived at home, he asked for leave and entered and gave me leave and I too
entered. He found milk in a cup and inquired: Where is this from? He was told:
It is a present for you from So and So. He called me and I responded: At your
service, Messenger of Allah. He said: Go to the Company of the Lounge and bring
them in. Abu Hurairah explains that the Company of the Lounge were men who
had no family, no property, no relations. They were the guests of the Muslims.
When the Holy Prophet received anything for charity he sent it to them and did
not retain anything out of it for himself. When he received a gift he sent for them
and shared it with them. On this occasion I resented his sending for them. I said to
myself: What will this milk amount to among so many? I am more deserving of it
than anyone else, so that by drinking it I might gain some strength. When they
come he will command me to give it to them. I do not expect that anything will
reach me out of this milk. But there was no escape from obeying Allah and His

Messenger. So I went to them and called them; they came and sought permission, which was granted and took their seats. The Holy Prophet called me and I responded: At your service, Messenger of Allah. He said: Take the milk and give it to them. I took the cup and would give it to one man who would drink his fill and return it to me, and I would give it to the next one who would do the same. I went on doing this till the cup reached the Holy Prophet. By that time all had drunk their fill. He took the cup and put it on his hand, looked at me, smiled and said: Aba Hirr? I said: At your service, Messenger of Allah. He said: Now you and I are left. I said: That is true, Messenger of Allah. He said: Then sit down and drink. I drank, but he went on saying: Drink; till I said: By Him Who has sent you with the truth, I can find no more room for it. He said: Then give it to me. So I gave him the cup. He praised Allah, pronounced the name of Allah and drank what was left of the milk (Bokhari).

506. Muhammad ibn Sirin relates of Abu Hurairah who said: I recall when I used to fall unconscious in the space between the pulpit of the Holy Prophet and the chamber of Ayesha, and every passer by would put his foot on my neck imagining that I was mad. Indeed, I was not mad; I was hungry (Bokhari).

507. Ayesha relates that when the Holy Prophet died his armour was pledged with a Jew for thirty measures of barley (Bokhari and Muslim).

508. Anas relates: The Holy Prophet had pledged his armour for a quantity of barley, and I went to him with some barley bread and smelly fat. The family of the Holy Prophet never possessed a measure of wheat between them at morning or evening, and they were nine houses (Bokhari).

509. This *hadith* is the same as No. 472.

510. Ayesha relates: The mattress of the Holy Prophet was of leather stuffed with the husk of the date-palm tree (Bokhari).

511. Ibn Umar relates: We were sitting with the Holy Prophet when a man of the Ansar came and greeted him and turned back. The Holy Prophet said to him: Brother from the Ansar, how is my brother Sa'ad ibn Ubadah? He answered: Well. The Holy Prophet asked: Which of you will come along to visit him? He stood up and we stood up with him. We were more than ten persons, and we had not a shoe, or leather sock, or cap or shirt. We walked through the barren plain till we came to Sa'ad's place. His people stood back from him and the Holy Prophet and his companions who were with him went up to him (Muslim).

512. Imran ibn Husain relates that the Holy Prophet said: The best of you are those who are my contemporaries, then those who come immediately after them, then those who come immediately after them (he said this twice or three times) then they will be followed by those who will testify but who will not be asked to testify, they will embezzle and will not keep trust, will make vows and will not fulfil them, and corpulence will prevail among them (Bokhari and Muslim).

513. Abu Umamah relates that the Holy Prophet said: Son of Adam, if you were to spend that which is spare it would be the better for you, and if you hold it back it would be the worse for you. You will not be blamed for keeping that which you need. Begin spending upon those who are dependent upon you (Tirmidhi).

514. Ubaidullah ibn Mohsin Ansari relates that the Holy Prophet said: He who begins the day secure as to his life, in good physical condition and possessing one day's provision is as if the world and all it contains were bestowed upon him (Tirmidhi).

515. Abdullah ibn Amr ibn 'As relates that the Holy Prophet said: He who accepts Islam, and is bestowed provision that suffices for his needs and Allah makes him content with what He has given him has achieved true prosperity (Muslim).

516. Fazalah ibn Ubaid relates that he heard the Holy Prophet say: Felicitation for him who is guided to Islam and has provision that suffices him and is content (Tirmidhi).

517. Ibn Abbas relates that the Holy Prophet went to bed hungry for several successive nights and his family had no supper and their bread was mostly of barley (Tirmidhi).

518. Fazalah ibn Ubaid relates that when the Holy Prophet led the Prayer some people fell down from their standing posture on account of starvation. They were of the Company of the Lounge. The rustics started saying that they were afflicted with madness. After concluding the service the Holy Prophet would go over to them and would say to them: If you knew what there is for you with Allah, the Exalted, you would wish to augment your starvation and lack of provision (Tirmidhi).

519. Miqdad ibn Ma'dikarib relates that he heard the Holy Prophet say: No man fills a vessel worse than his stomach. A few mouthfuls that would suffice to keep his back upright are enough for a man, but if he must eat more, then he should fill one third with food, one third with drink and leave one third for easy breathing (Tirmidhi).

520. Abu Umamah Iyas ibn Thalabah relates that the companions of the Holy Prophet one day brought up the subject of the world before him whereupon he said: Do you not hear, do you not realise? Abstention is part of faith, abstention is part of faith (Abu Daud).

521. Jabir ibn Abdullah relates that the Holy Prophet sent us under the command of Abu Ubaidah to an encounter with a caravan of the Quraish and provisioned us with a leather bag of dried dates without anything else. Abu Ubaidah rationed us on one date per day. Being asked: How did you manage? Jabir replied: We would suck it as does a child and drink some water on top of it. This carried us on till night. We would also shake down leaves of trees with our staffs, dip them in water and eat them. We reached the coast and saw something like a sand dune stretched along the beach. When we approached it we found it was a whale. Abu Ubaidah said: This is carrion, but after some reflection added: We have been sent by the Messenger of Allah and are employed in the cause of Allah. You are driven by necessity and it is lawful for you to eat of it. We subsisted on it for a month and put on weight, and we were three hundred in number. We used to take out skinfuls of grease through its eyes and would carve out pieces of meat as large as an ox. On one occasion Abu Ubaidah selected thirteen of us and seated them in the socket of its eye. He took one of its ribs and stood it up and made our tallest camel pass under it fully accoutered and all. When we left we took with us large pieces of its boiled meat as provision. When we returned to Medina we presented ourselves before the Holy Prophet and mentioned all this to him. He said: This was provision made for you by Allah. Have you any of its meat with you so that you would give it to us to eat? Thus we sent some of it to the Holy Prophet and he ate of it (Muslim).

522. Asma' bint Yazid relates that the sleeves of the shirt of the Holy Prophet reached down to his wrist (Abu Daud and Tirmidhi).

523. Jabir relates: On the day of the Moat we were digging when a very hard piece of rock was encountered. The Holy Prophet was told of it and said: I shall descend into the moat. He stood up and it was noticed that he had tied a piece of rock over his stomach. We had not tasted anything for three days. He took up a spade and struck the hard piece of rock with it and it became like sand. I asked the Holy Prophet's permission to go home and said to my wife: I have seen the Holy Prophet in a condition that I am unable to endure. Have you anything in the house? She said: I have some barley and a lamb. I slaughtered the lamb and ground down the barley and we put the meat in the cooking pot. Then I went to the Holy Prophet. In the meantime the flour had been kneaded and the meat in the pot was nearly cooked. I said to the Holy Prophet: I have some food, Messenger of Allah, will you come with one or two? He asked: How many should there be? I told him. He said: Many would be good. Tell your wife not to take the pot off the fire nor the bread from the oven till I arrive. Then he said to the Emigrants and the Helpers: Let us go. They all stood up.

I went to my wife and said: Bless you, the Holy Prophet, the Emigrants, the Helpers and the whole company are coming over. She said: Did he ask you? I said: Yes. The Holy Prophet said to his companions: Enter, but do not crowd in. Then he started breaking up the bread and putting meat on it. He would take from the pot and the oven, then cover them up and approach his companions and hand it over to them. He would then go back and uncover the pot and oven. He continued to break up the bread and putting meat on it till all had eaten their fill and some was left over. Then he said to my wife: Eat of it, and send it as a present, for people have been afflicted with hunger (Bokhari and Muslim). Another version is: When the moat was being dug I perceived the signs of hunger on the Holy Prophet: so I returned to my wife and said to her: Have you anything in the house? I have perceived the signs of severe hunger on the Holy Prophet. She brought out a leather bag in which there was a measure of barley and we had a home-reared lamb. I slaughtered the lamb and she prepared the flour for baking. I then cut up the meat and put it in the cooking pot. Then I turned to go to the Holy Prophet and my wife said to me: Do not humiliate me in the eyes of the Holy Prophet and those who are with him. When I came to him I said to him in a low tone: Messenger of Allah, we have slaughtered a small lamb and have ground a measure of barley. Please come with a few people. The Holy Prophet thereupon announced in a loud tone: O ye of the moat, Jabir has prepared an entertainment for you, so come along all of you; and addressing me he said: Do not take the pot off the fire, nor bake the dough till I arrive. So I came home and the Holy Prophet came leading the people. My wife said: It will all rebound on you. I said: I have only done what you told me. She brought out the dough and the Holy Prophet spat into it and blessed it, and then advanced towards the cooking pot and spat into it and blessed it. Then he said: Summon the woman who bakes, and let her bake along with you, and let her ladle out from the cooking pot, but do not take it off the fire. There were altogether a thousand of them. Verily, all of them ate till they left the food and went off; while our pot still bubbled as before and the dough was being baked as before.

524.   Anas relates: Abu Talha said to Umm Sulaim: I have perceived a weakness in the voice of the Holy Prophet in which I have recognised the effect of hunger. Have you, then, anything. She said: Yes; and brought out some pieces of barley bread. Then she took a head-covering of hers and wrapped them up in a portion of it and concealed the parcel under a cloth which she made me wear and sent me off to the Holy Prophet. I took it along and found the Holy Prophet seated in the mosque among people. I stood near them and the Holy Prophet asked me: Have you been sent by Abu Talha? I said: Yes. He asked: To invite us to a meal? I said: Yes. The Holy Prophet said: Let us go. They began to walk and I walked with them till I came to Abu Talha and told him what had happened. He called out to Umm Sulaim: The Holy Prophet has come with a large company and we have nothing to feed them with. She said: Allah and His Messenger know best. Abu Talha went and met the Holy Prophet and brought him in. The Holy Prophet said: Bring whatever you have, Umm Sulaim. So she brought the same pieces of bread. He asked them to be broken and then she squeezed the container of butter over them and they were greased. Then the Holy Prophet blessed them and said: Permit ten to come in. Abu Talha called in ten; they ate their fill and went out. Then the Holy Prophet said: Permit ten to come in; they were called, ate and went out. This went on till everyone had eaten his fill. They were seventy or eighty in all (Bokhari and Muslim).

Another version is: When all had eaten, that which was left was collected and it was as much as there was in the beginning. Another version is: After eighty persons had eaten, the Holy Prophet and the people of the house ate and there was a quantity left over. Another version is: Enough was left over to be sent to the neighbours. Another version is: Anas relates: I went to the Holy Prophet one day and found him sitting among his companions, having bandaged his waist. I asked someone: Why has the Messenger of Allah bandaged his waist? I was told: On account of hunger. I went to Abu Talha, the husband of Umm Sulaim, and said: Father, I have seen the Holy Prophet with his waist bandaged. I asked one of his companions why that was and he said: On account of hunger. Abu Talha went to my mother and asked: Have you anything. She said: Yes, I have pieces of bread and some dry dates. Were the Holy Prophet to come alone we could feed him his fill, but if he came in company there would not be enough. Anas then went on to relate the *hadith* in full.

57.
On Contentment, Chastity and Moderation in Spending.

Allah, the Exalted, has said:

181. There is no creature that moves in the earth but it is for Allah to provide it with sustenance (11.7).

182. These alms are for the deserving poor who are detained in the cause of Allah and are unable to move about in the land. Those who lack knowledge of their circumstances consider them to be free from want because of their abstaining from soliciting alms. They can be known from their appearance. They do not importune people (2.274).

183. Those who are neither extravagant nor niggardly in spending, but keep a balance between the two (25.68).

184. I have created men, high and low, that they should worship Me. I desire no support from them, nor do I desire that they should feed Me (51.57-58).

525. Abu Hurairah relates that the Holy Prophet said: Self-sufficience does not mean plenty of provisions; it is self sufficience of the spirit (Bokhari and Muslim).

526. This *hadith* is the same as No. 515.

527. Hakim ibn Hizam relates: I asked the Holy Prophet and he gave me; I asked again and he gave me; I asked again and he gave me and said: Hakim, riches are pleasant and sweet. He who acquires them by the way, they are a source of blessing for him; but they are not blessed for him who seeks them out of greed. He is like one who eats but is not filled. The upper hand is better than the lower. I said to him: Messenger of Allah, by Him Who has sent you with the Truth I shall not, after you, ask anyone for anything till I depart this life. Abu Bakr would call Hakim to bestow something upon him, but he would not accept it. Then Umar would call him but he would not accept anything. So Umar said: I ask the Muslims to bear witness that I offer Hakim his share of the spoils that Allah has appointed for him but he refuses to take it. Thus Hakim did not take anything from anyone after the Holy Prophet till his death (Bokhari and Muslim).

528. Abu Burdah relates that Abu Musa Ash'ari said: Six of us who accompanied the Holy Prophet in a campaign had but one camel between us which we rode by turns. Our feet were wounded and my nails also fell out. We had wrapped up our feet in rags and that is why the campaign became known as the Campaign of Rags. Abu Burdah says: Abu Musa related this but regretted having done it, saying: I wish I had not mentioned it; as he disliked disclosing anything concerning his exploits (Bokhari and Muslim).

529. Amr ibn Taghlib relates that some spoils or prisoners were brought to the Holy Prophet and he distributed them, giving to some and not to others. Then he was told that those whom he had not given anything were displeased. On this he praised Allah and glorified Him and said: It is true that I give to one and pass over another, while the one I leave out is dearer to me than the one to whom I give. I give to those in whose hearts I perceive anxiety and unease; others I leave to that which Allah has put in their hearts of good and self-sufficience. Of these is Amr ibn Taghlib. The latter in relating this remarked: I would certainly not exchange these words of the Holy Prophet for red camels (Bokhari).

530. This *hadith* is the same as No. 298 related by Abu Hurairah.

531. Abu Sufyan relates that the Holy Prophet said: Do not ask with importunity. If one of you asks me for something and I give it to him with reluctance, there is no blessing in what I give him (Muslim).

532. Auf ibn Malik Ashj'ai relates: Seven, eight or nine of us were with the Holy Prophet on one occasion when he said: Will you not make a covenant with the Messenger of Allah? We had only shortly before made our covenant. So we said: We have made our covenant with you, Messenger of Allah. He repeated: Will you not make your covenant with the Messenger of Allah? So we extended our hands and said: We have already made our covenant with you, Messenger of Allah. What covenant shall we now make with you? He said: That you will worship Allah and will not associate aught with Him, that you will observe the five *salats*, will obey Allah (here he said something in a low tone and added) and will not ask anyone for anything. Thereafter I have noticed that if a riding whip fell from the hand of one of them he would not ask anyone to restore it to him (Muslim).

533. Ibn Umar relates that the Holy Prophet said: If one of you persists in asking he will face Allah without a shred of flesh on his face (Bokhari and Muslim).

534. Ibn Umar relates that the Holy Prophet in the course of an address from the pulpit concerning charity and abstention from begging said: The upper hand is better than the lower; the upper is the spending hand the lower is the begging one (Bokhari and Muslim).

535. Abu Hurairah relates that the Holy Prophet said: He who makes a habit of asking reaches out for a brand of fire, then let him refrain or persist (Muslim).

536. Samurah ibn Jundub relates that the Holy Prophet said: Begging is an injury that a person inflicts upon his face except in the case of asking a ruler for something, or asking for something in extreme need (Tirmidhi).

537. Ibn Mas'ud relates that the Holy Prophet said: He who suffers from hunger and seeks relief from men will not be relieved, but he who seeks relief from Allah will be relieved sooner or later (Abu Daud and Tirmidhi).

538. Thauban relates that the Holy Prophet said: He who gives me a guarantee that he will not ask anyone for anything, for him I shall guarantee Paradise. I said: I give you the guarantee. Then Thauban never asked anyone for anything (Abu Daud).

539. Qabisah ibn Mukhariq relates that he had guaranteed an obligation and came to the Holy Prophet to seek assistance in discharging it. The Holy Prophet said: Wait till something comes to me for charity and I shall give you out of it. He added: Qabisah, asking is not lawful except for three persons. One, a person who assumes a guarantee may ask till the guarantee is discharged and should then refrain. Two, a person whose substance is destroyed by a calamity may ask till he attains a sufficiency. Three, a person who is afflicted by hunger and three men of understanding from his people affirm that he is so afflicted, till he attains a sufficiency. All other asking is unlawful and he who indulges in it eats that which is unlawful (Muslim).

540. This *hadith* is the same as No. 266.

58.
On Acceptance of that which is Bestowed without Asking or Desire

541. Umar relates: The Holy Prophet would bestow a bounty upon me and I would say: Bestow it upon someone who is in greater need of it than I am. He said: Take it when it comes to you without asking and without desiring it and make it your property. Then use it yourself or give it away in charity. As for the rest do not put yourself out to acquire it. Abdullah ibn Umar would not ask anyone for anything, nor refuse anything that was given him (Bokhari and Muslim).

59.
On Earning by Hand and Refraining from Asking and Hastening towards Giving

Allah, the Exalted, has said:

185. When the Prayer is finished, then disperse in the land and seek of Allah's grace (62.11).

542.   Zubair ibn Awam relates that the Holy Prophet said: That one of you should take up his cords, go to the mountain, carry a pile of wood on his back, sell it and thereby make his face secure against the chastisement of Allah would be better for him than asking people, whether they give him or not (Bokhari).

543.   Abu Hurairah relates that the Holy Prophet said: That one of you should carry a pile of wood is better for him than asking from someone whether he gives him or not (Bokhari and Muslim).

544.   Abu Hurairah relates that the Holy Prophet said: David the Prophet ate only out of his earnings from his labour (Bokhari).

545.   Abu Hurairah relates that the Holy Prophet said: Zakariah was a carpenter.

546.   Miqdad ibn Ma'dikarib relates that the Holy Prophet said: No one has eaten better food than that procured through the labour of his hands. David the Prophet of Allah ate only out of his earnings from his labour (Bokhari).

60.

On Generosity and Spending in a Good Cause trusting in Allah

Allah, the Exalted, has said:

186.   Whatever you spend, He will foster it (34.40).

187.   Whatever of your pure wealth you spend in the cause of Allah, and undoubtedly you spend it to seek the favour of Allah, its benefit accrues to yourselves. Whatever of your pure wealth you spend, it will be paid back to you in full and you will not be wronged (2.273).

188.   Whatever of your pure wealth you spend, Allah has full knowledge thereof (2.274).

547.   Ibn Mas'ud relates that the Holy Prophet said: Only two persons are worthy of being envied; a person upon whom Allah bestows riches and gives him the power to spend in a righteous cause; and a person upon whom Allah bestows wisdom by which he judges and which he teaches (Bokhari and Muslim).

548.   Ibn Mas'ud relates that the Holy Prophet asked: Which of you loves the property of his heir more than his own property? He was told: Messenger ot Allah, there is not one of us but loves his own property better. He said: His property is that which he has sent forward; that which he holds back belongs to his heir (Bokhari).

549.   This *hadith* is the same as the first part of No. 139.

550.   Jabir relates that the Holy Prophet never said no to anyone who asked him for anything (Bokhari and Muslim).

551. This *hadith* is the same as No. 297.

552. Abu Hurairah relates that the Holy Prophet said: Allah, the Exalted, says: Spend, son of Adam, you will also be spent upon (Bokhari and Muslim).

553. Abdullah ibn Amr ibn 'As relates that a man asked the Holy Prophet. What in Islam is best? He answered: To feed people and to greet everyone with the greeting of peace whether you know them or not (Bokhari and Muslim).

554. This *hadith* is the same as No. 138.

555. This *hadith* is the same as No. 513 with the addition: The upper hand is better than the lower (Muslim).

556. Anas relates that whenever in Islam a person asked the Holy Prophet anything he gave it to him. A man came to him and he gave him a flock of sheep scattered over a valley. When he returned to his people he said to them: O my people, accept Islam for Muhammad bestows on a scale that leaves no fear of poverty. Even when a person became a Muslim out of a worldly motive, in a short while Islam became dearer to him than the world and all in it (Muslim).

557. Umar relates that the Holy Prophet distributed some property and I said to him: Messenger of Allah, the others were more deserving than these. He said they have given me a choice. Either they should ask me openly and I would give them, or they might charge me with miserliness and I am not a miser (Muslim).

558. Jubair ibn Mut'im relates that while he walked with the Holy Prophet during his return from Hunain some rustics caught hold of him and began asking him for a portion of the spoils. They pushed him under a tree and someone snatched away his cloak. The Holy Prophet came to a halt and said: Restore my cloak to me; had I at my disposal bounties of the number of the leaves of this thorny tree I would have distributed all of them among you and you would not have found me a miser, or a liar, or a coward (Bokhari).

559. Abu Hurairah relates that the Holy Prophet said: Wealth is not diminished by charity; Allah augments the honour of one who forgives, and one serves another for the sake of Allah but Allah exalts him in rank (Muslim).

560. Amr ibn Sa'ad Anmari relates that he heard the Holy Prophet say: Three things I can guarantee, and remember well what I am going to tell you: No one's wealth is diminished by charity; Allah augments the honour of him who endures a wrong steadfastly; and no one starts begging but Allah inflicts poverty upon him. He also said: Remember well what I am going to tell you: The world is made up of four kinds of people: One, a person upon whom Allah bestows wealth and knowledge and he minds his duty to his Lord in respect of them, strengthens the ties of kinship and acknowledges the rights of Allah in them. Such a one is in the best position. Two, a person upon whom Allah bestows knowledge but no wealth and he is sincere and says: Had I possessed wealth I would have acted like the other one; that is his resolve. His reward is the same as that of the other. Three, a person upon whom Allah bestows wealth but no knowledge and he squanders his wealth ignorantly, does not mind his duty to his Lord in respect of it, does not discharge the obligations of kinship and does not acknowledge the rights of Allah in it. Such a one is in the worst position. Four, a person upon whom Allah bestows neither wealth nor knowledge, and he says: Had I possessed wealth I would have acted like this one. This is his resolve. They are both equal in sinfulness (Tirmidhi).

561.   Ayesha relates that they slaughtered a goat and distributed most of its meat. Then the Holy Prophet asked: Is any of it left? She answered: Nothing is left of it except a shank. He said: All of it is saved except the shank (Tirmidhi).

562.   Asma' bint Abu Bakr relates that the Holy Prophet said to her: Do not hold back, else Allah will hold back from you. Another version is: Spend and do not accummulate, and do not keep back what is spare, else Allah will hold back from you (Bokhari and Muslim).

563.   Abu Hurairah relates that he heard the Holy Prophet say: The case of a miser and a generous one is like that of two persons who are clad in steel armour from their breasts up to their collar bones. When the generous one spends, his armour expands till it covers his fingers and his toes. When the miser makes up his mind to spend something every ring of the armour sinks into his flesh. He tries to loosen it but it is not loosened (Bokhari and Muslim).

564.   Abu Hurairah relates that the Holy Prophet said: If a person gives away in charity to the value of even a date out of his lawful earnings (and Allah accepts only that which is pure) Allah accepts it with His right hand and fosters it for him, as one of you tends a foal, till it becomes like a mountain (Bokhari and Muslim).

565.   Abu Hurairah relates that the Holy Prophet said: While a man was walking through a barren tract of land he heard a voice proceeding from a cloud saying: Water the garden of So and So. Thereupon the cloud advanced in a certain direction and rained its water over a rocky piece of land. The streamlets flowed into a large channel. This man followed the channel till it encircled a garden and he saw the owner of the garden standing in its midst working with his spade spreading the water. He asked him: Servant of Allah, what is your name? He told him his name, which was the same that he had heard from the cloud. The owner of the garden then asked him: Servant of Allah, why did you ask me my name? He answered: I heard a voice from the cloud from which this water has come, saying: Water the garden of So and So; and I would like to know what do you do with it. He said: Now that you ask me I will tell you. I estimate the produce of the garden, then give away one third in charity, use one third for my family and self and restore one third to the garden (Muslim).

61.
On Prohibition of Niggardliness

Allah, the Exalted, has said:

189. He who is niggardly and is indifferent, and rejects that which is right, will have his way to misery made easy by Us. His wealth shall not avail him when he perishes (92.9.12).

190. Whoso is rid of the covetousness of his mind, it is those who shall prosper (64.17).

566. This *hadith* is the same as No. 205.

62.
On Self-Sacrifice and Service

Allah, the Exalted, has said:

191. They give them preference over their own selves, even when they themselves are destitute (59.10).

192. They feed the poor, the orphan and the captive for the love of Allah (76.9).

567. Abu Hurairah relates that a man came to the Holy Prophet and said: I am famishing. He sent word to one of his wives and she sent back word: By Him Who has sent thee with the Truth I have nothing but water. Then he sent word to another and received back the same reply. He sent word in turn to everyone of them and the same reply came back. Then he said: Who will make this one his guest? One of the Ansar said: Messenger of Allah, I will. So he took him home and said to his wife: Honour the guest of the Holy Prophet. Another version is: He asked his wife: Have you anything? She answered: Nothing, except a little for the children. He said: Beguile them with something, and when they should ask for food put them to sleep. When the guest comes in put out the light, and make him feel that we are also eating. So they sat down and the guest ate and they passed the night hungry. When he came to the Holy Prophet in the morning, the latter said to him: Allah was well pleased with that which you did about your guest last night (Bokhari and Muslim).

568. Abu Hurairah relates that the Holy Prophet said: The food of two suffices for three and the food of three suffices for four (Bokhari and Muslim). Muslim also relates from Jabir that the Holy Prophet said: The food of one suffices for two, the food of two suffices for four, and the food of four suffices for eight.

569. Abu Sa'id Khudri relates: While we were on a journey with the Holy Prophet a man came riding his mount and began turning his eyes right and left, whereupon the Holy Prophet said: Whoever can spare a mount should offer it to him who has none, and whoever has spare food should offer it to him who has none: and he went on specifying every type of provision till we thought none of us had any right to what might be spare (Muslim).

570. Sahl ibn Sa'ad relates that a woman brought a woven piece of stuff to the Holy Prophet and said to him: I have woven this with my own hands so that you might wear it. He accepted it feeling the need for it and later came out wearing it as his loin cloth. Someone present said: How nice it is. Give it to me to wear. The Holy Prophet said: Very well. Then he sat among us awhile, then went and sent it out folded to the man. Some of those present said to him: You did not do well. The Holy Prophet wore it as he had need of it, and you asked him for it, knowing that he never declines a request. He said: Indeed, I did not ask him for it that I might wear it. I asked him for it so that it might serve as my shroud. In fact it served as his shroud.

571. Abu Musa relates that the Holy Prophet said: When the Ash'aris are faced with scarcity in battle or while they are at home in Medina they collect all they have by way of provisions in a sheet and then divide it equally among themselves. Thus they are of me and I am of them (Bokhari and Muslim).

63.

On Aspiring after that which is Blessed

Allah, the Exalted, has said:

193.   After this should the aspirants aspire (83.27).

572. Sahl ibn Sa'ad relates that drink was brought to the Holy Prophet and he drank of it. On his right was a boy and on his left were older people. He said to the boy: Would you permit that I should give the rest of this drink to those on my left? The boy said: Messenger of Allah, I would certainly not give preference to anyone else over myself in respect of that which might come to me from you. So he handed over the rest of the drink to him. (Bokhari and Muslim).

573. Abu Hurairah relates that the Holy Prophet said: While Job, the Prophet, was bathing naked a gold locust dropped on him. He tried to secure it in a piece of cloth, when he heard his Lord calling him: Job, have I not made you independent of that which you see? Job made answer: Indeed, by Thy Honour, but I am not indifferent towards Thy blessings (Bokhari).

64.
On the Excellence of the Grateful Rich

Allah, the Exalted, has said:

194. He who spends to promote the cause of Allah, and works righteousness, and testifies to the truth of that which is right, will have his way to prosperity made easy by Us (92.6-8).

195. But the righteous one who spends his wealth to be purified, and who owes no favour to anyone which is to be repaid, his purpose being only to win the pleasure of his Lord, the Most High, will be kept away from the Fire. Surely will he be well pleased with Him (92.18-22).

196. If you give alms openly that is indeed good, but if you give secretly to the poor, it is even better for your own selves; thereby will He remove from you many of your ills. Allah is well aware of that which you do (2.272).

197. Never will you attain to the highest degree of virtue unless you spend in the cause of Allah out of that which you love; and whatever you spend, Allah surely knows it well (3.93).

574.   This *hadith* is the same as No. 547.

575.   Ibn Umar relates that the Holy Prophet said: Only two are to be envied: he upon whom Allah bestows the Quran and he conforms to it through the hours of the night and day; and he upon whom Allah bestows wealth and he spends it in the cause of Allah, through the hours of the night and day (Bokhari and Muslim).

576.   Abu Hurairah relates that some of the poor Emigrants came to the Holy Prophet and said: The wealthy shall walk away with all high ranks and lasting bounties. He asked: How is that? They answered: They pray as we do and observe the fast as we do; but they spend in charity and we cannot, and they free slaves and we cannot. He said: Shall I instruct you in something whereby you will overtake those who are ahead of you and will keep ahead of those who are behind you and no one will excel you unless he does that which you do? They said: Surely, Messenger of Allah. He said: Glorify and magnify and give praise to Allah thirty-three times on the termination of each Prayer service. Shortly after they came back to him and said: Our wealthy brethren having heard what we are doing have started doing the same. Said the Holy Prophet: This is Allah's grace. He bestows it upon whomsoever He wills (Bokhari and Muslim).

65.
On Death and Restraint of Desire

Allah, the Exalted, has said:

198. Everyone shall suffer death, and you shall be paid your full recompense on the Day of Judgment. He who is kept away from the Fire and is admitted to Paradise has indeed attained felicity. The life of this world is but illusory enjoyment (3.186).

199. No person knows what he will earn tomorrow and no person knows in what land he will die (31.35).

200. When their time arrives they cannot tarry a single hour nor can they go ahead (16.62).

201. O ye who believe, let not your properties or your children beguile you from the remembrance of Allah. Whoever behaves in that way, it is they who are the losers. Spend out of that with which We have provided you before death comes upon one of you and he should say: Lord, why didst Thou not grant me respite for a while, that I could give alms and be of the righteous? Allah will not grant respite to any when his appointed time has come. Allah is well aware of that which you do (63.10-12).

202. When death approaches one of them, he will supplicate: Lord send me back that I may act righteously in the life that I have departed from. That cannot be: it is only an utterance of his. Behind them is a barrier right up to the day when they shall be raised up again. . . . . Did you imagine that We had created you without purpose, and that you would not be brought back to Us (23.100-116)?

203. Is it not time that the hearts of those who believe should feel humbled at the remembrance of Allah and of that which has come down to them of the truth? Let them not be like those who were given the Book before them and the term of Allah's favour was prolonged for them, so that their hearts were hardened and most of them became disobedient (57.17).

577. This *hadith* is the same as No. 474.

578. Abdullah ibn Umar relates that the Holy Prophet said: If a Muslim has something that would entail a testamentary direction he should not let two nights pass without executing a written testament (Bokhari and Muslim). Muslim specifies three nights. Ibn Umar said: Since I heard the Holy Prophet say this I have not let a night pass without having my will by me.

579. Anas relates that the Holy Prophet drew a number of lines, and indicated that one of them represented man and another represented death and said: He continues like this till the nearest line (i.e. death) overtakes him.

580. Ibn Mas'ud relates that the Holy Prophet drew a rectangle and in the middle of it he drew a line lengthwise the upper end of which protruded beyond the rectangle. Across this middle line he drew a number of short lines. He indicated that the figure represented man, that the encircling rectangle was death, the middle line stood for his desires and the short lines across it were the trials and tribulations of life. He said: If one of these misses him he falls a victim to one of the others (Bokhari).

581. This *hadith* is the same as No. 93.

582. Abu Hurairah relates that the Holy Prophet said: Remember often the terminator of pleasures (i.e. death) (Tirmidhi).

583. Ubayy ibn Ka'ab relates that when a third of the night passed the Holy Prophet would get up and call out: Ye people, remember Allah; the calamity has arrived, followed by another. Death has arrived with all it comprises; death has arrived with all it comprises. On one occasion I said to the Holy Prophet: Messenger of Allah, I call down blessings on you repeatedly: how much of them shall I devote to you? He said: As much as you would wish. I said. A quarter? He said: If you wish; but it would be better for you were to increase it. I said: Half? He said: Whatever you wish, but it would be better for you were you to increase it. I said: Two-thirds? He said: As you wish; but it would be better for you if you were to increase it. I said: Shall I devote all my supplications to blessings on you? He said: In that case it would take care of all thy worries and thy sins will be forgiven (Tirmidhi).

66.
On Permission for Men to visit Graves

584. Buraidah relates that the Holy Prophet said: I had forbidden you visiting graves; but now you might visit them (Muslim). One version is: He who wishes might visit graves for they remind us of the hereafter.

585. Ayesha relates that when it was the turn of the Holy Prophet to stay with me, he would go forth during the latter part of the night to Baqi'ah (the cemetery) and his greeting was: Peace be on you dwellers of this home of the faithful. May you be given on the Day of Judgment according to the term appointed that which you have been promised. We shall, if Allah so wills, join you. Forgive, O Allah, the dwellers of Baqi'ah (Muslim).

586. Buraidah relates that the Holy Prophet taught that any of them visiting a cemetery should say: Peace be on you dwellers of this home of believers and Muslims, and we, if Allah so wills, shall join you. I supplicate for peace for you and for ourselves (Muslim).

587. Ibn Abbas relates that the Holy Prophet passed by some graves in Medina. He faced towards them and said: Peace be on you dwellers of the graves. May Allah forgive you and us. You are our heralds and we are following you (Tirmidhi).

67.
On the Undesirability of Praying for Death

588. Abu Hurairah relates that the Holy Prophet said: No one of you should wish for death, for if he is virtuous it is possible that he might add to his good works, and if he is an evil doer he might be able to remedy his past (Bokhari and Muslim).

Muslim's version is: No one of you should wish or pray for it before it comes to him. When he dies his actions will be terminated; and in the case of a believer his age only adds to good for him.

589. This *hadith* is the same as No. 40.

590. Qais ibn Hazum relates: We went to visit Khubaib ibn Arat in his illness. He had had his blood let at seven places. He said: Our companions who have passed on before have lost nothing in respect of the world and we have found that the only place for it is in the earth. Had the Holy Prophet not forbidden us praying for death, I would have prayed for it. Thereafter we visited him again and he was repairing a wall. He said: There is a reward for a Muslim in respect of everything on which he spends money except when he commits it to clay (Bokhari and Muslim).

68.
On Piety and Discarding the Doubtful

Allah, the Exalted, has said:

204. You thought it to be a light matter, while in the sight of Allah it was a grievous thing (24.16).

205. Thy Lord is on the watch (89.15).

591. Nu'man ibn Bashir relates that he heard the Holy Prophet say: That which is lawful is clear and also that which is unlawful, and between the two is that which is doubtful of which most people are not aware. He who keeps off the doubtful secures his faith and his honour, but he who falls into the doubtful falls into the unlawful, like a shepherd who grazes his flock in the vicinity of a protected pasture and runs the risk that some of his flock might stray into the pasture. Mind, every king has a pasture. Beware, Allah's pasture is that which He has forbidden. Hearken! In the body there is a lump of flesh, when it is healthy the whole body is healthy and when it is corrupted the whole body is corrupted (Bokhari and Muslim).

592. Anas relates that the Holy Prophet saw a dry date lying in the street and said: Were I not afraid that it might have been meant for charity I would have eaten it (Bokhari and Muslim).

593. Nawas ibn Sam'an relates that the Holy Prophet said: Virtue is good behaviour, and sin is that which troubles your mind and you are afraid that people should come to know of it (Muslim).

594. Wabisa ibn Ma'bad relates: I went to the Holy Prophet and he asked me: Have you come to inquire after virtue? I said: Indeed. He said: Ask your heart. Virtue is that which satisfies the soul and comforts the heart; and sin is that which perturbs the soul and troubles the heart, even if people should pronounce it lawful and should seek your views on such matters (Ahmad and Darmi).

595. Uqbah ibn Harith relates that he married a daughter of Abu Ihab ibn Aziz. Thereafter a woman came to him and said that she had given suck to both of them. Uqbah said to her: I have no knowledge that you have suckled me, nor did you tell me. Then he rode to the Holy Prophet in Medina and put the matter to him. He said: Now that this has been said how can you continue? So Uqbah put her aside and she married someone else (Bokhari).

596. Hasan ibn Ali relates: I learnt from the Holy Prophet: Give up that which raises a doubt in your mind and adhere to that concerning which you have no doubt (Tirmidhi).

597. Ayesha relates: Abu Bakr had a slave who used to pay him a manumission fee, and Abu Bakr ate of it. One day he brought something as his fee and Abu Bakr ate of it. The slave asked him: Do you know what this was? Abu Bakr asked: What was it? He said: In the Days of Ignorance I used to act as soothsayer for a person. In fact it was no soothsaying; it was all deception. Now on meeting me he gave me this thing, which you have eaten, on that account. Thereupon, Abu Bakr put his hand into his mouth and threw out the contents of his stomach (Bokhari).

598. Nafi' relates that Umar appointed four thousand dirhems for each of the early Emigrants, but for his son he appointed only three thousand five hundred. When asked: He is also an Emigrant, why have you appointed a smaller sum for him? He said: His father emigrated with him; meaning he was not like one who migrated by himself (Bokhari).

599. Atiyyah ibn Urwah relates that the Holy Prophet said: No one can attain complete righteousness till he gives up that in the doing of which there is no harm so as to safeguard himself against that which is harmful (Tirmhidhi).

69.
On the Desirability of Withdrawal from Corruption

Allah, the Exalted, has said:

206.   Flee ye, therefore, unto Allah; surely, I am a plain Warner unto you from Him (50.51).

600.   Sa'ad ibn Abi Waqqas relates that he heard the Holy Prophet say: Allah loves a servant who is righteous, self-sufficient and retiring (Muslim).

601.   Abu Sa'id Khudri relates that someone asked the Holy Prophet: Who is the best man? He answered: A believer who strives in the cause of Allah with his self and his property. The man asked: And next after him? He said: One who withdraws into a narrow valley and worships his Lord. Another version is: One who is mindful of his duty to Allah and safeguards people against his own mischief (Bokhari and Muslim).

602.   Abu Sa'id Khudri relates that the Holy Prophet said: The time comes when the best property of a Muslim will be a flock of goats with which he withdraws to the top of a mountain or to a rainy spot so as to safeguard his faith against all manner of tribulation (Bokhari).

603.   Abu Hurairah relates that the Holy Prophet said: Every Prophet has tended goats. He was asked: And did you? He answered: Yes. I tended them for a few coins for the Meccans (Bokhari).

604.   Abu Hurairah relates that the Holy Prophet said: The best life is that of a person who, holding the reins of his horse, flies on its back in the cause of Allah, wherever he detects a note of danger or sound of battle, seeking death or martyrdom wherever he is expected. Or, it is that of a person who carries on with a few goats on the top of some mountain, or in some valley, observing *salat*, praying the *Zakat*, worshipping his Lord, till death overtakes him, not intervening in the affairs of people except for good (Muslim).

70.
On Intercourse with People in a Beneficent Manner

Allah, the Exalted, has said:

207.   Assist one another in piety and rectitude (5.3).

71.
On Courtesy and Humility

Allah, the Exalted, has said:

208.   Extend kindness and affection to the believers who follow thee (26.216).

209. *O ye who believe, whoso from among you turns back from his religion let him remember that in his stead Allah will soon bring a people whom He will love and who will love Him, who will be kind and considerate towards the believers and firm and unyielding towards the disbelievers (5.55).*

210. *O mankind, We have created you from male and female, and We have divided you into tribes and sub-tribes for greater facility of intercourse. Verily, the most honoured from among you in the sight of Allah is he who is the most righteous among you (49.14).*

211. *Ascribe not purity to yourselves. He knows best him who is truly righteous (53.33).*

212. *The occupants of the elevated places will call out to men whom they know by their distinguishing marks: Your numbers availed you not, nor your haughty claims. Pointing to the inmates of heaven they will ask: Are these the people about whom you swore that Allah will not extend mercy to them? Allah will say to the people of heaven: Enter Paradise; no fear shall come upon you nor shall you grieve (7.49-50).*

605. Iyaz ibn Himar relates that the Holy Prophet said: Allah has revealed to me that you should be courteous so that no one should hold himself above another nor transgress against another (Muslim).

606. This *hadith* is the same as no. 559.

607. Anas passed near some children and offered them the greeting of peace and said: The Holy Prophet used to do the same (Bokhari and Muslim).

608. Anas relates that a girl of Medina would take hold of the Holy Prophet's hand and take him where she wished (Bokhari).

609. Aswad ibn Yazid relates that Ayesha was asked: What did the Holy Prophet do inside his house? She answered: He occupied himself with helping members of his family, and when the time of *salat* came he would go out for *salat* (Bokhari).

610. Tamim ibn Usaid relates: I presented myself before the Holy Prophet while he was delivering an address and said: Messenger of Allah, a stranger has come inquiring about his faith. He knows nothing about his faith. The Holy Prophet thereupon interrupted his address and came to me. A chair was brought for him and he sat down upon it and started instructing me in what Allah had taught him. Then he reverted to his address and completed it (Muslim).

611. Anas relates that when the Holy Prophet finished eating his meal he would lick his three fingers. He said: If food should fall from the hand of any of you he should remove the damaged portion and eat the rest, and not leave it for Satan. You should wipe out the vessel from which you eat, for you do not know which part of your food is blessed (Muslim).

612. This *hadith* is the same as No. 603.

613. Abu Hurairah relates that the Holy Prophet said: I would accept an invitation to a meal even if the food was only a shoulder or shank of lamb, and I would accept a gift even if it was no more than the same (Bokhari).

614. Anas relates that the Holy Prophet had a she-camel called Adhba' which would not let itself be outstripped. A desert Arab came riding his young camel which outstripped it. This grieved the Muslims. The Holy Prophet perceiving it said: It is Allah's way that He puts down whatever raises itself in the world (Bokhari).

72.
On Condemnation of Arrogance and Self-Esteem

Allah, the Exalted, has said:

213.   We bestow the home of the hereafter on those who desire not self-aggrandisement in the earth, nor corruption; and the end is for the righteous (29.84).

214.   Do not tread haughtily upon the earth (17.38).

215.   Do not puff up thy cheeks with pride before people, nor tread haughtily upon the earth. Surely, Allah loves not any arrogant boaster (31.19).

216.   Korah was of the people of Moses, but he oppressed them . . . Then we caused the earth to swallow him up and his dwelling (28.77-82).

615. Abdullah ibn Mas'ud relates that the Holy Prophet said: He who has a particle of arrogance in his heart will not enter Paradise. Someone said: A person likes handsome clothes and shoes. The Holy Prophet said: Arrogance means rejecting the truth out of self-esteem and looking down on people (Muslim).

616. This *hadith* is the same as No. 160.

617. This *hadith* is part of No. 254.

618. This *hadith* is the same as No. 256.

619. Abu Hurairah relates that the Holy Prophet said: Allah will not look on the Day of Judgment upon one who wears his loin-cloth low out of pride (Bokhari and Muslim).

620. Abu Hurairah relates that the Holy Prophet said: There are three to whom Allah will not speak, nor will he purify them or look at them and who will be afflicted with painful torment: an aged adulterer, a lying ruler, and an arrogant beggar (Muslim).

621.   Abu Hurairah relates that the Holy Prophet said: Allah, the Lord of honour and glory, says: Honour is My loin-cloth and Greatness My cloak. Whoever contests either of them with Me, shall I afflict with torment (Muslim).

622.   Abu Hurairah relates that the Holy Prophet said: While a man was walking along clad in a mantle in which he took delight, his hair combed, his tread haughty, Allah caused him to be swallowed up. Now, he will continue to struggle and sink in the earth till the Day of Judgment (Bokhari and Muslim).

623.   Salamah ibn Akwa'a relates that the Holy Prophet said: A man continues to behave haughtily till he is counted among the arrogant and is afflicted with that with which they are afflicted (Tirmidhi).

73.
On Good Behaviour

Allah, the Exalted, has said:

217.   Thou dost most surely possess high moral excellences (68.5).

218.   Those who suppress their anger and forgive people (3.135).

624.   Anas relates that the Holy Prophet was the best behaved of all people (Bokhari and Muslim).

625.   Anas relates: I have never felt any velvet or silk softer than the palm of the Holy Prophet, nor have I smelt any fragrance more agreeable than the smell of the Holy Prophet. I served him for ten years. He never said: Ugh! to me; nor did he say of anything I had done: Why did you do it? or, of anything I had not done: Why did you not do thus and thus? (Bokhari and Muslim).

626.   Sa'ab ibn Jassamah relates: I presented a wild ass to the Holy Prophet but he declined it. When he perceived my disappointment in my face he said: I have declined it as I have assumed the pilgrim's garb (Bokhari and Muslim).

627.   This *hadith* is the same as No. 593.

628.   Abdullah ibn Amr ibn 'As relates that the Holy Prophet did not indulge in loose talk, nor did he listen to it. He used to say: The best of you are those who have the best character (Bokhari and Muslim).

629.   Abu Darda' relates that the Holy Prophet said: Nothing will be heavier in the balance of a believing servant on the Day of Judgment than good behaviour. Allah abhors one who is given to loose talk (Tirmidhi).

630.   Abu Hurairah relates that the Holy Prophet was asked: What is that the pursuit of which would admit a person to Paradise? He answered: Being mindful of one's duty to Allah and good behaviour. Then he was asked:

What is that indulgence in which would push a person into the Fire? He answered: The mouth and genitals (Tirmidhi).

631. Abu Hurairah relates that the Holy Prophet said: The most perfect of believers in respect of their faith are those whose behaviour is most excellent and the best of you are those who behave best towards their wives (Tirmidhi).

632. Ayesha relates that she heard the Holy Prophet say: A believer can attain the rank of one who fasts during the day and spends the night in Prayer through his good behaviour (Abu Daud).

633. Abu Umamah Bahili relates that the Holy Prophet said: I guarantee a home within the boundary of Paradise for one who will give up showing off, even if he is in the right; and a home in the middle of Paradise for one who will give up lying even in fun; and a home on the heights of Paradise for one whose behaviour is excellent (Abu Daud).

634. Jabir relates that the Holy Prophet said: The dearest and closest of you to me on the Day of Judgment will be those who are the best behaved of you; and the most abhorrent of you to me and the farthest of you from me will be the pompous, the boastful and the arrogant (Tirmidhi).

74.

On Gentleness and Forbearance

Allah, the Exalted, has said:

219.   Those who suppress their anger and forgive people and Allah loves the benevolent (3.135).

220.   Make forbearance thy rule and enjoin equity and turn away from the ignorant (7.200).

221.   Good and evil are not alike. Repel evil with that which is best and, lo, he between whom and thyself was enmity is as though he were a warm friend. But none attains to this save those who are steadfast and none attains to this save those who are granted a large share of good (41.35-36).

222.   The wronged one who endures with fortitude and forgives indeed achieves a matter of high resolve (42.44).

635. Ibn Abbas relates that the Holy Prophet said to Ashajj Abd al-Qais: You possess two qualities which Allah loves: gentleness and endurance (Muslim).

636. Ayesha relates that the Holy Prophet said: Allah is Gentle and loves gentleness in all things (Bokhari and Muslim).,

637. Ayesha relates that the Holy Prophet said: Allah is Gentle and loves gentleness and bestows upon gentleness that which He does not bestow upon harshness or anything else (Muslim).

638. Ayesha relates that the Holy Prophet said: Gentleness adorns everything and its absence leaves everything defective (Muslim).

639. Abu Hurairah relates that a rustic passed water in the mosque and some people got up to rough-handle him, whereupon the Holy Prophet said: Let go of him and pour a bucket of water over it to wash it out. You have been raised up to make things easy and not to make them hard (Bokhari).

640. Anas relates that the Holy Prophet said: Make things easy and do not make them hard; and cheer people up and do not repel them (Bokhari and Muslim).

641. Jarir ibn Abdullah relates that he heard the Holy Prophet say: He who lacks gentleness lacks all good (Muslim).

642. This *hadith* is the same as No. 48.

643. Shaddad ibn Aus relates that the Holy Prophet said: Allah has prescribed benevolence towards everything. When you must kill a living thing do it in the best manner and so also when you slaughter an animal. Sharpen your knife and reduce its suffering (Muslim).

644. Ayesha relates: Wherever the Holy Prophet was given a choice he adopted the easier course, unless it was sinful, in which case he avoided it more than anyone else. Nor did he ever seek revenge for a personal wrong, unless it involved violation of a divine command in which case he exacted a penalty for the sake of Allah (Bokhari and Muslim).

645. Ibn Mas'ud relates that the Holy Prophet said: Shall I tell you of those whom the Fire is forbidden to touch? It is forbidden to touch every accessible, easy, soft, gentle one (Tirmidhi).

75.
On Forgiveness and Forbearance

Allah, the Exalted, has said:

223. Make forbearance thy rule and enjoin equity and turn away from the ignorant (7.200).

224. Forbear generously (15.86).

225. Let them forgive and forbear. Do you not desire that Allah should forgive you (24.23)?

226. Those who forgive people, and Allah loves the benevolent (3.135).

227. The wronged one who endures with fortitude and forgives, indeed achieves a matter of high resolve (42.44).

646. Ayesha relates that she asked the Holy Prophet: Did you experience a day harder than the day of the battle of Uhud? He answered: Indeed I experienced them at the hands of thy people and the hardest of them was the day of Aqabah when I presented myself to Abd Yalail ibn Abd Kulal and he made no response to that which I had desired. So I left grieved and depressed and felt no relief till I arrived at Qarn Tha'alib. Then I raised my head and saw a cloud that was shielding me from the sun in which I beheld Gabriel who called me and said: Allah has heard what your people have said to you and the response they have made to you and has sent the Angel of the Mountains to you so that you may direct him to do what you might wish done to them. Then the Angel of the Mountains called to me, offered me the greeting of peace and said: Muhammad, indeed Allah has heard what thy people have said to thee. I am the Angel of the Mountains and my Lord has sent me to thee so that you might give me your direction concerning that which you would wish done to them. If you would so wish I would press down upon them the two great mountains. The Holy Prophet answered him: Indeed not, I am hoping that Allah will make out of their issue such as would worship Allah, the One, not associating aught with Him (Bokhari and Muslim).

647. Ayesha relates that the Holy Prophet never struck anyone, neither a servant nor a maid, but, of course, he fought in the cause of Allah. He never exacted retribution for any injury done him, but, of course, imposed penalties for violation of divine injunctions (Muslim).

648. Anas relates: I was walking with the Holy Prophet who had on a Najrani cloak which had a stiff border. A rustic came up and taking hold of the side of his cloak jerked it violently. I noticed that the violence of the jerk had bruised the base of the neck of the Holy Prophet. The rustic said: O Muhammad, direct that I be given out of Allah's provision that is with you. The Holy Prophet turned to him and smiled and directed that he be given something (Bokhari and Muslim).

649. Ibn Mas'ud relates: I can recall seeing the Holy Prophet while he recounted that a Prophet of Allah who was beaten and wounded by his people kept wiping the blood away from his face and supplicated: Allah do forgive my people for they know not (Bokhari and Muslim).

650. This *hadith* is the same as No. 45.

76.
On Endurance of Hurt

Allah, the Exalted, has said:

228.   Those who control their tempers and forgive people, and Allah loves the benevolent (3.135).

229.   The wronged one who endures with fortitude and forgives, indeed achieves a matter of high resolve (42.44).

651. This *hadith* is the same as No. 320.

77.
On Indignation against Violation of Injunctions

Allah, the Exalted, has said.

230. Whoso honours that which is declared sacred by Allah may be sure that it counts for good with his Lord (22.31).

231. If you help the cause of Allah, He will help you and make your steps firm (47.8).

652. Uqbah ibn Amr relates that a man came to the Holy Prophet and said: I am delayed by the morning Prayer service because of So and So who leads it and prolongs it. I have never seen the Holy Prophet so provoked into admonition as he was then. He said: Some of you make people dislike the faith. Whoever leads the Prayer should keep it brief for among the congregation are all types, old, young and those who have to attend to affairs (Bokhari and Muslim).

653. Ayesha relates that the Holy Prophet on returning from a journey, saw a light curtain which I had slung along a platform before my chamber and which bore some pictures. His face changed colour and he wiped out the pictures and said: Ayesha, on the Day of Judgment those who make likenesses of Allah's creatures will be subject to the severest torment (Bokhari and Muslim).

654. Ayesha relates that the Quraish were worried about the case of a Makhzumi woman who had committed theft and wondered who should intercede on her behalf with the Holy Prophet. Some said: Who can venture to do so except Usamah ibn Zaid who is much loved by the Holy Prophet? So Usamah spoke to him and the Holy Prophet said to him: Do you seek to intercede in the matter of the limits prescribed by Allah? Then he stood up and made an address in which he said: Those who were before you were ruined because they would let off a high-placed one if he committed theft and would exact the prescribed penalty from a poor one who stole. I call Allah to witness that were Fatimah, daughter of Muhammed, to steal, I would cut off her hand (Bokhari and Muslim).

655. Anas relates that the Holy Prophet noticed spittal in the mosque in the direction of the *qibla*. He changed colour, stood up and scraped it away with his own hand, and said: When you stand in Prayer you are in communion with your Lord, and He is between you and the *qibla*. Let no one, therefore, cast out his spittal in that direction, but only to his left or under his foot. Then he took up a corner of his cloak, spat into it and folded it up and said: Or, he should do like this (Bokhari and Muslim).

78.

On the Duty of Public Officials to deal Kindly with People

Allah, the Exalted, has said:

232. Extend kindness and affection to the believers who follow thee (26.216).

233. Allah enjoins equity and benevolence and graciousness as between kindred, and forbids evil designs, ill behaviour and transgression. He admonishes you that you may take heed (16.91).

656. This *hadith* is the same as No. 285.

657. Ma'qil ibn Yasam relates that he heard the Holy Prophet say: Allah will forbid Paradise to one whom He appoints in authority over people and who plays them false, die when he might (Bokhari and Muslim). Another version is: Even the fragrance of Paradise will not reach him, if he does not look after them with goodwill and sincerity. Muslim's version is: If a person is in charge of the affairs of the Muslims and does not strive diligently to promote their welfare, he will not enter Paradise with them.

658. Ayesha relates that she heard the Holy Prophet say in her house: Allah, when one who is placed in authority over my people is hard on them, be Thou hard on him also, and when such a one is gentle with them be Thou gentle with him also (Muslim).

659. Abu Hurairah relates that the Holy Prophet said: Authority among the Bani Israel was exercised by Prophets, when a Prophet died he was succeeded by a Prophet. I will not be succeeded by a Prophet, but there will be successors after me, a large number of them. He was asked: Messenger of Allah, then what do you command us? He said: Fulfil the covenant of allegiance with them one after the other, and render to them that which is due to them: and ask Allah for that which is due to you. Allah will call them to account in respect of that which is committed to them (Bokhari and Muslim).

660. This *hadith* is part of No. 194.

661. Abu Maryam Azdi relates that he said to Mu'awiah: I heard the Holy Prophet say: If Allah places someone in authority over the Muslims and he puts up a barrier between himself and their needs and objects and poverty, Allah will put up a barrier between Himself and his needs and objects and poverty on the Day of Judgment. So Mu'awiah appointed a man to keep a check on the needs of people (Abu Daud and Tirmidhi).

79.

On a Just Ruler

Allah, the Exalted, has said:

234. Allah enjoins equity and benevolence (16.91).

235. Act justly, verily Allah loves the just (49.10).

662. This *hadith* is the same as No. 379.

663. Abdullah ibn Amr ibn 'As relates that the Holy Prophet said: The just will be placed in columns of light in the presence of Allah. They will be those who act justly in their decisions, their families and the affairs committed to them (Muslim).

664. Auf ibn Malik relates that he heard the Holy Prophet say: Your best rulers will be those whom you love and who love you, and for whom you pray and who pray for you; and your worst rulers will be those whom you hate and who hate you, and whom you curse and who curse you. We asked: Messenger of Allah, shall we not boycott them? He said: Not so long as they maintain the Prayer services; not so long as they maintain the Prayer services (Muslim).

665. Iyah ibn Himar relates that he heard the Holy Prophet say: The dwellers of Paradise will be of three types: a just ruler who spends in charity having been given the capacity; a man merciful and tender towards every relative and Muslim; and a pious man with a family who refrains from asking (Muslim).

80.

On Obedience to Authority

Allah, the Exalted, has said:

236. O ye who believe, obey Allah and obey his Messenger and those who are in authority among you (4.60).

666. Ibn Umar relates that the Holy Prophet said: A Muslim is obligated to hear and obey whether he likes it or not, except when he is required to do something that is sinful, in which case there is no obligation to hear or to obey (Bokhari and Muslim).

667. Ibn Umar relates: When we covenanted with the Holy Prophet to hear and obey, he would say to us: As far as you can (Bokhari and Muslim).

668. Ibn Umar relates that he heard the Holy Prophet say: He who fails to obey in any respect shall meet his Lord on the Day of Judgment and will have no excuse to offer: and he who dies without having sworn allegiance will die in error (Muslim). Another version is: He who dies having discarded his association with the community dies in error.

669. Anas relates that the Holy Prophet said: Hear and obey even if a negro slave whose head is like a grape is placed in authority over you (Bokhari).

670. Abu Hurairah relates that the Holy Prophet said: You are obligated to hear and to obey in prosperity and adversity, willingly or unwillingly, and even when you are treated unjustly (Muslim).

671. Abdullah ibn Umar relates: We were on a journey with the Holy Prophet and made camp. Some were busy putting up their tents, some were occupied with sports and others with their cattle when the herald of the Holy Prophet announced that it was time for the Prayer service. We gathered round the Holy Prophet and he addressed us, saying: Every Prophet before me was under obligation to instruct his people in that which he knew was good and to warn them against that which he apprehended was evil. As to you, you will be secure in the early part of your history and later you will encounter misfortune and that which you will dislike. One misfortune will make its predecessor appear light. One calamity will arrive and a believer will say: This is ruin; and it will pass and another will approach and he will say: This is the one, this is the one. Then he who desires to be rescued from the Fire and to enter Paradise should face his end while he believes in Allah and the Last Day, and should deal with others as he wishes to be dealt with. He who should have sworn allegiance to one leader and should have committed his hand and his heart to him should obey him to the limit of his capacity. If another should contest the authority of that leader he should be committed to the sword (Muslim).

672. Wail ibn Hujr relates that Salamah ibn Yahid Jo'ffi asked the Holy Prophet: Tell me, if our rulers should be such that they should require from us their due and should refuse to render to us our due, what would be your direction for us? The Holy Prophet turned away from him, but he repeated his question, whereupon the Holy Prophet said: Hear them and obey them. They are accountable for their obligations and you are accountable for yours (Muslim).

673. Abdullah ibn Mas'ud relates that the Holy Prophet said: There will be discrimination after me and things that you will dislike. He was asked: Messenger of Allah, how would you direct those of us who should encounter these things? He answered: Discharge your obligations and supplicate Allah for your rights (Bokhari and Muslim).

674. Abu Hurairah relates that the Holy Prophet said: He who obeys me obeys Allah and he who disobeys me disobeys Allah, and he who obeys my appointee obeys me and he who disobeys my appointee disobeys me (Bokhari and Muslim).

675. Ibn Abbas relates that the Holy Prophet said: If a person experiences something unpleasant at the hands of a ruler he should bear it with equanimity, for he who departs from obedience a hand's breadth dies in error (Bokhari and Muslim).

676. Abu Bakr relates that he heard the Holy Prophet say: He who dishonours the ruler is dishonoured by Allah (Tirmidhi).

81.

On Prohibition of Asking for Office

Allah, the Exalted, has said:

237. We bestow the home of the hereafter on those who desire not self-aggrandisement in the earth, nor corruption; and the end is for the righteous (28.84).

677. Abdur Rahman ibn Samurah relates that the Holy Prophet said to him: Do not ask for public office. If you are given it without asking you will be helped in discharging its responsibilities, but if you are given it on asking for it you will be its captive. If you vow to do a thing and then find a better alternative adopt the latter and expiate your vow (Bokhari and Muslim).

678. Abu Dharr relates that the Holy Prophet said to him: Abu Dharr, I find you are weak and I desire for you what I desire for myself. Do not seek authority even over two people, nor take up the guardianship of an orphan's property (Muslim).

679. Abu Dharr relates: I said to the Holy Prophet: Will you not appoint me to public office? He patted me on the shoulder and said: Abu Dharr, you are weak and office is a trust and is a source of limitation and remorse on the Day of Judgment except for him who takes it up with a full sense of responsibility and duly discharges its obligations (Muslim).

680. Abu Hurairah relates that the Holy Prophet said: You will be greedy after public office, but remember that it will be a source of humiliation on the Day of Judgment (Bokhari).

82.

On Selecting Good Advisors

Allah, the Exalted, has said:

238. Friends on that day will be enemies of each other, except the righteous (43.68).

681. Abu Sa'id Khudri and Abu Hurairah relate that the Holy Prophet said: Whenever Allah raises a Prophet or appoints a vicegerent he has two counsellors, one counsels him to good and incites him to it and the other counsels him to evil and incites him to it. He alone escapes evil who is safeguarded by Allah (Bokhari).

682. Ayesha relates that the Holy Prophet said: When Allah desires good for a ruler He furnishes him with a sincere counsellor who reminds him when he forgets and assists him if he remembers; and when He desires for him something other than good He furnishes him with an evil counsellor who does not remind him if he forgets and does not assist him if he remembers (Abu Daud).

83.

On Refusal to appoint to Public Office

683. Abu Musa Ash'ari relates that he called on the Holy Prophet with two of his cousins and one of them said to him: Messenger of Allah, appoint us to some office out of that which Allah has committed to you. The other also said something to the same effect. The Holy Prophet said: I do not appoint anyone to public office who asks for it or desires it (Bokhari and Muslim).

84.

On Modesty

684. Ibn Umar relates that the Holy Prophet passed by a man of the Ansar who was rallying his brother on his modesty. The Holy Prophet said: Leave him alone, for modesty is part of faith (Bokhari and Muslim).

685. Imran ibn Husain relates that the Holy Prophet said: Modesty only results in good (Bokhari and Muslim). Muslim's version is: Modesty is all good.

686. Abu Hurairah relates that the Holy Prophet said: Faith has more than sixty or seventy elements, the greatest of them is the affirmation: There is none worthy of worship save Allah; and the least of them is removal from a path of that which causes inconvenience. Modesty is also an element of faith (Bokhari and Muslim).

687. Abu Sa'id Khudri relates that the Holy Prophet was more modest than a virgin behind her veil and that when something displeased him we could perceive it from his face (Bokhari and Muslim).

85.

On Keeping a Secret

Allah, the Exalted, has said:

239.   Fulfil every covenant, for you will be called to account for it (17.35).

688. Abu Sa'id Khudri relates that the Holy Prophet said: On the Day of Judgment of the people in the lowest position in the sight of Allah will be the man who consorts with his wife and then publishes her secret (Muslim).

689. Abdullah ibn Umar relates that when Hafsah, daughter of Umar, became a widow Umar met Usman ibn Affan and said to him: If you should be willing, I would give Hafsah in marriage to you. Usman said: I shall consider the matter. Umar relates: I waited for a few days and then Usman met me and said: It has come to me that I should not marry just yet. Then

I met Abu Bakr and said to him: If you should be willing I would give Hafsah in marriage to you. Abu Bakr remained silent and did not say a word which went harder with me than the reaction of Usman. I had waited only a few days when the Holy Prophet asked for her hand in marriage and I married her to him. Thereafter when Abu Bakr met me he said: You might perhaps have been offended when you made the proposal about Hafsah and I said nothing in reply. I said: Yes, that is so. He said: The only thing that stood in my way was that the Holy Prophet had mentioned her and I could not disclose the Holy Prophet's secret. Had the Holy Prophet not made an offer, I would have agreed to the proposal (Bokhari).

690. Ayesha relates that on one occasion when all the wives of the Holy Prophet were with him together, his daughter Fatimah came in walking. She walked exactly like the Holy Prophet. When he saw her he welcomed her and asked her to be seated at his side and whispered something to her at which she sobbed violently. When he perceived her grief he whispered to her again at which she smiled. I said to her: The Holy Prophet chose you, leaving aside his wives, to speak secretly to you and yet you cried! When he left I asked her: What did the Holy Prophet say to you? She said: I will not reveal the secret of the Holy Prophet. When the Holy Prophet died I said to her: I adjure you by the right I have in respect of you to tell me what the Holy Prophet told you. She said: Now, yes. When he whispered to me the first time he told me that every year Gabriel used to hear him recite the Quran and then recite it back to him once or twice, and that this time he had done it twice. He said: I see that my time is now approaching. Then be mindful of your duty to Allah and be steadfast, for I shall be an excellent forerunner for you. On this I cried as you saw. When he perceived my distress he whispered to me the second time and said: Fatimah, are you not pleased that you will be the first among the believing women; on which I smiled as you saw (Bokhari and Muslim).

691. Thabit relates that Anas said: The Holy Prophet chanced upon me when I was playing among the boys and greeted us and despatched me on an errand for him which delayed my return to my mother. When I got to her she asked: What had detained you? I said: The Holy Prophet sent me on an errand. She asked: What was the errand? I said: It was secret. She said: Do not tell anyone the secret of the Holy Prophet. Anas said to Thabit: Were I to tell it to anyone I would tell you (Muslim).

86.

On Fulfilment of Covenants

Allah, the Exalted, has said:

240. Fulfil every covenant, for you will be called to account for it (17.35).

241. Fulfil the covenant of Allah when you make one (16.92).

242. O ye who believe, fulfil your pledges (5.2).

243. O ye who believe, why do you say that which you do not? Most odious is it in the sight of Allah that you should say that which you do not (61.3-4).

692. This *hadith* is the same as No. 201.

693. Abdullah ibn Amr ibn 'As relates that the Holy Prophet said: There are four qualities which, if they are found in a person, prove him a thorough hypocrite. If a person has one of them, he has one quality of hypocrisy until he gets rid of it. These are: when he is entrusted with something he embezzles, when he talks he lies, when he promises he breaks his promise and when he contends he reviles (Bokhari and Muslim).

694. Jabir relates: The Holy Prophet said to me: When the revenues of Bahrain are received, I shall give you thus, and thus and thus. But he died before the revenues were received. When they were received Abu Bakr caused it to be announced: Anyone to whom the Holy Prophet had made a promise or owed anything should come forward. So I went to him and said to him: The Holy Prophet had said to me thus and thus. He took a double handful out of the money and gave it to me. I counted it and found it was five hundred dirhems. He said to me: Take twice as much more (Bokhari and Muslim).

87.

On Safeguarding a Good Practice

Allah, the Exalted, has said:

244. Allah would not withdraw a favour that He has conferred upon a people, until they change their own attitude towards Him (13.12).

245. Be not like the woman who having made strong yarn breaks it into pieces (16.93).

246. Let them not be like those who were given the Book before them and the term of Allah's favour was prolonged for them, so that their hearts were hardened (57.17).

247. But they did not observe it duly (57.28).

695. This *hadith* is the same as No. 155.

88.

On Cheerfulness and Soft Speech

Allah, the Exalted, has said:

248.   Continue to be kindly gracious towards the believers (15.89).

249.   If thou hadst been rough and hard-hearted they would surely have dispersed from around thee (3.160).

696.   Adiyy ibn Hatim relates that the Holy Prophet said: Shield yourselves against the Fire even if it be only with half a date given in alms, and one who cannot afford even that much should at least utter a good word (Bokhari and Muslim).

697.   Abu Hurairah relates that the Holy Prophet said: A good word is charity (Bokhari and Muslim).

698.   This *hadith* is the same as No. 121.

89.

On Clarity of Discourse

699.   Anas relates that the Holy Prophet would repeat his words three times so that his meaning was fully grasped, and when he came upon a party of people and greeted them he would repeat the salutation three times (Bokhari).

700.   Ayesha relates that the Holy Prophet spoke simply so that all those who listened to him understood him (Abu Daud).

90.

On Listening with Attention

701.   Jarir ibn Abdullah relates that the Holy Prophet asked him on the occasion of the Farewell Pilgrimage to tell the people to be quiet, and then said: Do not revert to disbelief after me, cutting off each other's heads (Bokhari and Muslim).

91.
On Economy in Preaching

Allah, the Exalted, has said:

250. Call unto the way of thy Lord with wisdom and goodly exhortation (16.126).

702. Shaqiq ibn Salamah relates: Ibn Mas'ud used to preach to us every Thursday. A man said to him: Abu Abdur Rahman, I wish you would preach to us every day. He said: What stops me from doing it is the fear lest I should bore you. I adopt the same method in preaching to you that the Holy Prophet adopted in preaching to us out of fear of boring us (Bokhari and Muslim).

703. Amr ibn Yassir relates that he heard the Holy Prophet say: The length of a person's Prayer and the brevity of his sermon testify to his intelligence. Make your Prayer long and your sermons short (Muslim).

704. Mu'awiah ibn Hakam Sulamiqq relates: While I was in Prayer with the Holy Prophet one of the congregation happened to sneeze and I responded with: Allah have mercy on you. On this the congregation reproved me with their looks. To this I reacted with: May you lose your mothers, why are you staring at me? Thereupon they started beating their hands against their legs. Then I understood that they wanted me to be silent, so I restrained myself. May my father and mother be the ransom of the Holy Prophet, I have not known a better instructor before him or after him. When he finished the Prayer, he did not remonstrate with me, or beat me, or reprove me. He said: During Prayer no talk is permissible. It is all praise and glorification and recitation of the Quran. He added something in the same vein. I said: Messenger of Allah, I have newly emerged from Ignorance and Allah has favoured us with Islam. There are still some men among us who go to consult soothsayers. He said: You should not go to them. Then I said: There are some of us who are guided by omens. He said, these are things that come up in their minds. They should not be influenced by them (Muslim).

705. This *hadith* comprises the first part of No. 158.

92.
On Dignity and Calmness

Allah, the Exalted, has said:

251. The true servants of the Gracious One are those who walk upon the earth with humility and when they are accosted by the ignorant ones their response is: Peace (25.64).

706. Ayesha relates: I never saw the Holy Prophet laugh outright so that the interior of his mouth could be seen. He only smiled (Bokhari and Muslim).

93.
On Walking Sedately to the Mosque

Allah, the Exalted, has said:

252.   Whoso venerates the sacred signs of Allah may be sure that it counts as the righteousness of the heart for him (22.33).

707.   Abu Hurairah relates that he heard the Holy Prophet say: When the Prayer service is about to commence, do not come running to it. Come to it walking calmly. Then join in the service at the stage of your arrival and make up afterwards what you might have missed. (Bokhari and Muslim). Muslim adds: For when one of you makes up his mind to join the *salat*, he is already in the *salat*.

708.   Ibn Abbas relates that he was with the Holy Prophet in the return from Arafat on the day of the Pilgrimage. The Holy Prophet heard behind him an uproar of shouting and of beating and driving the camels. He pointed towards it with his whip and said: O ye people, proceed calmly. There is no virtue in rushing forward (Bokhari).

94.
On Honouring the Guest

Allah, the Exalted, has said:

253.   Has an account of the honoured guests of Abraham reached thee? When they came to him they said: Peace on you. He returned their salutation: On you be peace; and murmured to himself: They appear to be strangers. Then he went quietly to his household and brought a fat roasted calf and placing it before them said: Will you not eat (51.25-28)?

254.   His people hurried to him wild with indignation, and before this also they were given to all manner of ill-behaviour. Lot remonstrated with them: O my people, my daughters are your pure spouses. So fear Allah and do not humiliate me in the presence of my guests. Is there not among you any man of intelligence (11.79)?

709.   This *hadith* is the same as No. 316.

710.   Abu Shuraih Khalid ibn Amr Khuza'i relates that he heard the Holy Prophet say: He who believes in Allah and the Last Day should honour his guest according to his right. He was asked: What is his right, Messenger of Allah? He answered: A day and a night, and hospitality for three days. That which might be beyond this is charity (Bokhari and Muslim). Muslim adds: It is not permissible for a Muslim to stay so long with his brother as to involve him in sin. He was asked: Messenger of Allah, how would he involve him in sin? He answered: By prolonging his stay so that the host has nothing left with which to exercise hospitality.

95.
On Good News and Felicitation

Allah, the Exalted, has said:

255.   *Give glad tidings to My servants who listen to the Word and follow the best thereof (39.18-19).*

256.   *Their Lord gives them glad tidings of mercy from Him, and of His pleasure, and of gardens wherein there shall be lasting bliss for them (9.21).*

257.   *Rejoice in the Garden that you were promised (41.31).*

258.   *We gave him glad tidings of a gentle son (37.102)*

259.   *Our messengers came to Abraham with glad tidings (11.70).*

260.   *His wife was standing by and she too was perturbed, whereupon We conveyed to her the glad tidings of the birth of Isaac, and beyond Isaac of Jacob (11.72).*

261.   *The angels called to him as he stood praying in the chamber: Allah gives you glad tidings of Yahya (3.40).*

262.   *Call to mind when the angels said to Mary: Allah, through His word gives thee glad tidings of a son named the Messiah (3.46).*

711.   Abdullah ibn Abi Aufa relates that the Holy Prophet gave Khadijah the glad tidings of a house of pearls in which there would be no noise and no cause for fatigue (Bokhari and Muslim).

712.   Abu Musa Ash'ari relates that one day he made his ablutions in his house and then set forth with the determination that he would stick to the Holy Prophet and spend the day in his company. So he came to the mosque and inquired about him and was told that he had gone in a certain direction. He says: I followed after him, inquiring about him till he entered Bi'r Aris. I sat down at the door till he had completed his ablutions. Then I went to him and saw that he was seated on the platform of the well, having drawn up his loin cloth to his knees and suspended his feet into the well. I greeted him and returned to the door and said to myself: I shall be the Holy Prophet's doorman

today. Presently Abu Bakr came and knocked on the door, I said: Who is that? He said: Abu Bakr. I said: Wait a moment. Then I went to the Holy Prophet and said: Messenger of Allah, Abu Bakr is at the door asking permission to come in. He said: Give him permission and greet him with the promise of Paradise. I returned and said to Abu Bakr: You may enter, and the Messenger of Allah greets you with the promise of Paradise. Abu Bakr entered and sat down beside the Holy Prophet on the platform, drawing up his loin cloth to the knees and suspending his feet into the well, as the Holy Prophet had done. I returned to the door and sat down. I had left my brother at home, making his ablutions and intending to join me. I said to myself: If Allah desires good for him, He will bring him here. Someone knocked at the door and I said: Who is that? He said: Umar ibn Khattab. I said: Wait a moment; and went to the Holy Prophet and after greeting him said: Umar is at the door asking permission to enter. He said: Give him permission and greet him with the promise of Paradise. I went back to Umar and said to him: You have permission and the Messenger of Allah greets you with the promise of Paradise. He entered and sat down with the Holy Prophet on the platform on his left and suspended his feet into the well. I returned to the door and sat down and said to myself: If Allah desires good for my brother, He will bring him here.

Someone knocked at the door and I said: Who is that? He said: Usman ibn Affan. I said: Wait a moment; and went and told the Holy Prophet. He said: Give him permission and greet him with the promise of Paradise together with a misfortune that shall afflict him. I returned to him and said: You may enter, and the Messenger of Allah greets you with the promise of Paradise, together with a misfortune that shall afflict you. He entered and finding the platform full sat down on the other side of it opposite to them. Sa'id ibn Musayyab has said that the order in which they sat down indicated the juxtaposition of the places of their burial (Bokhari and Muslim).

Another version adds: The Holy Prophet directed me to guard the door. When Usman was told he said: Praise be to Allah, I seek His help.

713. Abu Hurairah relates: We were sitting with the Holy Prophet, and Abu Bakr and Umar were also of the company, when the Holy Prophet got up and left us. When some time passed we began to worry lest he should meet with trouble in our absence. I was the first to be agitated and set out in search of him till I came to a garden wall of the Banu Najjar. I went round searching for an entrance, but did not find one. However, I espied a small channel of water coming from a well outside, which entered the garden through the wall. I squeezed myself through the hole and reached the Holy Prophet. He said: Abu Hurairah? I replied: The same, Messenger of Allah. He asked: What is the matter? I answered: You were with us. Then you left and did not return for quite a while. We were afraid lest you should meet with trouble without us. We were agitated, I being the first. So I came to this wall and squeezed in through the hole like a fox, and the others are following me. He gave me his shoes and said: Abu Hurairah, take these and whoever you should encounter outside this wall who affirms in full sincerity of belief that there is none worthy of worship save Allah, greet him with the promise of Paradise (Muslim).

714. Ibn Shamasah relates: We were present with Amr ibn 'As when he was in extremity. He wept for a long time and turned his face to the wall. His son tried to comfort him, saying: Father, did not the Holy Prophet give you this good news? Did he not give you that good news? Then he turned his face towards us and said: Our best preparation is the affirmation: There is none worthy of worship save Allah, and Muhammad is His Messenger. I have passed through three stages. I recall when no one was a bitterer enemy of the Holy Prophet than myself: nor was anything dearer to me than that if I had the power I would put an end to him. Had I died in that condition, I would have been one of the denizens of the Fire. When Allah put Islam in my heart, I went to the Holy Prophet and said: Extend your right hand, so that I might swear allegiance to you. He put forth his right hand, but I withdrew my hand. He said: What is the matter, Amr? I said: I wish to make a condition. He asked: What condition do you wish to make? I answered: That my sins will be forgiven. He said: Know you not that Islam wipes out all that has gone before it, that Migration wipes out all that has gone before it, and that the Pilgrimage wipes out all that has gone before it? Thereafter, no one was dearer to me than the Holy Prophet nor was anyone more glorious than him in my eyes. So bright was his glory that I could not look at his face for any length of time, so that if I were asked to describe him I would not be able to as I had not looked at him long enough. Had I died in that condition I could have hoped to be one of the dwellers of Paradise. Thereafter we were made responsible for many things, and I know not how I shall fare with respect to them. When I die no mourner or fire should attend my bier. When you bury me throw the earth gently over me and tarry over my tomb for the space of time it takes to slaughter a camel and distribute its meat, so that I should draw comfort from your presence and can consider what answer shall I make to the messengers of my Lord (Muslim).

96.
On Saying Farewell and Parting Advice

Allah, the Exalted, has said:

263. The same did Abraham enjoin upon his sons and also Jacob: Sons of mine, truly Allah has chosen this religion for you, then live every moment in submission to Allah, so that death whenever it comes should find you in a state of submission to Him. Were you present when Jacob faced the hour of death and he asked his sons: Who will you worship after I am gone? They answered: We will worship thy God and the God of thy fathers Abraham and Ishmael and Isaac, the One God, and to Him have we submitted ourselves (2.133-134).

715. This *hadith* is part of No. 349.

716. Malik ibn Huyairis relates: We came to the Holy Prophet, a group of young men of about the same age, and we stayed with him for twenty days. He was a most kind and considerate person. He perceived that we were eager to return to our people. He inquired from us about those we had left behind, and we told him. Then he said: Now return to your people and stay with them and instruct them and direct them and observe such *salat* at such a time and such *salat* at such a time. When the time for a *salat* arrives one of you should call out the *Azan* and the oldest of you should lead the service (Bokhari and Muslim) Bokhari in his version adds: Observe the *salat* as you have seen me observe it.

717. This *hadith* is the same as No. 376.

718. Salim ibn Abdullah ibn Umar relates that when a person was about to set out on a journey Abdullah ibn Umar would say to him: Draw near that I might bid farewell to you as the Holy Prophet used to bid farewell to us. I commit to Allah your faith, your trust and your terminal actions (Tirmidhi).

719. Abdullah ibn Yazid Khatmiyy relates that when he bade farewell to a force the Holy Prophet would say: I commit to Allah your faith, your trust and your terminal actions (Abu Daud).

720. Anas relates that a man came to the Holy Prophet and said: Messenger of Allah, I am about to set out on a journey, kindly bestow some provision on me. He said: May Allah provide you with righteousness. The man said: Please add to it. He said: And may He forgive your sins. The man repeated: Please add some more. The Holy Prophet said: And may He facilitate for you the doing of good, wherever you may be (Tirmidhi).

97.
On Consultation and Praying for Good

Allah, the Exalted, has said:

264. Take counsel with them in matters of administration (3.160).

265. Their affairs are administered by mutual consultation (42.39).

721. Jabir relates: The Holy Prophet used to instruct us in the method of praying for guidance in respect of all matters like teaching us a chapter of the Quran. He would say: When one of you contemplates entering upon an enterprise, he should say two *raka'as* of voluntary Prayer and then supplicate: Allah, I seek good from Thee because of Thy knowledge, and seek power from Thee because of Thy power, and beg of Thee because of Thy vast grace, for

Thou hast power and I have no power, and Thou hast knowledge and I have no knowledge, and Thou knowest well all that is hidden. Allah, if Thou knowest that this matter is good for me in respect of my faith, my subsistence and the ultimate in my affairs, then grant me power over it, and make it easy for me and bless it for me. But if Thou knowest that it is bad for me in respect of my faith, my subsistence or the ultimate in my affairs, then remove it from me and keep me away from it, and grant me power to do good wherever it may be and then make me pleased with it. The supplicant should specify the particular affair (Bokhari).

98.
On Varying the Route of Return

722. Jabir relates that on the occasion of the two festivals the Holy Prophet would proceed to the service along one route and return from it by another (Bokhari).

723. Ibn Umar relates that the Holy Prophet proceeded by way of Shajarah and returned by way of Mu'arras. He entered Mecca by the Higher Pass and left it by the Lower Pass (Bokhari and Muslim).

99.
On Preferring the Right Hand for Performance of all Good Acts

Allah, the Exalted, has said:

266. He who is given his record in his right hand will say: Come read my record (69.20).

267. Those on the right (and what will those on the right be?) and those on the left (and what will those on the left be?) (59.9-10).

724. Ayesha relates that the Holy Prophet liked to use his right hand for everything; for his ablutions, for combing his hair and for putting on his shoes (Bokhari and Muslim).

725. Ayesha relates that the Holy Prophet's right hand was used for his ablutions and for eating his food; and his left hand was used in his toilet and for other similar purposes (Abu Daud).

726. Umm Atiyyah relates that the Holy Prophet directed them, when they were to wash the body of his daughter Zainab, to begin with her right side and with the parts that are washed in ablutions (Bokhari and Muslim).

727. Abu Hurairah relates that the Holy Prophet said: When any of you puts on his shoes he should begin with the right foot, and when he puts them off he should begin with the left; so that the right foot should be the first to be shod and the last to be unshod (Bokhari and Muslim).

728. Hafsah relates that the Holy Prophet used his right hand for eating, drinking and putting on his clothes, and used his left hand for purposes beside these (Abu Daud).

729. Abu Hurairah relates that the Holy Prophet said: When you put on your clothes or make your ablutions, begin with your right side (Abu Daud and Tirmidhi).

730. Anas relates that when the Holy Prophet returned to Mina he came to the jamarah and pelted it. Then he came back to his place and offered the sacrifice. Then he said to the barber: Take from here; and indicated the right side of his head and then the left. Then he distributed his hair among the people (Bokhari and Muslim). Another version is: When he had pelted the jamarah and offered the sacrifice and was ready for the shave, he indicated to the barber the right side of his head and was shaved on that side. Then he called Abu Talha Ansari and gave his hair to him. Then he indicated the left side of his head and was shaved on that side. He gave the hair to Abu Talha and said: Distribute it among the people.

100.
On Table Manners

731. This *hadith* is the same as No. 301.

732. Ayesha relates that the Holy Prophet said: When any of you begins to eat he should pronounce the name of Allah, the Exalted. If he forgets to do it in the beginning, he should say: In the name of Allah, first and last (Abu Daud and Tirmidhi).

733. Jabir relates that he heard the Holy Prophet say: If a person remembers Allah when he enters his house and when he eats, Satan says to his cronies: You will not find here lodging or food. If he enters without the remembrance of Allah, Satan says: You have secured lodging. Then if he does not remember Allah at the time of eating, Satan says: You have secured both lodging and food (Muslim).

734. Huzaifah relates: When we were present at a meal with the Holy Prophet, we would not stretch forth our hands towards the food until he had started eating. On one occasion when we were with him a girl rushed in, as if she was famishing, and made for the food, but the Holy Prophet seized her hand. Then a rustic came in as if he was starving and he seized his hand also and said: Satan considers that food lawful for himself in which the name of Allah is not pronounced. He brought this girl to make it lawful through her, but I seized her hand. Then he brought this rustic to make it lawful through him, but I seized his hand also. Now by Him in Whose hands is my life, I have

Satan's hand in my grasp also along with their hands. Then he pronounced the name of Allah and began to eat (Muslim).

735. Umayyah ibn Makhsi relates that the Holy Prophet was sitting while a man was eating. He did not pronounce the name of Allah till only a mouthful of the food was left. When he raised it to his mouth he said: In the name of Allah, first and last. The Holy Prophet smiled at this and said: Satan continued to eat with him, but when he pronounced the name of Allah, Satan threw out all that he had eaten (Abu Daud and Nisai).

736. Ayesha relates that the Holy Prophet was eating in the company of his companions when a rustic came and ate up the food in two mouthfuls. The Holy Prophet said: If he had pronounced the name of Allah, it would have sufficed for all of you (Tirmidhi).

737. Abu Umamah relates: When the Holy Prophet finished a meal he would say: All praise is due to Allah, praise which is pure, perpetual and full of blessings which is indispensable and to which one cannot be indifferent, O Lord (Bokhari).

738. Mu'az ibn Anas relates that the Holy Prophet said: He who eats a meal and says at the end: All praise is due to Allah, Who has given me this to eat and provided it for me without any effort on my part or any power; will have all his preceding sins forgiven him (Tirmidhi).

101.
On Not Finding Fault with Food and Praising It

739. Abu Hurairah relates that the Holy Prophet never found fault with food. If he desired it he ate it, and if he disliked it he left it (Bokhari and Muslim).

740. Jabir relates that the Holy Prophet asked for sauce and was told that there was nothing but vinegar. He called for it and began to eat his food with it exclaiming: What excellent sauce is vinegar; what excellent sauce is vinegar. (Muslim).

102.
On the Response of one Fasting to an Invitation

741. Abu Hurairah relates that the Holy Prophet said: When any of you is invited to a meal, he should accept the invitation. Then if he is fasting he should pray for the host, and if he is not fasting he should eat (Muslim).

103.

On a Person who is Invited being Accompanied by Another

742. Abu Mas'ud Badri relates: A man prepared some food for the Holy Prophet and invited him along with four others. But a fifth also went along with them. Arrived at the door, the Holy Prophet said to the host: This one has followed us. You may permit him, if you will, and if you wish he will retire. He said: Messenger of Allah, indeed I invite him (Bokhari and Muslim).

104.

On Eating what is in front of One

743. This *hadith* is the same as No. 301.
744. This *hadith* is the same as No. 160.

105.

On Prohibition of Eating Two Dates or other Fruits Together

745. Jabalah ibn Suhaih relates: We were with Abdullah ibn Zubair during a year of famine and were given a ration of dates. Passing by us when we were eating Abdullah ibn Umar would say: Do not eat two dates together, for the Holy Prophet prohibited it, except with the permission of one's companions (Bokhari and Muslim).

106.

On Eating without being Filled

746. Wahshi ibn Harb relates that some of the companions of the Holy Prophet said to him: Messenger of Allah, we eat but are not satisfied. He said: Perhaps you eat separately. They said: That is so. He told them: Eat together and pronounce the name of Allah over your food. It will be blessed for you. (Abu Daud).

107.

On Eating from the Side of the Vessel

747. Ibn Abbas relates that the Holy Prophet said: Blessing descends upon food in its middle, so eat from the sides of the vessel and do not eat from its middle (Tirmidhi).

748. Abdullah ibn Busr relates: The Holy Prophet had a cauldron called *gharra*, which took it four men to carry. When his companions had finished their forenoon voluntary Prayer, *gharra* would be brought full of broth and they would sit down round it. When their number was large the Holy Prophet would sit down on his haunches. A rustic once said: What kind of sitting is that? On which the Holy Prophet said: Allah has made me a courteous servant and has not made me a fierce tyrant. Then he said: Eat from the sides of the cauldron and leave the higher part of it. That will be blessed (Abu Daud).

108.

On Dislike of Eating while Leaning against a Pillow

749. Wahl ibn Abdullah relates that the Holy Prophet said: I do not eat while reclining against a pillow (Bokhari).

750. Anas relates that he saw the Holy Prophet lying on his back, with his knees raised eating a date (Muslim).

109.

On Eating with Hands

751. Ibn Abbas relates that the Holy Prophet said: When one of you has finished eating he should not wipe his fingers without first licking his fingers or having them licked (Bokhari and Muslim).

752. Ka'ab ibn Malik relates that he saw the Holy Prophet eat with three fingers and having finished, lick them (Muslim).

753-755. These three *ahadith* are comprised in No. 165.

756. Anas relates that the Holy Prophet when he finished eating would lick his three fingers and say: If a mouthful of food should fall from the hand of any of you, he should pick it up, remove any uncleanness from it and eat it and not leave it for Satan. He also told us to wipe out the vessel, saying: You do not know which part of your food is blessed (Muslim).

757. Sa'id ibn Harith relates that he asked Jabir whether it was obligatory to wash for Prayer after eating cooked food. He said: No. In the time of the Holy Prophet we seldom had such food. Nor did we have napkins. When we ate such food we wiped our fingers against our palms, forearms or feet. It was not necessary to repeat our ablutions for Prayer on that account. (Bokhari).

110.
On Saving Food

758, 759. These two *ahadith* are comprised in No. 568. •

111.
On Drinking Water

760. Anas relates that the Holy Prophet when he drank would stop three times for taking breath (Bokhari and Muslim).

761. Ibn Abbas relates that the Holy Prophet said: Do not drink in one draught like a camel, but in two or three. Pronounce the name of Allah when you start drinking and praise Him when you finish. (Tirmidhi).

762. Abu Qatadah relates that the Holy Prophet forbade breathing inside the vessel when drinking (Bokhari and Muslim).

763. Anas relates that milk mixed with water was brought to the Holy Prophet when on his right was seated a rustic and on his left Abu Bakr. He drank from it and handed the rest to the rustic saying: The right has preference (Bokhari and Muslim).

764. This *hadith* is the same as No. 572.

112.
On the Undesirability of Drinking directly from a Water-skin etc.

765. Abu Sa'id Khudri relates that the Holy Prophet forbade any one drinking directly from a water-skin (Bokhari and Muslim).

766. Abu Hurairah relates that the Holy Prophet forbade drinking directly from a water-skin (Bokhari and Muslim).

767. Kabashah bint Thabit relates: The Holy Prophet visited me and drank from a suspended water-skin through its mouth standing; I stood up and cut off the mouth to preserve it as a memento (Tirmidhi).

113.
On the Undesirability of Blowing upon Drink

768. Abu Sa'id Khudri relates that the Holy Prophet forbade blowing over drink. A man asked: What about straws floating about on the surface? He answered: Pour them out. The man said: My thirst is not quenched with one draught. The Holy Prophet said: Then take breath, but put away the vessel from your mouth (Tirmidhi).

769. Ibn Abbas relates that the Holy Prophet forbade breathing into or blowing upon a vessel from which one drinks (Tirmidhi).

114.

On Drinking Standing or Sitting

770. Ibn Abbas relates that he gave the Holy Prophet Zam Zam water to drink and he drank it standing (Bokhari and Muslim).

771. Nazal ibn Sabrah relates that Ali arrived at the Bab-ar-Rahbrah (Kufa) and drank water standing and said: I saw the Holy Prophet doing what you have seen me doing (Bokhari).

772. Ibn Umar relates: In the time of the Holy Prophet we ate walking and we drank standing (Tirmidhi).

773. Amr ibn Su'aib relates on the authority of his father and grandfather that they saw the Holy Prophet drink standing and sitting (Tirmidhi).

774. Anas relates that the Holy Prophet forbade a person drinking standing. Qatadah asked Anas: What about eating? He said: That would be worse (Muslim). Another version is that he reproved drinking standing.

775. Abu Hurairah relates that the Holy Prophet said: No one of you should drink standing (Muslim).

115.

On Turns in Drinking

776. Abu Qatadah relates that the Holy Prophet said: He who serves drink to others should be the last to drink himself (Tirmidhi).

116.

On Drinking Vessels

777. Anas relates that the Holy Prophet was at Zaura. When the time of Prayer approached, those whose houses were close by went over to wash and the rest remained with the Holy Prophet. A stone mug was brought for him in which there was some water. It was small enough for him to spread his hand over it. He performed his ablutions and it sufficed for all the others also. Anas was asked: How many of you were there? He said: Eighty or more (Bokhari and Muslim). Another version is: The Holy Prophet called for a vessel containing water. He was brought a wide shallow vessel with a little water in it. He put his fingers in it. Anas says: I kept looking at the water pouring from between his fingers. I estimated the number of those who performed their ablutions with it as being between seventy and eighty.

778. Abdullah ibn Zaid relates: The Holy Prophet came to us and we put out water for him in a brass vessel for his ablutions (Bokhari).

779. Jabir relates: The Holy Prophet came to the house of a man of the Ansar with a companion and said to him: If you have some water in the water-skin left over from last night give it to us for drink, else we shall drink from some stream (Bokhari).

780. Huzaifah relates: The Holy Prophet forbade us wearing silk or brocade and drinking out of gold or silver vessels, and said: These are for them (non-Muslims) in this world and for you in the hereafter (Bokhari and Muslim).

781. Umm Salamah relates that the Holy Prophet said: He who drinks from a silver vessel kindles the fire of hell in his belly (Bokhari and Muslim). Muslim's versions are: He who eats or drinks out of a gold or silver vessel; and: He who drinks out of a gold or silver vessel kindles the fire of hell in his belly.

117.
On Clothes, their Material and Colours

. Allah, the Exalted, has said:

268. Children of Adam, We have created for you raiment which covers your nakedness and is a source of adornment; but the raiment of righteousness is best (7.27).

269. He has made for you garments that protect you in heat and cold and coats of mail that protect you in battle (16.82).

782. Ibn Abbas relates that the Holy Prophet said: Wear white clothes for they are best and use them as shrouds for your dead (Tirmidhi).

783. Samurah relates that the Holy Prophet said: Wear white for that is purest and most elegant and shroud your dead in it (Nisai and Hakim).

784. Bra'a relates: The Holy Prophet was of middle height. I saw him wearing a red mantle than which I have never seen anything more elegant (Bokhari and Muslim).

785. Wahb ibn Abdullah relates: I saw the Holy Prophet in Mecca at Batha. He was in a tent made of red leather. Bilal came out with water with

which the Holy Prophet had made his ablutions. Some people obtained a few drops of it and some had to be content with receiving the wetness off others. Then the Holy Prophet came out wearing a red mantle. I can recall noticing the whiteness of his shanks. He made his ablutions and Bilal recited the call of Prayer. I kept following the movement of his face to the right and left when he recited: Come to Prayer, Come to Prosperity. Then a short spear was planted in front and the Holy Prophet advanced and led the Prayer. Dogs and donkeys passed in front of him (beyond the spear) without let or hindrance (Bokhari and Muslim).

786. Abi Ramtha Rifa'a Tamimi relates: I saw the Holy Prophet wearing two green garments (Abu Daud and Tirmidhi).

787. Jabir relates that the Holy Prophet entered Mecca on the day it fell wearing a black turban (Muslim).

788. Abu Sa'id Amr ibn Hurais relates: I recall seeing the Holy Prophet wearing a black turban both ends of which fell over his shoulders (Muslim). Another version is: The Holy Prophet made an address and he was wearing a black turban both ends of which fell over his shoulders (Muslim). Another version is: The Holy Prophet made an address and he was wearing a black turban.

789. Ayesha relates that the Holy Prophet was shrouded in three pieces of white cotton Yemeni cloth, which did not include a shirt or a turban (Bokhari and Muslim).

790. Ayesha relates that one day the Holy Prophet went out wearing a cloak made of black hair which bore representations of the saddle of a camel (Muslim).

791. Mughirah ibn Shu'bah relates: I was with the Holy Prophet one night during a journey, when he asked me: Have you some water with you? I replied in the affirmative. Then he dismounted and walked away into the darkness. When he returned I poured out water from a vessel and he washed his face. He was wearing a woollen long coat and could not extract his arms from his sleeves till he pulled them inside the coat and brought them out from below it and then washed his forearms. Then he passed his hands over his head. I stretched out my hand to take off his socks, but he said: Leave them. I put them on after I had washed my feet; and he passed his hands over them (Bokhari and Muslim).

One version has it: He was wearing a tight-sleeved Syrian long coat. Another version says: This incident took place during the campaign of Tabuk.

118.

On Dress and the Manner of Wearing it

792. Umm Salamah relates that out of all garments the Holy Prophet liked a shirt best (Abu Daud and Tirmidhi).

793. Asma' bint Yazid relates that the sleeves of the shirt of the Holy Prophet reached down to his wrists (Abu Daud and Tirmidhi).

794. Ibn Umar relates that the Holy Prophet said: He who lets down his loin cloth out of pride will find that Allah will not look at him on the Day of Judgment. On this Abu Bakr submitted: Messenger of Allah, my loin cloth is apt to slide down unless I take care of it. The Holy Prophet said: You are not of those who let it down out of pride (Bokhari).

795. This *hadith* is the same as No. 619.

796. Abu Hurairah relates that the Holy Prophet said: The portion of a loin cloth worn below the ankles is condemned to the Fire (Bokhari).

797. Abu Dharr relates that the Holy Prophet said: There are three to whom Allah will not speak on the Day of Judgment, nor will He look at them or purify them. He repeated this three times. Abu Dharr said: They are lost and ruined! Who are they, Messenger of Allah? He said: One who lets down his garments out of pride, one who boasts of favours done to another and one who promotes the sale of his wares with false oaths (Muslim). One version has it: One who lets down his loin cloth.

798. Ibn Umar relates that the Holy Prophet said: On the Day of Judgment Allah will not look upon one who lets down his loin cloth, shirt or turban out of pride (Abu Daud and Nisai).

799. Jabir ibn Sulaim relates: I saw a man whose direction was obeyed by everyone; no one did other than that which he said. I asked: Who is he? I was told: He is the Messenger of Allah. I said twice: On you be peace, Messenger of Allah. He said: Do not say: On you be peace. This is the greeting of the dead. Say, instead: Peace be on you. I asked: Are you the Messenger of Allah? He answered: I am the Messenger of Allah, Who, when you are afflicted and call on Him, will remove your afflictions; Who, when you are afflicted with famine and call on Him, will cause food to grow for you; and Who, if you lose your mount in a barren and desert land and call on Him, will restore it to you. I said to him: Instruct me. He said: Do not revile any one. (Since then I have never abused anyone, neither a freeman, nor a slave, nor a camel, nor a goat). He continued: Do not disdain the doing of the least good; and talk to your brother with a cheerful face. That is part of goodness. Hold up your loincloth half way up to the knee, and at least above the ankles; for letting it down is prideful and contemptuous, and Allah dislikes pride. If someone charges you with defaults from which he thinks you suffer, do not charge him with defaults from which you think he suffers, for the penalty for his default will overtake him (Abu Daud and Tirmidhi).

800. Abu Hurairah relates: To a person who had been engaged in Prayer while his loin cloth had been hanging down, the Holy Prophet said: Go and perform your ablutions again. The man went and came back after having performed them. The Holy Prophet said: Go and make your ablutions. Someone present said to the Holy Prophet: Messenger of Allah, you ask him to perform his ablutions and then you keep silent. He said: He says his Prayer while his loin cloth is hanging down. Allah does not accept the Prayer of a man who lets down his loin cloth (Abu Daud).

801. Qais ibn Bishr Taghlibi relates that his father, who kept company with Abu Darda' told him: There was a man in Damascus who was a companion of the Holy Prophet, who was called Ibn al-Hanzaliyyah. He liked solitude and did not spend much time in the company of people. He spent most of his time in *salat,* and when he had finished he occupied himself with glorifying and magnifying Allah, till he went home. He passed by us one day when we were sitting with Abu Darda'. The latter said to him: Tell us something which might be useful for us and the telling of which would not harm you. He said: The Holy Prophet despatched a scouting party and when they returned one of them came to the company in which the Holy Prophet was and said to his neighbour, in the course of conversation: I wish you had seen us when we met the enemy and one of them took up his spear and struck one of us and he returned his attack and said: Take this from me and I am only a Ghifari boy. Now what do you think of this? The neighbour said: I think he lost his merit because of his boast. He said: I see no harm in it. They began to argue till the Holy Prophet heard them and said: Glory be to Allah, he could be both rewarded and praised. Abu Darda' seemed pleased with this and raising his head began to repeat: Did you hear the Holy Prophet say this? and Ibn al-Hanzaliyyah kept answering: Indeed; till I said to Abu Darda': Would you mount on his knees?

Ibn al-Hanzaliyyah passed by us another day and Abu Darda' said to him: Tell us something that might be useful for us and the telling of which would not harm you. He said: The Holy Prophet told us that he who spends on making provision for a horse is like one who extends his hand in spending for charity and does not restrain it. He passed by us another day and Abu Darda' said to him: Tell us something that might be useful for us and the telling of which would not harm you. He said: The Holy Prophet once said: Khuraim Usaidi would be an excellent person were it not for his long hair and his low hanging loin cloth. This reached the ears of Khuraim and he hastened to trim down his hair with a pair of scissors to his ears and to raise his loin cloth halfway up to his knees.

On another occasion he passed by us and Abu Darda' said to him: Tell us something that might be useful for us and the telling of which would not harm you. He said that he had heard the Holy Prophet say, while returning from an expedition: You are returning to your brothers so put your saddles and clothes in order till you begin to look elegant. Allah does not like untidiness (Abu Daud).

802. Abu Sa'id Khudri relates that the Holy Prophet said: The loin cloth of a Muslim should be half way below the knees; but there is no harm if it is above the ankles. That which hangs below the ankles is in the Fire. Allah will not look at one who lets down his loin cloth out of pride (Abu Daud).

803. Ibn Umar relates: I passed near the Holy Prophet and my loin cloth was hanging low. He said to me: Abdullah, pull up your loin cloth. I pulled it up. He said: More. I pulled it up more and have ever since worn it high. Someone asked: How high? He said: Half-way up to the knees (Muslim).

804. Ibn Umar relates that the Holy Prophet said: On the Day of Judgment Allah will not look upon one who trails his loin cloth along out of pride. Umm Salamah asked: What should the women do with their skirts? He said: They might lower them a hand's breadth. She said: Their feet would still be uncovered. He said: Let them lower them an arm's length but no more (Abu Daud and Tirmidhi).

119.

On Giving up Smart Clothing out of Humility

805. Mu'az ibn Anas relates that the Holy Prophet said: One who having the capacity to wear rich garments abstains from wearing them out of a sense of humility before Allah will be called by Allah on the Day of Judgment in priority to all others and will be given the choice to put on whichever of the mantles of faith he prefers (Tirmidhi).

120.

On Moderation in Dress

806. Amr ibn Shuaib relates on the authority of his father and grandfather that the Holy Prophet said: Allah likes to see the mark of his bounty on His servant (Tirmidhi).

121.

On Prohibition of Wearing Silk for Men

807. Umar ibn Khattab relates that the Holy Prophet said: Do not wear silk, for he who wears it in this life shall not wear it in the hereafter (Bokhari and Muslim).

808. Umar ibn Khattab relates that he heard the Holy Prophet say: Silk is worn by him who has no share in the hereafter (Bokhari and Muslim).

809. Anas relates that the Holy Prophet said: He who wears silk in this life shall not wear it in the hereafter (Bokhari and Muslim).

810. Ali relates: I saw the Holy Prophet take a piece of silk in his right hand and a piece of gold in his left and heard him say: The wearing of these two is unlawful for the males among my followers (Abu Daud).

811. Abu Musa Ash'ari relates that the Holy Prophet said: Wearing of silk and gold has been made unlawful for the males among my followers and lawful for the females (Tirmidhi).

812. Huzaifah relates: The Holy Prophet forbade us eating or drinking out of gold or silver vessels, and wearing of silk and brocade or sitting on them (Bokhari).

122.

On Permission to wear Silk in case of Skin Disorders

813. Anas relates that the Holy Prophet permitted Zubair and Abdur Rahman ibn Auf to wear silk because they suffered from itch (Bokhari and Muslim).

123.

On Prohibition of Sitting and Riding on Skins of Wild Animals

814. Mu'awiah relates that the Holy Prophet said: Do not ride on saddles made of silk or leopard skin (Abu Daud).

815. Abu Malih relates on the authority of his father that the Holy Prophet prohibited the use of the skins of wild animals (Abu Daud and Tirmidhi). Another version is: He forbade skins of wild animals being used as floor coverings.

124.

On Supplication on Wearing New Articles

816. Abu Sa'id Khudri relates that when the Holy Prophet wore a new article he would name it, for instance, turban, or shirt or cloak and would supplicate: Allah, Thine is the praise that Thou hast given it to me to wear. I beg of Thee its good and the good of the purpose for which it has been made, and seek Thy protection against its evil and the evil of the purpose for which it has been made (Abu Daud and Tirmidhi).

125.

On Beginning with the Right Side when Dressing

This topic has already been dealt with (see chapter 99).

126.
On Sleeping

817, 818. These two *ahadith* are comprised in No. 80.

819. Ayesha relates that the Holy Prophet used to offer eleven *raka'as* of voluntary Prayers in the latter part of the night. When the dawn broke he offered two brief *raka'as* and then rested on his right side till the *muezzin* came to tell him that the congregation had assembled (Bokhari and Muslim).

820. Huzaifah relates: When the Holy Prophet lay down for sleep at night he would place his hand under his cheek and supplicate: Allah, with Thy name I die and return to life; and when he woke up he supplicated: All praise is to Allah Who has brought us back to life after He had caused us to die and to Him is the return. (Bokhari).

821. Ya'ish ibn Tighfah Ghifari relates that his father said: I was lying down in the mosque on my belly when someone poked me with his foot and said: Such lying down is displeasing to Allah. I looked up and saw that it was the Holy Prophet (Abu Daud).

822. Abu Hurairah relates that the Holy Prophet said: When a person sits down in company in which there is no remembrance of Allah, he incurs loss and displeasure from Allah; and when a person lies down and does not remember Allah, he incurs loss and displeasure from Allah. (Abu Daud).

127.
On Lying Down on One's Back

823. Abdullah ibn Yazid relates that he saw the Holy prophet lying down on his back in the mosque with one foot resting on the other (Bokhari and Muslim).

824. Jabir ibn Samurah relates that after the Dawn Prayer the Holy Prophet would sit cross-legged among his companions till the sun became quite bright (Abu Daud).

825. Ibn Umar relates that he saw the Holy Prophet seated in the courtyard of the Ka'aba with his arms encircling his raised knees (Bokhari).

826. Qailah bint Makhramah relates that she saw the Holy Prophet seated with his arms encircling his knees and that when she perceived his attitude of awed humility she trembled with awe of him (Tirmidhi).

827. Sharid ibn Su'ud relates: The Holy Prophet passed by me when I was sitting with my left hand against my back, supporting myself on the flesh below my thumbs. On seeing me in this position he said: Do you prefer sitting like those with whom Allah is wroth (Abu Daud)?

128.
On Sitting in Company

828. Ibn Umar relates that the Holy Prophet said: Let no one ask another to give up his seat to him; but make room and sit at ease. If a person gave up his seat for Ibn Umar he would not take it (Bokhari and Muslim).

829. Abu Hurairah relates that the Holy Prophet said: When someone gets up from among company and returns to it he is the best entitled to occupy the seat he had left (Muslim).

830. Jabir ibn Samurah relates: When we came to the Holy Prophet we sat down at the extremity of the company (Abu Daud).

831. Salman Farisi relates that the Holy Prophet said: If a person takes a bath on Friday, cleans himself thoroughly, oils his hair, uses such perfume as is available, sets forth for the mosque, does not intrude between two persons, offers the prescribed portion of the Prayer and listens in silence to the Imam his sins committed since the previous Friday are forgiven (Bokhari).

832. Amr ibn Shuaib relates on the authority of his father and grandfather that the Holy Prophet said: It is not permissible for a person to intrude between two people without their consent (Abu Daud and Tirmidhi). Abu Daud's version is: No one should sit between two persons without their permission.

833. Huzaifah ibn Yaman relates that the Holy Prophet cursed a person who should sit in the middle of a circle (Abu Daud). Tirmidhi's version on the authority of Mijlaz is: Someone went and sat in the middle of a circle, whereupon Huzaifah said: Cursed is, according to Muhammad, or Allah has cursed through Muhammad, one who sits in the middle of a circle.

834. Abu Sa'id Khudri relates that he heard the Holy Prophet say: The best companies are those in which there is plenty of room (Abu Daud).

835. Abu Hurairah relates that the Holy Prophet said: If a person sits in company which indulges in vain talk and before leaving it supplicates: Holy art Thou, O Allah, and Thine is the praise: I bear witness that there is none worthy of worship save Thyself; I ask Thy forgiveness and turn to Thee; he is forgiven his participation in that company (Tirmidhi).

836. Abu Barzah relates that towards the end the Holy Prophet when he was about to leave a company would supplicate: Holy art Thou, O Allah, and Thine is the praise; I bear witness that there is none worthy of worship save Thyself; I ask Thy forgiveness and turn to Thee. Someone said to him: Messenger of Allah, you have taken to saying something you used not to say before. He said: This is an expiation of that which goes on in the company (Abu Daud and Muslim).

837. Ibn Umar relates that it was seldom that the Holy Prophet would leave a company without supplicating in these terms: Allah, bestow upon us of Thy fear that should serve as a barrier between us and our sins; and of Thy obedience that should serve to carry us to Thy Paradise; and of the certainty of faith that should render the misfortunes of this world easy for us to endure. Allah, bestow upon us the benefit of our hearing and our sight and our other faculties so long as Thou dost grant us life and make them survive us; and afflict with our rancour those who might oppress us, and help us against those who are at enmity with us; and do not afflict us with misfortune in our faith, and do not make the world our principal concern, or the ultimate limit of our knowledge; and do not grant authority over us to one who would not show mercy to us (Tirmidhi).

838. Abu Hurairah relates that the Holy Prophet said: Those who leave a company in which there has been no remembrance of Allah, leave it like the corpses of donkeys, and suffer remorse (Abu Daud).

839. Abu Hurairah relates that the Holy Prophet said: A company in which there is no mention of Allah, the Exalted, and no supplication for blessings on their Prophet will be afflicted with remorse. If Allah wills He might punish them and if He wills He might forgive them (Tirmidhi).

840. This *hadith* is the same as No. 822.

129.

On Dreams

Allah, the Exalted, has said:
270. Of His signs is your sleep by night and by day (30.24).

841. Abu Hurairah relates that he heard the Holy Prophet say: Nothing is left of Prophethood but glad tidings. On being asked: What are glad tidings? he replied: True dreams (Bokhari).

842. Abu Hurairah relates that the Holy Prophet said: When the time draws near, the dream of a believer will not be falsified, and the dream of a believer is one of the forty-six elements of Prophethood (Bokhari and Muslim). One version adds: The most truthful of you in their talk will see true dreams most.

843. Abu Hurairah relates that the Holy Prophet said: He who sees me in his dream is as if he had seen me in his waking state, for Satan cannot assume my likeness (Bokhari and Muslim).

844. Abu Sa'id Khudri relates that he heard the Holy Prophet say: When any of you sees a dream that he likes, it is from Allah. He should praise Allah for it and relate it (one version says: he should not relate it except to those he likes). When he sees one that he dislikes, it is from Satan. He should seek Allah's protection against it and should not mention it to anyone. Then it will not cause him any harm (Bokhari and Muslim).

845. Abu Qatadah relates that the Holy Prophet said: A true dream is from Allah and a confused dream is from Satan. He who sees something in a dream that he dislikes should spit out three times to the left and should seek

Allah's protection against Satan. It will then cause him no harm (Bokhari and Muslim).

846. Jabir relates that the Holy Prophet said: When one of you sees a disagreeable dream he should spit out three times to the left, should seek Allah's protection against Satan three times and should turn over in bed (Muslim).

847. Wathilah ibn Asqa'a relates that the Holy Prophet said: The greatest lies are that a person should assert a false paternity, or should set forth a false dream, or should attribute to me something I have not said (Bokhari).

130.

On Multiplying the Greeting of Peace

Allah, the Exalted, has said:

271.　O ye who believe, enter not houses other than your own until you have obtained leave and have saluted the inmates thereof (24.28).

272.　When you enter houses, greet your people with the salutation of peace, a greeting from your Lord full of blessings and purity (24.62).

273.　When you are greeted with a salutation greet with a better salutation, or return the same (4.87).

274.　Has an account of the honoured guests of Abraham reached thee? When they came to him they said: Peace on you. He returned their salutation: On you be peace (51.25).

848. This *hadith* is the same as No. 553.

849. Abu Hurairah relates that the Holy Prophet said: When Allah created Adam He said to him: Go and offer the salutation of peace to that company of angels sitting there and then listen to the greeting they return to you, for that will be your greeting and that of your progeny. Adam said to the angels: Peace be on you; and they responded with: Peace be on you and the mercy of Allah; adding "the mercy of Allah" to his greeting (Bokhari and Muslim).

850. Bra'a ibn 'Azib relates: The Holy Prophet enjoined the following seven upon us: Visiting the sick, following a funeral, calling down the mercy of Allah upon one who sneezes, supporting the weak, helping the oppressed, multiplying the greeting of peace, and fulfilling vows (Bokhari and Muslim).

851. This *hadith* is the same as No. 381.

852. Abdullah ibn Salam relates that he heard the Holy Prophet say: O ye people, multiply the greeting of peace, feed people, strengthen the ties of kinship and be in Prayer when others are asleep, you will enter Paradise in peace (Tirmidhi).

853. Tufail ibn Ubayy ibn Ka'ab relates that he would visit Abdullah ibn Umar in the morning and would accompany him into the market place. Abdullah would offer the greeting of peace to every petty shopkeeper, trader and poor person. One day when I came to him he asked me to accompany him into the market place. I said to him: What will you do in the market place? You do not stop to buy anything, nor do you inquire about any article or its price, nor do you sit down with any company. Let us sit down here and talk. He retorted: O man of the belly (Tufail had somewhat of a belly) we shall go into the market place to greet everyone we meet with the salutation of peace (Malik).

131.
On the Manner of Greeting

854. Imran ibn Husain relates: A man came to the Holy Prophet and said: Peace be on you. The Holy Prophet returned his greeting and the man sat down. The Holy Prophet said: Ten (meaning the man had earned the merit of ten good deeds). Another one came and said: Peace be on you and the mercy of Allah. The Holy Prophet returned his greeting and the man sat down. The Holy Prophet said: Twenty. A third one came and said: Peace be on you and the mercy of Allah and His blessings. The Holy Prophet returned his greeting and he sat down. The Holy Prophet said: Thirty (Abu Daud and Tirmidhi).

855. Ayesha relates: The Holy Prophet said to me: Here is Gabriel. He greets you with the salutation of peace. I said: Peace be on him and the mercy of Allah and His blessings (Bokhari and Muslim).

856. This *hadith* is the same as No. 699.

857. Miqdad relates in the course of a long *hadith*: We used to set aside for the Holy Prophet his share of the milk. He would come at night and offer his greeting in a tone that did not disturb the sleeping but was heard by the waking. In fact the Holy Prophet came and offered his greeting as he was wont. (Muslim).

858. This *hadith* is included in No. 869.

859. This *hadith* is included in No. 862.

860. This *hadith* is included in No. 799.

132.
On the Order of Greeting

861. Abu Hurairah relates that the Holy Prophet said: A rider should greet a pedestrian, a pedestrian should greet one who is sitting and a small party should greet a large party (Bokhari and Muslim). Bokhari's version adds: A younger one should greet an older one.

862. Abu Umamah relates that the Holy Prophet said: The person closest to Allah is one who anticipates others in greeting (Abu Daud). Tirmidhi's version is: The Holy Prophet was asked: Messenger of Allah, when two persons meet who should greet the other first? He answered: The one who is closer to Allah.

133.
On Repetition of Greeting

863. Abu Hurairah, in the course of the *hadith* relating to the person who was at fault in performing his *salat*, states that he came up to the Holy Prophet and saluted him. The Holy Prophet returned his greeting and said: Go back and repeat your *salat* for you have not performed it properly. He went back, performed the *salat* and came up to the holy Prophet and saluted him. This happened three times (Bokhari and Muslim).

864. Abu Hurairah relates that the Holy Prophet said: When one of you meets a brother he should salute him. Then if they are separated by a tree or a wall or a rock, he should salute him again when they meet (Abu Daud).

134.
On Greeting when Entering Home

Allah, the Exalted, has said:

275. When you enter houses, salute your people with the greeting of peace, a greeting from your Lord full of blessings and purity (24.62).

865. Anas relates that the Holy Prophet said to him: Son, when you enter your home greet your people with the salutation of peace. It would be a source of blessing for you and for the members of your family (Tirmidhi).

135.
On Greeting Children

866. This *hadith* is the same as No. 607.

136.
On Greeting Women

867. Sahl ibn Sa'ad relates: There was a woman among us who would put beetroot in a kettle and add some ground barley and cook them together. When we returned from the Friday service we would greet her and she would offer it to us (Bokhari).

868. Umm Hani bint Abu Talib relates: I went to the Holy Prophet on the day of the fall of Mecca. He was taking a bath while Fatimah was holding up a cloth to screen him. I offered him the salutation of peace (Muslim).

869. Asma' bint Yazid relates: The Holy Prophet passed by us, a party of women, and greeted us (Abu Daud). The version of Tirmidhi is: The Holy Prophet passed through the mosque one day and there was a party of women seated in the mosque. He signified his greeting by raising his hand.

870. Omitted.

137.
On Greeting Non-Muslims

871. Anas relates that the Holy Prophet said: When the people of the Book greet you, you should respond with: And on you (i.e. be peace). (Bokhari and Muslim).

872. Usamah ibn Zaid relates that the Holy Prophet passed by a company of people which comprised Muslims, idol worshippers and Jews, and he greeted them with the salutation of peace (Bokhari and Muslim).

138.
On Greeting when Arriving and Departing

873. Abu Hurairah relates that the Holy Prophet said: When one of you arrives in an assembly he should greet those present, and so also when he decides to depart. The first is not more obligatory than the last (Abu Daud and Tirmidhi).

139.

On Asking Permission to Enter

Allah, the Exalted, has said:

276.   O ye who believe, enter not houses other than your own until you have obtained leave and have saluted the inmates thereof (24.28).

277.   When your children attain puberty they should ask leave in the same manner as their seniors (24.60).

874.   Abu Musa Ash'ari relates that the Holy Prophet said: Leave is to be asked three times. Then if leave is granted you may enter; otherwise go back (Bokhari and Muslim).

875.   Sahl ibn Sa'ad relates that the Holy Prophet said: Asking for leave has been prescribed in order to restrain the eyes (Bokhari and Muslim).

876.   Ribi' ibn Hirash relates: A man of the Bani A'amir told us that he asked the Holy Prophet for leave to enter when he was at home, saying: May I enter? The Holy Prophet said to his servant: Go out and instruct this one in the manner of asking leave. Tell him to say: Peace be on you. May I come in? The man heard this and said: Peace be on you. May I come in? The Holy Prophet then gave him leave and he went in (Abu Daud).

877.   Kildah ibn Hanbal relates that he visited the Holy Prophet and entered without a greeting. The Holy Prophet said to him: Go back and say: Peace be on you. May I come in (Abu Daud and Tirmidhi)?

140.

On Mentioning One's Name when Asking Leave

878.   Anas relates in the course of his well-known *hadith* relating to the ascension of the Holy Prophet: Then Gabriel ascended with me to the nearest heaven and asked for the gate to be opened. He was asked: Who is there? He said: Gabriel. He was asked: Who is with you? He answered: Muhammad. Then he ascended to the second heaven and asked for the gate to be opened. He was asked: Who is there? He said: Gabriel. He was asked: Who is with you? He answered: Muhammad. In the same way to the third, fourth and all of them. At the gate of each he was asked: Who is there? and he said: Gabriel (Bokhari and Muslim).

879.   Abu Dharr relates: I went out one night and saw the Holy Prophet walking alone. I began to walk in the shadow of the moon, but he looked in my direction and saw me and asked: Who is there? I answered: Abu Dharr (Bokhari and Muslim).

880. Umm Hani relates: I went to the Holy Prophet. He was taking a bath and Fatimah was screening him. He asked: Who is there? and I answered: It is I, Umm Hani (Bokhari and Muslim).

881. Jabir relates: I went to the Holy Prophet and knocked on the door. He asked: Who is there? I said: I. He repeated I? I? as if he disliked it (Bokhari and Muslim).

141.

On Sneezing and Yawning

882. Abu Hurairah relates that the Holy Prophet said: Allah likes a sneeze and dislikes a yawn. When one of you sneezes and says: Praise be to Allah; it becomes obligatory upon every Muslim who hears him to respond with: Allah have mercy on you. But a yawn is from Satan. When one of you feels like yawning he should suppress it as far as he can, for Satan laughs when any of you yawns (Bokhari).

883. Abu Hurairah relates that the Holy Prophet said: When any of you sneezes he should say: Praise be to Allah; and his brother or companion should respond with: May Allah have mercy on you; to which he should reply: May Allah guide you and improve your condition (Bokhari).

884. Abu Musa relates that he heard the Holy Prophet say: When one of you sneezes and praises Allah, you should respond with: May Allah have mercy on you; but if he does not praise Allah, make no response (Muslim).

885. Anas relates that two men sneezed in the presence of the Holy Prophet. He responded to one with: May Allah have mercy on you; and did not respond to the other. The latter said: So and So sneezed and you responded to him; I sneezed and you did not respond. The Holy Prophet answered: He praised Allah and you did not praise Him (Bokhari and Muslim).

886. Abu Hurairah relates that when the Holy Prophet sneezed he covered his mouth with his hand or a piece of cloth and suppressed the sound (Abu Daud and Tirmidhi).

887. Abu Musa relates that the Jews would sneeze in the presence of the Holy Prophet hoping that he would respond with: May Allah have mercy on you; but he responded with: May Allah guide you and improve your condition (Abu Daud Tirmidhi).

888. Abu Sa'id Khudri relates that the Holy Prophet said: When one of you yawns he should close his mouth with his hand, else Satan would enter (Muslim).

142.

On Shaking Hands etc.

889. Abu Khattab Qatadah relates: I inquired from Anas: Was handshake customary among the companions of the Holy Prophet? He said: Yes (Bokhari).

890. Anas relates that when the people of the Yemen came the Holy Prophet said: The people of Yemen have come to you. They are the first who practised handshake (Abu Daud).

891. Bra'a relates that the Holy Prophet said: When two Muslims meet and shake hands they are forgiven their sins before they part (Abu Daud).

892. Anas relates that a man asked the Holy Prophet: Messenger of Allah, when one of us meets a brother or a friend should he bow to him? He said: No. The man said: Should he seize his hand and shake it? He said: Yes (Tirmidhi).

893. Safwan ibn Assal relates that a Jew asked his fellow to take him to the Holy Prophet, and when they came to him they inquired from him about the nine clear signs (and here follows the recital of the *hadith* concluding with) and they kissed his hands and feet and said: We bear witness that you are a Prophet. (Tirmidhi).

894. Ibn Umar relates at the end of a recital: Then we approached the Holy Prophet and kissed his hand (Abu Daud).

895. Ayesha relates that Zaid ibn Harithah came to Medina, and the Holy Prophet was in my house at the time. Zaid came and knocked at the door. The Holy Prophet hurried to him, trailing his cloak, embraced him and kissed him (Tirmidhi).

896. This *hadith* is the same as No. 121.

897. This *hadith* is the same as No. 227.

143.

On Visiting the Sick

898. This *hadith* is the same as No. 241.

899. This *hadith* is the same as No. 240.

900. Abu Hurairah relates that the Holy Prophet said: Allah, the Lord of honour and glory, will say on the Day of Judgment: Son of Adam, I was sick and you did not visit me. The man will exclaim: Lord, how could I visit You and You are Lord of the worlds! Allah will say: Did you not know that My servant So and So was sick and you did not visit him. Did you not realise that if you had visited him you would have found Me with him? Son of Adam, I asked you for food and you did not feed Me. The man will exclaim: Lord, how could I feed You while You are the Lord of the worlds! Allah will say: Did you not know that My servant So and So asked you for food and you did not feed him? Did you not realise that if you had fed him you would have found your reward with Me? Son of Adam, I asked you for drink and you did not give Me to drink. The man will exclaim: Lord, how could I have given You to drink when You are the Lord of the worlds! Allah will say: My servant So and So asked you for a drink and you did not give him to drink. Did you not realise that if you had given him to drink you would have found its reward with Me? (Muslim).

901. Abu Musa Ash'ari relates that the Holy Prophet directed: Visit the sick, feed the hungry and procure the freedom of captives (Bokhari).

902. Thauban relates that the Holy Prophet said: When a Muslim visits a brother Muslim who is ailing he is among the *Kharfah* of Paradise till he returns from his visit. The Holy Prophet was asked: Messenger of Allah, what is the *Kharfah* of Paradise? He answered: Its fruits (Muslim).

903. Ali relates that he heard the Holy Prophet say: When a Muslim visits an ailing Muslim in the morning, seventy thousand angels keep calling down blessings on him till the evening; and if he visits him in the evening, seventy thousand angels keep calling down blessings on him till the morning, and he is allotted an orchard of fruit trees in Paradise (Tirmidhi).

904. Anas relates that a Jewish boy who served the Holy Prophet fell ill and the Holy Prophet visited him and sat down near his head and said to him: Accept Islam. The boy looked at his father who was close to him and who answered: Obey, Abul Qasim; whereupon the boy declared his acceptance of Islam. When the Holy Prophet left him he affirmed: All praise is due to Allah Who has delivered him from the Fire (Bokhari).

144.
On Prayer for the Sick

905. Ayesha relates that when anyone complained to the Holy Prophet of pain or suffered from a boil or an injury he would touch the earth with his forefinger and then raise it and say: In the name of Allah, I seek blessing from the dust of our earth which contains the saliva of some of us whereby our sick are healed by the command of Allah (Bokhari and Muslim).

906. Ayesha relates that when the Holy Prophet visited any member of his family who was sick he would touch the invalid with his right hand and would supplicate: O Allah, Lord of mankind, remove the affliction and bestow healing, Thou art the Healer, there is no healing save Thy healing, a healing that leaves no ill behind (Bokhari and Muslim).

907. Anas relates that he said to Thabit: Shall I beat off thy ailment as the Holy Prophet used to beat off ailments? He said: Please do; whereupon Anas supplicated: O Allah, Lord of mankind, Remover of affliction, bestow healing, for Thou art the Healer, there is no healer save Thyself, a healing that leaves no ill behind (Bokhari).

908. Sa'ad ibn Abi Waqqas relates that the Holy Prophet visited him during his illness and supplicated: O Allah, bestow healing on Sa'ad; O Allah, bestow healing on Sa'ad; O Allah, bestow healing on Sa'ad (Muslim).

909. Usman ibn Abul 'As relates that he complained to the Holy Prophet of an ache that afflicted his body, who told him: Place thy hand on the part of thy body that aches and say *Bismillah* three times, and then repeat seven times: I seek the protection of the Honour and Might of Allah from the evil that afflicts me and that I apprehend (Muslim).

910. Ibn Abbas relates that the Holy Prophet said: If a person visits an invalid who is not on the point of death and supplicates seven times: I beseech Allah the Glorious, Lord of the Glorious Throne, to bestow healing on thee: Allah will heal him of his sickness (Abu Daud and Tirmidhi).

911. Ibn Abbas relates that the Holy Prophet visited a rustic who was ailing. When he visited an invalid he was wont to say: Have no fear. The ailment will prove purifying, if God wills (Bokhari).

912. Abu Sa'id Khudri relates that Gabriel came to the Holy Prophet and inquired: Muhammad, are you in pain? He answered: Yes. Gabriel said: In the name of Allah, I cleanse thee of all that troubles thee and from the mischief of every person and of every envious eye. May Allah heal thee. In the name of Allah, I cleanse thee (Muslim).

913. Abu Sa'id Khudri and Abu Hurairah both bear witness that the Holy Prophet said: If a person says: There is none worthy of worship save Allah, Great is Allah; his Lord responds to him and affirms: There is none worthy save I, and I am Great. When he says: There is none worthy of worship save Allah, the One, He has no associate; He affirms: There is none worthy of worship save I Alone. I have no associate. When he says: There is none worthy of worship save Allah, His is the kingdom and His the praise; He affirms: There is none worthy of worship save I; Mine is the praise and Mine is the Kingdom. When he says: There is none worthy of worship save Allah, and there is no strength to resist evil nor power to do good except through Allah; He affirms: There is none worthy of worship save I, and there is no strength to resist evil nor power to do good except through Me. The Holy Prophet added: He who says this in his illness and dies thereafter will not be devoured by the Fire (Tirmidhi).

145.
On Inquiring about the Sick

914. Ibn Abbas relates that Ali ibn Abu Talib came out of the chamber of the Holy Prophet during the illness of the latter which proved fatal and the people asked him: Abu Hasan, how is the Holy Prophet this morning? He answered: Praise be to Allah, he is in good condition (Bokhari).

146.
On what one should say on the Approach of Death

915. Ayesha relates that she heard the Holy Prophet say, when he was resting against her in his last illness: Allah, forgive me and have mercy on me and join me to the Companion on high (Bokhari and Muslim).

916. Ayesha relates that she observed the Holy Prophet when he was in extremity put his hand in a cup of water which was close to him and wipe his face with it, saying: Allah, help me over the hardship and agony of death (Tirmidhi).

147.
On Kindness towards one facing Death

917. This *hadith* is the first part of No. 22.

148.
On Giving Expression to Suffering

918. This *hadith* is the same as No. 38.
919. This *hadith* is the first part of No. 6.
920. Qasim ibn Muhammad relates that Ayesha said: Oh, my headache; whereupon the Holy Prophet said: Indeed, I would say: Oh, my headache (Bokhari).

149.
On Urging a Dying One to affirm the Unity of Allah

921. Mu'az relates that the Holy Prophet said: He whose last words are: There is none worthy of worship save Allah; shall enter Paradise (Abu Daud and Hakim).
922. Abu Sa'id Khudri relates that the Holy Prophet said: Urge your dying ones to affirm: There is none worthy of worship save Allah (Muslim).

150.
On Closing the Eyes of one who has Died and Praying for him

923. Umm Salamah relates: The Holy Prophet came to Abu Salamah when his eyes had become glazed. He closed them and said: When the soul is taken possession of, the sight also follows it. Thereupon the members of Abu Salamah's family fell to bewailing him. The Holy Prophet admonished them: Pray for only that which is good for yourselves, for the angels say Amen to your supplications. Then he prayed: Allah, forgive Abu Salamah and exalt his rank among those who are rightly guided, and be Thou the Guardian of those he has left behind him and forgive him and us, O Lord of the worlds, and make his grave spacious and illumine it for him (Muslim).

151.

On what should be said when a Person Dies

924. Umm Salamah relates that the Holy Prophet said: When you visit an invalid or one just dead say only that which is good, for the angels say Amen to whatever you say. She adds: When Abu Salamah died I came to the Holy Prophet and said: Messenger of Allah, Abu Salamah has died. He directed me: Supplicate: Allah, do forgive me and him and bestow upon me a better future. I supplicated as he had directed, and Allah bestowed upon me one better than he, even Muhammad (Muslim).

925. Umm Salamah relates: I heard the Holy Prophet say: When a person is afflicted by misfortune and supplicates: To Allah we belong and to Him shall we return; Allah compensate me in my misfortune and bestow upon me better than that which I have lost; Allah compensates him in his misfortune and bestows upon him better than he has lost. Umm Salamah adds: When Abu Salamah died, I supplicated as the Holy Prophet had directed and indeed Allah bestowed upon me better than him whom I had lost, that is to say, I was asked in marriage by the Holy Prophet (Muslim).

926. Abu Sa'ad relates that the Holy Prophet said: When a child of a servant of Allah dies, Allah inquires from His angels: Have you taken into custody the soul of the child of My servant? They answer: Yes. Then He inquires: Have you taken into custody the soul of the flower of his heart? They answer: Yes. Then He inquires: Then what did My servant say? They answer: He praised Thee and affirmed: To Allah we belong and to Him we shall return. On which Allah will say: Build for My servant a mansion in Paradise and name it: The House of Praise (Tirmidhi).

927. This *hadith* is the same as No. 32.

928. This *hadith* is part of No. 29.

152.

On Silent Shedding of Tears in Grief

929. Ibn Umar relates that the Holy Prophet visited Sa'ad ibn Ubadah in his illness. He was accompanied by Abdur Rahman ibn Auf, Sa'ad ibn Abi Waqqas and Abdullah ibn Mas'ud. The Holy Prophet on seeing Sa'ad began to weep and his companions also wept. He told them: Listen well. Allah does not punish the shedding of tears or the grief of the heart, but punishes or forgives the utterances of this; and he pointed to his tongue (Bokhari and Muslim).

930. This *hadith* is part of No. 29.

931. Anas relates that the Holy Prophet came to his son Ibrahim when he was in extremity and his eyes began to run, whereupon Abdur Rahman ibn Auf exclaimed: Messenger of Allah, even you? The Holy Prophet said: Ibn Auf, this is but the tenderness of the heart. He wept again and said: The eye sheds tears and the heart is sorrowful, but we utter only that which should please our Lord. We are indeed grieved, Ibrahim, by thy parting (Bokhari).

153.

On Safeguarding Knowledge of the Condition of a Dead Body

932. Abi Rafi' Aslam, freedman of the Holy Prophet, relates that the Holy Prophet said: He who washes a dead body and safeguards his knowledge of it is forgiven by Allah forty times (Hakim).

154.

On Participating in Funeral Prayers

933. This *hadith* is the same as No. 36.

934. This *hadith* is the same as No. 37.

935. Umm Atiyyah relates: We were forbidden to follow funerals but the prohibition was not harsh (Bokhari and Muslim).

155.

On the Desirability of large Participation in Funeral Prayers

936. Ayesha relates that the Holy Prophet said: If as many as a hundred Muslims should participate in the funeral service of a person who dies, all of them interceding for him, their intercession would be granted (Muslim).

937. This *hadith* is the same as No. 433.

938. Marthad ibn Abdullah Yazni relates that when Malik ibn Hubairah conducting a funeral service found a paucity of participants he would divide them into three rows, explaining that the Holy Prophet had said: If three rows of suppliants pray for the deliverance of a deceased person he would be admitted to Paradise (Abu Daud and Tirmidhi).

156.
On the Contents of Funeral Prayers

939. Abu Abdur Rahman Auf ibn Malik relates: The Holy Prophet led the funeral prayer over a deceased person and I preserved his prayer in my memory. He supplicated: Allah, do forgive him and have mercy on him and make him secure and overlook his shortcomings, and bestow upon him an honoured place in Paradise, and make his place of entry spacious, and wash him clean with water and snow and ice, and cleanse him of all wrong as Thou dost cleanse a piece of white cloth of dirt, and bestow upon him a home better than his home and a family better than his family and a spouse better than his spouse, and admit him into Paradise, and shield him from the torment of the grave and the torment of the Fire. Hearing him I wished I had been that corpse (Muslim).

940. Abu Hurairah and Abu Qatadah and Abu Ibrahim Ash'ari on the authority of his father relate that the Holy Prophet supplicated over a funeral in the following terms: Allah, do forgive our living and our dead and our young ones and old ones and our males and our females and those of us who are present and those of us who are absent. Allah, he whom Thou dost grant life from among us let him live in accordance with Islam and he whom Thou dost cause to die from among us cause him to die in the faith. Allah, do not deprive us of the reward of one who has died and do not put us to trial after him (Abu Daud and Tirmidhi).

941. Abu Hurairah relates that he heard the Holy Prophet say: When you pray over a dead body do it with the utmost sincerity (Abu Daud).

942. Abu Hurairah relates that the Holy Prophet supplicated in a funeral Prayer: Allah, Thou art his Lord, and Thou didst create him and guide him to Islam, and Thou hast taken possession of his soul, and Thou knowest well his secret and overt acts. We have approached Thee interceding for him. Do Thou forgive him (Abu Daud).

943. Wathilah ibn Asqa'a relates: The Holy Prophet conducted the funeral prayer of a deceased Muslim when we were also of the company, and I heard him supplicate: Allah, So and So, son of So and So is under Thy protection and is a follower of Thy commandments, do Thou shield him from the torment of the grave and the torment of the Fire, Thou dost keep faith and art worthy of all praise. Allah, do forgive him and have mercy on him. Indeed Thou art the Most Forgiving, the Ever Merciful (Abu Daud).

944. Of Abdullah ibn Aufa it is related that in conducting the funeral prayer of his daughter he called four *takbirs* and after the fourth *takbir* he continued standing for the space of time between two *takbirs* seeking forgiveness for her and praying for her. When he finished he said: The Holy Prophet used to do like this. Another version is: He called four *takbirs* and remained standing in prayer for a while till I imagined he would call a fifth *takbir*. Then he saluted to the right and the left. When he came away we asked him: How was this? He answered: I would add nothing to that which I saw the Holy Prophet do; or, he said: Thus did the Holy Prophet (Hakim).

157.
On Speedy Burial

945. Abu Hurairah relates that the Holy Prophet said: Prepare a funeral briskly; for should the deceased be righteous you would speed him towards good and should he be otherwise you would be laying aside evil from your necks (Bokhari and Muslim).

946. This *hadith* is the same as No. 447.

158.
On Speedy Payment of the Debts of a Deceased Person

947. Abu Hurairah relates that the Holy Prophet said: The soul of a deceased believer is held back on account of his debt till the debt is discharged (Tirmidhi).

948. Husain ibn Wuhuh relates that Talha ibn Bra'a ibn Hazib fell ill and the Holy Prophet came to inquire after him. After he had seen him he said: I conceive that Talha's end is near. Let me know when it comes and prepare his funeral quickly for it is not fitting that the corpse of a Muslim should be detained among his family (Abu Daud).

159.
On Admonition in a Graveyard

949. Ali relates: We were in Baqi'ah cemetery with a funeral when the Holy Prophet came and sat down and we gathered round him. He had a pointed stick in his hand. He bent down and began to scrape the ground with his stick. Then he said: Everyone of you has his place determined in the Fire or in Paradise. He was asked: Messenger of Allah, shall we then rest content with that which has been determined for each of us? He answered: Go on striving. For everyone that has been made easy which has been created for him (Bokhari and Muslim).

160.
On Praying for the Deceased after Burial

950. Uthman ibn Affan relates that after the burial of a deceased person the Holy Prophet would stop for a while and urge: Seek forgiveness for your brother and pray for steadfastness for him, for he is now being questioned (Abu Daud).

951. This *hadith* is part of No. 714.

161.
On Giving of Alms on behalf of a Deceased Person

Allah, the Exalted, has said:

278.   They supplicate: Lord, forgive us and our brethren who preceded us in the faith (59.11).

952. Ayesha relates that a man said to the Holy Prophet: My mother has died suddenly. I believe that if she could have spoken she would have given away something in charity. Would it count as meritorious on her part if I were to give away something in charity on her behalf? He answered: Yes (Bokhari and Muslim).

953. Abu Hurairah relates that the Holy Prophet said: When a person dies his actions come to an end except in respect of three matters that he leaves behind: a continuing charity, knowledge from which benefit could be derived and righteous issue who pray for him (Muslim).

162.
On Praise of a Deceased Person

954. Anas relates that some companions of the Holy Prophet passed a funeral and praised the person who had died, upon which the Holy Prophet said: It has become incumbent. Then they passed another funeral and spoke ill of the person who had died and the Holy Prophet said: It has become incumbent. Umar ibn Khattab inquired from the Holy Prophet; What has become incumbent? He answered: That one you praised and Paradise became incumbent for him, and of the other you spoke ill and the Fire became incumbent for him. You are the witnesses of Allah upon the earth (Bokhari and Muslim).

955. Abu Aswad relates: I came to Medina and was sitting with Umar ibn Khattab when a funeral passed and those present praised the goodness of the deceased. On this Umar said: It has become incumbent. Then another funeral passed and those present praised the goodness of the deceased. Again Umar said: It has become incumbent. Then a third funeral passed and those present condemned the vileness of the deceased. This time also Umar said: It has become incumbent. On this I inquired: Commander of the Faithful, what is it that has become incumbent? He answered: I said only that which the Holy Prophet had said. He said: Allah will admit into Paradise any Muslim whose goodness is attested to by four people. We asked: Should there be only three? He answered: Even if there should be only three. Then we asked: Should there be only two? He answered: Even if there should be only two. We refrained from asking him about one (Bokhari).

163.
On the Good Fortune of one who loses Small Children

956. Anas relates that the Holy Prophet said: When a Muslim dies three of whose children had died before attaining puberty Allah will admit him to Paradise by His grace having mercy on them (Bokhari and Muslim).

957. Abu Hurairah relates that the Holy Prophet said: A Muslim, three of whose children die, will not be touched by the Fire, except symbolically (Bokhari and Muslim).

958. Abu Sa'id Khudri relates that a woman came to the Holy Prophet and said: Messenger of Allah, the men relate that which they hear from you, then appoint for us also a day when we could come to you to learn from you that which Allah has taught you. He said: Get together on such and such a day. They gathered together and the Holy Prophet taught them out of that which Allah had taught him and then said: Any of you who loses three children will be shielded by them from the Fire. One of the women asked: And should there be two. He answered: Even if there should be two (Bokhari and Muslim).

164.
On Weeping and Trembling over the Remains of Wrongdoers

959. Ibn Umar relates that when the Holy Prophet reached Hijr, the land of Thamud, he admonished his companions: Do not pass by these tormented ones, except with running eyes, and should you be dry-eyed do not pass near them, lest that should afflict you which afflicted them (Bokhari and Muslim). Another version is: When the Holy Prophet passed by Hijr, he admonished his companions: Do not enter the dwelling-places of those who had wronged themselves except with running eyes lest that should afflict you which afflicted them. Then he covered up his head and hastened the pace of his mount till he had emerged from the valley.

165.

On Setting Out on a Journey

960. This *hadith* is part of No. 21.

961. Sakhar ibn Wada'a Ghamidi relates that the Holy Prophet supplicated: Allah, bless the mornings of my people. Whenever he despatched a scouting party or an army he despatched it in the first part of the day. Sakhar was a merchant. He always despatched his goods in the early part of the day. His commerce flourished and his wealth increased (Abu Daud and Tirmidhi).

166.

On Travelling in Company under a Leader

962. Ibn Umar relates that the Holy Prophet said: If people knew that which I know of the hazards of travelling alone no rider would set forth on a journey alone at night (Bokhari).

963. Amr ibn Shuaib relates on the authority of his father and grandfather that the Holy Prophet said: One rider is a satan, two riders are two satans and three riders are a caravan (Abu Daud, Tirmidhi and Nisai).

964. Abu Sa'id Khudri and Abu Hurairah relate that the Holy Prophet said: When three people set out on a journey they should appoint one of themselves as leader (Abu Daud).

965. Ibn Abbas relates that the Holy Prophet said: The best company is four, the best scouting party is four hundred and the best army is four thousand; and an army of twelve thousand will not be vanquished for want of numbers (Abu Daud and Tirmidhi).

167.

On the Rules of Journeying

966. Abu Hurairah relates that the Holy Prophet said: When you travel through fertile land give the camels their share from the land and when you travel through barren land hasten your pace and thus husband their strength; and when you make camp for the night leave the track alone for it is also the track of the beasts and of insects during the night (Muslim).

967. Abu Qatadah relates that when in the course of a journey the Holy Prophet made camp in the latter part of the night he would lie down on his right side, and when he made camp a short while before dawn he would stretch out and raising his arm would rest his head on his palm (Muslim).

968.   Anas relates that the Holy Prophet said: You should make it a rule to travel by night for the earth is folded during the night (Abu Daud).

969.   Abu Tha'labah Khushini relates that on making camp people would scatter among dunes and valleys till the Holy Prophet said: Your dispersing among these dunes and valleys is from Satan. Thereafter when they made camp they kept close to one another (Abu Daud).

970.   Sa'ad ibn Amr relates that the Holy Prophet passed by a camel whose belly was sticking to his back whereupon he said: Be mindful of your duty to Allah in respect of these dumb animals. Ride them while they are in good condition and slaughter them and eat their meat when they are in good condition (Abu Daud).

971.   Abdullah ibn Ja'afar relates: The Holy Prophet made me ride pillion with him one day and confided something to me which I shall never disclose to anyone. I pride myself that he did not screen himself from me behind a wall or the trunk of a date palm. To this Barqani has added: Then the Holy Prophet entered a garden belonging to an Ansari and saw therein a camel which, when it perceived his presence, groaned and its eyes began to run. The Holy Prophet approached it and patted it on the hump and the base of its head; and inquired: Who is the owner of this camel? To whom does it belong? An Ansari youth came forward and said: Messenger of Allah, it is mine. He said: Do you not fear Allah in the matter of these beasts of which He has made you owner? This camel complains to me that you starve it and work it hard (Abu Daud).

972.   Anas relates: When we made camp we unsaddled our beasts before saying our Prayers.

168.

On Helping a Companion

973.   This *hadith* is the same as No. 569.

974.   Jabir relates that when he was preparing for an expedition the Holy Prophet addressed us: O ye company of Emigrants and Helpers, there are among you people who have no money and no kinsfolk, then let every one of you associate with himself two or three of them for there is nothing for it but that everyone should ride a mount one by one in turn. So I associated two or three with me and I rode my camel turn by turn equally with them (Abu Daud).

975.   Jabir relates that the Holy Prophet always brought up the rear so as to help drive the weaker animals faster, to give a lift to pedestrians and to pray for them (Abu Daud).

169.

On Supplication when Starting on a Journey

Allah, the Exalted, has said:

279. He has made for you vessels and beasts whereon you ride, that you may settle yourselves firmly on their backs and when you are securely seated thereon you may remember the favour of your Lord and say: Holy is He who has subjected this to us, while we had not the strength to subdue it by ourselves. To our Lord surely shall we return (43.13-15).

976. Ibn Umar relates that when the Holy Prophet mounted his camel to set out on a journey he would recite: Allah is Great; three times, and would supplicate: Holy is He Who has subjected this to us while we had not the strength to subdue it ourselves. To our Lord surely shall we return. Allah, we beseech Thee for virtue and righteousness and such action during this journey as would please Thee. Allah make this journey easy for us and fold up its length for us. Allah, Thou art the Companion in this journey and the Guardian of those we leave behind. Allah, I seek Thy protection from the hardships of the journey and that I should encounter anything grievous on my return respecting my property or my family or my children. On his return he would repeat the supplication and would add: We return in safety, turning to our Lord, worshipping Him and praising Him (Muslim).

977. Abdullah ibn Sarjis relates that when the Holy Prophet set out on a journey he supplicated seeking Allah's protection against the hardships of the journey, and the encountering of anything grievous on return, and incurring any loss after gain, and the plaint of a wronged one, and witnessing anything disagreeable concerning property or family (Muslim).

978. Ali ibn Rabi'a relates: I was with Ali ibn Abu Talib when a mount was brought to him. When he put his foot in the stirrup he said: In the name of Allah; and when he had settled himself on its back he affirmed: Holy is He Who has subjected this to us, while we had not the strength to subdue it by ourselves. To our Lord surely shall we return (43. 14,15). Then he affirmed three times: All praise is due to Allah; and then he affirmed three times: Allah is Great; and then he affirmed: Holy art Thou. I have wronged my soul, do Thou forgive me, for none forgives sins save Thyself; and then he laughed. He was asked: Commander of the Faithful, why did you laugh? He answered: I saw the Holy Prophet do as I have done and then he laughed; and I asked him: Messenger of Allah, why did you laugh? And he answered me: Your Lord, Holy is He, is pleased with His servant when he says forgive me my sins knowing that there is none beside Me who can forgive sins (Abu Daud and Tirmidhi).

170.

On Glorification while Climbing and Descending

979. Jabir relates: When we climbed a height we proclaimed: Allah is Great; and when we descended from a height we proclaimed Holy is Allah (Bokhari).

980. Ibn Umar relates that when the Holy Prophet and his forces climbed a height they proclaimed: Allah is Great; and when they descended they proclaimed: Holy is Allah (Abu Daud).

981. Ibn Umar relates that when the Holy Prophet returned from Hajj or Umra, wherever he climbed a height he repeated: Allah is Great, three times, and would then proclaim: There is none worthy of worship save Allah, the One, without associate. His is the Kingdom and His the praise, and He has power over all things. We return in safety, turning to our Lord, worshipping Him, prostrating ourselves before Him and praising Him. Allah has fulfilled His promise. He has helped His servant and has alone vanquished the hosts (Bokhari and Muslim). Muslim adds: When he returned from a battle or an expedition or Hajj or Umra.

982. Abu Hurairah relates that a person said to the Holy Prophet: Messenger of Allah, I intend to proceed on a journey; will you advise me? He told him: Adhere to righteousness, and whenever you climb a height proclaim: Allah is Great. When the man turned to go, the Holy Prophet supplicated: Allah, fold up the distance for him and make his journey easy for him (Tirmidhi).

983. Abu Musa Ash'ari relates: We were with the Holy Prophet on a journey and when we scaled a height we would proclaim aloud: There is none worthy of worship save Allah; and: Allah is Great! The Holy Prophet admonished us: O people, take it easy. He on whom you call is not deaf or absent. He is with you; Hearing, Nigh (Bokhari and Muslim).

171.

On the Supplication of a Traveller

984. Abu Hurairah relates that the Holy Prophet said: Three supplications are assured of acceptance without a doubt: the plaint of a wronged one; the prayer of a traveller; and the prayer of a father for his child, (Abu Daud and Tirmidhi).

172.

On Supplication against Apprehended Mischief

985. Abu Musa Ash'ari relates that when the Holy Prophet apprehended mischief from a people, he supplicated: Allah, we confront them with Thee and seek Thy protection against their mischief.

173.
On Supplication on Arrival

986. Khaulah bint Hakim relates that she heard the Holy Prophet say: He who arrives at the goal of his journey and supplicates: I seek the protection of Allah's perfect words against the mischief of that which He has created; will suffer no harm from anything till he marches away from that place (Muslim).

987. Ibn Umar relates that when during a journey the Holy Prophet was overtaken by night he would say: O earth, Allah is my Lord and thy Lord. I seek Allah's protection from thy evil, and the evil of that which is in thee, and the evil of that which is created in thee, and the evil of that which moves about on thee; and I seek His protection against the mischief of a lion, a black serpent, every kind of snake, a scorpion, dwellers of towns, the breeder and the born (Abu Daud).

174.
On Speedy Return from a Journey

988. Abu Hurairah relates that the Holy Prophet said: A journey is a torment. It deprives a person of food, drink and sleep. When you have accomplished the purpose of a journey you should return home quickly (Bokhari and Muslim).

175.
On Returning Home by Day

989. Jabir relates that the Holy Prophet said: When any of you has been away from home for a period, he should not return home at night. Another version is that the Holy Prophet forbade a person returning home by night (Bokhari and Muslim).

990. Anas relates that the Holy Prophet would not return home from a journey by night. He came home during the morning or the afternoon (Bokhari and Muslim).

176.
On Glorification on Returning Home

991. Anas relates: We returned from a journey with the Holy Prophet and when Medina came into view he began to repeat: We are returning safe, turning to our Lord, worshipping Him and praising Him; and he kept it up till we entered the town (Muslim).

177.
On Proceeding to the Mosque on Return

992. Ka'ab ibn Malik relates that when the Holy Prophet returned from a journey he proceeded straight to the mosque and offered two *raka'as* of voluntary Prayer (Bokhari and Muslim).

178.
On a Woman being Prohibited from Travelling Alone

993. Abu Hurairah relates that the Holy Prophet said: It is not permissible for a woman that she should travel for a day and a night unless she is accompanied by someone related to her within the prohibited degrees (Bokhari and Muslim).

994. Ibn Abbas relates that he heard the Holy Prophet say: No man should be in the company of a woman unless there is present someone who is related to her within the prohibited degrees, nor should she travel save in the company of such a relative. Someone asked him: Messenger of Allah, my wife is about to set out for Hajj and my name has been put down for such and such expedition. He told him: Go and perform the Hajj with your wife (Bokhari and Muslim).

179.
On the Excellence of Reading the Quran

995. Abu Umamah relates that he heard the Holy Prophet say: Keep reading the Quran for it will intercede for its readers on the Day of Judgment (Muslim).

996. Nawas ibn Sama'an relates that he heard the Holy Prophet say: The Quran will be summoned on the Day of Judgment along with those who kept it company in this life and acted in conformity with it. It will be heralded by the second and third chapters and these will plead on behalf of those who kept company with them (Muslim).

997. Uthman ibn Affan relates that the Holy Prophet said: The best of you are those who learn the Quran and teach it (Bokhari).

998. Ayesha relates that the Holy Prophet said: He who recites the Quran fluently will be in the company of the noble and virtuous; and he who recites the Quran haltingly and with difficulty will have a double reward (Bokhari and Muslim).

999. Abu Musa Ash'ari relates that the Holy Prophet said: The case of a believer who recites the Quran is that of fruit which is fragrant and delicious;

and the case of a believer who does not recite the Quran is that of fruit which has no fragrance but is sweet to the taste; and the case of a hypocrite who recites the Quran is that of fruit which is fragrant but tastes bitter; and the case of a hypocrite who does not recite the Quran is that of fruit which has no fragrance and tastes bitter (Bokhari and Muslim).

1000. Umar ibn Khattab relates that the Holy Prophet said: Allah will exalt many people through this Book, and will abase many because of it (Muslim).

1001. This *hadith* is the same as No. 575.

1002. Bra'a ibn 'Azib relates that a person was reciting *sura* Al-Kahf (Chapter 18) while his horse was close to him secured by two ropes. A cloud spread over the horse and advanced towards it whereupon it began to frolic. In the morning the man came to the Holy Prophet and mentioned the incident to him. He said: This was comfort that descended by virtue of the recitation of the Quran (Bokhari and Muslim).

1003. Ibn Mas'ud relates that the Holy Prohet said that when a person recites one letter from the Book of Allah that is one good deed equal to ten good deeds the like of it. I do not say that ALM is a letter, but A is a letter, L is a letter and M is a letter (Tirmidhi).

1004. Ibn Abbas relates that the Holy Prophet said: He in whose heart there is nothing of the Quran is like a house in ruin (Tirmidhi).

1005. Abdullah ibn Amr ibn 'As relates that the Holy Prophet said: One who is given to reciting the Quran will be told on the Day of Judgment: Go on reciting and ascending, and recite slowly as was thy wont in life, for thy station, will be where the last verse of thy recitation will end (Abu Daud and Tirmidhi).

180.

On Safeguarding the Quran

1006. Abu Musa relates that the Holy Prophet said: Safeguard the Quran in your memories, for by Him in Whose hands is the life of Muhammad, it escapes sooner from memory than does a camel from its rope (Bokhari and Muslim).

1007. Ibn Umar relates that the Holy Prophet said: The case of one who has the Quran by heart is like that of one who has a camel secured by a rope. If he watches it, he retains it; and if he neglects it, it wanders away (Bokhari and Muslim).

181.

On Good Recitation of the Quran

1008. Abu Hurairah relates that he heard the Holy Prophet say: Allah does not lend ear so joyously to anything as he does to the recitation of the Quran by a

Prophet who has a beautiful voice and recites well and audibly (Bokhari and Muslim).

1009. Abu Musa Ash'ari relates that the Holy Prophet said to him: You have been granted one of the tunes of David (Bokhari and Muslim). Muslim has added: I wish you could have seen me when I was listening to your recitation last night.

1010. Bra'a ibn 'Azib relates: I heard the Holy Prophet recite *sura* Al-Tin (Chapter 95) during the evening service. I have never heard anyone recite in a more beautiful voice than his (Bokhari and Muslim).

1011. Bashir ibn Abd al-Munzir relates that the Holy Prophet said: He who does not recite the Quran tunefully is not one of us (Abu Daud).

1012. This *hadith* is the same as No. 449.

182.
On Special Chapters and Verses

1013. Abu Sa'id Rafi' relates: The Holy Prophet said to me: Shall I tell you before you go out of the mosque which is the greatest chapter of the Quran? and he took hold of my hand. When we were about to issue from the mosque I said to him: Messenger of Allah, you had said you would tell me which is the greatest chapter of the Quran. He answered: The opening chapter which contains the seven oft-repeated verses and the Great Quran which has been bestowed upon me (Bokhari).

1014. Abu Sa'id Khudri relates that the Holy Prophet said concerning the recitation of *sura* Al-Ikhlas (Chapter 112): By Him in Whose hands is my life, it is equal to the recitation of one third of the Quran. Another version is: The Holy Prophet inquired from his companions: Would any of you find it burdensome to recite one third of the Quran in the course of a night? They considered it difficult and said: Which of us would have the strength to do that, Messenger of Allah? He said: *sura* Al-Ikhlas is one third of the Quran (Bokhari).

1015. Abu Sa'id Khudri relates that a man heard another recite *sura* Al-Ikhlas repeatedly. In the morning he came to the Holy Prophet and mentioned this to him belittling it. The Holy Prophet said to him: By Him in Whose hands is my life, it is equal to one third of the Quran (Bokhari).

1016. Abu Hurairah relates that the Holy Prophet said that the *sura* Al-Ikhlas (Chapter 112) equals one third of the Quran (Muslim).

1017. Anas relates that a man said to the Holy Prophet: Messenger of Allah, I love *sura* Al-Ikhlas. He told him: Love of it will admit you to Paradise (Tirmidhi).

1018. Uqbah ibn 'Amir relates that the Holy Prophet said: Know you not that last night certain verses were revealed the like of which has never been known; *sura* Al-Falaq and *sura* Al-Nas (Chapters 113 and 114) (Muslim).

1019. Abu Sa'id Khudri relates that the Holy Prophet used to seek protection against the *jinn* and the evil eye till *suras* Al-Falaq and Al-Nas were revealed. After they were revealed he took to them and discarded everything beside them (Tirmidhi).

1020. Abu Hurairah relates that the Holy Prophet said: There is a *sura* in the Quran comprising thirty verses which continued its intercession on behalf of a man till he was forgiven. It is *sura* Al-Mulk (Chapter 67) (Abu Daud and Tirmidhi).

1021. Abu Mas'ud Badri relates that the Holy Prophet said: If a person recites the last two verses of *sura* Al-Baqarah at night, they suffice him (Bokhari and Muslim).

1022. Abu Hurairah relates that the Holy Prophet admonished: Do not convert your houses into graves. Indeed, Satan runs away from a house in which *sura* Al-Baqarah is recited (Muslim).

1023. Ubayy ibn Ka'ab relates: The Holy Prophet asked me: Abu Mundhir, do you know which verse of the Book of Allah is the grandest? I answered: the verse of the *Kursi* (2.256). He poked me in the chest and said: Felicitations on your knowledge, Abu Mundhir (Muslim).

1024. Abu Hurairah relates: The Holy Prophet had appointed me to watch over the Sadqa Fitr (alms given on the occasion of the Festival at the end of Ramadhan) and during the night one sneaked up and started stealing from the alms and I caught hold of him and said: I will take you to the Holy Prophet; but he pleaded: I am in need and I have a large family and we are in sore distress. So I let him go. Next morning the Holy Prophet asked me: Abu Hurairah, what did your prisoner do last night? I answered: Messenger of Allah, he pleaded his need and that of his family, so I took pity on him and let him go. The Holy Prophet said: He told you a lie and will return. So I realized that he would come back as the Holy Prophet had said and I kept watching for him. He sneaked up again and started taking from the alms and I said to him: I shall take you to the Holy Prophet. He pleaded: I am in need and have a large family; let me go and I shall not come back. So I took pity on him and let him go. Next morning the Holy Prophet said to me: Abu Hurairah, how did your prisoner of last night behave? I answered: Messenger of Allah, he pleaded his need and that of his family and I took pity on him and let him go. He said: He told you a lie and will come back again. So I watched for him a third time. He sneaked up to steal from the alms when I caught him and said: I shall take you to the Holy Prophet and this is the last of the three times you promised that you will not come back and you came back. He pleaded: Let me go, and I will tell you some phrases which will be of benefit to you before Allah. I asked him: What are they? He answered: When you go to bed recite the verse of the Chair (2. 256) for it will be a guardian over you on behalf of Allah and Satan will not be able to approach you till morning. So I let him go. Next morning the Holy Prophet asked me: How did your prisoner behave last night? And I answered: Messenger of Allah, he said he would teach me some phrases which would be of benefit to me before Allah. So I let him go. He asked: What are those phrases? I answered: He said to me: When you go to bed recite the verse of the Chair from its beginning to its end and told me that this would guard me on behalf of Allah and Satan would not be able to approach me till the morning. The Holy Prophet observed: This time he told you the truth and yet he is a liar. Abu Hurairah, do you realise who was speaking to you during these three nights? I answered: No. The Holy Prophet answered: It was Satan (Bokhari).

1025. Abu Darda' relates that the Holy Prophet said: He who commits to memory the first ten verses of *sura* Al-Kahf (Chapter 18) will be secure against Anti-Christ. One version is: the last ten verses of *sura* Al-Kahf (Muslim).

1026. Ibn Abbas relates: While Gabriel was sitting with the Holy Prophet a sound was heard from above and Gabriel raised his head and said: A door has been opened from heaven which had not been opened up to this day. Then an angel descended from it and Gabriel said: This angel has descended to the earth and had not descended before till this day. He saluted the Holy Prophet and said: Be glad of the two lights that have been bestowed upon you which had not been bestowed upon any Prophet before you: The opening chapter of the Book and the last verses of *sura* Al-Baqarah (Chapter 2). Whenever you recite even a word of this it will be bestowed upon you (Muslim).

183.

On Gathering together for Recitation of the Quran

1027. Abu Hurairah relates that the Holy Prophet said: Whenever people gather together in one of the houses of Allah for recitation of the Quran and teaching it to one another, comfort descends upon them, mercy covers them, angels spread their wings over them and Allah makes mention of them to those around Him (Muslim).

184.

On the Excellence of Ablutions

Allah, the Exalted, has said:

280. O ye who believe, when you make ready for Prayer, wash your faces and your hands up to the elbows, and pass your wet hands over your heads, and wash your feet up to the ankles. Should you have consorted with your spouses, purify yourselves by bathing. Should you be ill or on a journey, or

one of you comes from the privy, or you have consorted with
your spouses and you find not water, then have recourse to
pure dust and having placed your hands on it pass them over
your faces and forearms. Allah desires not to put you in a
difficulty, but desires to purify you and to complete His
favour unto you that you may be grateful (5.7).

1028. Abu Hurairah relates that he heard the Holy Prophet say: My people
will be called on the Day of Judgment bright faced, white-limbed, from the
effects of their ablutions; then whoever of you can afford to extend his brightness
let him do so (Bokhari and Muslim).

1029. Abu Hurairah relates: I heard my friend say: The adornment of a
believer in Paradise will reach as far as the water with which he performs his
ablutions reaches (Muslim).

1030. Usman ibn Affan relates: The Holy Prophet said: He who makes his
ablutions carefully will find that his defaults depart from his body, even from
below his nails (Muslim).

1031. Usman ibn Affan relates: I saw the Holy Prophet perform his
ablutions as I do mine and said: One who performs his ablutions in this fashion
will have his past sins forgiven him, and his walking to the mosque and his Prayer
will earn extra merit (Muslim).

1032. This *hadith* is the same as No. 129.

1033. Abu Hurairah relates that the Holy Prophet came to the cemetery
and said: Peace be on you dwellers in the home of a believing people. We shall join
you, if Allah so wills. I would have loved to have had a view of our brethren.
Someone of those present inquired: Are we not your brethren, Messenger of
Allah? He answered: You are my companions. Our brethren are those who have
not yet arrived in this world. He was asked: How will you recognise those of your
followers, Messenger of Allah, who have not yet arrived? He answered: Tell me;
if a man has horses with white foreheads and white fetlocks and they are mixed
with pure black horses, will he not be able to recognise his own? They answered:
Certainly, Messenger of Allah. He said: Well, then, my people will come bright
faced, white-limbed from the effects of their ablutions; and I shall arrive at the
Reservoir of Abundance ahead of them (Muslim).

1034. This *hadith* is the same as No. 131.

1035. This *hadith* is the first part of No. 25.

1036. Umar ibn Khattab relates that the Holy Prophet said: Everyone of
you who performs his ablutions carefully and then affirms: I bear witness that
there is none worthy of worship save Allah, the One, without associate; and I bear
witness that Muhammad is His Servant and Messenger; will find all eight gates of
Paradise open for him. He can enter by whichever he prefers (Muslim). Tirmidhi
adds: and supplicates: Allah, make me of those who turn to Thee in repentance
and make me of those who purify themselves.

185.
On the Excellence of Azan

1037. Abu Hurairah relates that the Holy Prophet said: If people realised the beneficence of calling the *Azan* and standing in the first row for Prayer and they could secure these privileges only through drawing lots they would draw lots for them; and if they knew the merit of coming early to Prayer they would vie with each other in hastening to it; and if they appreciated the value of the dawn and evening Prayers they would come to them even if they had to crawl on all fours (Bokhari and Muslim).

1038. Mu'awiah relates that he heard the Holy Prophet say: The *muezzins* (those who call the *Azan*) will have the longest necks (i.e. will be the most exalted) on the Day of Judgment (Muslim).

1039. Abdullah ibn Abdur Rahman ibn Abi Sa'as'ah relates that Abu Sa'id Khudri said to him: I notice that you are fond of goats and the desert. When you are among your goats in the desert and call the *Azan* raise your voice for whoever of the *jinn* and men and whatever hears the farthest sound of the voice of the *muezzin* shall bear witness to it on the Day of Judgment. This I heard from the Holy Prophet (Bokhari).

1040. Abu Hurairah relates that the Holy Prophet said: When the *Azan* is called Satan turns his back on it and rushes away exploding so that he does not hear the words of the call. When the call is finished he comes back till the *iqamah* is called, when he runs away again and returns when that is finished and begins to distract the minds of the worshippers, whispering: Think of this, recall that; matters which the worshipper had not previously in mind, till he does not know how much he has prayed (Bokhari and Muslim).

1041. Abdullah ibn Amr ibn 'As relates that he heard the Holy Prophet say: When you hear the *Azan* repeat after the *muezzin* what he says, then call down Allah's blessings on me, for whoever calls down blessings on me Allah sends down blessings on him ten times in return, then beg of Allah for me *wasilah*, which is a station in Paradise of which only one of all the servants of Allah will be held worthy and I am hoping that I shall be that one. Whoever begs *wasilah* for me it becomes incumbent upon me to intercede for him (Muslim).

1042. Abu Sa'id Khudri relates that the Holy Prophet said: When you hear the *Azan*, repeat after the *muezzin* what he says (Bokhari and Muslim).

1043. Jabir relates that the Holy Prophet said: For him who after hearing the *Azan* supplicates: Allah, Lord of this perfect call and of the Prayer about to be performed, bestow on Muhammad *wasilah* and exaltation and raise him to the praiseworthy station that Thou hast promised him; it becomes incumbent upon me to intercede on the Day of Judgment (Bokhari).

1044. Sa'ad ibn Abi Waqqas relates that the Holy Prophet said: He who after hearing the *Azan* affirms: I bear witness that there is none worthy of worship save Allah, the One, without associate and that Muhammad is His Servant and Messenger; I am pleased with Allah as my Lord, with Muhammad as His

Messenger and with Islam as my faith; will have his sins forgiven (Muslim).

1045. Anas relates that the Holy Prophet said: A supplication made between the *Azan* and *Iqamah* is not rejected (Abu Daud and Tirmidhi).

186.
On the Excellence of the Salat

Allah, the Exalted, has said:

281. Prayer shields a votary against indecency and misbehaviour (29.46).

1046. Abu Hurairah relates that he heard the Holy Prophet say: Tell me if one of you had a stream running at his door and he should take a bath in it five times every day would any dirt be left upon him? He was answered: No dirt would be left on him. The Holy Prophet observed: This is the case of the five Prayers. Allah wipes out all faults in consequence of them (Bokhari and Muslim).

1047. This *hadith* is the same as No. 432.

1048. This *hadith* is the same as No. 437.

1049. This *hadith* is the same as No. 130.

1050. Uthman ibn Affan relates that he heard the Holy Prophet say: For every Muslim who on the approach of the time of a prescribed Prayer makes his ablutions carefully and thereafter bows and prostrates himself in Prayer with humility, this serves as atonement for his past sins so long as he avoids major ones; and this is for always (Muslim).

187.
On the Excellence of the Dawn and Afternoon Prayers

1051. Abu Musa relates that the Holy Prophet said: He who is constant in the dawn and afternoon Prayers will enter Paradise (Bokhari and Muslim).

1052. Abu Zuhair Umarah ibn Ruwaibah relates that he heard the Holy Prophet say: He who is constant in the Prayer before sunrise and the Prayer before sunset will not enter the Fire (Muslim).

1053. This *hadith* is the same as No. 392.

1054. Abu Hurairah relates that the Holy Prophet said: A succession of angels visits you during the night and also during the day and they get together during the dawn Prayer and the afternoon Prayer. Then those of them who had spent the night among you ascend to heaven and Allah inquires from them (though He knows better than they): What conditions did you leave My servants in? They answer: They were praying when we came to them and they were praying when we left them (Bokhari and Muslim).

1055. Jarir ibn Abdullah Bajali relates: We were with the Holy Prophet one night when the moon was full. He looked at it and said: You will surely behold your Lord as you are beholding this moon without any perturbation. If you can so manage that you should not neglect the Prayer before sunrise and the Prayer before sunset, do it (Bokhari and Muslim).

1056. Buraidah relates that the Holy Prophet said: He who misses the afternoon Prayer renders his works vain (Bokhari).

188.
On the Excellence of Walking to the Mosque

1057. Abu Hurairah relates that the Holy Prophet said: For him who proceeds to the mosque, morning or evening, Allah prepares an entertainment in Paradise every time he proceeds, morning or evening (Bokhari and Muslim).

1058. Abu Hurairah relates that the Holy Prophet said: He who makes his ablutions at home and then walks to one of the houses of Allah to discharge an obligation imposed on him by Allah, one step of his wipes out a sin and another step raises his status (Muslim).

1059. This *hadith* is the same as No. 137.

1060. This *hadith* is the same as No. 136.

1061. Abu Musa relates that the Holy Prophet said: The person whose Prayer brings him the highest reward is the one who walks farthest to it; and he who waits so that he might say his Prayer in congregation has a higher reward than one who says it alone and goes to bed (Bokhari and Muslim).

1062. Buraidah relates that the Holy Prophet said: To those who walk to the mosque in dark nights give glad tidings of full light on the Day of Judgment (Abu Daud and Tirmidhi).

1063. This *hadith* is the same as No. 131.

1064. Abu Sa'id Khudri relates that the Holy Prophet said: When you see a person frequenting the mosque, bear witness to his faith, for Allah, the Lord of honour and glory has said: He alone can service the mosques of Allah who believes in Allah and the Last Day (9.18) (Tirmidhi).

189.
On the Excellence of Waiting for Prayer

1065. Abu Hurairah relates that the Holy Prophet said: So long as you continue in the mosque for the purpose of Prayer and are not able to return home solely because of Prayer you will be deemed to be occupied in Prayer (Bokhari and Muslim).

1066. Abu Hurairah relates that the Holy Prophet said: The angels call down blessings on everyone of you who continues in his place of Prayer in a state of purity after the Prayer is finished, saying: Allah, forgive him; Allah have mercy on him (Bokhari).

1067. Anas relates that on one occasion the Holy Prophet was delayed coming to the mosque for the evening Prayer till midnight. After the Prayer finished he turned to us and said: Some people said their Prayer and went and slept, but you who waited were accounted as if you were occupied with Prayer throughout (Bokhari).

190.

On the Excellence of Congregational Prayer

1068. Ibn Umar relates that the Holy Prophet said: Prayer with the congregation is twenty seven times more beneficent than Prayer performed by oneself (Bokhari and Muslim).

1069. Abu Hurairah relates that the Holy Prophet said: The Prayer of a person with the congregation is twenty five times more beneficent than his Prayer at home or in his shop, and that is because when he performs his ablutions carefully and then proceeds to the mosque for the sole purpose of the Prayer, every step that he takes raises his status and wipes out his sin. While he is in his place of Prayer in a state of purity the angels keep calling down blessings on him saying: Allah, send down blessings on him; Allah, have mercy on him. He is deemed to be occupied in Prayer while he waits for it (Bokhari and Muslim).

1070. Abu Hurairah relates that a blind person came to the Holy Prophet and submitted: Messenger of Allah, I have no one to guide me to the mosque; and he asked his permission that he might say his Prayers at home. The Holy Prophet gave him leave but as soon as he turned away the Holy Prophet called him and asked him: Can you hear the call to Prayer? He answered: Yes. The Holy Prophet said: Then respond to it (Muslim).

1071. Ibn Umm Maktum relates that he said to the Holy Prophet: Messenger of Allah, Medina abounds in reptiles and wild beasts and being blind I cannot see my way to the mosque. He said: If you can hear the words of the call: Come to Prayer; Come to Salvation; then respond to them (Abu Daud).

1072. Abu Hurairah relates that the Holy Prophet said: By Him in Whose hands is my life, I have sometimes thought that I would ask for fuel to be collected and the *Azan* to be called, and would appoint someone to lead the Prayer and then go to those who absent themselves from Prayer and set fire to their houses before their eyes (Bokhari and Muslim).

1073. Ibn Mas'ud said: He who would love to meet Allah tomorrow in a state of obedience to His will should take care of these Prayers when he is summoned for them. Allah has expounded to your Prophet the ways of guidance and these Prayers are a part of them. If you were to say these Prayers at home as does this laggard you would depart from the way of your Prophet, and if you depart from it you would have gone astray. I have known a time when only a confirmed hypocrite would stay away from them. Some of us were brought to the mosque supported between two men till they reached their place in the row (Muslim). Another version is: The Messenger of Allah taught us the ways of guidance, and part of them is Prayer in the mosque from which the *Azan* is called.

1074. Abu Darda' relates that he heard the Holy Prophet say: If there are three in a village or even in the desert and they do not join in Prayer, Satan would surely overcome them. So always gather together for Prayer, for a wolf would rend a solitary sheep (Abu Daud).

191.
On Urging joining the Dawn and Evening Prayers

1075. Uthman ibn Affan relates that he heard the Holy Prophet say: He who says the evening Prayer in congregation is as if he had spent half the night in voluntary Prayer, and he who says the dawn Prayer in congregation is as if he had spent the whole night in voluntary Prayer (Muslim). Tirmidhi's version is: He who says the evening Prayer in congregation is as if he had spent half the night in voluntary Prayer, and he who says the evening and dawn Prayers in congregation is as if he had spent the whole night in voluntary Prayer.

1076. This *hadith* is the same as No. 1037.

1077. Abu Hurairah relates that the Holy Prophet said: The hypocrites find no Prayer so burdensome as the dawn and evening Prayers and yet if they knew of their beneficence they would come to them even if they had to crawl on all fours (Bokhari and Muslim).

192.
On Safeguarding the Prescribed Prayers

Allah, the Exalted, has said:

282. Be watchful over Prayers, particularly over the Prayer the hour of which approaches when you are pre-occupied (2.239).

283. Then if they repent and observe Prayer and pay the Zakat, leave them alone (9.5).

1078. This *hadith* is the same as No. 314.

1079. Ibn Umar relates that the Holy Prophet said: Islam is based on five articles: Bearing witness that there is none worthy of worship save Allah and that Muhammad is the Messenger of Allah, observing Prayer, paying the *Zakat*, Pilgrimage to the House of Allah and observing the Fast of Ramadhan (Bokhari and Muslim).

1080.   This *hadith* is the same as No. 393.

1081.   This *hadith* is the same as No. 210.

1082.   Jabir relates that he heard the Holy Prophet say: Giving up Prayer is tantamount to disbelief and paganism (Muslim).

1083.   Buraidah relates that the Holy Prophet said: That which distinguishes us from the disbelievers and hypocrites is our commitment to Prayer. He who gives it up falls into disbelief (Tirmidhi).

1084.   Shaqiq ibn Abdullah relates that the companions of the Holy Prophet did not consider neglect of any obligation as mounting to disbelief except neglect of Prayer (Tirmidhi).

1085.   Abu Hurairah relates that the Holy Prophet said: The first item in respect of which a person would be called to account on the Day of Judgment will be Prayer. If that is found in order he would be successful and prosper, but if that is not in order he would be ruined and lost. In case of a shortcoming in his obligations the Lord of honour and glory will say: Look, if among the voluntary actions of My servant there is anything that would make up the shortcomings in respect of his obligations. All his obligations would be checked up in that manner (Tirmidhi).

193.
On the Excellence of the First Row

1086.   Jabir ibn Samurah relates: The Holy Prophet came up to us and said: Why do you not stand in rows as do the angels before their Lord? We inquired: Messenger of Allah, how do the angels range themselves before their Lord? He answered: They fill each row beginning with the first and stand close together (Muslim).

1087.   This *hadith* is the same as No. 1037.

1088. ˆ Abu Hurairah relates that the Holy Prophet said: The best rows of men in Prayer are the first ones and the worst are the last ones and the best rows of women in Prayer are the last ones and the worst are the first (Muslim).

1089.   Abu Sa'id Khudri relates that the Holy Prophet perceiving a tendency among his companions that they preferred to stand in back rows said to them: Come forward and be close to me and let those who come after be close to you. If a people begin to fall behind, Allah puts them behind (Muslim).

1090.   This *hadith* is the same as No. 352.

1091.   Anas relates that the Holy Prophet said: Keep your rows straight, for keeping them straight is part of the due observance of Prayer (Bokhari and Muslim).

1092. Anas relates: We stood up for Prayer and the Holy Prophet joining us said: Make your rows straight and stand shoulder to shoulder for I can observe you from the back of my head (Bokhari and Muslim). Bokhari adds: We used to stand shoulder to shoulder and foot to foot.

1093. This *hadith* is the same as No. 161.

1094. Bra'a ibn 'Azib relates: The Holy Prophet would pass between the rows from one end to the other putting our chests and shoulders in line, saying: Do not be out of line, else your hearts will be out of line; and would add: Allah and His angels send down blessings on the front rows (Abu Daud).

1095. Ibn Umar relates that the Holy Prophet said: Arrange your rows, shoulder to shoulder, closing your ranks, not pressing hard on the arms of your brethren but not leaving gaps for Satan. He who closes a gap in a row will be joined to Allah's mercy and he who breaks a row will be cut off from Allah's mercy (Abu Daud).

1096. Anas relates that the Holy Prophet directed: Close your ranks, do not make them wide spaced and put your necks in line; for by Him in whose hands is my life, I can see Satan entering through the gaps in the rows like a lamb (Abu Daud).

1097. Anas relates that the Holy Prophet directed: Fill the front row, then the one next to it. If there is any deficiency it should be in the last row (Abu Daud).

1098. Ayesha relates that the Holy Prophet said: Allah and His angels send down blessings on those who are in the right side of the rows (Abu Daud).

1099. Bra'a ibn 'Azib relates: When we were at Prayer behind the Holy Prophet we liked to be on his right, so that at the end of the Prayer he should be seated facing us. On one occasion I heard him supplicate: Lord, shield me from Thy chastisement on the day on which Thou wilt raise Thy servants (Muslim).

1100. Abu Hurairah relates that the Holy Prophet directed: Put the Imam in the middle and close the gaps in the rows (Abu Daud).

194.
On the Excellence of Voluntary Prayers

1101. Umm Habibah relates that she heard the Holy Prophet say: Allah prepares a house in Paradise for every Muslim who offers twelve *raka'as* of voluntary Prayer every day beyond that which is prescribed (Muslim).

1102. Ibn Umar relates: I have offered, in the company of the Holy Prophet two *raka'as* of voluntary Prayer before the noon Prayer and two *raka'as* after it, and two *raka'as* after the Friday service, and two after the sunset Prayer and two after the evening Prayer (Bokhari and Muslim).

1103. Abdullah ibn Mughaffal relates that the Holy Prophet said: Between every *Azan* and *Iqamah* there is a Prayer; between every *Azan* and *Iqamah* there is a Prayer; between every *Azan* and *Iqamah* there is a Prayer, for him who so wishes (Bokhari and Muslim).

195.
On Emphasis on two Raka'as before Dawn Prayer

1104. Ayesha relates that the Holy Prophet never omitted four *raka'as* before the noon prayer and two *raka'as* before the dawn Prayer (Bokhari).

1105. Ayesha relates that the Holy Prophet did not attach more importance to any voluntary Prayer than to the two *raka'as* before the dawn Prayer (Muslim).

1106. Ayesha relates that the Holy Prophet said: The two *raka'as* before the dawn Prayer are better than the world and all it contains (Muslim). Another version is: Are dearer to me than the whole world.

1107. Bilal relates that he went to apprise the Holy Prophet of the approach of the hour of the dawn Prayer, but Ayesha diverted his attention to some other matter till it began to be light. Then Bilal rose and informed the Holy Prophet of the hour of Prayer and followed it up with a reminder. But the Holy Prophet did not come out immediately. When he came out he led the Prayer. Then Bilal told him that Ayesha had diverted his attention to something else and this had delayed him warning the Holy Prophet of the hour of Prayer till it began to be light. Yet the Holy Prophet had taken time to come out. He said: I was occupied with my two *raka'as*. Bilal said: Messenger of Allah, you let the light spread. The Holy Prophet replied: Even if the light had spread more than it had, I would have offered the two *raka'as* well and handsomely (Abu Daud).

196.
On the Manner of Offering the two Raka'as at Dawn

1108. Ayesha relates that the Holy Prophet would offer two brief *raka'as* between the *Azan* and *Iqamah* of the dawn Prayer (Bokhari and Muslim). Another version is: He offered the two *raka'as* so abbreviating them that I wondered whether he had recited the Fatihah. Muslim's version is: He would offer the two *raka'as* when he heard the *Azan* and made them brief. Still another version is: With the light of the dawn.

1109. Hafsah relates that the Holy Prophet offered two brief *raka'as* after the *muezzin* had called the *Azan* for the dawn Prayer and it began to be light (Bokhari and Muslim). Muslim's version is: After it began to be light the Holy Prophet did not offer anything but two brief *raka'as*.

1110. Ibn Umar relates that the Holy Prophet offered his voluntary Prayer at night two *raka'as* by two *raka'as* and at the end concluded with an odd *raka'a*. Then he would offer two *raka'as* before the dawn Prayer so brief as if he could hear the *Iqamah* being called (Bokhari and Muslim).

1111. Ibn Abbas relates that in his two *raka'as* before the dawn Prayer, the Holy Prophet recited the verse: Affirm: We believe in Allah and in that

which has been sent down to us . . . (2.137) in the first *raka'a* and the verse:
We believe in Allah and bear thou witness we are obedient to Allah (3.53) in
the second *raka'a*. One version says: The verse: Let us agree upon one matter
which is the same for you and for us . . . (3.65) in the second *raka'a* (Muslim).

1112. Abu Hurairah relates that the Holy Prophet recited *sura*
Al-Kafirun (Chapter 109) and *sura* Al-Ikhlas (Chapter 112) in the two *raka'as*
before the dawn Prayer (Muslim).

1113. Ibn Umar relates: I observed the Holy Prophet for a month
reciting chapters 109 and 112 in the two *raka'as* before the dawn Prayer
(Tirmidhi).

197.
On Relaxation after the Two Raka'as

1114. Ayesha relates that after offering his two *raka'as* the Holy Prophet
would lie down on his right side (Bokhari).

1115. Ayesha relates that between the evening and dawn Prayers the
Holy Prophet would offer eleven *raka'as,* ten of them two by two and the last
one by itself. When the *muezzin* made the call for *Fajr* and it became light and
he came to apprise the Holy Prophet, he would get up and offer two brief
raka'as and then lie down on his right side till the *muezzin* came to him for the
Iqamah (Muslim).

1116. Abu Hurairah relates that the Holy Prophet said: When you have
offered your two *raka'as* before *Fajr* you can lie down on your right side (Abu
Daud and Tirmidhi).

198.
On the Sunnahs of the Noon Prayer

1117. Ibn Umar relates: I offered two *raka'as* before *Zohar* and two after
it in the company of the Holy Prophet (Bokhari and Muslim).

1118. Ayesha relates that the Holy Prophet never omitted four *raka'as*
before *Zohar* (Bokhari).

1119. Ayesha relates: When the Holy Prophet was in my house he would
offer four *raka'as* before *Zohar,* then go and lead the Prayer and come back
and offer two *raka'as*. He would lead the *Maghrib* Prayer and come back and
offer two *raka'as*. When he had led the *Isha* Prayer he would come in and offer
two *raka'as* (Muslim).

1120. Umm Habibah relates that the Holy Prophet said: One who does
not neglect four *raka'as* before *Zohar* and four after it will be shielded against
the Fire (Abu Daud and Tirmidhi).

1121. Abdullah ibn Sa'id relates that the Holy Prophet would offer four *raka'as* after the declining of the sun before the noon Prayer and said: This is the hour when the gates of heaven are opened and I desire that some righteous action on my part should rise to heaven during this hour (Tirmidhi).

1122. Ayesha relates that if the Holy Prophet could not offer four *raka'as* before *Zohar* he offered them after *Zohar* (Tirmidhi).

199.
On the Sunnahs of the Afternoon Prayer

1123. Ali ibn Abi Talib relates that the Holy Prophet was wont to offer four *raka'as* before *Asr* and followed them up with salutation on the favourite angels and those who follow them from among the believers and Muslims (Tirmidhi).

1124. Ibn Umar relates that the Holy Prophet supplicated: May Allah have mercy on one who offers four *raka'as* before *Asr* (Abu Daud and Tirmidhi).

1125. Ali ibn Abi Talib relates that the Holy Prophet was wont to offer two *raka'as* before *Asr* (Abu Daud).

200.
On the Sunnahs of the Sunset Prayer

1126. Abdullah ibn Mughaffal relates that the Holy Prophet said: Offer two *raka'as* before *Maghrib;* and he repeated it twice, adding the last time: He who may so wish (Bokhari).

1127. Anas relates: I noticed the principal companions of the Holy Prophet hastening to the mosque before *Maghrib* (to offer *sunnahs*) (Bokhari).

1128. Anas relates: In the time of the Holy Prophet we used to offer two *raka'as* after sunset before *Maghrib*. He was asked: Did the Holy Prophet offer them? He answered: He saw us offering them; and did not order us or forbid us (Muslim).

1129. Anas relates: When we were in Medina and the *muezzin* called the *Azan* for *Maghrib* the worshippers hastened to the mosque and offered two *raka'as,* so much so that a stranger noticing so many doing so would sometimes imagine that the congregational Prayer had been concluded (Muslim).

201.
On the Sunnahs of the Evening Prayer

See Nos. 1102 and 1103 above.

202.
On the Sunnahs of the Friday Prayer

1130. This *hadith* merely refers to No. 1102 above.

1131. Abu Hurairah relates that the Holy Prophet said: When you finish the Friday Prayer, offer four *raka'as* thereafter (Muslim).

1132. Ibn Umar relates that the Holy Prophet did not offer any *sunnahs* in the mosque after Friday Prayer, but returned to his house and offered two *raka'as* there (Muslim).

203.
On the Preference of Offering Voluntary Prayer at Home

1133. Zaid ibn Thabit relates that the Holy Prophet said: Offer your Prayers in your homes for, with the exception of the prescribed Prayers, the best Prayer is that which is offered at home (Bokhari and Muslim).

1134. Ibn Umar relates that the Holy Prophet said: You should offer the voluntary part of your Prayers at home also. Do not turn your homes into graves (Bokhari and Muslim).

1135. Jabir relates that the Holy Prophet said: When you have finished your Prayer in the mosque you should offer the rest of your Prayer at home for Allah will bless your home because of your Prayer (Muslim).

1136. Umar ibn Ata relates that Nafi' ibn Jubair sent him to Saib ibn Ukht to inquire from him about what Mu'awiah had said about his Prayer. Saib told him: I offered the Friday Prayer with him and when the Imam had said the *salam* I stood up in my place and offered the *sunnahs*. When Mu'awiah went inside he sent for me and told me: Never do again what you did just now. Once you have finished the Friday Prayer do not immediately continue with the *sunnah* unless you have spoken to someone or have shifted your place, for the Holy Prophet commanded us that we should not follow up the congregational Prayer with *sunnah* unless we had talked to someone or had shifted our place (Muslim).

204.

On the Importance of Vitr

1137. Ali has said: *Vitr* (odd) Prayer is not obligatory like the prescribed Prayers but the Holy Prophet always offered *Vitr* and said: Allah is One and loves *Vitr*. So offer *Vitr* Prayers, O ye who follow the Quran (Abu Daud and Tirmidhi).

1138. Ayesha relates: The Holy Prophet offered *Vitr* Prayers in the first part of the night, or in the middle of it, or in its latter part, in which case he finished his *Vitr* Prayer at dawn (Bokhari and Muslim).

1139. Ibn Umar relates that the Holy Prophet said: Make the end of your voluntary Prayer at night *Vitr* (Bokhari and Muslim).

1140. Abu Sa'id Khudri relates that the Holy Prophet said: Offer your *Vitr* Prayer before dawn (Muslim).

1141. Ayesha relates that the Holy Prophet would offer his voluntary Prayer while she was sleeping in front of him and when the time came for his *Vitr* Prayer he would wake her up and proceed with his *Vitr* Prayer (Muslim). Another version is: When the time came for his *Vitr* Prayer, he would say to me: Ayesha, wake up and offer your *Vitr* Prayer.

1142. Ibn Umar relates that the Holy Prophet said: You should welcome the dawn by completing your *Vitr* Prayer (Abu Daud and Tirmidhi).

1143. Jabir relates that the Holy Prophet said: He who apprehends that he might not be able to get up in the latter part of the night should offer his *Vitr* Prayer during the early part of the night, but he who is eager to get up in the latter part should offer his *Vitr* Prayer at that time for in the latter part of the night there is the presence of angels and Prayer at that time is best (Muslim).

205.

On the Excellence of the Forenoon Voluntary Prayer

1144. Abu Hurairah relates: The Holy Prophet directed me to observe fast for three days in every month and to offer two *raka'as* during the forenoon and to offer *Vitr* before going to sleep (Bokhari and Muslim).

1145. This *hadith* is the same as No. 118.

1146. Ayesha relates that the Holy Prophet used to offer four *raka'as* during the forenoon and added to them whatever Allah wished (Muslim).

1147. Umm Hani bint Abu Talib relates: I went to the Holy Prophet on the day of the fall of Mecca and found that he was taking a bath. When he had finished he offered eight *raka'as* of voluntary Prayers. This was during the forenoon (Bokhari and Muslim).

206.
On the Time of the Forenoon Voluntary Prayer

1148. Zaid ibn Arqam saw some people offering voluntary Prayer in the early morning and observed: Would that they knew that voluntary Prayer a little later is better, for the Holy Prophet said: The time of the forenoon Prayer for those who turn wholly to Allah is when the sun warms up (Muslim).

207.
On the Excellence of Voluntary Prayer in Entering a Mosque

1149. Abu Qatadah relates that the Holy Prophet said: When any of you enters the mosque he should not sit down till he has offered two *raka'as* (Bokhari and Muslim).
1150. Jabir relates: I came to the Holy Prophet when he was in the mosque and he said to me: Offer two *raka'as* (Bokhari and Muslim).

208.
On Offering Prayer after Ablutions

1151. Abu Hurairah relates that the Holy Prophet said to Bilal: Tell me, Bilal, of your most hopeful action since your acceptance of Islam, for I have heard the echo of your footsteps in Paradise in front of me. Bilal replied: I do not consider any of my actions more hopeful than that whenever I have performed my ablutions during the day or night I have each time offered by way of Prayer that which had been prescribed for me (Bokhari and Muslim).

209.
On the Excellence of Friday Prayer and its due Preparation

Allah, the Exalted, has said:
284.   When the Prayer is finished then disperse in the land
and seek of Allah's grace, and remember Allah much that
you may prosper (62.11).

1152. Abu Hurairah relates that the Holy Prophet said: The best of days on which the sun rises is Friday; on that day was Adam created, on that day he was admitted to the garden and on that day was he expelled therefrom (Muslim).
1153. This *hadith* is the same as No. 128.

1154. Abu Hurairah relates that the Holy Prophet said: The five daily Prayers and the Friday Prayer to the next Friday Prayer and the observance of *Ramadhan* to the observance of the next *Ramadhan* atone for all defaults in between so long as major defaults are shunned (Muslim).

1155. Abu Hurairah and Ibn Umar relate that they heard the Holy Prophet say from his wooden pulpit: Let my people beware of neglecting the Friday Prayer, else Allah will set a seal upon their hearts and they will be counted among the negligent ones (Muslim).

1156. Ibn Umar relates that the Holy Prophet said: When one of you prepares for the Friday Prayer let him take a bath (Bokhari and Muslim).

1157. Abu Sa'id Khudri relates that the Holy Prophet said: Bath on Friday is obligatory on every adult (Bokhari and Muslim).

1158. Samurah relates that the Holy Prophet said: He who performs his ablutions for the Friday Prayer adopts the easier course and it is good, but a bath is better (Abu Daud and Tirmidhi).

1159. This *hadith* is the same as No. 831.

1160. Abu Hurairah relates that the Holy Prophet said: He who takes a full bath on Friday and repairs early to the mosque is as if he had sacrificed a camel for winning Allah's pleasure; and he who proceeds to the mosque later than him is as if he had sacrificed a cow; and he who goes later than him is as if he had sacrificed a chicken; and he who goes last is as if he had sacrificed an egg. When the Imam arrives the angels crowd in to listen to his address (Bokhari and Muslim).

1161. Abu Hurairah relates that concerning Friday the Holy Prophet said: There is on that day a brief space of time during the service when whatever supplication a Muslim servant of Allah makes is granted (Bokhari and Muslim).

1162. Abu Burdah ibn Abu Musa Ash'ari relates: Abdullah ibn Umar asked me: Did you hear your father relate anything from the Holy Prophet concerning a special moment during the Friday service? I told him: Yes, I heard him say that he heard the Holy Prophet say: That moment occurs between the Imam ascending the pulpit and the end of the service (Muslim).

1163. Aus ibn Aus relates that the Holy Prophet said: Your best day is Friday, so you should be diligent on that day in calling down blessings on me for your blessings are conveyed to me (Abu Daud).

210.
On Prostration in Gratitude for Divine Favours

1164. Sa'ad ibn Abi Waqqas relates: We started from Mecca for Medina in the company of the Holy Prophet. As we approached Azwara he dismounted and raised his hands in supplication and prayed for a while and then fell into prostration and remained thus for a long time. Then he stood up and raised his hands in supplication and prayed for a while and then fell into prostration. He did this three times and then explained to us: I supplicated my Lord in intercession for my people and He granted me one third of them, whereupon I fell into prostration before my Lord, thanking Him. Then I raised my head and supplicated my Lord for my people, and He granted me another third of them, whereupon I fell into prostration before my Lord, thanking Him. Again I raised my head and supplicated my Lord for my people and He granted me the last third of them, on which I fell into prostration before my Lord (Abu Daud).

211.
On the Excellence of Prayer at Night

Allah, the Exalted, has said:

285. At night also wake up for the recitation of the Quran, an additional favour unto thee. It may be that thereby thy Lord will raise thee to a praiseworthy station (17.80).

286. They withdraw themselves from their beds in the latter part of the night for Prayer (32.17).

287. They slept but little at night (51.18).

1165. This *hadith* is the same as No. 98.

1166. Ali relates that the Holy Prophet visited Fatimah and him one night and inquired of them: Do you not offer Prayer at night (Bokhari and Muslim)?

1167. Salim ibn Abdullah ibn Umar relates on the authority of his father that the Holy Prophet said: Abdullah is an excellent man only if he were to offer his voluntary Prayer at night. Salim adds that after this Abdullah slept but little at night (Bokhari and Muslim).

1168. This *hadith* is the same as No. 155.

1169. Abdullah ibn Mas'ud relates that mention was made before the Holy Prophet of a man who slept through the night till after dawn, on which he observed: He is a man in whose ears (or ear) Satan has urinated (Bokhari and Muslim).

1170. Abu Hurairah relates that the Holy Prophet said: When a person sleeps Satan ties three knots at the base of his head, muttering over each: The night is long, sleep on. If he wakes up and remembers Allah, one of the knots is loosened. Then if he gets up and makes his ablutions another one is loosened. If he says his Prayer, he is free of all of them and he begins his morning in a happy cheerful mood. Otherwise he gets up in a disagreeable, slothful mood (Bokhari and Muslim).

1171. This *hadith* is the same as No. 852.

1172. Abu Hurairah relates that the Holy Prophet said: The best month for fasting next after Ramadhan is Muharram, and the best Prayer next after the prescribed Prayers is Prayer at night (Muslim).

1173. Ibn Umar relates that the Holy Prophet said: Night Prayer is a succession of two *raka'as* at a time, and when you perceive the approach of dawn add a single *raka'a* to make an odd number (Bokhari and Muslim).

1174. Ibn Umar relates that the Holy Prophet offered a succession of two *raka'as* at night followed by a single *raka'a* (Bokhari and Muslim).

1175. Anas relates that the Holy Prophet would not fast during a month till we began to think he would not fast in this month, and he would go on observing the fast till we thought he would not omit fasting at all during the month, and if one wanted to see him offering prayer at night one could do that or if one wanted to see him at sleep at night one could do that (Bokhari).

1176. Ayesha relates that the Holy Prophet offered eleven *raka'as* at night, of which every prostration lasted for a long enough space of time to permit a person to recite fifty verses. Thereafter he would offer two brief *raka'as* before *Fajr* and then recline on his right side till the *muezzin* came to call him for *Fajr* (Bokhari).

1177. Ayesha relates that the Holy Prophet never offered more than eleven *raka'as* at night during Ramadhan or at any other time. He would offer four *raka'as* long and perfect, and then four of the same type and then three. I asked him: Messenger of Allah, do you sleep before offering *Vitr?* He answered: Ayesha, my eyes sleep but my heart does not (Bokhari and Muslim).

1178. Ayesha relates that the Holy Prophet slept during the early part of the night and stood in Prayer during the latter part (Bokhari and Muslim).

1179. This *hadith* is the same as No. 103.

1180. This *hadith* is the same as No. 102.

1181. Jabir relates that the Holy Prophet was asked: Which Prayer is best? He answered: The one in which the worshipper makes a long stand (Muslim).

1182. This *hadith* is comprehended in No. 150.

1183. Jabir relates that he heard the Holy Prophet say: Every night there is a brief space of time during which whatever of good pertaining to this life or the next a Muslim supplicates for, it is granted him (Muslim).

1184. Abu Hurairah relates that the Holy Prophet said: He who gets up for the night Prayer should start it with two brief *raka'as* (Muslim).

1185. Ayesha relates that the Holy Prophet started his night Prayer with two brief *raka'as* (Muslim).

1186. Ayesha relates that if the Holy Prophet missed his night Prayer through indisposition or the like he offered twelve *raka'as* during the day (Muslim).

1187. Umar ibn Khattab relates that the Holy Prophet said: If a person is unable to offer the whole or part of that which it is customary for him to offer during the night and he offers it at any time between *Fajr* and *Zohar*, it is written down for him as if he had offered it during the night (Muslim).

1188. Abu Hurairah relates that the Holy Prophet said: Allah will have mercy on a man who gets up at night for his voluntary Prayer and awakens his wife for the same purpose and if she hesitates he sprinkles water over her face to make her get up, and Allah will have mercy on a woman who gets up at night to offer voluntary Prayer and awakens her husband for the same purpose and if he hesitates sprinkles water over his face to make him get up (Abu Daud).

1189. Abu Hurairah and Abu Sa'id relate that the Holy Prophet said: If a man awakens his wife at night and they offer Prayer (or offer two *raka'as*) they are both recorded among those who remember Allah (Muslim).

1190. This *hadith* is the same as No. 147.

1191. Abu Hurairah relates that the Holy Prophet said: If one of you stands up for Prayer at night and finds it difficult to recite the Quran accurately not being able to keep track of what he is saying, he should go back to sleep (Muslim).

212.
On Voluntary Prayer during Ramadhan

1192. Abu Hurairah relates that the Holy Prophet said: He who maintains voluntary Prayer throughout Ramadhan out of sincerity of faith and in hope of earning merit will have his past sins forgiven him (Bokhari and Muslim).

1193. Abu Hurairah relates that the Holy Prophet would persuade people to offer voluntary Prayer during Ramadhan but would not order them imperatively. He said: He who maintains voluntary Prayer throughout Ramadhan, out of sincerity of faith and in hope of earning merit, will have his past sins forgiven him (Muslim).

213.
On Voluntary Prayer during the Night of Decrees

Allah, the Exalted, has said:

288. Surely, We sent down the Quran during the Night of Decrees. How shouldst thou know what is the Night of Decrees? The Night of Decrees is better than a thousand months. Therein descend angels and the Spirit by the command of their Lord with their Lord's decrees concerning every matter. It is all peace, till the break of dawn (97.2-6).

289. We revealed it in a blessed Night (44.4).

1194. Abu Hurairah relates that the Holy Prophet said: He who offers voluntary Prayer during the Night of Decrees out of sincerity of faith and in hope of earning merit will have his past sins forgiven him (Bokhari and Muslim).

1195. Ibn Umar relates that some of the companions of the Holy Prophet dreamt that the Night of Decrees was among the last seven nights of Ramadhan, whereupon the Holy Prophet said: I see that your dreams all agree upon the last seven nights. Whoever, then, seeks the Night of Decrees should look for it among the last seven nights of Ramadhan (Bokhari and Muslim).

1196. Ayesha relates that the Holy Prophet used to go into retreat in the mosque during the last ten days of Ramadhan and said: Look for the Night of Decrees among the last ten nights of Ramadhan (Bokhari and Muslim).

1197. Ayesha relates that the Holy Prophet said: Look for the Night of Decrees among the odd nights of the last ten nights of Ramadhan (Bokhari).

1198. Ayesha relates that when the last ten days of Ramadhan began the Holy Prophet kept awake the whole night and would awaken his wife and was most diligent in worship (Bokhari and Muslim).

1199. Ayesha relates that the Holy Prophet strove in worship during Ramadhan more than he strove at any other time and he strove in the last ten days of Ramadhan more than he strove during its earlier part (Muslim).

1200. Ayesha relates: I asked the Holy Prophet: Messenger of Allah, tell me, in case I should realise which night is the Night of Decrees, how should I supplicate in it? He answered: Supplicate: Allah, Thou art Most Forgiving and dost love forgiveness, then do Thou forgive me (Tirmidhi).

214.
On the Excellence of Brushing of Teeth etc.

1201. Abu Hurairah relates that the Holy Prophet said: Did I not apprehend that it would be burdensome on my people (or on people) I would prescribe the brushing of teeth before every Prayer (Bokhari and Muslim).

1202. Huzaifah relates that when the Holy Prophet woke up from sleep he brushed his teeth (Bokhari and Muslim).

1203. Ayesha relates: We used to prepare for the Holy Prophet his toothbrush and the water for his ablutions so that whenever Allah awakened him during the night he could brush his teeth and make his ablutions and offer Prayer (Muslim).

1204. Anas relates that the Holy Prophet said: I have impressed upon you repeatedly the importance of brushing your teeth (Bokhari).

1205. Shuraih ibn Hani relates: I asked Ayesha what is the first thing that the Holy Prophet did upon entering his house? She answered: He brushed his teeth (Muslim).

1206. Abu Musa Ash'ari relates I went to the Holy Prophet and noticed a bit of the bark of his toothbrush on his tongue (Bokhari and Muslim).

1207. Ayesha relates that the Holy Prophet said: Brushing the teeth purifies the mouth and is agreeable to the Lord (Nisai and Ibn Khuzaimah).

1208. Abu Hurairah relates that the Holy Prophet said: These are five demands of nature: Circumcision, removal of pubic hair, paring of nails, removal of the hair in the armpits and cutting close the hair on the lips (Bokhari and Muslim).

1209. Ayesha relates that the Holy Prophet said: There are ten demands of nature: Cutting close the hair on the lips, letting the beard grow, brushing the teeth, cleaning out the nose, paring the nails, washing out the base of the fingers, removal of the hair in the armpits and the removal of pubic hair, washing the affected parts after a call of nature. The narrator of the *hadith* says that he has forgotten the tenth and thinks that it might possibly be the rinsing of the mouth (Muslim).

1210. Ibn Umar relates that the Holy Prophet said: Cut down close the hair on the lips and let the beard grow (Bokhari and Muslim).

215.

On the Obligation of Paying the Zakat

Allah the Exalted, has said:

290.   Observe Prayer and pay the Zakat (2.44).

291.   They had only been commanded to worship Allah, devoting themselves wholly to Him in full sincerity, and to observe Prayer, and to pay the Zakat. This is the enduring faith (98.6).

292.   Take a portion of their wealth as alms, that thou mayest purify them thereby and provide for their uplift and welfare (9.103).

1211. This *hadith* is the same as No. 1079.

1212. Talha ibn Ubaidullah relates: A man from Nejd with rumpled hair came to the Holy Prophet. His voice reached our ears but we could not understand what he was saying till he approached close to the Holy Prophet and we understood that he was inquiring about Islam. The Holy Prophet said to him: There are five obligatory Prayers in twenty four hours. He said: Am I under obligation beyond these? The Holy Prophet answered: No, unless you were to offer voluntary Prayer; and went on to say: Then there is the fast of the

month of Ramadhan. The man asked: Am I under obligation beyond it? The
Holy Prophet repeated: No, unless you were to observe voluntary fasts. Then
the Holy Prophet mentioned to him the *Zakat* and he made the same inquiry
and the Holy Prophets gave the same answer. The man then turned away
saying: Allah is my witness that I shall not add anything to this, nor shall I
detract anything from it. On this the Holy Prophet observed: He will prosper if
he proves truthful (Bokhari and Muslim).

1213.   This *hadith* is comprehended in No. 210.

1214.   This *hadith* is the same as No. 393.

1215.   Abu Hurairah relates: When the Holy Prophet died and Abu Bakr
became Khalifa and of the Arabs some repudiated their obligations and Abu
Bakr said he would fight them, Umar said to him: How will you fight them
while the Holy Prophet said: I have been commanded to fight those who fight
me till they should affirm: There is none worthy of worship save Allah. Then
whoever affirms this, his life and property will be secure except to the extent of
his obligations, and his responsibility is to Allah. Abu Bakr answered him: I
shall certainly fight those who make a distinction between Prayer and *Zakat*.
Zakat is obligatory in respect of wealth. Allah is my witness that if they hold
back from me the nose-rope of a camel that they paid to the Holy Prophet, I
shall fight them for their holding it back. Umar said thereafter: I then
understood that Allah had made the matter of fighting plain to Abu Bakr and
I recognised that he was in the right (Bokhari and Muslim).

1216.   Abu Ayub relates that a man asked the Holy Prophet: Tell me
what should I do to be admitted to Paradise. He answered him: Worship
Allah, associating naught with Him, observe Prayer, pay the *Zakat* and
strengthen the ties of kinship (Bokhari and Muslim).

1217.   Abu Hurairah relates: A rustic came to the Holy Prophet and
said: Messenger of Allah, tell me what I should do so that I should enter
Paradise. He answered him: Worship Allah and do not associate anything with
Him, and observe Prayer, and pay the obligatory *Zakat*, and observe the fast of
Ramadhan. The man said: By Him in Whose hands is my life I will not add
anything to this. When he turned away the Holy Prophet said to those around
him: He who would be pleased to look at someone out of the dwellers of
Paradise should look at that one (Bokhari and Muslim).

1218.   Jarir ibn Abdullah relates: I made a covenant with the Holy
Prophet to observe Prayer, to pay the *Zakat* and to have the welfare of every
Muslim at heart (Bokhari and Muslim).

1219.   Abu Hurairah relates that the Holy Prophet said: A person having
gold or silver who does not pay the *Zakat* due on it should know that on the
Day of Judgment his gold and silver will be melted into slabs which will then
be heated in the fire of hell and his side and forehead and back will be
branded therewith. When the slabs will become cool they will be heated up
again and the branding will be continued during a day the extent of which will

be equal to fifty thousand years till the people will have been judged and he will be shown his way to Paradise or to the Fire.

He was asked: Messenger of Allah, what about camels? He answered: In the same way the owner of camels who does not discharge what is due in respect of them (and what is due includes their milk on the day they are taken to water) will be thrown on his face in a wide level plain on the Day of Judgment to be trampled upon by the camels. These camels will be strong and fat and not one from among them will be missing. They will trample him under their feet and will tear him apart with their teeth. When the last of them will have passed over him the first of them will begin the process over again through a day the extent of which will be equal to fifty thousand years till all men have been judged and he will be shown his way to Paradise or to the Fire.

Then he was asked: Messenger of Allah, what about cows and goats? He answered: The same will be the case of one who owns cows and goats and does not discharge his obligation in respect of them. On the Day of Judgment he will be thrown on his face in a wide level plain when none of the animals will be missing and none will be without horns. They will gore him with their horns and will trample him under their feet and when one side has finished the other side will begin, throughout a day, the extent of which will be equal to fifty thousand years till all men have been judged and he will be shown his way to Paradise or to the Fire.

He was asked: Messenger of Allah, what about horses? He answered: Horses may be divided into three groups: those that are a burden for their owner, those that are a screen for him and those that make their owner worthy of reward. As to those who are a burden for their owner they are the ones who are reared for show or for pride or for causing injury to the Muslims. They will be a cause of torment for their owner. The ones that are a screen for their owner are those that are reared by him for the cause of Allah and he does not forget that which is due to Allah in respect of their backs and their necks. They are his screen. Those that make their owner worthy of reward are the ones that are reared in meadows and gardens for being used in the cause of Allah by the Muslims. Whatever they eat from these meadows and gardens is written down as good works of their owner, so much so that even their droppings and their urine counts for an equal number of good works for him. Every rope that is used up in their jumping and every height from which they jump and every hoof mark that they make counts for an equal number of good works for him. When their owner leads them through a stream and they drink from it, whether their owner intended them to do so or not, every mouthful that they drink counts as good works for him.

He was asked: Messenger of Allah, what about donkeys? He answered: No specific direction has been revealed to me with regard to donkeys but the following peerless verse is comprehensive: Then whoso will have done the smallest particle of good will see it, and whoso will have done the smallest particle of ill will also see it (99.8-9) (Bokhari and Muslim).

216.

On Fasting

Allah, the Exalted, has said:

293.   O ye who believe, fasting is prescribed for you during a fixed number of days, as it was prescribed for those before you, so that you may safeguard yourselves against moral and spiritual ills. But whoso from among you should be ailing or should be on a journey shall complete the reckoning by fasting on a corresponding number of other days; and for those who find fasting a strain hard to bear is an expiation, the feeding of a poor person, if they can afford it. Whoso carries through a good work through eager obedience, it is the better for him. If you had knowledge you would realise that it is better for you that you should fast. The month of Ramadhan is the month in which the Quran began to be revealed, the Book which comprises guidance for mankind and clear proofs of guidance and divine Signs which discriminate between truth and falsehood. Therefore, he who from among you witnesses this month should fast through it. But whoso is ailing or is on a journey should complete the reckoning by fasting on a corresponding number of other days (2. 184 - 186).

1220.   Abu Hurairah relates that the Holy Prophet said: Allah, the Lord of honour and glory says: All other deeds of man are for himself, but his fasting is purely for Me and I shall reward him for it. The fast is a shield. When any of you is fasting he should eschew loose talk and noisy exchanges. Should anyone revile him or seek to pick a quarrel with him, he should respond with: I am observing a fast. By Him in Whose hands is the life of Muhammad, the breath of one who is fasting is purer in the sight of Allah than the fragrance of musk. One who fasts experiences two joys: he is joyful when he breaks his fast, and he is joyful by virtue of his fast when he meets his Lord (Bokhari and Muslim). Bokhari adds: Allah says: He abstains from food and drink and from indulging his passion for My sake. A fast is undertaken for My sake and I shall bestow the reward for it. Other good works are rewarded only ten times. Muslim's version adds: A man's good works carry a multiple reward, from ten times to seven hundred times. Allah says: A fast is an exception, for it is observed for My sake and I shall bestow the reward for it. He who observes a fast gives up his passion and his food for My sake. For such a one there are two joys; a joy when he breaks his fast and a joy when he meets his Lord. His breath is purer in the estimation of Allah than the fragrance of musk.

1221.   Abu Hurairah relates that the Holy Prophet said: He who spends a pair of anything in the cause of Allah will be called from the gates of Paradise:

Servant of Allah, this gate is better for thee. Thus, he who is constant in Prayer will be called from the gate of Prayer; and he who is eager in striving in the cause of Allah will be called from the gate of striving; and he who is regular in fasting will be called from the gate called Rayyan; and he who is munificent in charity will be called from the gate of charity. Abu Bakr said: May my father and mother be thy sacrifice, Messenger of Allah, those who are called from these gates shall want for nothing, but will any one be called from all these gates? He answered: Yes, and I am hoping you will be one of them (Bokhari and Muslim).

1222. Sa'ad ibn Sahl relates that the Holy Prophet said: There is a gate of Paradise called Rayyan through which only those will enter on the Day of Judgment who are regular in observing the fast and no one else. A call will go forth: Where are those who observed the fast regularly? and they will step forth and no one beside him will enter through that gate. After they shall have entered the gate will be closed and no one else will enter thereby (Bokhari and Muslim).

1223. Abu Sa'id Khudri relates that the Holy Prophet said: When a servant of Allah observes the fast for a day for the sake of Allah, He thereby repels the Fire from him a distance of seventy years of journeying (Bokhari and Muslim).

1224. Abu Hurairah relates that the Holy Prophet said: He who observes the fast during Ramadhan out of sincerity of faith and in hope of earning merit will have his past sins forgiven him (Bokhari and Muslim).

1225. Abu Hurairah relates that the Holy Prophet said: When Ramadhan arrives the gates of Paradise are opened and the gates of hell are locked up and satans are put in chains (Bokhari and Muslim).

1226. Abu Hurairah relates that the Holy Prophet said: Start the fast with observing the new moon and terminate it with observing it. If you are unable to observe it by reason of the sky being overcast postpone the fast by a day (Bokhari and Muslim). Muslim adds: If you are unable to observe the new moon at the end of Ramadhan, observe the fast for the thirtieth day.

217.
On Munificent Charity etc. during Ramadhan

1227. Ibn Abbas relates that the Holy Prophet was the most generous of men and he was at his most bountiful during Ramadhan when Gabriel visited him every night and recited the Quran to him. During this period the bounty of the Holy Prophet waxed faster than the rain-bearing breeze (Bokhari and (Muslim).

1228. This *hadith* is the same as No. 1198.

218.
On Prohibition of Fasting

1229. Abu Hurairah relates that the Holy Prophet said: Do not observe the fast on two days preceding Ramadhan, but this does not apply to one who has made a practice of it (Bokhari and Muslim).

1230. Ibn Abbas relates that the Holy Prophet said: Do not anticipate Ramadhan. Start the fast with observing the new moon and terminate it with observing it. If the sky is overcast let the month run to thirty days (Tirmidhi).

1231. Abu Hurairah relates that the Holy Prophet said: When the middle of Sha'ban arrives do not observe a fast during the rest of it (Tirmidhi).

1232. Ammar ibn Yasir said: He who observes the fast on a doubtful day disobeys the Holy Prophet (Abu Daud and Tirmidhi).

219.
On Supplication on Observing the New Moon

1233. Talha ibn Ubaidullah relates that, on seeing a new moon, the Holy Prophet would supplicate: Allah, do Thou cause the appearance of this moon to be a harbinger of peace, faith, security and Islam for us. Thy Lord, O moon, and mine is Allah. May this be a moon presaging guidance and good (Tirmidhi).

220.
On Breakfast during Ramadhan

1234. Anas relates that the Holy Prophet said: Take breakfast before the fast begins; there is blessing in breakfast (Bokhari and Muslim).

1235. Zaid ibn Thabit relates: We ate breakfast during Ramadhan with the Holy Prophet and then stood up for Prayer. He was asked what was the interval of time between the two. He said: The time required for the recital of fifty verses (Bokhari and Muslim).

1236. Ibn Umar relates that the Holy Prophet had appointed two *muezzins*, Bilal and Ibn Umm Maktum. He said: Bilal calls the *Azan* while it is still night. So continue your breakfast till Ibn Umm Maktum calls it. There was in fact only a brief interval between the two (Bokhari and Muslim).

1237. Amr ibn 'As relates that the Holy Prophet said: The difference between our observance of the fast and that of the People of the Book is the eating of breakfast (Muslim).

221.

On the Time of Breaking the Fast etc.

1238. Sahl ibn Sa'ad relates that the Holy Prophet said: My people will adhere to good as long as they do not delay the breaking of the fast (Bokhari and Muslim).

1239. Abu Atiyyah relates: Masruq and I visited Ayesha and Masruq said to her: There are two of the companions of the Holy Prophet neither of whom holds back from any type of good; one of them goes forward in breaking his fast and offering *Maghrib* Prayer and the other retards both. She asked: Who is the one who goes forward in breaking his fast and offering *Maghrib?* He answered: Abdullah ibn Mas'ud. She observed: The Holy Prophet did the same (Muslim).

1240. Abu Hurairah relates that the Holy Prophet said: Allah, the Lord of honour and glory says: Of My servants I love most those who are foremost in breaking their fasts (Tirmidhi).

1241. Umar ibn Khattab relates that the Holy Prophet said: When the night approaches from the East and the day retreats in the West and the sun has set, the one observing the fast breaks it (Bokhari and Muslim).

1242. Abdullah ibn Aufa relates: We were with the Holy Prophet in the course of a journey when he was observing a voluntary fast. When the sun set he said to someone: So and So, dismount and prepare the ground roast barley for us. He answered: Messenger of Allah, if you would let it be dark. He repeated: Dismount and prepare the barley for us. The man said: There is daylight still. The Holy Prophet said a third time: Dismount and prepare the barley for us. On this the man dismounted and prepared the dish. The Holy Prophet ate of it and pointing to the East said: When you perceive the night approaching from that direction let the one observing the fast break it (Bokhari and Muslim).

1243. Salman ibn 'Amir Dhabi relates that the Holy Prophet said: Break your fast with a date, else with water for it is pure (Abu Daud and Tirmidhi).

1244. Anas relates: The Holy Prophet used to break his fast before offering *Maghrib* with fresh dates, failing that with dry dates and failing that he would swallow a few mouthfuls of water (Abu Daud and Tirmidhi).

222.

On Safeguarding the Fast

1245. This *hadith* is part of No. 1220.

1246. Abu Hurairah relates that the Holy Prophet said: If a person does not eschew falsehood and false conduct, Allah has no need that he should abstain from food and drink (Bokhari).

223.
On Miscellaneous Matters concerning the Fast

1247. Abu Hurairah relates that the Holy Prophet said: Should any of you eat or drink in forgetfulness of the fast, he should continue his fast till the end, for Allah has fed him and given him to drink (Bokhari and Muslim).

1248. Laqit ibn Sabarah relates: I asked the Holy Prophet to inform me about the ablutions. He answered: Carry out the ablutions completely in all respects, and remember that you clean out the base of your fingers and wash out your nose well, but be careful in this last if you should be observing the fast (Abu Daud and Tirmidhi).

1249. Ayesha relates: Should the Holy Prophet have consorted with a wife he would take a bath and start the fast (Bokhari and Muslim).

1250. Ayesha and Umm Salamah relate: Should the Holy Prophet have consorted with a wife he would start and complete his fast as usual (Bokhari and Muslim).

224.

On the Excellence of Fasting in the Months of Muharram and Sha'ban etc.

1251. This *hadith* is the same as No. 1172.

1252. Ayesha relates: The Holy Prophet did not observe the voluntary fast so often in any month as in Sha'ban for he observed the fast throughout Sha'ban. One version has it: He observed the fast during the greater part of Sha'ban (Bokhari and Muslim).

1253. Mujiba Bahiliyyah relates on the authority of her father or uncle that he visited the Holy Prophet and returned and visited him again after the interval of a year. In the meantime his appearance and condition had changed. When he came to him the second time he asked him: Messenger of Allah, do you recognise me? The Holy Prophet inquired: Who are you? He answered: I am the Bahili who visited you last year. The Holy Prophet said: You were quite handsome, what has altered you so much? He answered: Since I parted from you, I have not eaten except at night. The Holy Prophet observed: You have tormented yourself needlessly. You should observe the fast during Ramadhan and on one day in every other month. He urged: Permit me to do more for I am strong. The Holy Prophet said: Then observe the fast during two days in every month. He said: Permit me to do more. The Holy Prophet said: Observe the fast on three days in every month. He pleaded for more. The Holy Prophet said: During the four sacred months fast for three days and abstain from fasting for three days alternately (Abu Daud).

225.

On the Excellence of Fasting in the First Ten Days of Zil Hajj

1254. Ibn Abbas relates that the Holy Prophet said: There are no days during which righteous action is so pleasing to Allah as righteous action in these days (meaning the first ten days in Zil Hajj). He was asked: Messenger of Allah, not even striving in the cause of Allah? He answered: Not even striving in the cause of Allah except in the case of one who goes forth with his life and his property and does not come back with either (Bokhari).

226.

On the Excellence of Fasting on the Day of Arafat and the Tenth Day of Muharram

1255. Abu Qatadah relates: The Holy Prophet was asked about observing the fast on the day of *Arafat*. He said: It atones for the sins of the preceding year and the subsequent year (Muslim).

1256. Ibn Abbas relates that the Holy Prophet himself observed the fast on the tenth day of Muharram and directed that it should be observed as a fast (Bokhari and Muslim).

1257. Abu Qatadah relates that the Holy Prophet was asked about observing the fast on the tenth day of Muharram and answered: It atones for the sins of the preceding year (Muslim).

1258. Ibn Abbas relates that the Holy Prophet said: If I survive till the next year I shall fast on the ninth day of Muharram (Muslim).

227.

On the Excellence of Fasting on the First Six Days of Shawal

1259. Abu Ayub relates that the Holy Prophet said: He who observes the fast throughout Ramadhan and then follows it up with observing the fast on the first six days of Shawal is as if he had observed the fast throughout the year (Muslim).

228.

On the Desirability of Fasting on Monday and Thursday

1260. Abu Qatadah relates that the Holy Prophet was asked about observing the fast on Monday and answered: That is the day on which I was born and the day on which I received the call (or the day on which I received revelation) (Muslim).

1261. Abu Hurairah relates that the Holy Prophet said: A man's deeds are reported on Mondays and Thursdays and I prefer that I should be observing the fast when my deeds are reported (Tirmidhi).

1262. Ayesha relates that the Holy Prophet was diligent in observing the fast on Monday and Thursday (Tirmidhi).

229.

On the Desirability of Fasting on Three Days in every Month

1263. This *hadith* is the same as No. 1144.

1264. Abu Darda' relates (here follows the immediately preceding *hadith*).

1265. This *hadith* is comprehended in No. 150.

1266. Mu'azah Adawiah relates that she asked Ayesha: Did the Holy Prophet observe fast on three days during every month? And she said: Yes. I asked her: During which part of the month did he fast? She answered: He did not mind which part it was (Muslim).

1267. Abu Dharr relates that the Holy Prophet said: If you observe fast on three days in a month, then make them the days of the 13th, 14th and 15th nights of the moon (Tirmidhi).

1268. Qatadah ibn Milhan relates: The Holy Prophet directed us to observe the fast on the three white days of every month, meaning the days of the 13th, 14th and 15th nights of the moon (Abu Daud).

1269. Ibn Abbas relates that the Holy Prophet never omitted observance of the fast on white days, whether he was stationary or was on a journey (Nisai).

230.

On the Excellence of Providing for the Breaking of the Fast etc.

1270. Zaid ibn Khalid Juhni relates that the Holy Prophet said: He who provides for the breaking of the fast of another earns the same merit as the one who was observing the fast without diminishing in any way the reward of the latter (Tirmidhi).

1271. Umm Ammarah relates that the Holy Prophet visited her and she put some food before him. He asked her to eat also. She said: I am fasting. On this he observed: Angels call down blessings on a person who should be fasting when other people eat in his presence till they finish (or till they have eaten their fill) (Tirmidhi).

1272. Anas relates that the Holy Prophet came to visit Sa'ad ibn Ubadah who brought bread and olive oil and presented it to him. The Holy

Prophet partook of it and said: Those who were fasting have broken their fast with you and the righteous have eaten your food while the angels were calling down blessings on you (Abu Daud).

231.
On Retreat

1273. Ibn Umar relates that the Holy Prophet used to go into retreat in the mosque during the last ten days of Ramadhan (Bokhari and Muslim).

1274. Ayesha relates that the Holy Prophet went into retreat during the last ten days of Ramadhan till Allah caused his death. Thereafter his wives used to go into retreat (Bokhari and Muslim).

1275. Abu Hurairah relates that the Holy Prophet went into retreat for ten days in the month of Ramadhan but in the year in which he died he went into retreat for twenty days (Bokhari).

232.
On Pilgrimage

Allah, the Exalted, has said:

294. Pilgrimage to the House is a duty laid upon people which they owe to Allah, those of them who can afford the journey thither. Those who repudiate it should remember that Allah is Independent of all creatures (3.98).

1276. This *hadith* is the same as No. 1079.

1277. Abu Hurairah relates: The Holy Prophet addressed us and said: O ye people, Allah has prescribed the Pilgrimage for you, so mind that you perform it. A man asked: Messenger of Allah, is it prescribed every year? The Holy Prophet kept silent till the man had repeated his question three times. Then the Holy Prophet observed: Had I said yes, it would have become obligatory and you could not have offorded it; then he added: Leave me alone so long as I do not impose anything on you. Some who were before you were ruined by their habit of asking too many questions and differing with their Prophets. Thus when I direct you to do something carry out my direction as far as it is within your power and when I forbid you anything then leave it altogether (Muslim).

1278. Abu Hurairah relates that the Holy Prophet was asked: Which action is best? He answered: Faith in Allah and His Messenger. He was asked: And thereafter? He answered: Faith in Allah and His Messenger. He was asked: And thereafter? He answered: Striving in the cause of Allah. He was asked: And after that? He answered: Pure Pilgrimage (Bokhari and Muslim).

1279. Abu Hurairah relates that he heard the Holy Prophet say: He who performs the Pilgrimage without indulging in vain talk or committing any default returns from the Pilgrimage as pure as he was on the day his mother bore him (Bokhari and Muslim).

1280. Abu Hurairah relates that the Holy Prophet said: Umrah followed by another Umrah atones for that which is between the two and the only reward of the Pilgrimage is Paradise (Bokhari and Muslim).

1281. Ayesha relates: I asked the Holy Prophet: Messenger of Allah, we consider that striving in the cause of Allah is the best deed, then shall we not go forth in the cause of Allah? He answered: The best striving in the cause of Allah for you is the Pilgrimage (Bokhari).

1282. Ayesha relates that the Holy Prophet said: Allah does not relieve more people from chastisement of the Fire on any day than on the Day of *Arafat* (Muslim).

1283. Ibn Abbas relates that the Holy Prophet said: Umrah performed during Ramadhan equals the Pilgrimage (or equals Pilgrimage in my company) (Bokhari and Muslim).

1284. A woman asked the Holy Prophet: Messenger of Allah, the Pilgrimage has been imposed by Allah on his servants at a time when my father has reached extreme old age and has not the strength to ride an animal. Shall I perform the Pilgrimage on his behalf? He answered: Yes (Bokhari and Muslim).

1285. Laqit ibn 'Amir relates that he came to the Holy Prophet and said: My father is a very old man who has not the strength to perform the Pilgrimage or Umrah or to undertake the journey. The Holy Prophet said: Perform the *Hajj* and Umrah on behalf of your father (Abu Daud and Tirmidhi).

1286. Saib ibn Yazid relates: I was seven years old when I was taken to Pilgrimage at the same time when the Holy Prophet performed the Pilgrimage (Bokhari).

1287. This *hadith* is the same as No. 181.

1288. Anas relates that the Holy Prophet performed the Pilgrimage on a camel which also carried his provisions (Bokhari).

1289. Ibn Abbas relates: Ukaz and Majinnah and Zulmajez were trade markets in pre-Islamic days. In Islam people imagined that it would be sinful to carry on trade and commerce during the Pilgrimage, whereupon the verse was revealed: It is no sin for you to seek any of the bounties of your Lord during the days of the Pilgrimage (2.199) (Bokhari).

233.
On Striving in the Cause of Allah

Allah, the Exalted, has said:

295. Fight the idolators all together, as they fight you all together, and know that Allah is with the righteous (9.36).

296. *Fighting is ordained for you, while it is repugnant to you. It may be that you dislike a thing which is good for you, and it may also be that you prefer a thing and it may be the worse for you. Allah knows all and you know not (2.217).*

297. *Go forth, without equipment or with equipment, and strive in the cause of Allah with your belongings and your persons (9.41).*

298. *Allah has purchased of the believers their persons and their belongings in return for the promise that they shall have Paradise, for they fight in the cause of Allah and they slay the enemy or are themselves slain. This is a promise that He has made incumbent upon Himself as set out in the Torah, and the Gospel and the Quran; and who is more faithful to his promises than Allah? Rejoice, then, in the bargain that you have made with Him; that indeed is the supreme triumph (9.111).*

299. *Those of the believers who remain at home, except those who are disabled, and those who strive in the cause of Allah with their belongings and their persons are not equal. Allah has exalted in rank those who strive with their belongings and their persons above those who remain at home. To all Allah has promised good. Allah has exalted those who strive above those who remain at home with the promise of a great reward, in the shape of degrees of excellence to be bestowed by Him, and forgiveness and mercy. Allah is Most Forgiving, Ever Merciful (4.96-97).*

300. *O ye who believe, shall I guide you to a commerce that will deliver you from a painful chastisement? It is that you believe in Allah and His Messenger, and strive in the cause of Allah with your belongings and your persons, that is the better for you, did you but know. He will forgive you your sins and will admit you to gardens beneath which rivers flow, and to pure and pleasant dwellings in Gardens of Eternity. That is the supreme triumph (61.11-14).*

1290. This *hadith* is the same as No. 1278.

1291. This *hadith* is the same as No. 314.

1292. This *hadith* is comprehended in No. 1278.

1293. Anas relates that the Holy Prophet said: To be occupied in the cause of Allah a morning or evening is better than the world and all it contains (Bokhari and Muslim).

1294. Abu Sa'id Khudri relates that a man came to the Holy Prophet

and asked: Who is the best of mankind? He answered: A believer who strives
with his person and his property in the cause of Allah. The man asked: And
after him? He said: A believer who worships Allah in a mountain valley and
spares people all mischief (Bokhari and Muslim).

1295.   Sahl ibn Sa'ad relates that the Holy Prophet said: Patrolling the
frontier for a day is better than the world and all it contains. Your being
allotted a strip in Paradise no wider than your horse-whip is better than the
world and all it contains. Being occupied with striving in the cause of Allah for
a morning or an evening is better than the world and all it contains (Bokhari
and Muslim).

1296.   Salman relates that he heard the Holy Prophet say: Patrolling the
frontier for a day and a night is better than a month's fasting and voluntary
Prayer at night and should such a one die while engaged in such patrolling,
that with which he was occupied and his provision will both be continued and
he will be shielded against the trials of the grave (Muslim).

1297.   Fuzalah ibn Ubaid relates that the Holy Prophet said: Death puts
an end to all action, except in the case of one who patrols the frontier in the
cause of Allah, for his activity continues to grow till the Day of Judgment and
he is shielded against the trials of the grave (Abu Daud and Tirmidhi).

1298.   Uthman relates that he heard the Holy Prophet say: Patrolling the
frontier for a day in the cause of Allah is better than a thousand days of other
good works (Tirmidhi).

1299.   Abu Hurairah relates that the Holy Prophet said: To him who
goes forth in His cause, impelled only by the desire to strive in His cause, and
by faith in Him and by his affirmation of the truth of His Messengers, Allah
guarantees that He will admit him to Paradise or bring him back to the home
from which he issued forth together with the reward or spoils achieved by him.
By Him in Whose hands is Muhammad's life such a one will suffer no injury
in the cause of Allah but that he will appear on the Day of Judgment in the
same condition in which he was on the day when he received the injury, its
colour will be the colour of blood and its smell will be like the fragrance of
musk. By Him in Whose hands is Muhammad's life, were it not that it would
be hard upon the Muslims, I would not tarry behind any party whatever that
goes forth to fight in the cause of Allah; but I have not the means to provide
transportation for them nor have they and it would be hard on them to remain
behind while I went forth. By Him in Whose hands is Muhammad's life, I
would wish to fight in the cause of Allah and be killed, and to fight again and
be killed, and to fight again and be killed (Muslim).

1300.   Abu Hurairah relates that the Holy Prophet said: Everyone who is
injured in the cause of Allah will appear on the Day of Judgment with his
wound bleeding, its colour the colour of blood and its smell like the fragrance
of musk (Bokhari and Muslim).

1301.   Mu'az relates that the Holy Prophet said: Paradise becomes
incumbent for a Muslim who fights for the cause of Allah for the briefest

space. He who receives a wound or a bruise in the cause of Allah, will appear on the Day of Judgment with it as it was; its colour that of saffron and its smell like the fragrance of musk (Abu Daud and Tirmidhi).

1302. Abu Hurairah relates that a companion of the Holy Prophet came upon a valley in which there was a spring of sweet water which pleased him greatly. He reflected: I wish I could withdraw from people and settle in this valley; but I shall do it only with the permission of the Holy Prophet. He mentioned this to the Holy Prophet who said to him: Do not do this, for one's standing ready in the cause of Allah is better than his Prayers in his home through seventy years. Would you not wish that Allah should forgive you and admit you to Paradise? Then fight in the cause of Allah. Paradise becomes incumbent for those who fight in the cause of Allah even for the briefest space (Tirmidhi).

1303. Abu Hurairah relates that the Holy Prophet was asked: Messenger of Allah, what other good deed equals striving in the cause of Allah? He answered: You have not the strength to carry it out. The question was repeated twice or three times and each time he answered: You have not the strength to carry it out. He then added: The case of one who strives in the cause of Allah is like that of a person who should observe the fast and the Prayers and should carry out Allah's commandments in a humble spirit and should not interrupt his observance of the fast or his participation in Prayer till the return of the one who is striving in the cause of Allah (Bokhari and Muslim). Bokhari's version is: A man asked the Holy Prophet: Messenger of Allah, tell me of some action that should be equal to Jehad in its merit. He answered: I do not know of any; and added: Have you the strength that when a person goes forth to strive in the cause of Allah you should enter the mosque and stand in Prayer and not interrupt it and observe the fast and not break it (till he should return)? The man said: Who would have the strength to do this?

1304. Abu Hurairah relates that the Holy Prophet said: The best life is that of a person who stands ready in the cause of Allah holding the bridle of his pony and flies on its back to the spot whence he hears any intimation of danger or anxiety seeking slaughter or death; or that of a person on the top of a hill or in a valley who observes Prayer, pays the *Zakat* and worships his Lord till he is overtaken by death and does not concern himself with the affairs of anyone except the doing of good (Muslim).

1305. Abu Hurairah relates that the Holy Prophet said: There are a hundred grades in Paradise which Allah has prepared for those who strive in the cause of Allah and the distance between any two of those grades is like the distance between heaven and earth (Bokhari).

1306. Abu Sa'id Khudri relates that the Holy Prophet said: Paradise becomes incumbent for a person who is pleased with Allah as his Lord and with Islam as his faith and with Muhammad as Messenger. Abu Sa'id was pleased with this and requested the Holy Prophet to repeat it. He repeated it and added: There is something else by which Allah exalts a servant a hundred grades in Paradise, the distance between any two grades being like the distance between heaven and earth. Abu Sa'id asked: What is that, Messenger of Allah? He answered: Striving in the cause of Allah, striving in the cause of Allah (Muslim).

1307. Abu Bakr ibn Abu Musa Ash'ari relates that he heard his father say in the face of the enemy: The Holy Prophet said: The gates of Paradise are under the shadow of swords. Thereupon a man of lowly condition stood up and inquired: Abu Musa, did you indeed hear the Holy Prophet say that? He answered: Yes. The man then turned towards his companions and saluted them in farewell. He then broke the scabbard of his sword and threw it away and walked with his sword into the enemy ranks and fought till he was killed (Muslim).

1308. Abdullah ibn Jubair relates that the Holy Prophet said: The Fire will not touch one whose feet are covered with dust in striving for the cause of Allah (Bokhari).

1309. This *hadith* is the same as No. 451.

1310. Ibn Abbas relates that he heard the Holy Prophet say: The Fire will not touch two pairs of eyes; one that sheds tears out of fear of Allah and the other that keeps watch through the night in the cause of Allah (Tirmidhi).

1311. This *hadith* is the same as No. 179.

1312. Abu Umarah relates that the Holy Prophet said: The best charity is providing the shade of a tent in the cause of Allah, or providing a servant for one who strives in the cause of Allah, or providing a young she-camel for one striving in the cause of Allah (Tirmidhi).

1313. This *hadith* is the same as No. 178.

1314. Abu Sa'id Khudri relates that the Holy Prophet sent an expedition to Bani Lahyan and directed that out of every two men one should join the expedition and the reward of both will be equal (Muslim). Another version is: Let one out of every two men go forth: and added: whichever of you remains behind and looks well after the family and property of the one who has joined the expedition shall have his reward equal to half of the reward of the one who goes forth.

1315. Bra'a relates: A man in armour came to the Holy Prophet and asked: Messenger of Allah; shall I go and fight; or shall I become a Muslim? He answered: Become a Muslim and fight. He became a Muslim and fought and was slain, upon which the Holy Prophet said: He strove a little and was rewarded much (Bokhari and Muslim).

1316. Anas relates that the Holy Prophet said: No one who enters Paradise wishes to return to this world even if he should be given all that the world contains, except a martyr who yearns that he should return to the world and be slain ten times on account of the honour that he experiences by virtue of his martyrdom. One version has it: On account of that which he experiences of the excellence of martyrdom (Bokhari and Muslim).

1317. Abdullah ibn Amr ibn 'As relates that the Holy Prophet said:

Allah forgives everything to a martyr except his debt (Muslim). Another version is: Being slain in the cause of Allah atones for everything except debt (Muslim).

1318. This *hadith* is the same as No. 219.

1319. This *hadith* is the same as No. 89.

1320. Anas relates: The Holy Prophet went forth with his companions and arrived at Badr ahead of the idolators and directed: Let no one of you go forward ahead of me. When the idolators approached, the Holy Prophet said: Now stand up and proceed towards the Paradise whose extent comprehends the heaven and the earth; whereupon Umair ibn Hamam inquired: Messenger of Allah, does Paradise comprehend the heavens and the earth? He answered: Yes. Umair ejaculated: Well, well. The Holy Prophet asked him: What has urged you to say well, well? He answered: Messenger of Allah, I uttered these words to express the hope that I might become a dweller of Paradise. The Holy Prophet told him: You are one of its dwellers. He took out some dates from his quiver and began eating them. Then he said: Were I to survive till I finish eating these dates, that would be a long interval. So he threw away the remaining dates and rushed into the fighting and was slain (Muslim).

1321. Anas relates that some people came to the Holy Prophet and requested that he should send some men with them who should teach them the Quran and the *Sunnah*. He sent with them seventy men of the Ansar who were known as *qaris* (Reciters) among them my maternal uncle Haram. These people used to recite the Quran and occupied themselves at night with teaching and learning it. During the day, they brought water to the mosque and gathered wood for fuel which they sold and with the proceeds of which they purchased food for those who remained in attendance in the mosque and the needy. These people were sent by the Holy Prophet with those who had asked for them but were slaughtered treacherously on the way. While they were being slaughtered, they supplicated: O Allah, convey from us to our Prophet that we have reached Thee and are pleased with Thee and that Thou art pleased with us. A man approached Haram from his back and transfixed him with his spear, whereupon Haram ejaculated: By the Lord of the Ka'aba I have achieved my purpose. The Holy Prophet informed his companions: Your brethren have been slaughtered and they supplicated: O Allah convey from us to our Prophet that we have reached Thee and are pleased with Thee and that Thou art pleased with us (Bokhari and Muslim).

1322. This *hadith* is the same as No. 109.

1323. This *hadith* is a part of No. 1551.

1324. Anas relates that Umm Haritha ibn Suraqoh came to the Holy Prophet and said: Messenger of Allah, will you tell me about Haritha (he had been killed on the day of Badr) for if he is in Paradise I must bear it with fortitude and if not I might give vent to my grief. The Holy Prophet said to her: Umm Haritha, there are many grades in Paradise and your son has achieved *Firdaus*, the high (Bokhari).

1325. Jabir ibn Abdullah relates: The dead body of my father whose nose and ears had been cut off by the enemy was brought and placed before the Holy Prophet. I got up to uncover his face when the people stopped me and the Holy Prophet said: The angels continue to cover him with their wings (Bokhari and Muslim).

1326. This *hadith* is the same as No. 57.

1327. Anas relates that the Holy Prophet said: He who supplicates sincerely for martyrdom is granted it, even though he is not slain (Muslim).

1328. Abu Hurairah relates that the Holy Prophet said: A martyr does not suffer when he is slain anymore than one of you suffers from being bitten by an ant (Tirmidhi).

1329. Abdullah ibn Abi Aufa relates: On one of the occasions when the Holy Prophet encountered the enemy he waited for the decline of the sun and in the meantime stood up and addressed the people saying: Do not desire a brush with the enemy and continue to supplicate Allah for security. But when you meet the enemy be steadfast and remember that Paradise lies under the shadow of swords. Then he supplicated: Allah, Revealer of the Book, Driver of the clouds, Defeater of hosts, vanquish them and succour us against them (Bokhari and Muslim).

1330. Sahl ibn Sa'ad relates that the Holy Prophet said: Two supplications are not turned down (or are seldom turned down), a supplication while the *azan* is being called and a supplication during battle when the fighting warms up. (Abu Daud).

1331. Anas relates: When the Holy Prophet went into battle, he would supplicate: Allah Thou art my Support and my Helper. I turn to Thee and fight with the strength bestowed by Thee (Abu Daud and Tirmidhi).

1332. This *hadith* is the same as No. 985.

1333. Ibn Umar relates that the Holy Prophet said: There is good in the forehead of horses till the Day of Judgment (Bokhari and Muslim).

1334. Urwah Bariqi relates that the Holy Prophet said: There is good in the forehead of horses till the Day of Judgment and reward and spoils (Bokhari and Muslim).

1335. Abu Hurairah relates that the Holy Prophet said: He who rears a horse for service in the cause of Allah, believing in Allah and relying on His promise, will find that its fodder and drink and droppings and urine will all be credited to him in the scales on the Day of Judgment (Bokhari).

1336. Abu Mas'ud relates: A man came to the Holy Prophet with a dromedary wearing a nose rope and said: This is in the cause of Allah. The Holy Prophet answered him: You will have in return for it on the Day of Judgment seven hundred dromedaries every one of them wearing a nose rope (Muslim).

1337. Uqbah ibn 'Amir Juhni relates that he heard the Holy Prophet say from the pulpit: Hearken! In the verse: Make ready for them whatever you can of armed strength (8.61); armed strength means archery; armed strength means archery (Muslim).

1338. Uqbah ibn 'Amir Juhni relates that he heard the Holy Prophet say: Soon many lands will be opened to you and Allah will help you, so let no one neglect his skill in archery (Muslim).

1339. Uqbah ibn 'Amir Juhni relates that the Holy Prophet said: He who is instructed in archery and neglects it is not of us (or he is guilty of disobedience) (Muslim).

1340. Uqbah ibn 'Amir Juhni relates that he heard the Holy Prophet say: Allah will admit three people to Paradise on account of one arrow: First, the one who makes it with a good motive, secondly, the one who shoots it, and, thirdly, the one who hands it up for shooting. So learn archery and riding. I prefer that you should learn archery rather than riding. He who gives up archery after having been instructed in it because of lack of interest neglects a bounty (Abu Daud).

1341. Sulama ibn Akwa relates: The Holy Prophet passed by a group who were practising archery and said to them: Practise archery, children of Ishmael, for your ancestor was an archer (Bokhari).

1342. Amr ibn Abusah relates that he heard the Holy Prophet say: He who shoots an arrow in the cause of Allah has merit equal to the freeing of a slave (Abu Daud and Tirmidhi).

1343. Abu Yahya Kharaim ibn Fatik relates that the Holy Prophet said: He who spends in the cause of Allah has his reward seven hundred times (Tirmidhi).

1344. This *hadith* is the same as No. 1223.

1345. Abu Hurairah relates that the Holy Prophet said: He who observes the fast for a day in the cause of Allah will find that Allah has dug a moat between him and the Fire as wide as the distance between heaven and earth (Tirmidhi).

1346. Abu Hurairah relates that the Holy Prophet said: He who dies without having fought in the cause of Allah and without having thought of it in his mind dies with one characteristic of hypocrisy within him (Muslim).

1347. Jabir relates: We were together with the Holy Prophet in an expedition when he said: There are in Medina men who are with you so far as merit is concerned wherever you journey and whatever valley you traverse. They have only been prevented by illness (or by some other cause) from being with you, but they are your partners in reward (Bokhari and Muslim).

1348. This *hadith* is substantially the same as No. 8.

1349. Abdullah ibn Amr ibn 'As relates that the Holy Prophet said: There is no company or group which fights in the cause of Allah and gathers spoils and is delivered safe but has received two-thirds of its reward in this life. And there is no group or company which suffers and is defeated but that its full reward is awaited (Muslim).

1350. Abu Hurairah relates that a man asked the Holy Prophet's permission to travel and he told him: The travel for my people is striving in the cause of Allah, the Lord of honour and glory (Abu Daud).

1351. Abdullah ibn Amr ibn 'As relates that the Holy Prophet said: The return from an expedition after its completion is as meritorious as the fighting.

1352. Saib ibn Yazid relates: When the Holy Prophet returned from the battle of Tabuk, people went out from Medina to meet him and I also met him with other boys at Thaniyyah-til-Wada'a (Abu Daud). Bokhari's version is: We went to Thaniyyah-til-Wada'a with other boys to meet the Holy Prophet.

1353. Abu Hurairah relates that the Holy Prophet said: He who did not take part in fighting or equip a fighter or look well after the family of a fighter would be afflicted by severe misfortune before the Day of Judgment (Abu Daud).

1354. Anas relates that the Holy Prophet said: Strive against the idolators with your belongings, your persons and your tongues (Abu Daud).

1355. Nu'man ibn Muqarrin relates: I have witnessed that when the Holy Prophet did not begin fighting in the early part of the day, he postponed it till the declining of the sun and the starting of the breeze. Then help would arrive from Allah (Abu Daud and Tirmidhi).

1356. Abu Hurairah relates that the Holy Prophet said: Desire not an encounter with the enemy, but when you meet the enemy be steadfast (Bokhari and Muslim).

1357. Abu Hurairah and Jabir relate that the Holy Prophet said: War is a matter of tactics (Bokhari and Muslim).

, 234.

On Martyrdom without Fighting

1358. Abu Hurairah relates that the Holy Prophet said: There are five who are martyrs; he who dies of the plague, he who dies of cholera, he who dies of drowning, he who is killed by the falling of a wall and he who becomes a martyr by fighting in the cause of Allah (Bokhari and Muslim).

1359. Abu Hurairah relates that the Holy Prophet asked: Whom do you consider a martyr? He was answered: Messenger of Allah, he who is slain in the cause of Allah is a martyr. He said: Then there will be few martyrs among my people. He was asked: Messenger of Allah, who is then a martyr? He answered: He who is slain in the cause of Allah is a martyr, he who dies in the cause of Allah is a martyr, he who dies of the plague is a martyr, he who dies of cholera is a martyr, he who dies of drowning is a martyr (Muslim).

1360. Abdullah ibn Amr ibn 'As relates that the Holy Prophet said: He who is killed in defence of his property is a martyr (Bokhari and Muslim).

1361. Sa'id ibn Zaid ibn Amr ibn Nufail relates that he heard the Holy Prophet say: He who dies in the defence of his property is a martyr, he who dies in his own defence is a martyr, he who dies in defence of his faith is a martyr, he who dies in defence of his family is a martyr (Abu Daud and Tirmidhi).

1362. Abu Hurairah relates: A man came to the Holy Prophet and asked: Messenger of Allah, tell me if a person comes intending to take away my property, what shall I do? He answered: Do not give it to him. The man asked: but what if he should fight me? The Holy Prophet said: Then fight him. The man asked: If he should kill me? Then you are a martyr. The man asked: If I should kill him? The Holy Prophet answered: He will be in the Fire. (Muslim).

235.
On the Excellence of Freeing a Slave

Allah, the Exalted, has said:

301.   But he attempted not the scaling of the height. How shouldst thou know what the scaling of the height is? It is the freeing of a slave (90.12-14).

1363. Abu Hurairah relates that the Holy Prophet said: He who frees a Muslim slave will have every one of his limbs delivered from the Fire in return for each of the limbs of the slave (Bokhari and Muslim).

1364. This *hadith* is part of No. 117.

236.
On Benevolence towards Slaves

Allah, the Exalted, has said:—

302.   Worship Allah and associate naught with Him, and be benevolent towards parents, and kindred, and orphans, and the needy, and the neighbour who is a kinsman, and the neighbour who is not related to you, and your associates and the wayfarer, and those who are under your control (4.37).

1365. Ma'arur ibn Su'ud relates: I saw Abu Dharr wearing a cloak and I noticed that his slave was wearing the like of it. I inquired from him about this and he explained that in the time of the Holy Prophet he had a sharp exchange with a man and shamed him by making a reference to his mother. Thereupon the Holy Prophet said to me: You still have traces of pre-Islamic culture in you. Your servants are your brothers whom your Lord has placed under your authority. He who has a brother under his authority should feed him out of that which he eats himself and should clothe him as he clothes himself. Do not assign a task to them which is beyond their strength and if you do so help them in carrying it out (Bokhari and Muslim).

1366. Abu Hurairah relates that the Holy Prophet said: When a servant of yours brings you your food, if you do not ask him to sit down with you, you should at least give him a morsel or two out of it, for he has laboured in preparing it (Bokhari).

237.
On the Excellence of a Servant who discharges his Duty to Allah and his Duty to his Master

1367. Ibn Umar relates that the Holy Prophet said: A slave who serves his master well and worships Allah well will have a double reward (Bokhari and Muslim).

1368. Abu Hurairah relates that the Holy Prophet said: A pious, diligent slave has a double reward (Bokhari and Muslim).

1369. Abu Musa Ash'ari relates that the Holy Prophet said: A slave who worships his Lord duly and discharges diligently and obediently the obligations he owes to his master will have a double reward (Bokhari).

1370. Abu Musa Ash'ari relates that the Holy Prophet said: There are those who will have a double reward. One, a man of the People of the Book who believes in his Prophet and believes in Muhammad; two, a slave who discharges duly the obligation he owes to Allah and the obligation he owes to his master, and three, a man who owns a female slave and trains her well and educates her well and feeds her and marries her (Bokhari and Muslim).

238.
On the Excellence of Worship during Disturbances

1371. Ma'qail ibn Yasir relates that the Holy Prophet said: To carry out worship when conditions are disturbed is equal to emigration to me (Muslim).

239.

On the Excellence of Fair Dealing

Allah, the Exalted, has said:

303.   Whatever of good you do, Allah knows it well (2.216).
304.   O my people, give full measure and full weight with justice and do not defraud people by making short delivery (11.86).

305.   Woe unto those who give short measure; those who, when they take by measure from other people take it full; but when they give by measure to others or weigh out to them give them less. Do not such people know that they will be raised up again unto a terrible day, the day when mankind will stand before the Lord of the worlds? (83.2-7).

1372.   Abu Hurairah relates that a man came to the Holy Prophet and was harsh in demanding the repayment of his loan. The companions were about to take hold of him when the Holy Prophet said: Leave him alone, for one to whom an obligation is due is entitled to make a demand and he added: Give him a camel of the same age as the camel that is due to him. He was told that only a better camel than the one due to the creditor was available. The Holy Prophet said: Give him the better one for the best of you are those who discharge their obligations best (Bokhari and Muslim).

1373.   Jabir relates that the Holy Prophet said: Allah will have mercy on a man who is easy when he sells and when he buys and when he demands the discharge of an obligation due to him (Bokhari).

1374.   Abu Qatadah relates that he heard the Holy Prophet say: He who desires that Allah should deliver him from the discomfort of the Day of Judgment should grant respite to one who is in straitened circumstances or should remit the debt altogether (Muslim).

1375.   Abu Hurairah relates that the Holy Prophet said: A man had dealings with people and instructed his agent: When you come to one who is in straitened circumstances, forbear, maybe that Allah will forbear when our turn comes. When he met Allah, He forbore (Bokhari and Muslim).

1376.   Abu Mas'ud Badri relates that the Holy Prophet said: A man before you was called to account and nothing good was found to his credit except that he had dealings with people and was in easy circumstances and had instructed his agents that they should forbear in the case of those in straitened circumstances. Allah, the Lord of honour and glory, said: I am more worthy of this quality. Forbear from him (Muslim).

1377.   Huzaifah relates that a man was brought before Allah upon whom He had bestowed wealth and He asked him: How did you conduct yourself in the world? He answered (and it is not possible to conceal anything from Allah): Lord, thou didst bestow wealth upon me from Thyself and I carried on business with people with it and it was my habit to forbear. I was easy with one who was in easy circumstances and granted respite to one who was in straitened circumstances. Thereupon Allah, the Exalted, said: I am more worthy of these qualities than you are; and He commanded: Forbear against this servant of Mine. Uqbah ibn Amr and Abu Mas'ud Ansari affirm that they heard the Holy Prophet say this (Muslim).

1378. Abu Hurairah relates that the Holy Prophet said: He who grants respite to one in straitened circumstances or gives up a portion of his claim against him, will be sheltered by Allah under the shadow of His throne on the Day of Judgment when there will be no other shade than His shade (Tirmidhi).

1379. Jabir relates that the Holy Prophet purchased a camel from him and weighed out to him more than its price (Bokhari and Muslim).

1380. Abu Safwan Su'ud ibn Qais relates: Makhramah Abdi and I procured some drapery from Hajar and the Holy Prophet came to us and purchased a pair of trousers from us. We had a person who weighed in the price of the stuff sold. The Holy Prophet said to him: Weigh in and add a little to it (Abu Daud and Tirmidhi).

240.
On Knowledge

Allah, the Exalted, has said:

306. Keep up the supplication: Lord bestow on me an increase of knowledge (20.115).

307. Ask them: Can those who know be like those who know not (39.10)?

308. Allah will exalt in rank those from among you who believe and those to whom knowledge is given (58.12).

309. Of the servants of Allah it is those who possess knowledge who fear Him (35.29).

1381. Mu'awiah relates that the Holy Prophet said: Upon him for whom Allah desires good, He bestows understanding of the Faith (Bokhari and Muslim).

1382. This *hadith* is the same as No. 547.

1383. This *hadith* is the same as No. 163.

1384. This *hadith* is the last part of No. 177.

1385. Abdullah ibn Amr ibn 'As relates that the Holy Prophet said: Convey to people my directions though only in the shape of one verse; and you may borrow events from Bani Ismail without harm. But he who deliberately attributes to me something which is not true should prepare his seat in the Fire (Bokhari).

1386. Abu Hurairah relates that the Holy Prophet said: For him who follows a path for seeking knowledge, Allah will ease the way to Paradise (Muslim).

1387. Abu Hurairah relates that the Holy Prophet said: He who calls another to guidance will have a reward equal to the reward of him who follows him; this will not diminish the reward of either of them (Muslim).

1388. This *hadith* is the same as No. 953.

1389. This *hadith* is the same as No. 481.

1390. Anas relates that the Holy Prophet said: He who issues forth in search of knowledge is busy in the cause of Allah till he returns from his quest (Tirmidhi).

1391. Abu Sa'id Khudri relates that the Holy Prophet said: A believer never has his fill of knowledge till he ends up in Paradise (Tirmidhi).

1392. Abu Umamah relates that the Holy Prophet said: A learned one is as much above a worshipper as I am above the least of you; and he added: Allah, His angels and all those in the heavens and the earth even the ants in their heaps and the fish in the water call down blessings on those who instruct people in beneficent knowledge (Tirmidhi).

1393. Abu Darda' relates that he heard the Holy Prophet say: For him who adopts a path seeking knowledge, Allah eases the way to Paradise and angels spread their wings for a seeker of knowledge, being pleased with his occupation, and all that are in the heavens and the earth, including the fish in the water, ask for forgiveness for a learned one. A learned one is superior to a worshipper as the moon is superior to all the planets. The divines are heirs of the Prophets and the Prophets do not leave an inheritance of dirhems and dinars but only of knowledge. He who acquires knowledge acquires a vast portion (Abu Daud and Tirmidhi).

1394. Ibn Mas'ud relates that he heard the Holy Prophet say: May Allah prosper the affairs of a person who hears something from me and conveys it to others as he heard it, for sometimes one who hears from another remembers it better than the original hearer himself (Tirmidhi).

1395. Abu Hurairah relates that the Holy Prophet said: He who is asked about knowledge and conceals it will be bridled on the Day of Judgment with a bridle of Fire (Abu Daud and Tirmidhi).

1396. Abu Hurairah relates that the Holy Prophet said: He who acquires knowledge through which the pleasure of Allah, the Lord of honour and glory, might be sought only so that he might attain through it something that he desires of the world will not perceive even the fragrance of Paradise on the Day of Judgment (Abu Daud).

1397. Abdullah ibn Amr ibn 'As relates that he heard the Holy Prophet say: Allah will not roll up knowledge by withdrawing it from people but will put it out of reach through the death of divines with the result that when there are no divines people will adopt ignorant ones as their leaders and will ask them for guidance and they will render their opinions without knowledge. They will be astray themselves and will lead others astray (Bokhari and Muslim).

241.

On Praise of Allah and His Gratitude

Allah, the Exalted, has said:

310. Keep Me, therefore, constantly in mind, I shall keep you in mind, and be grateful to Me and be not unmindful of the bounties that I have bestowed upon you. (2.153).

311. If you will use My bounties beneficently, I will surely multiply them unto you. (14.8).

312. Proclaim: All Praise belongs to Allah (17.112).

313. The end of their prayer will be: All praise belongs to Allah, the Lord of the worlds. (10.11).

1398. Abu Hurairah relates that on the night of his Ascent the Holy Prophet was presented with two cups, one containing liquor and the other containing milk. He looked at them and took the one that had milk in it. Thereupon Gabriel said to him: All praise be to Allah who has guided you to that which is in accord with human nature. Had you selected liquor your people would have gone astray (Muslim).

1399. Abu Hurairah relates that the Holy Prophet said: Every matter of importance which is not begun with the praise of Allah, remains defective (Abu Daud).

1400. This *hadith* is the same as No. 926.

1401. This *hadith* is the same as No. 140.

242.

On Calling down Blessings on the Holy Prophet

Allah, the Exalted, has said:

314. Allah sends down blessings on the Prophet, and His angels invoke blessings on him. O ye who believe, do you also invoke blessings on him and salute him with the salutation of peace (33.57).

1402. Abdullah ibn Amr ibn 'As relates that he heard the Holy Prophet say: He who calls down blessings on me, Allah sends down blessings on him ten times (Muslim).

1403. Ibn Mas'ud relates that the Holy Prophet said: The closest to me on the Day of Judgment will be those who call down blessings on me most (Tirmidhi).

1404. Aus ibn Aus relates that the Holy Prophet said: The best of your days is Friday, then invoke blessings upon me frequently on that day, for your invocation is conveyed to me. He was asked: Messenger of Allah, how will our invocation be conveyed to you when you will have mixed with the earth? He answered: God has forbidden the earth from damaging the bodies of the Prophets (Abu Daud).

1405. Abu Hurairah relates that the Holy Prophet said: May humiliation afflict the man in whose presence mention is made of me and he does not invoke blessings upon me (Tirmidhi).

1406. Abu Hurairah relates that the Holy Prophet said: Do not make my grave a place of festivity but invoke blessings upon me for your blessing will reach me, wherever you may be (Abu Daud).

1407. Abu Hurairah relates that the Holy Prophet said: Whenever anyone invokes blessings upon me Allah will restore my soul to me so that I will respond to his invocation (Abu Daud).

1408. Ali relates that the Holy Prophet said: A miser is one who does not invoke blessings upon me when I am mentioned in his presence (Tirmidhi).

1409. Fuzala ibn Ubaid relates: The Holy Prophet heard someone supplicate in his Prayer without glorification of Allah and without invoking blessings upon the Holy Prophet. Concerning him, the Holy Prophet observed: That one was in a hurry; then he called him and said to him (or to someone beside him): When one of you is in Prayer he should begin with Praise of his Lord and His glorification and then invoke blessings on the Prophet and then supplicate as he may wish (Abu Daud and Tirmidhi).

1410. Abu Muhammad Ka'ab ibn Ujrah relates: The Holy Prophet came to us and we asked him: Messenger of Allah, we know how to salute you but how shall we invoke blessings upon you? He answered: Say: O Allah, send down thy blessings on Muhammad and the people of Muhammad as Thou didst send down Thy blessings on the people of Abraham, Thou art indeed the Praiseworthy, the Glorious. O Allah, foster Muhammad and the people of Muhammad as Thou didst foster the people of Abraham, for Thou art the Praiseworthy, the Glorious (Bokhari and Muslim).

1411. Abu Mas'ud Badri relates: We went to the Holy Prophet and we were in the company of Sa'ad ibn Ubadah and Bashir ibn Sa'ad asked the Holy Prophet: Messenger of Allah, we are commanded by Allah to invoke blessings on you, then how shall we invoke blessings on you? The Holy Prophet remained silent till we wished that he had not asked him this question. After a while the Holy Prophet said: Say: O Allah, send down Thy blessings on Muhammad and on the people of Muhammad as Thou didst send down Thy blessings on Abraham, and foster Muhammad and the people of Muhammad as Thou didst foster the people of Abraham. Indeed Thou art the Praiseworthy, the Glorious; and the salutation is as you know (Muslim).

1412. Abu Humaid Sa'idi relates: The Holy Prophet was asked: How shall we invoke blessings on thee? He answered: Say: O Allah, send down Thy blessings on Muhammad and on his wives and on his progeny as Thou didst send down Thy blessings on Abraham and foster Muhammad and his wives and his progeny as Thou didst foster Abraham. Indeed Thou art the Praiseworthy, the Glorious (Bokhari and Muslim).

243.
On the Remembrance of Allah

Allah, the Exalted, has said:

315.   Verily, the remembrance of Allah possesses the highest beneficence (29.46).

316.   Keep Me, therefore, constantly in mind, I shall keep you in mind (2.153).

317.   Remember thy Lord in thy mind with humility and fear, in low tones, morning and evening and be not neglectful (7.206).

318.   And remember Allah much that you may prosper (62. 11).

319.   For men who submit themselves wholly to Allah, and women who submit themselves wholly to Him, and men who believe and women who believe and men who are obedient and women who are obedient, and men who are truthful and women who are truthful, and men who are steadfast and women who are steadfast, and men who are humble and women who are humble, and men who give alms and women who give alms, and men who fast and women who fast, and men who guard their chastity and women who guard their chastity and men who remember Allah much and women who remember Him, Allah has prepared forgiveness and a great reward (33.36).

320.   O ye who believe, remember Allah much; and glorify Him morn and eve (33.42).

1413.   Abu Hurairah relates that the Holy Prophet said: There are two phrases that are easy on the tongue, but are heavy in the balance and are loved by the Gracious One: Glorified be Allah and His is the Praise; Glorified be Allah, the Lord of Majesty (Bokhari and Muslim).

1414.   Abu Hurairah relates that the Holy Prophet said: That I should say: Glory be to Allah, and to Allah belongs all Praise, and there is none worthy of worship save Allah, and Allah is Great; is dearer to me than the whole universe (Muslim).

1415.   Abu Hurairah relates that the Holy Prophet said: He who recites: There is none worthy of worship save Allah the One, Who has no associate, His is the Kingdom and His the Praise and He has Power over all things; a hundred times during the day will have merit equal to that of freeing ten slaves and a hundred good actions will be credited to him and a hundred of his defaults will be wiped out and he will be safeguarded against Satan till the end of the day; and no one will exceed him in doing good except one who recites these phrases more often than him. He also said: The defaults of one even if they be like the foam of the sea will be wiped out if he recites a hundred times in the day: Holy is Allah and to Him belongs all praise (Bokhari and Muslim).

1416. Abu Ayub Ansari relates that the Holy Prophet said: He who recites: There is none worthy of worship save Allah, the One, Who has no associate, His is the Kingdom and His the Praise, and He has Power over all things; ten times is like one who sets free four persons from among the descendants of Ishmael (Bokhari and Muslim).

1417. Abu Dharr relates that the Holy Prophet said to him: Shall I tell you what phrase is most agreeable to Allah? The phrase most agreeable to Allah is: Holy is Allah and worthy of all Praise (Muslim).

1418. Abu Malik Ash'ari relates that the Holy Prophet said: Cleanliness is half of faith, and the phrase: All Praise belongs to Allah; fills the balance, and the phrase: Holy is Allah and all praise belongs to Allah; fills the space between the heavens and the earth (Muslim).

1419. Sa'ad ibn Abi Waqqas relates that a rustic came to the Holy Prophet and begged him: Do teach me phrases that I should recite. The Holy Prophet answered him: Recite: There is none worthy of worship save Allah the One, Who has no associate. Allah is the greatest and much praise is due to Allah. Holy is Allah the Lord of the worlds and there is no strength to resist evil, nor power to do good except through Allah, the Mighty, the Wise. The man said: All this is for my Lord, is there anything for me? The Holy Prophet said: Recite: O Allah, forgive me and have mercy on me and guide me and provide for me (Muslim).

1420. Thauban relates that when the Holy Prophet finished his Prayer he asked forgiveness three times and recited: Allah, Thou art the Bestower of Peace and from Thee is peace. Blessed art Thou, O Lord of glory and honour. One of the narrators of the *hadith* was asked: In what terms did the Holy Prophet seek forgiveness? He answered: The Holy Prophet used to say: I beseech Allah for forgiveness, I beseech Allah for forgiveness (Muslim).

1421. Mughirah ibn Shu'bah relates that when the Holy Prophet finished his Prayer, he would recite: There is none worthy of worship save Allah, the One, Who has no associate, His is the Kingdom and His the Praise and He has power over all things. Allah, none may obstruct what Thou dost bestow and none may bestow what Thou dost hold back and to a man of means his means will avail nothing against Thee (Bokhari and Tirmidhi).

1422. Abdullah ibn Zubair used to recite after every Prayer: There is none worthy of worship save Allah, the One, Who has no associate; His is the Kingdom and His the Praise and He has power over all things. There is no strength to resist evil nor power to do good except through Allah. There is none worthy of worship, save Allah. We worship none save Him; His is the bounty and the grace and for Him is all excellent praise; there is none worthy of worship save Allah. We hold to Him with full sincerity of faith though the disbelievers may resent it. The Holy Prophet used to celebrate Allah's Greatness in those terms after every Prayer (Muslim).

1423. This *hadith* is the same as No. 576.

1424. Abu Hurairah relates that the Holy Prophet said: He who recites after every Prayer: Holy is Allah; thirty three times and: To Allah belongs all Praise; thirty three times; and recites: Allah is Great; thirty three times; and completes the century with reciting: There is none worthy of worship save Allah, the One, Who has no associate; His is the Kingdom and His the Praise and He has power over all things: will have his sins forgiven though they may be like the foam of the sea (Muslim).

1425. Ka'ab ibn Ujrah relates that the Holy Prophet said: There are phrases, one who recites them after every prescribed Prayer will never be frustrated, that is to say, celebration of Divine Holiness thirty three times, of His Praise thirty three times and of His Greatness thirty four times (Muslim).

1426. Sa'ad ibn Abi Waqqas relates that the Holy Prophet used to seek protection after his Prayers with these phrases: Allah, I seek Thy protection from cowardice and miserliness and from being brought to a state of helplessness and seek Thy protection from the trials of this life and from the trials of the grave (Bokhari).

1427. Mu'az relates that the Holy Prophet took hold of his hand and said: Mu'az, Allah knows that I love you and I admonish you, Mu'az, that you should never omit reciting after every Prayer: Allah, assist me in remembering Thee and being grateful to Thee and performing Thy worship in an excellent manner (Abu Daud).

1428. Abu Hurairah relates that the Holy Prophet said: When you reach the stage in your Prayer of bearing witness you should seek the protection of Allah from four contingencies, saying: Allah, I seek Thy protection from the torment of hell, from the torment of the grave, from the trials of life and death and from the mischief of the Anti-Christ (Muslim).

1429. Ali relates that the Holy Prophet when he was in Prayer, would supplicate towards the end of the Prayer after bearing witness and before the concluding salutation: Allah forgive me that which I have sent on and that which is to come, that which I have done covertly and that which I have done overtly and that in which I have been guilty of excess and those of my defaults of which Thou hast better knowledge than I have. Thou dost advance one and Thou dost put one back. There is none worthy of worship save Thee (Muslim).

1430. Ayesha relates that in his bowing and prostration the Holy Prophet recited repeatedly: Holy art Thou, O Allah our Lord, and Thine is the Praise. Forgive me, O Allah (Bokhari and Muslim).

1431. Ayesha relates that the Holy Prophet repeated in his bowing and prostration: The Glorious, the Most Holy Lord of the angels and of the Spirit (Muslim).

1432. Ibn Abbas relates that the Holy Prophet said: In bowing glorify the Lord and in prostration exert yourself in supplication. Thus will you ensure acceptance of your supplications (Muslim).

1433. Abu Hurairah relates that the Holy Prophet said: A servant is closest to his Lord when he is in prostration, so multiply your supplications in prostration (Muslim).

1434. Abu Hurairah relates that the Holy Prophet would supplicate in his prostration: Allah forgive me all my sins small and great, first and last, overt and covert (Muslim).

1435. Ayesha relates: One night I missed the Holy Prophet from his bed so I cast about and discovered that he was in bowing and prostration and was reciting: Holy art Thou and Thine is the Praise and there is none worthy of worship save Thee. One version has it: My hand came up against his feet while he was in prostration and his feet were erect and he was supplicating: Allah I seek the protection of Thy pleasure against Thy wrath and the protection of Thy forgiveness against Thy chastisement and Thy protection against Thyself. I have not the capacity to enumerate Thy Praise. Thou art as Thou hast described Thyself (Muslim).

1436. Sa'ad ibn Abi Waqqas relates: We were with the Holy Prophet when he said: Would any of you have the strength to perform a thousand good deeds in a day? One of those present asked him: How might a thousand good deeds be performed? He answered: If one glorifies the Lord a hundred times he would be credited with a thousand good deeds or a thousand of his faults would be wiped out (Muslim).

1437. This *hadith* is the same as No. 118.

1438. Juwairiah bint Harith (wife of the Holy Prophet) relates that the Holy Prophet went out from her one morning after the dawn Prayer while she was still in her place where she had offered her Prayer and came back after the sun had risen and she was still sitting at her place, whereupon he said: Have you continued in the same condition in which I left you? She said: Yes. The Holy Prophet then said: After I left you, I recited four phrases three times. If they were weighed against that which you have said this morning they would prove weightier. They are: Holy is Allah and worthy of all Praise, as many times as the number of all His creation and according to His pleasure and corresponding to the weight of His throne and the number of His words (Muslim). Another version is: Holy is Allah the number of His creation, Holy is Allah according to His pleasure, Holy is Allah corresponding to the weight of his Throne, Holy is Allah the number of His words. Tirmidhi's version is: Shall I teach you phrases which you might recite? Holy is Allah, the number of His creation, Holy is Allah the number of His creation, Holy is Allah the number of His creation; Holy is Allah according to His pleasure, Holy is Allah according to His pleasure, Holy is Allah according to His pleasure; Holy is Allah corresponding to the weight of His

Throne, Holy is Allah corresponding to the weight of His Throne, Holy is Allah corresponding to the weight of His Throne; Holy is Allah the number of His words, Holy is Allah the number of His words, Holy is Allah the number of His words.

1439.   Abu Musa Ash'ari relates that the Holy Prophet said: The case of one who remembers his Lord and of one who does not remember his Lord is like that of the living and the dead (Bokhari). Muslim's version is: The case of a house in which Allah is remembered, and of one in which Allah is not remembered is like that of the living and the dead.

1440.   Abu Hurairah relates that the Holy Prophet said: Allah, the Exalted, said: I am to a servant of Mine as he imagines Me to be. I am with him when he remembers Me. If he remembers Me in his mind I remember him in My mind; and if he remembers Me in company I remember him in better company (Bokhari and Muslim).

1441.   Abu Hurairah relates that the Holy Prophet said: The *mufarridun* will outstrip the rest. He was asked: Who are the *mufarridun?* He answered: The men who remember Allah much and the women who remember Allah much (Muslim).

1442.   Jabir relates that he heard the Holy Prophet say: The best remembrance of Allah is: There is none worthy of worship save Allah (Tirmidhi).

1443.   Abdullah ibn Busr relates that a man asked the Holy Prophet: Messenger of Allah, the ordinances of Islam appear to me a host, so kindly tell me something to which I should hold fast. He answered him: Let thy tongue be constantly occupied with the remembrance of Allah (Tirmidhi).

1444.   Jabir relates that the Holy Prophet said: For him who says: Holy is Allah and to Him belongs all praise; a date tree is planted in Paradise (Tirmidhi).

1445.   Ibn Mas'ud relates that the Holy Prophet said: The night of my Ascent I met Abraham and he said to me: Muhammad, convey my *salam* to your people and tell them that Paradise is a vast plain of pure soil and sweet water and that its trees cry: Holy is Allah, all praise is due to Allah, there is none worthy of worship save Allah, and Allah is Great (Tirmidhi).

1446.   Abu Darda' relates that the Holy Prophet said: Shall I tell you what is your best action, the purest in the estimation of kings, that which raises your rank to the highest, is better for you than spending gold and silver, and is better for you than that you should encounter the enemy and cut off their necks, they cutting off yours? Tell us indeed; they answered; and he said: It is the remembrance of Allah, the Exalted (Tirmidhi).

1447.   Sa'ad ibn Abi Waqqas relates that he was with the Holy Prophet when the latter came to a woman who had a heap of date stones (or pebbles) in front of her by which she counted her glorification of Allah; and he said to her: Shall I instruct you in a method that will be easier (or better) for you than this? Say: Holy is Allah the number of those He has created in the heaven, Holy is

Allah the number of those He has created in the earth, Holy is Allah the number of those between the two, Holy is Allah the number of those He will create; and then say: Allah is Great; in the same way; and: All praise belongs to Allah; in the same way; and: There is none worthy of worship save Allah; in the same way; and: There is no strength to resist evil and no power to do good except through Allah; in the same way (Tirmidhi).

1448. Abu Musa relates: The Holy Prophet said to me: Shall I inform you of one of the treasures of Paradise? I said: Certainly, Messenger of Allah. He said: It is: There is no strength to resist evil, nor power to do good except through Allah (Bokhari and Muslim).

244.

On Remembrance of Allah in all Situations

Allah, the Exalted, has said:

321.   In the creation of the heavens and the earth and in the alternation of night and day there are indeed Signs for people of understanding, who remember Allah, standing, sitting and lying on their sides (3. 191-192).

1449. Ayesha relates that the Holy Prophet remembered Allah on all occasions (Muslim).

1450. Ibn Abbas relates that the Holy Prophet said: If one of you when he consorts with his wife were to supplicate: In the name of Allah, keep us away from Satan, O Allah, and keep Satan away from that which Thou mightest bestow upon us; then if a child is decreed for them it would be shielded against all harm by Satan (Bokhari and Muslim).

245.

On Supplication on Retiring and Rising

1451. Huzaifah and Abu Dharr relate that the Holy Prophet supplicated on retiring at night: With Thy name, O Allah, I expire and return to life; and supplicated on rising: All praise belongs to Allah Who has brought me back to life after He had caused me to die, to Him is the return (Bokhari).

246.
On Remembrance in Company

Allah, the Exalted, has said:

322. Continue thy companionship with those who call on their Lord, morning and evening, seeking His pleasure and look not beyond them (18.29).

1452. Abu Hurairah relates that the Holy Prophet said: Allah has angels who patrol the streets looking for people who occupy themselves with the remembrance of Allah, and when they find a company so occupied they call to one another: Come to your duty; and they cover them with their wings up to the sky. Then their Lord inquires from them (and He Himself knows best): What are My servants saying? They report: They proclaim Thy Holiness and Greatness, and praise Thee and glorify Thee. He inquires: Have they seen Me? They answer: No, they have not seen Thee. He inquires: What if they saw Me? They answer: If they saw Thee they would be more diligent in Thy worship and Thy glorification and in proclaiming Thy Holiness. Then He inquires: What do they ask of Me. They answer: They ask of Thee Paradise. He inquires: Have they seen it? They answer: No Lord, they have not seen it. He inquires: What if they saw it? They answer: If they saw it they would desire it more and seek it more and yearn more for it. He inquires: From what do they seek protection? They answer: They seek protection from the Fire. Then He inquires: Have they seen it? They answer: No, they have not seen it. He inquires: What if they saw it? They answer: If they saw it they would run from it more and would fear it more. Then He says: I call upon you to witness that I forgive them. One of the angels then says: Among them is So and So. He is not one of them. He came to them for some purpose of his own. Allah says: They are a company whose associate shall not be frustrated (Bokhari and Muslim).

Muslim's version is: Allah has angels who travel constantly looking for companies who foregather for the remembrance of Allah. When they find one so occupied they sit down with them and cover one another with their wings so that the space between them and the sky is filled. When the company disperses the angels get up and ascend to heaven. Allah, the Lord of honour and glory, asks them (and He Himself knows best): Whence do you come? They answer: We come from some of Thy servants in the earth who proclaim Thy Holiness and Greatness and Unity and praise Thee and supplicate Thee. He inquires: What do they ask of Me? They answer: They ask of Thee Thy Paradise. He inquires: Have they seen My Paradise? They answer: No, Lord. Then He inquires: What if they were to see My Paradise? They say: They also seek Thy protection. He inquires: From what do they seek My protection? They answer: From Thy Fire, Lord. He inquires: Have they seen my Fire? They say: No. He inquires: What if they were to see My Fire? They add: And they ask Thy forgiveness. Then He says: I have forgiven them, and bestowed upon them what they ask for and have granted them My protection against that from which they seek protection. They say: Lord, there is among them one, So and So, a sinful creature who only passed by and sat down among them. He says: Him also have I forgiven. They are a company whose associate shall not be frustrated.

1453. Abu Sa'id Khudri and Abu Hurairah relate that the Holy Prophet said: When a company foregathers for the remembrance of Allah its members are surrounded by angels and are covered by mercy, and comfort descends upon them and Allah makes mention of them to those around Him (Muslim).

1454. Harith ibn Auf relates that while the Holy Prophet was seated in the mosque surrounded by people, three men came in. While two of them approached him and the third turned away, of the two, one perceived an opening between those who were seated and took his seat there and the other sat down behind those who were seated. When the Holy Prophet finished his talk, he said: I shall tell you about these three. One of them sought refuge with Allah and Allah gave him shelter. The second felt shy and Allah forbore from him. The third turned away and Allah turned away from him (Bokhari and Muslim).

1455. Abu Sa'id Khudri relates that Mu'awiah came into the mosque and saw a company seated therein. He asked them: What causes you to be seated here? They answered: We are gathered for the remembrance of Allah. He inquired: Do you call Allah to witness that that is your only purpose? They answered: That is so. He told them: I did not put you on oath out of any suspicion. No one situated like me *vis-a-vis* the Holy Prophet has narrated so little about him. The Holy Prophet on one occasion came upon a company of his companions and inquired: What has brought you together? They answered: We are seated together remembering Allah and praising Him for having guided us to Islam and having conferred this favour upon us. He inquired: Do you call Allah to witness that that is your only purpose? They answered: Allah is our witness that that is our only purpose. He said: I did not put you on oath out of any suspicion, but Gabriel came to me and told me that Allah takes pride in you among the angels. (Muslim).

247.

On Remembrance of Allah Morn and Eve

Allah, the Exalted, has said:

323. Remember thy Lord in thy mind with humility and fear, in low tones morning and evening, and be not neglectful (7. 206).

324. And glorify thy Lord with His Praise before the rising of the sun and before its setting (20. 131).

325. And glorify thy Lord with His praise morning and evening (40.56).

326. This light now illumines houses which Allah has ordained that they be exalted and in which His name is commemorated. Therein is He glorified morn and eve by men whom neither trade nor traffic beguiles from the remembrance of Allah (24. 37-38).
327. We subjected the people of the mountains to him. They celebrated the praises of Allah with him morn and eve (38.19).

1456. Abu Hurairah relates that the Holy Prophet said: He who recites morn and eve: Holy is Allah and all praise belongs to Him; a hundred times, will not be exceeded by any one in good works on the Day of Judgment unless by one who shall have recited the same like him or more (Muslim).

1457. Abu Hurairah relates: A man came to the Holy Prophet and said: Messenger of Allah, what torment I endured last night from the sting of a scorpion. He told him: Had you said before retiring: I seek the protection of the perfect words of Allah from the mischief of whatever He has created; it would have done you no harm (Muslim).

1458. Abu Hurairah relates that when the Holy Prophet rose in the morning he recited: Allah, with Thy favour have we arrived at the morning and with Thy favour do we live and we die and to Thee is the return; and when he retired in the evening he recited: Allah, with Thy favour have we arrived at the evening and with Thy favour do we live and we die and to Thee is the return (Abu Daud and Tirmidhi).

1459. Abu Hurairah relates that Abu Bakr said to the Holy Prophet: Messenger of Allah, instruct me in that which I should recite morn and eve. He said: Recite: Allah, Originator of the heavens and the earth, Knower of the unseen and the seen, Lord of all things and their Master, I bear witness that there is none worthy of worship save Thee, and I seek Thy protection from the evil of my mind and the evil of Satan and his incitement towards setting up Thy equals. The Holy Prophet said: Recite these morn and eve and on retiring to bed (Abu Daud and Tirmidhi).

1460. Ibn Mas'ud relates that the Holy Prophet would say in the evening: We have arrived at the evening and so has the land by the favour of Allah, and all praise belongs to Allah, and there is none worthy of worship save Allah, the One, Who has no associate. The narrator says: I think he would also say: His is the Kingdom and His the Praise, and He has power over all things. Lord, I ask thee for all the good of this night and the good of that which will follow it, and seek Thy protection against the evils of this night and the evil of that which will follow it. Lord, I seek Thy protection against sloth and the mischief of dotage, and seek Thy protection against the torment of the Fire and the torment of the grave. In the morning he would substitute the word morning for the word evening (Muslim).

1461. Abdullah ibn Khubaib relates that the Holy Prophet said to him:

Recite the *sura* Al-Ikhlas and the two chapters following it three times, morning and evening, and they will suffice thee in all respects (Abu Daud and Tirmidhi).

1462. Uthman ibn Affan relates that the Holy Prophet said: He who recites three times every morning and every evening: In the name of Allah, with Whose name there is protection against every kind of harm in the earth and in the heaven, and He is the All-Hearing, All-Knowing; will not be harmed by anything (Abu Daud and Tirmidhi).

248.

On the Supplication on Retiring

Allah, the Exalted, has said:

> *328. In the creation of the heavens and the earth and in the alternation of the night and the day there are indeed signs for people of understanding who remember Allah, standing, sitting and lying on their sides and ponder over the creation of the heavens and the earth (3. 191-192).*

1463. This *hadith* is a part of No. 1451.

1464. Ali relates that the Holy Prophet said to Fatimah and him: When you go to bed proclaim Allah's Greatness thirty-three times and His Holiness thirty-three times and praise Him thirty-three times. One version has Greatness thirty-four times, and another has Holiness thirty-four times. (Bokhari and Muslim).

1465. Abu Hurairah relates that the Holy Prophet said: When one of you goes to bed he should sweep the mattress with a piece of cloth for he knows not what might have fallen on it after he left it, and should supplicate: With Thy name, Lord, have I reclined my side and with Thy name shall I raise it. If Thou shouldst detain my spirit then have mercy on it, and if Thou shouldst restore it then guard it against that against which Thou dost guard Thy righteous servants (Bokhari and Muslim).

1466. Ayesha relates that when the Holy Prophet came to bed he would cup his hands and blow upon his palms and recite the last two chapters of the Quran and then pass his hands over his body (Bokhari and Muslim). Another version is: He would cup his hands and blow upon them and recite the last three chapters of the Quran into them and then pass them over his body beginning with his head and face and continuing over the front of his body. He did this three times.

1467. Bra'a ibn 'Azib relates that the Holy Prophet said to him: When you go to bed make your ablutions as for Prayer then lie on your right side and recite: Allah, I commit my soul to Thee and turn my attention to Thee and commit my affairs to Thee, and rest my back towards Thee, yearning for

Thee and in fear of Thee. There is no refuge and no asylum against Thee save in Thyself. I believe in the Book that Thou hast revealed and in the Prophet whom Thou hast sent. Then if you die you will die a believer in the true faith. Let these words be your last words at night (Bokhari and Muslim).

1468. Anas relates that when the Holy Prophet went to bed he recited: All praise belongs to Allah who has given us to eat and drink and has fulfilled our designs and has provided us with shelter, when there are so many who have no one to fulfil their designs or to give them shelter (Muslim).

1469. Huzaifah relates that when the Holy Prophet went to bed he would put his right hand under his cheek and supplicate: Allah, shield me against Thy torment on the Day on which Thou wilt raise up Thy servants (Tirmidhi). Abu Daud relates the same on the authority of Hafsah, adding: He would repeat it three times.

249.
On Supplications

Allah, the Exalted, has said:

329.   Your Lord has said: Call on Me: I will respond to you (40. 61).

330.   Call upon your Lord in humble entreaty in secret. He loves not those who exceed the bounds (7.56).

331.   When My servants inquire from thee concerning Me, tell them I am close. I respond to the call of the supplicant when he calls on Me (2.187).

332.   Or, Who responds to the afflicted person when he calls upon Him, and removes the affliction (27. 63)?

1470. Nu'man ibn Bashir relates that the Holy Prophet said: Prayer is worship (Abu Daud and Tirmidhi).

1471. Ayesha relates that the Holy Prophet preferred prayers that are comprehensive and discarded others (Abu Daud).

1472. Anas relates that the supplication most often made by the Holy Prophet was: Lord, bestow upon us the best of this world and the best of the hereafter, and deliver us from the torment of the Fire (Bokhari and Muslim). Muslim adds: When Anas prayed he made the same supplication, and if he made any other, he included this one in it.

1473. Ibn Mas'ud relates that the Holy Prophet supplicated: Allah, I beseech Thee for guidance, righteousness, chastity and self-sufficiency (Muslim).

1474. Tariq ibn Ushaim relates that when a man became a Muslim the Holy Prophet would instruct him in Prayer and then direct him to supplicate in these terms: Allah, forgive me and have mercy on me, and guide me and forbear from me and provide for me (Muslim). Another version is: A man came to the Holy Prophet and asked: Messenger of Allah, how shall I supplicate my Lord? He answered: Say: Allah, forgive me and have mercy on me and forbear from me and provide for me. These will comprehend thy life and thy hereafter.

1475. Abdullah ibn Amr ibn 'As relates that the Holy Prophet supplicated: Allah, Director of hearts, direct our hearts to Thy obedience (Muslim).

1476. Abu Hurairah relates that the Holy Prophet said: Seek Allah's protection against being sorely tried, encountering ill-luck, evil fortune and the exultation of your enemies (Bokhari and Muslim).

1477. Abu Hurairah relates that the Holy Prophet supplicated: Allah, direct me aright in my faith which is the guardian of my affairs, and direct me aright in my life in which I have my being, and set right my hereafter which is my resort, and make my life wax in every type of good, and make my death a comfort from all ill (Muslim).

1478. Ali relates that the Holy Prophet said to him: Recite: Allah, guide me and keep me straight. Another version is: Allah, I beseech Thee for guidance and straightness (Muslim).

1479. Anas relates that the Holy Prophet supplicated: Allah, I seek Thy protection against helplessness and sloth, and against cowardice, dotage and miserliness; and I seek Thy protection against the torment of the grave and the trials of life and death. Another version adds: and from oppressive indebtedness and the tyranny of people (Muslim).

1480. Abu Bakr relates that he asked the Holy Prophet to teach him some supplication which he might recite in his Prayer. He told him: Supplicate: Allah, I have wronged my soul greatly and no one forgives sins save Thee, then accord me forgiveness from Thyself and have mercy on me, indeed Thou art the Most Forgiving, Ever Merciful (Bokhari and Muslim).

1481. Abu Musa relates that the Holy Prophet supplicated thus: Allah, forgive me my defaults and my mistakes and my excesses in my affairs and that which Thou knowest better than I. Allah, forgive me that which I said in seriousness or in fun or by mistake or deliberately, and I am guilty of all these. Allah, forgive me that which I have sent on and that which is to come and that which I did covertly and that which I did overtly and that which Thou knowest better than me. Thou dost advance one and thou dost put one back and hast power over all things (Bokhari and Muslim).

1482. Ayesha relates that the Holy Prophet would supplicate: Allah, I seek Thy protection from the evil of that which I have done and the evil of that which I have not done (Muslim).

1483. Ibn Umar relates: Of the supplications of the Holy Prophet was: Allah, I seek Thy Protection against the declining of Thy favour and the changing of Thy security and the suddenness of Thy wrath and all Thy anger (Muslim).

1484, Zaid ibn Arqam relates that the Holy Prophet would supplicate: Allah, I seek Thy protection against the declining of Thy favour and dotage and the torment of the grave. Allah, bestow on my soul its righteousness and purify it. Thou art the Best to purify it and Thou art its Guardian and its Master. Allah, I seek Thy protection against knowledge that profits not and a heart that fears not and a mind that is not satisfied and a prayer that is not responded to (Muslim).

1485. Ibn Abbas relates that the Holy Prophet would supplicate: Allah, to Thee I submit, in Thee I believe, in Thee I put my trust, to Thee I turn, with Thy help I contend and from Thee I seek judgment. Then forgive me that which I have sent on and that which is to come and that which I did covertly and that which I did overtly. Thou dost advance one and Thou dost put one back. There is none worthy of worship save Thee. Some versions are: There is no strength to resist evil and no power to do good except through Allah (Bokhari and Muslim).

1486. Ayesha relates that the Holy Prophet would supplicate in these terms: Allah, I seek Thy protection from the trial and torment of the Fire and from the evils of wealth and privation (Abu Daud and Tirmidhi).

1487. Zaid ibn Ilaqah relates on the authority of his uncle Qatabah ibn Malik: The Holy Prophet would supplicate: Allah, I seek Thy protection against undesirable manners and acts and desires (Tirmidhi).

1488. Shakil ibn Humaid relates that he asked the Holy Prophet to teach him a supplication. He told him to supplicate: Allah, I seek Thy protection from the evil of my hearing and of my sight and of my tongue and of my heart and of my passions (Abu Daud and Tirmidhi).

1489. Anas relates that the Holy Prophet would supplicate: Allah, I seek Thy protection against leucoderma, lunacy, leprosy and all evil defects (Abu Daud).

1490. Abu Hurairah relates that the Holy Prophet would supplicate: Allah, I seek Thy protection against hunger for it is a bad bed-fellow and I seek Thy protection against dishonesty for it is the worst inner disorder (Abu Daud).

1491. Ali relates that a slave who had settled the terms of his freedom with his master came to Ali and said: I am not able to discharge my instalments according to the agreement and I ask you to help me. Ali said to him: Shall I teach you a supplication which the Holy Prophet taught me whereby Allah will discharge your obligation even if it were as heavy as a mountain. Do you supplicate: Allah, make that which is permissible sufficient for me so as to make me independent of that which is forbidden and of Thy grace bestow upon me a sufficiency which would make me independent of all beside Thee (Tirmidhi).

1492. Imran ibn Husain relates that the Holy Prophet taught his father two phrases of supplication: Allah, reveal to me my guidance and protect me against the evil of my mind (Tirmidhi).

1493. Abbas ibn Abd al-Muttalib relates: I asked the Holy Prophet: Messenger of Allah, instruct me in something that I should supplicate Allah for it. He said: Beg Allah for security. I waited for some days and went and asked him again: Messenger of Allah, instruct me in something that I should supplicate Allah for it. He said to me: Abbas, uncle of the Messenger of Allah, beg Allah for security in this life and in the hereafter (Tirmidhi).

1494. Shahr ibn Haushab relates: I asked Umm Salamah: Mother of the Faithful, what was the supplication most often made by the Holy Prophet when he was in your house? She said: His supplication most often was: Controller of hearts, make firm my heart in Thy faith (Tirmidhi).

1495. Abu Darda' relates that the Holy Prophet said: Of the supplications of David was: Allah, I beg of Thee Thy love and the love of those who love Thee and such conduct as should lead me to Thy love. Allah, make Thy love dearer to me than my soul and my family and dearer than cold water (Tirmidhi).

1496. Anas relates that the Holy Prophet said: Recite frequently: O Lord of glory and honour (Tirmidhi).

1497. Abu Umamah relates: The Holy Prophet made many supplications which we were not able to retain in our memories. So we said to him: Messenger of Allah, you make many supplications of which we do not remember any. He said: Shall I tell you something which shall comprehend all of them? Supplicate: Allah, I beg of Thee of good all that Thy Prophet Muhammad begged of Thee and seek Thy Protection against all the evil against which Thy Prophet Muhammad sought Thy protection. Thou art the One who is asked for help and it is for Thee to convey the guidance. There is no strength to resist evil nor power to do good except through Allah (Tirmidhi).

1498. Ibn Mas'ud relates: Of the supplications of the Holy Prophet was: Allah, I beg of Thee that which incites Thy mercy and Thy forgiveness and security against every sin and treasures of every virtue and achievement of Paradise and deliverance from the Fire (Hakim).

250.

On the Excellence of Supplication for Absent Ones

Allah, the Exalted, has said:

333. Those who come after them and supplicate: Lord, forgive us and our brethren who preceded us in the faith (59.11).

334. Beseech for the suppression of Thy frailties and ask forgiveness for the believing men and the believing women (47.20).

335. Our Lord, extend Thy forgiveness to me and to my parents and to all the believers on the day when the reckoning is held (14.42).

1499. Abu Darda' relates that he heard the Holy Prophet say: Whenever a Muslim supplicates on behalf of a brother in his absence an angel repeats: May you have also the like of it (Muslim).

1500. Abu Darda' relates that the Holy Prophet often said: A Muslim's prayer on behalf of his brother in his absence is responded to. An angel so appointed stands near him and each time he prays for his brother for some good the appointed angel says: Amen, and may you have the like of it (Muslim).

251.

On Miscellaneous Matters concerning Supplications

1501. Usamah ibn Zaid relates that the Holy Prophet said: He who has received some good from another and says to his benefactor: May Allah reward thee well; makes full recompense (Tirmidhi).

1502. Jabir relates that the Holy Prophet said: Do not call down ill upon yourselves or upon your children or upon your property lest it should be a moment of the acceptance of prayer and your prayer might be accepted (Muslim).

1503. This *hadith* is the same as No. 1433.

1504. Abu Hurairah relates that the Holy Prophet said: Your prayers will be accepted if you are not in a hurry and blurt out: I supplicated my Lord but he did not respond to my supplication (Bokhari and Muslim). Muslim's version is: A servant's prayer continues to be accepted so long as he does not supplicate for something sinful or something that would cut off the ties of kinship and is not in a hurry. Someone asked: Messenger of Allah, what would be hurry? He answered: A supplicant saying: I have prayed and prayed but have not found my prayer responded to; and getting tired and giving up praying.

1505. Abu Umamah relates that the Holy Prophet was asked: What prayer finds greatest acceptance? He answered: A prayer offered in the middle of the latter part of the night and in the last part of the prescribed Prayers (Tirmidhi).

1506. Ubadah ibn Samit relates that the Holy Prophet said: Whenever a Muslim supplicates Allah, Allah grants his supplication or averts some evil of the kind from him so long as he does not supplicate for something sinful or something that would cut off the ties of kinship. Upon this someone said: Then we shall supplicate plenty. The Holy Prophet said: Allah is more plentiful in responding (Tirmidhi). Hakim's version adds: Or lays up a reward for him like it.

1507. Ibn Abbas relates that the Holy Prophet when he was restless would supplicate: There is none worthy of worship save Allah, the Great, the Forbearing; there is none worthy of worship save Allah, Lord of the Great Throne; there is none worthy of worship save Allah, Lord of the heavens, Lord of the earth and Lord of the Noble Throne (Bokhari and Muslim).

252.

On the Miracles of the Saints

Allah, the Exalted, has said:

336. Hearken, the friends of Allah, that is those who believe and are ever mindful of their duty to Allah, shall certainly have no fear nor shall they grieve; for them are glad tidings in the hither life and also in the hereafter; that indeed is the supreme triumph (10.63-65).

337. Then take hold of the branch of the palm tree and shake it; it will shed fresh ripe dates upon thee. Thus eat and drink and wash and be at rest (19.26-27).

338. Whenever Zachariah entered her chamber he found some provision with her. One day he said to her: Mary, whence hast thou this? She answered: It is from Allah; surely Allah bestows upon whomsoever He pleases without measure (3.38).

339. Now that you have withdrawn from them and from that which they worship besides Allah, continue secure in the cave; your Lord will extend his mercy to you and will provide facilities for you in your present situation. The sun could be observed to move away from their cave on the right as it rose, and to turn away from them on the left when it set; and they were in a spacious hollow in the cave (18.18-19).

1508. Abdur Rahman ibn Abu Bakr relates that the Companions of the Lounge were poor people and the Holy Prophet said on one occasion: He who has food for two should take with him a third and he who should have food for four should take with him two more. Abu Bakr brought away three and the Holy Prophet took with him ten. Abu Bakr ate with the Holy Prophet and remained with him till after the evening Prayer and by the time he came home a part of the night had passed and his wife said to him: What kept you from your guests? He said: Have you not given them their food? She answered: They were offered food but they refused to eat till you should arrive. Abdur Rahman continues: I went and hid myself out of fear. Abu Bakr called me and rallied me in harsh terms and said: Now you eat and let it not prove agreeable to you. As for me, by Allah I shall not eat at all. Then it so happened that for every mouthful that we took from the top more than its equal rose up from the bottom till everyone had eaten his fill and the food had increased in quantity more than it was in the beginning. Abu Bakr looked at it and said to his wife: Sister of Bani Firas, what is this? She said: Delight of my eye, it is now three times of that which it was. Abu Bakr said: My oath not to eat of it was prompted by Satan; and he ate of it a mouthful also and then carried it to the Holy Prophet, where it remained till the morning. At that time the term of a treaty we had made with a tribe had expired and twelve of us had been appointed scouts, each of the twelve having some men under him, Allah alone knows how many were there with each. They all ate of that food.

Another version is: Abu Bakr took an oath that he would not eat of it, and his wife took an oath that whe would not eat of it and the guests swore they would not eat of it unless Abu Bakr ate. So he said: My oath was incited by Satan; and he called for the food and ate of it and they all ate. It so happened that for every mouthful they took there rose up from under it more than its equal. Abu Bakr said to his wife: Sister of Bani Firas, What is this? She answered: Delight of my eye, it is now more than it was when we started eating. Thus they all ate and sent the rest to the Holy Prophet. It is related that he also ate of it. Another version is: Abu Bakr said to Abdur Rahman: I have to go to the Holy Prophet. You take care of the guests and feed them before I get home. Abdur Rahman went and placed before them whatever there was and asked them to eat. They inquired: Where is our host? He urged them to eat. They retorted: We shall not eat till our host comes. He pleaded: Please accept our hospitality, for if he arrives and finds that you have not eaten he will be wroth with us. But they persisted in their refusal. Abdur Rahman says: I realised that Abu Bakr would be upset and so when he came I withdrew. He inquired: How did you fare? and was informed of what had happened. He called out: Abdur Rahman; but I kept silent. He then called out: You stupid lout, I put you on oath that if you hear my voice come forth. So I came out and said: Ask your guests. They said: He is telling the truth. He did bring the food to us. Then Abu Bakr said: You waited for me, but by Allah I shall not eat of this food this night. The guests said: We shall not eat, unless you eat also. Abu Bakr said: Ruin seize you, what is the matter with you that you do not accept our hospitality? Bring the food. It was brought, and he said: My oath was incited by Satan. He put forth his hand, pronounced the name of Allah and ate, and they also ate (Bokhari and Muslim).

1509.   Abu Hurairah relates that the Holy Prophet said: There were among the people before you men who were the recipients of revelation. Should there be one such from among my people it would be Umar (Muslim).

1510.   Jabir ibn Samurah relates that the people of Kufa complained to Umar against Sa'ad ibn Abi Waqqas and Umar appointed Ammar governor of Kufa in place of Sa'ad. Their complaint was that he did not even conduct the Prayer services properly. Umar sent for Sa'ad to Medina and said to him: Abu Ishaq, they complain that you did not conduct the Prayer services properly. Sa'ad replied: I conducted the services according to the model of the Holy Prophet without the least detraction. For instance, in the evening Prayer I made the first two *raka'as* long and the last two *raka'as* short. Umar said: This is what I too think about you, Abu Ishak; and he sent with him a man (or some men) to Kufa to inquire about him from the people of Kufa. The inquiry was made in every mosque and they all praised him; but in the mosque of Bani 'Abs a man stood up whose name was Usamah ibn Qatadah and who was known as Abu Sa'ad, who said: Now that we have been asked, I must say that Sa'ad did not accompany an expedition, did not distribute the spoils equitably and did not judge justly. On this Sa'ad said: I shall make three supplications concerning him: Allah, if this servant of Thine has lied seeking to show off and gain notoriety, then do Thou prolong his days and lengthen his period of adversity and afflict him with trials. Thereafter when the man was asked about his condition he would say: I am an old man, afflicted with trials, overtaken by the imprecation of Sa'ad. The narrator adds: I saw this man when his eyebrows fell over his eyes in his old age and he roamed the streets teasing the girls (Bokhari and Muslim).

1511. Urwah ibn Zubair relates that Arwah bint Aus laid a complaint before Marwan ibn Hakam, governor of Medina, alleging that Sa'id ibn Zaid ibn Amr ibn Nufail had taken possession of part of her land. Sa'id replied: Could I take her land after I had heard the pronouncement of the Holy Prophet? Marwan asked him: What did you hear from the Holy Prophet? He answered: I heard the Holy Prophet say: He who takes a hand's breadth of land unjustly shall wear round his neck a garland composed of seven earths. Marwan said: I shall not ask you for any proof after this. Sa'id responded with: Allah, if she is lying do Thou take away her sight and cause her to perish in her land. Urwah relates that she became blind before she died and was killed by falling into a pit while she was walking in her land concerning which she had raised a dispute and fell into a well and died, and that well became her grave.

1512. Jabir ibn Abdullah relates: My father called me the evening before Uhad and said: I believe I shall be among the first from among the companions of the Holy Prophet to be killed and after the Holy Prophet you are the one most dear to me. Discharge my debt and treat your sisters well. Next morning he was among the first to be killed and I buried him along with another in the same grave. Thereafter I was not happy that I should leave him with another in the grave, so I dug up his body after six months and he was in the same condition in which he was on the day I buried him, except for his ear. Then I buried him in a separate grave (Bokhari).

1513. Anas relates that two of the companions of the Holy Prophet (Usaid ibn Huzair and Abbad ibn Bishr) left the Holy Prophet late one dark night and perceived as if there were two lights in front of them; and when they separated each of them had one light in front of him till he arrived home (Bokhari).

1514. Abu Hurairah relates that the Holy Prophet sent a scouting party of twelve under the command of 'Asim ibn Thabit Ansari. They left, and when they arrived at Hudat which is between Usfan and Mecca, a sub-tribe of Huzail, called Banu Lehyan, was alerted about them, and they set out in pursuit of them with about a hundred archers following them in their footste,s. When 'Asim and his companions perceived them they took refuge on a piece of high ground. They were surrounded by their enemies and were told: If you will come down and surrender we promise that not one of you will be killed. Upon this 'Asim said: I will not get down on the promise of an unbeliever. Allah, do Thou convey our situation to Thy Prophet. The enemy shot arrows at them and killed 'Asim. Only three of the Muslims, Khubaib, Zaid ibn Dathanah and another, relied on their promise and came down. When the enemy had them in their power they took off the chords of their bows with which they tied them up securely. The third man said: This is the first contravention of your pledge. I will not accompany you and shall follow the example of my other companions. They pulled him and tried to drag him with them but he resisted going with them. So they killed him and carried Khubaib and Zaid ibn Dathanah with them and sold them in Mecca. All this had happened subsequent to the Battle of Badr. Khubaib was purchased by the heirs of Harith ibn 'Amir ibn Naufal ibn Abd Manaf, and it was Khubaib who had slain Harith in the Battle of Badr. Khubaib remained a prisoner with them till they agreed among themselves to kill him. He had borrowed a razor from one of the daughters of Harith and a child of hers came up to Khubaib who seated him in his lap while the razor was in his hand and the mother was not looking. When she noticed the situation of the child she was terrified and Khubaib, perceiving her terror, said to her: Are you afraid that I would kill him? I am not capable of such a thing. She used to say about him: I have never seen a prisoner better then Khubaib. I found him one day eating fresh grapes off a grapevine which he held in his hand while he was in chains. At that time there was no fruit available in Mecca. She used to say: I am sure it was food provided by Allah for Khubaib. When they took him out of the Sanctuary to execute him, Khubaib said to them: Let me offer two *raka'as* in Prayer. So they released him and he offered two *raka'as*; whereafter he said: I would have made my supplication longer did I not feel that you might think that I was afraid of death. He then supplicated: Allah count their number, slay them one by one and spare not one of them. He then recited: If I am slain a Muslim, I care not on which side I fall dead. My death is in the cause of Allah and if He so wills He would bless the severed portions of my limbs. It was Khubaib who set the example for every Muslim who might be slain in the cause of Allah to be steadfast and offer Prayer before execution. The Holy Prophet informed his companions of the event on the day when Khubaib and his comrade were executed.

Asim ibn Thabit had killed one of the chieftains of the Quraish in the Battle of Badr. When they were told that he had been slain they sent a few of their people to bring away something from which he might be identified, but Allah raised a cloud of bees (or wasps) which surrounded the corpse of 'Asim so that the envoys of the Quraish were not able to cut away any portion of his body as a memento (Bokhari).

1515. Ibn Umar relates: I never heard Umar say about anything: I conceive it to be thus and thus; but that it turned out to be as he had conceived it (Bokhari).

253.

On Prohibitions etc.

Allah, the Exalted, has said:

340.   Do not backbite one another. Would any of you like to eat the flesh of his dead brother? Surely you would loath such an imputation. Be mindful of your duty to Allah. Surely, Allah is Oft-Returning with compassion and is Ever Merciful (29.13).

341.   Follow not that of which thou has no knowledge; for the ear and the eye and the heart shall all be called to account (17. 37).

342.   He utters not a word, but there is by him an alert watcher who takes care to preserve it (50.19).

1516.   This *hadith* is comprehended in No. 310.

1517.   This *hadith* is comprehended in No. 213.

1518.   This *hadith* is the same as No. 1524.

1519.   Abu Hurairah relates that he heard the Holy Prophet say: A person says something thoughtlessly whereby he is conducted into the Fire farther than the distance between the east and the west (Bokhari and Muslim).

1520.   Abu Hurairah relates that the Holy Prophet said: A person says something, of the import of which he is not aware, and it pleases Allah, whereby Allah raises his status; and a person says something, of the import of which he is not aware, and it displeases Allah and it carries him into hell. (Bokhari).

1521.   Bilal ibn Harith Muzani relates that the Holy Prophet said: A man says something, not realising its import, which is pleasing to Allah, in consequence of which Allah decrees His pleasure for him till the day when he will meet Him; and a man says something, not realising its import, which displeases Allah, in consequence of which Allah decrees His displeasure for him till the day when he will meet Him (Malik and Tirmidhi).

1522.   Sufyan ibn Abdullah relates: I said to the Holy Prophet: Messenger of Allah, tell me something to which I should hold fast. He said: Affirm: My Lord is Allah; and then be steadfast. Then I said: Messenger of Allah, what is it that you are most afraid of in my case? He took hold of his tongue and said: Of this (Tirmidhi).

1523.   Ibn Umar relates that the Holy Prophet said: Do not indulge in much talk without remembrance of Allah, for much talk without remembrance of Allah hardens the heart and the person farthest from Allah will be the one who has a hard heart (Tirmidhi).

1524. Abu Hurairah relates that the Holy Prophet said: He whom Allah shields against the evil of that which is between his jaws and the evil of that which is between his legs will enter Paradise (Tirmidhi).

1525. Uqbah ibn 'Amir relates: I asked the Holy Prophet: Messenger of Allah, how can salvation be achieved? He answered: Control your tongue, take to your house and weep over your sins (Tirmidhi).

1526. Abu Sa'id Khudri relates that the Holy Prophet said: When a man gets up in the morning all his limbs entreat his tongue saying: Be regardful of Allah on our behalf for we but follow you; if you go straight we shall go straight and if you are awry we shall be awry (Tirmidhi).

1527. Mu'az relates: I asked the Holy Prophet: Messenger of Allah, tell me of something which should cause me to be admitted to Paradise and shall keep me away from the Fire. He answered: You have asked about a matter of great import but it is easy for one for whom Allah makes it easy. Worship Allah and associate not anything with Him, observe Prayer, pay the *Zakat*, observe the Fast of Ramadhan and perform the Pilgrimage if you can afford the journey. Then he added: Shall I inform you of the gates of goodness? The fast is a shield, charity puts out sins as water puts out fire and also the Prayer in the middle of the night. Then he recited: They withdraw themselves from their beds in the latter part of the night for Prayers and they call on their Lord in fear and hope and spend out of that which We have bestowed on them. No one knows what bliss is kept hidden from them, as a reward for what they used to do (32. 17-18).

Then he added: Shall I tell you of the root of the matter and of its contours and of its top? I said: Certainly, Messenger of Allah. He said: The root of the matter is Islam, its contours are Prayers and its top is striving in the cause of Allah. Then he asked: Shall I tell you of that which is at the bottom of all this? I said: Certainly, Messenger of Allah. Upon this he took hold of his tongue and said: Keep this under control. I inquired: Messenger of Allah, shall we be called to account in respect of that which we say? He answered: May your mother lose you, will people not be thrown face down into hell only on account of the harvest of the tongue (Tirmidhi)?

1528. Abu Hurairah relates that the Holy Prophet said: Do you know what backbiting is? He was answered: Allah and His Messenger know best. He said: Your saying of your brother that which he would dislike. Someone said: But if my brother should be as I say? The Holy Prophet said: If he should be as you say then you have been guilty of backbiting and if he should not be as you say you are guilty of a calumny (Muslim).

1529. This *hadith* is comprehended in No. 215.

1530. Ayesha relates: I said to the Holy Prophet: It is enough for you concerning Safayyah that she is thus and thus (some narrators have said that she made a reference to her short size). The Holy Prophet said: You have uttered a phrase which would suffice to pollute an ocean. Ayesha also relates: I mentioned something unpleasant about someone to the Holy Prophet. He said: I do not like to be told anything unpleasant about anyone even in return for so much and so much (Abu Daud and Tirmidhi).

1531. Anas relates that the Holy Prophet said: On the night of my Ascent I passed by some people whose nails were of copper and they were combing their faces and their chests with them. I inquired from Gabriel: Who are these? He said: These are people who eat the flesh of men and attack their reputations and honour (Abu Daud).

1532. This *hadith* is comprehended in No. 1575.

254.

On Prohibition of Listening to Idle Talk

Allah, the Exalted, has said:

343.   When they hear idle talk, they turn away from it (28. 56).

344.   Those who shun all that is vain (23: 4).

345.   The ear, the eye and the heart shall all be called to account (17. 37).

346.   When thou seest those who are engaged in vain discourse concerning Our Signs, keep away from them until they turn to some other topic. Should Satan cause thee to forget do not continue to sit with the unjust people after recollection (6. 69).

1533. Abu Darda' relates that the Holy Prophet said: He who defends the honour of a brother, Allah will shield his face against the Fire on the Day of Judgment (Tirmidhi).

1534. This *hadith* is part of No. 420.

1535. This *hadith* is part of No. 21.

255.

On Permissible Criticism

1536. Ayesha relates that a man asked for permission to see the Holy Prophet whereupon the latter said: Let him come in, he is the worst of his family (Bokhari and Muslim).

1537. Ayesha relates that the Holy Prophet said: I do not think that So and So, and So and So, understand anything of our faith (Bokhari).

1538. Fatimah bint Qais relates: I went to the Holy Prophet and said to him: Abu Jahm and Mu'awiah have made me a proposal of marriage. The Holy Prophet said: As to Mu'awiah, he is poor and has no property, as to Abu Jahm, he does not put away his rod from his shoulder (Bokhari and Muslim). Muslim's version is: Abu Jahm is given to beating women; and it has also been said that the reference is to his being most of the time on a journey.

1539. Zaid ibn Arqam relates: We went on an expedition with the Holy Prophet which proved very hard on people. In the course of it Abdullah ibn Ubayy said: Do not spend on those who are with the Messenger of Allah so that they may disperse; and also said: If we return to Medina, the one most honourable will drive out therefrom the one most mean. I went to the Holy Prophet and informed him of this and he sent for Abdullah ibn Ubayy, who denied on oath having said it. People began to say: Zaid has carried a false tale to the Holy Prophet. I was much grieved by this till *sura* Al-Munafiqun (Chapter 63) of the Holy Quran was revealed. Then the Holy Prophet sent for the hypocrites so that he might ask forgiveness for them but they turned their heads away out of arrogance (Bokhari and Muslim).

1540. Ayesha relates: Hindah, wife of Abu Sufyan, said to the Holy Prophet: Abu Sufyan is a stingy one and does not give me that much which would suffice for me and my children unless I take something from his property without his knowledge. The Holy Prophet said: Take that much which would suffice for thee and thy children according to what is customary (Bokhari and Muslim).

256.

On Carrying Tales

Allah, the Exalted, has said:

347. Backbiter, slanderer (68.11).
348. He utters· not a word, but there is by him an alert watcher who takes care to preserve it (50.19).

1541. Huzaifah relates that the Holy Prophet said: One who carries tales will not enter Paradise (Bokhari and Muslim).

1542. Ibn Abbas relates that the Holy Prophet passed by two graves and said: These two are in torment and not over a great matter, but indeed they are great sins. One of them carried tales and the other would not screen himself when passing water (Bokhari and Muslim).

1543. Ibn Mas'ud relates that the Holy Prophet said: Shall I tell you what *adha* is? It is carrying tales between people (Muslim).

257.

On Carrying Tales to those in Authority

Allah, the Exalted, has said:

349. Assist not one another in sin and transgression (5.3).

1544. Ibn Mas'ud relates that the Holy Prophet said: No companion of mine should convey to me anything unpleasant concerning another for I desire that when I meet you my mind should be clear with regard to everyone (Abu Daud and Tirmidhi).

258.

On Condemnation of being Double-Faced

Allah, the Exalted, has said:

350. They seek to hide from people but cannot hide from Allah. He is with them when they plot at night that which He does not approve of. Allah will bring to naught that which they do (4. 109).

1545. Abu Hurairah relates that the Holy Prophet said: You will find people with pedigrees. Those who were best before Islam will be best in Islam if they will comprehend the Faith aright. You will find the best people among those in authority such as will detest those who are double-faced and are thus the worst of people, approaching one with one bearing and another with another (Bokhari and Muslim).

1546. Muhammad ibn Zaid relates that some people said to his grandfather; Abdullah ibn Umar: We visit our rulers and say to them things contrary to that which we say when we leave them. Abdullah answered: In the time of the Holy Prophet we considered this hypocrisy (Bokhari).

259.

On Condemnation of Falsehood

Allah, the Exalted, has said:

351. Follow not that of which thou hast no knowledge (17. 37).

352. He utters not a word, but there is by him an alert watcher who takes care to preserve it (50.19).

1547. This *hadith* is the same as No. 54.

1548. This *hadith* is the same as No. 693.

1549. Ibn Abbas relates that the Holy Prophet said: He who relates as a dream that which he has not seen will be called upon to tie a knot between two grains of barley, and he who eavesdrops upon a people will have molten lead poured into his ears on the Day of Judgment, and he who paints the portrait of a person will be tormented and will be called upon to breathe into it a soul which he will not be capable of doing (Bokhari and Muslim).

1550. Ibn Umar relates that the Holy Prophet said: The greatest imposture is that a person should purport to show his eyes that which they have not seen (Bokhari). He adds: The meaning is that a person should relate something as having been seen by him in his dream which he did not in fact see.

1551. Samurah ibn Jundub relates: The Holy Prophet would often inquire from his companions: Has any of you seen a dream? Then whoever was able would relate his dream to him. One morning he related to us: Last night two persons came to me in my dream and said: Come with us. I accompanied them and we came upon a man who was lying on his back and another one standing near his head struck him on the head with a stone. When the stone hit the head of the person struck it rolled away from him. The striker went after the stone and caught it up and returned with it. In the meantime the head of the person who was hit recovered from its injury and the striker hit him again. I said to my two companions, Holy is Allah, what is this? They said: Proceed, proceed; and we proceeded and came to a man lying on his back and another one standing near him with a hooked bar of iron in his hand and approaching him from one side ripped open his mouth till his neck and ripped open his nostril till his neck and tore open his eye till his neck and then he turned to his other side and did the same on that side. By that time the first side of the man's face recovered from its injuries and the tormentor returned to the first side and repeated what he had done to it the first time. I said to my companions: Holy is Allah, what are these two at? They said to me: Proceed, proceed; and we proceeded and arrived near a pit which was like an oven out of which we could hear cries. We glanced into it and saw men and women naked who cried out when the flames reached them from below. I asked my companions, who are these? They said: Proceed, proceed; and we proceeded till we arrived at a stream the water of which was red like blood and a man was swimming in it. On the bank of the stream was another who had collected many pieces of rock. When the swimmer approached him, he would strike him with a piece of rock which would smash his face and he would start swimming again and as he approached the bank once more the man on the bank would strike him with a piece of rock which smashed his face. I inquired from my companions; who are these two? And they said: Proceed, proceed; and we proceeded till we came to a frightfully ugly person near a blazing fire which he started and round which he kept running. I asked my two companions: What is this? And they said: Proceed, proceed; and we proceeded till we came to a garden which was full of spring flowers and in the midst of the garden was a man so tall that I could not see his head as if it was hidden in the sky and around him were so many children as I had never seen before. I asked my companions: Who are these? And they said: Proceed, proceed; and we proceeded and arrived at a tree so enormous that I had not seen any so big nor so beautiful and my companions asked me to climb it and we all climbed and we beheld a city which was built of gold and silver bricks laid alternately. We came to the gate of the city and asked for the gate to be opened and it was opened for us and we entered and we saw therein people one half of whose bodies was the most beautiful that you could imagine and the other half the most ugly. There was a stream flowing through the middle of the city the water of which was pure white. My companions said to the people: Go and plunge into the stream. They did so and when they returned to us their ugliness had disappeared and they became wholly beautiful. My two companions said to me: This is the Garden of Eden and that is your residence. I raised my eyes and beheld a palace like a white cloud and they repeated: That is your residence. I said to them: May Allah bless you both, now let me enter it. They said: Not just yet but you will certainly enter it.

I said to them: I have witnessed many strange things this night. What is the meaning of that which I have seen? They said to me: We shall now tell you. The first person that you saw whose head was being smashed with a stone was one who had committed the Quran to memory and then forgotten it and neglected the prescribed Prayers. The person whose mouth and nostril and eye were ripped open to the neck was one who ran about from his home spreading forth lies which circulated through the world. The men and women in the oven were adulterers and adulteresses. The man you saw swimming in the stream being stoned was one who earned money by way of interest. The ugly man starting the fire was the guardian of hell. The very tall man in the garden was Abraham and the children around him were those who had died in their natural state. (Some of those around the Holy Prophet asked him: Messenger of Allah, would the children of the idolators be included among them? The Holy Prophet said: Yes, and the children of the idolators also). Those who were half handsome and half ugly were people who had mixed righteous conduct with evil and Allah forbore from them (Bokhari).

Another version is: I saw last night two men who took me to the Holy Land (and the account proceeds as in the version above and continues:) We arrived at a pit like an oven the upper part of which was narrow and the lower was wide and there was fire raging inside it. As the flames rose the inmates also rose till they were about to emerge from it and when the flames went down they went down with them. There were men and women in it, all naked. Then we arrived at a stream flowing with blood and with a man standing in the middle of it and another one on the bank with a heap of stones in front of him. The one in the middle wanted to get out of the stream but when he tried to get out the one on the bank struck him with a stone on his face which pushed him back to where he had been before. This happened every time he tried to get out. Then the two climbed a tree along with me and caused me to enter a house better than which I had never seen in which there were men old and young. I was told: The one you saw with his cheeks ripped open was a liar whose lies were repeated till the ends of the earth. He will be treated like this till the Day of Judgment. The one you saw whose head was smashed, was a man whom Allah had taught the Quran and who slept during the night ignoring it and would not act upon it during the day. He will be treated like that till the Day of Judgment. The first house that you entered was the dwelling of the believers and this house that you have seen is the dwelling of martyrs. I am Gabriel and this my comrade is Michael, now raise thy head; whereupon I raised my head and saw something like a cloud above me. I was told: This is your dwelling. I said: Leave me to enter my dwelling. They said: You have still a portion of your age that you have not completed. When you have completed it you will enter your dwelling (Bokhari).

260.

On the Need of Investigation

Allah, the Exalted, has said:

353. Follow not that of which thou hast no knowledge (17.37).

354. He utters not a word, but there is by him an alert watcher who takes care to preserve it (50.19).

1552. Abu Hurairah relates that the Holy Prophet said. It is enough to make a man a liar that he should go on repeating all that he might hear. (Muslim).

1553. Samurah relates that the Holy Prophet said: He who attributes something to me which he knows is false is one of the liars. (Muslim).

1554. Asma' relates that a woman asked the Holy Prophet: Messenger of Allah, I have a co-wife. Would it be sinful if I were to pretend that my husband had given me something which he had not given me? He answered: One who pretends having received something that was not given him is like one who wears two garments of falsehood (Bokhari and Muslim).

261.

On Prohibition of Giving False Evidence

Allah, the Exalted, has said:

355. Shun all words of falsehood (22.31).

356. Follow not that of which thou hast no knowledge (17.51).

357. He utters not a word, but there is by him an alert watcher who takes care to preserve it (50.19).

358. Surely, Thy Lord is on the watch (89.15).

359. Those who bear not false witness (25.73).

1555. This *hadith* is the same as No. 338.

262.
On Prohibition of Cursing

1556. Abu Zaid ibn Thabit ibn Dhahak relates that the Holy Prophet said: He who takes a false oath that if he is not telling the truth he might become a follower of a faith other than Islam is already as he describes himself. He who kills himself with an instrument will be tormented with that instrument on the Day of Judgment. A person cannot offer as a vow that which does not belong to him. Cursing a believer is equal to slaying him (Bokhari and Muslim).

1557. Abu Hurairah relates that the Holy Prophet said: It does not behove a righteous Muslim that he should be given to cursing (Muslim).

1558. Abu Darda' relates that the Holy Prophet said: Those who are given to cursing will neither be intercessors nor witnesses on the Day of Judgment (Muslim).

1559. Samurah ibn Jundub relates that the Holy Prophet said: Do not curse anyone with the curse or wrath of Allah or with the Fire (Abu Daud and Tirmidhi).

1560. Ibn Mas'ud relates that the Holy Prophet said that a believer is not given to taunting or cursing or indecent talk or abuse (Tirmidhi).

1561. Abu Darda' relates that the Holy Prophet said: When a person curses something the curse ascends to heaven and all the gates of heaven are closed against it. Then it descends to the earth and the gates of the earth are closed against it. Then it turns right and left and when it finds no exit it turns to the one who has been cursed and attaches itself to him if he should be deserving of it, but if not it returns to the one who uttered it (Abu Daud).

1562. Imran ibn Husain relates: While the Holy Prophet was on a journey a woman of the Ansar riding a she-camel abused it and cursed it. The Holy Prophet heard this and said: Take off the load from the she-camel and turn it loose for it has been cursed (Muslim).

1563. Abu Barazah Nadhlah ibn Ubaid Aslami relates: A girl on a she-camel which was also carrying a load suddenly encountered the Holy Prophet and the mountain pass became narrow for her people. She shouted at her she-camel and cursed it. The Holy Prophet said: The she-camel that has been cursed shall not accompany us (Muslim).

263.
On Permissibility of Cursing Sinners

Allah, the Exalted, has said:

360.   Take note, the curse of Allah is upon such wrong-doers (11.19).

361.   Thereupon a crier will call out: The curse of Allah is upon the wrongdoers (7. 45).

264.
On Prohibition of Abusing a Muslim Unjustly

Allah, the Exalted, has said:

362.   Those who malign believing men and believing women for that which they have not done shall bear the guilt of a calumny and a manifest sin (33. 59).

1564.   Ibn Mas'ud relates that the Holy Prophet said: Abuse of a Muslim is sin and his murder is disbelief (Bokhari and Muslim).

1565.   Abu Dharr relates that he heard the Holy Prophet say: Let no one reproach his brother with sin or disbelief else if he should not be deserving of the reproach it could rebound upon the one who utters it (Bokhari).

1566.   Abu Hurairah relates that the Holy Prophet said: If two people abuse each other the responsibility of it lies upon the one who started it unless the wronged one should transgress (Muslim).

1567.   This *hadith* is the same as No. 245.

1568.   Abu Hurairah relates that he heard the Holy Prophet say: He who falsely charges his female slave with adultery will be subjected to the punishment of adultery on the Day of Judgment (Bokhari and Muslim).

265.

On Prohibition of Abusing the Dead

1569. Ayesha relates that the Holy Prophet said: Do not abuse the dead for they have attained to that which they had sent forward (Bokhari).

266.

On Prohibition of Maligning

Allah, the Exalted, has said:

363. Those who malign believing men and believing women for that which they have not done shall bear the guilt of a calumny and a manifest sin (33. 59).

1570. Abdullah ibn Amr ibn 'As relates that the Holy Prophet said: A Muslim is one from whose tongue and hand the Muslims are secure, and an emigrant is one who abandons that which Allah has prohibited (Bokhari and Muslim).

1571. This *hadith* is part of No. 671.

267.

On Prohibition of Entertaining Ill-Feeling

Allah, the Exalted, has said:

364. All believers are brothers (49.11)

365. They will be kind and considerate towards the believers and firm and unyielding towards the disbelievers (5.55).

366. Muhammad is the Messenger of Allah. Those who are with him are unyielding towards the disbelievers, compassionate towards one another (48.30).

1572. Anas relates that the Holy Prophet said: Entertain no ill-will or envy nor indifference nor cut off intercourse; be servants of Allah, brethren to each other. It is not permissible for a Muslim to keep away from his brother for more than three days (Bokhari and Muslim).

1573. Abu Hurairah relates that the Holy Prophet said: The gates of Paradise are opened on Mondays and Thursdays and all are forgiven who do not associate anything with Allah except one who bears enmity towards a brother. With regard to them it is decreed; hold these two back till they have composed their differences (Muslim). Another version adds: Every Monday and Thursday the deeds of people are submitted to Allah.

268.
On Prohibition of Jealousy

Allah, the Exalted, has said:

367.   Do they envy people that which Allah has bestowed upon them out of His bounty (4.55)?

1574. Abu Hurairah relates that the Holy Prophet said: Beware of envy for envy devours good works as fire devours fuel (Abu Daud).

269.
On Prohibition of Spying

Allah, the Exalted, has said:

368.   Spy not (49.13).

369.   Those who malign believing men and believing women for that which they have not done shall bear the guilt of a calumny and a manifest sin (37.59).

1575. Abu Hurairah relates that the Holy Prophet said: Beware of suspicion for suspicion is great falsehood. Do not search for each other's faults nor spy nor hanker after that which others have nor envy nor entertain ill-will nor indifference and be Allah's servants, brethren to each other as you have been commanded. A Muslim is the brother of a Muslim; he does not wrong him or humiliate him nor is contemptuous towards him. Righteousness dwells here, righteousness dwells here; and he pointed to his chest. It is enough evil for a Muslim that he should look down upon a brother Muslim. Everything of a Muslim is forbidden to another Muslim, his blood, his honour and his property. Allah does not look to your bodies or to your features or to your works, He looks at your heart. Another version is: Do not entertain envy or ill-will and do not spy or search for faults, nor make false bids and be Allah's servants, brethren to each other. Another version is: Do not boycott or be indifferent or entertain ill-will or envy. Be Allah's servants, brethren to each other. Another version is: Do not boycott each other nor intervene upon another's deal (Muslim).

1576. Mu'awiah relates that he heard the Holy Prophet say: If you go about searching for the faults of Muslims you will corrupt them (Abu Daud).

1577. Ibn Mas'ud relates that a man was brought to him and he was told; This is So and So and his beard smells of liquor. Ibn Mas'ud said: We have been forbidden to search for faults, we can take note only of that which is overt (Abu Daud).

270.

On Prohibition of Suspicion

Allah, the Exalted, has said:

370. O ye who believe, eschew too much suspicion; for some suspicion might do much harm (49.13).

1578. This *hadith* is part of No. 1575.

271.

On Prohibition of Looking Down on People

Allah, the Exalted, has said:

371. O ye who believe, let no people deride another people, haply they may be better than themselves, nor let one group of women deride another, haply the last may be better than the first. Defame not your people nor call them names. Ill indeed it is to earn an evil reputation after having believed. Those who do not repent are the wrongdoers (49. 12).

372. Woe to every backbiter, slanderer (104. 2).

1579. This *hadith* is part of No. 1575.
1580. This *hadith* is the same as No. 615.
1581. Jundub ibn Abdullah relates that the Holy Prophet said: A man said: By Allah, He will not forgive So and So; whereupon Allah, the Lord of honour and glory, said: Who is he who takes an oath in My name that I will not forgive So and So. I have forgiven him and have deprived your good deeds of all merit (Muslim).

272.

On Prohibition of Exultation over Another's Misfortune

Allah, the Exalted, has said:

373. All believers are brothers (49. 11).

374. Those who desire the spread of indecency among the believers will have a painful chastisement in this world and in the hereafter (24. 20).

1582. Wathila ibn Asqa'a relates that the Holy Prophet said: Do not exult over the misfortune of a brother for Allah might have mercy on him and involve you in misfortune (Tirmidhi).

273.

On Prohibition of Deriding a Person's Descent

Allah, the Exalted, has said:

375. Those who malign believing men and believing women for that which they have not done shall bear the guilt of a calumny and a manifest sin (33.59).

1583. Abu Hurairah relates that the Holy Prophet said: Two matters are signs of disbelief on the part of those who indulge in them: Decrying a person's descent and bewailing the dead (Muslim).

274.

On Prohibition of Cheating

Allah, the Exalted, has said:

376. Those who malign believing men and believing women for that which they have not done shall bear the guilt of a calumny and a manifest sin (33.59).

1584. Abu Hurairah relates that the Holy Prophet said: He who raises a weapon against us is not one of us and he who cheats us is not one of us (Muslim). Muslim also records that the Holy Prophet passed by a heap of corn and on thrusting his arm into it his fingers felt a wetness, whereupon he asked the owner: What is this? He answered: Messenger of Allah, it was wetted by rain. The Holy Prophet said: Why did you not let it remain on top so that people could see it? He who cheats is not one of us.

1585. Abu Hurairah relates that the Holy Prophet said: Do not raise prices in competition (Bokhari and Muslim).

1586. Ibn Umar relates that the Holy Prophet prohibited raising prices in competition (Bokhari and Muslim).

1587. Ibn Umar relates: A man mentioned to the Holy Prophet that he was often deceived in dealings. The Holy Prophet said to him: When you enter into a transaction you should say: There should be no deception (Bokhari and Muslim).

1588. Abu Hurairah relates that the Holy Prophet said: He who plays false with another's wife or female slave is not one of us (Abu Daud).

275.

On Prohibition of Breach of Covenant

Allah, the Exalted, has said:

377.   O ye who believe fulfil your covenants (5.2).

378.   Fulfil your covenants for you will be called to account for your covenants (17.35).

1589. This *hadith* is the same as No. 693.

1590. Ibn Mas'ud and Ibn Umar and Anas relate that the Holy Prophet said: For everyone who breaks his covenant there will be a standard on the Day of Judgment. People will say: This standard proclaims a breach of covenant by So and So (Bokhari and Muslim).

1591. Abu Sa'id Khudri relates that the Holy Prophet said: Every breaker of covenant will have a standard over his back on the Day of Judgment the height of which will be according to the size of his breach. Hearken! there is no bigger breaker of covenant than a ruler who plays his people false (Muslim).

1592. Abu Hurairah relates that the Holy Prophet said: Allah, the Exalted, says there are three against whom I shall contend on the Day of Judgment. One, he who makes a covenant in My name and then defaults on it; two, he who sells a free man into slavery and devours his price; and three, he who hires a workman and having taken full work from him fails to pay him his wages (Bokhari).

1593. This *hadith* is the same as No. 797.

276.

On Prohibition of Following a Gift with Reproaches

Allah, the Exalted, has said:

379.   Those who spend their wealth in the cause of Allah, then follow not up that which they have spent with reproaches or injury (2.263).

380.   O ye who believe, render not vain your alms with reproaches or injury (2.265).

277.

On Prohibition of Pride and Arrogance

Allah, the Exalted, has said:

381.   Ascribe not purity to yourselves. He knows best him who is truly righteous (53. 33).

*382.   Blame attaches only to those who wrong others and
transgress in the earth without justification. For them there
is a painful chastisement (42. 43).*

1594.   Ayadh ibn Himar relates that the Holy Prophet said: Allah has
revealed to me that you should be humble, so that no one transgresses against
another, no one holds himself above another. (Muslim).

1595.   Abu Hurairah relates that the Holy Prophet said: When a person
says: People are ruined; it is he who ruins them (Muslim).

278.
On Prohibition of Boycott

Allah, the Exalted, has said:

*383.   All believers are brothers, so make peace between
your brothers (49. 11).*

384.   Assist not one another in sin and transgression (5. 3).

1596.   This *hadith* is the same as No. 1572.

1597.   Abu Ayesha relates that the Holy Prophet said: It is not
permissible for a Muslim that he should keep away from his brother for more
than three days so that when they meet they should turn away from each other.
The better of them is he who is the first to greet the other (Bokhari and
Muslim).

1598.   This *hadith* is the same as No. 1573.

1599.   Jabir relates that he heard the Holy Prophet say: Satan has
despaired that the Muslims would worship him in the Arabian Peninsula, so
he tries to bring about cessation of intercourse between them (Muslim).

1600.   Abu Hurairah relates that the Holy Prophet said: It is not
permissible for a Muslim to keep away from his brother for more than three
days. He who keeps away from his brother for more than three days and dies
in that condition will enter hell (Abu Daud).

1601.   Abu Khirash Hadrad relates that he heard the Holy Prophet say:
He who keeps away from his brother for a year is as if he had slain him (Abu
Daud).

1602.   Abu Hurairah relates that the Holy Prophet said: It is not
permissible for a believer to keep away from a believer for more than three
days. After the lapse of this period, he should go and meet him and salute
him. If he returns the salutation they will be sharers in the merit of
reconciliation. If he does not return the salutation he will be guilty of sin and
the former will be acquitted of the responsibility for the separation between
them (Abu Daud).

279.

On Prohibition of Two Conversing together excluding a Third

Allah, the Exalted, has said:

385. Secret conspiracy is a device of Satan (58.11).

1603. Ibn Umar relates that the Holy Prophet said: Where three are present two should not hold secret converse excluding the third (Abu Daud). Abu Saleh relates: I asked Ibn Umar: What if there should be four? He said: In that case there is no harm. Malik has reported in Muatta that Abdullah ibn Dinar relates: Ibn Umar and I were together in the house of Khalid ibn Uqbah when a man came to consult Ibn Umar. As I was the only other person present, Ibn Umar called another man in, which made us four and said to the two of us: Move away a bit, for I have heard the Holy Prophet say: Two should not hold converse together, excluding a third.

1604. Ibn Mas'ud relates that the Holy Prophet said: Where there are three of you, two should not hold converse together till the number increases, lest the third should be embarrassed (Bokhari and Muslim).

280.

On Prohibition of Cruelty

Allah, the Exalted, has said:

386. Be benevolent towards parents, and kindred, and orphans, and the needy, and the neighbour who is a kinsman, and the neighbour who is not related to you, and your associates and the wayfarer and those who are under your control. Surely Allah loves not the proud and the boastful (4. 57).

1605. Ibn Umar relates that the Holy Prophet said: A woman was tormented on account of a cat which she had shut up till it died. On that account she entered the Fire. She did not give it to eat or drink when she shut it up, nor did she leave it free to pick up its nourishment from among the rodents and insects of the earth (Bokhari and Muslim).

1606. Ibn Umar relates that he passed by some Quraish youths who were shooting arrows at a bird they had tied down, having made a bargain with the owner of the bird that he should have every arrow of theirs that missed. When they saw Ibn Umar they dispersed. Ibn Umar said: Who has done this? May Allah's curse be upon him who has done this. The Holy Prophet has cursed him who makes a target of a living thing (Bokhari and Muslim).

1607. Anas relates that the Holy Prophet forbade an animal being made a target (Bokhari and Muslim).

1608. Abu Ali Su'ud ibn Muqrin relates: I was one of seven Bani Muqrin and between us we had only one maid servant. The youngest of us happened to slap her and the Holy Prophet commanded that she should be set free (Muslim).

1609. Abu Mas'ud Badri relates: I was striking a slave with a whip when I heard a voice from behind me: Beware Abu Mas'ud. I had been so upset that I did not recognise the voice till the person drew near and I discovered it was the Holy Prophet and he was saying: Beware Abu Mas'ud, Allah has more power over you than you have over this slave; and I responded: I shall never strike a slave again. Another version is: The whip fell from my hand in awe of the Holy Prophet. Another version is: Messenger of Allah, I set him free to win the pleasure of Allah. The Holy Prophet observed: If you had not done that you would have been singed by the Fire (Muslim).

1610. Ibn Umar relates that the Holy Prophet said: The atonement for beating or slapping a slave on the face for something he has not done is that he should be set free (Muslim).

1611. Hisham ibn Hakim ibn Hizam relates that he passed by some non-Muslim peasants in Damascus who had been ordered to stand in the sun and over whose heads olive oil had been poured. He inquired: What is this? and was told: They are being tormented for recovery of tax. On this Hisham said: I bear witness that the Holy Prophet said: Allah will chastise those who torment people in this life. Then he went to the Governor and told him this, and he ordered the men to be released (Muslim).

1612. Ibn Abbas relates that the Holy Prophet was displeased at the sight of a donkey that had been branded on its face. Ibn Abbas said: I shall brand my donkey on the part of his body farthest from the face, and he ordered it to be branded on its hips. He was the first to do this (Muslim).

1613. Jabir ibn Abdullah relates that the Holy Prophet passed by a donkey that had been branded on its face and said: Allah's curse be on him who branded it (Muslim). Muslim also relates that the Holy Prophet forbade beating or branding an animal on its face.

281.

On Prohibition of Tormenting by Fire

1614. Abu Hurairah relates: The Holy Prophet sent us on an expedition and told us: If you find So and So, and So and So of the Quraish commit them to the fire. When we were about to set out he said to us: I had ordered you to burn So and So, and So and So. But it is Allah alone who chastises with fire. So if you find them, execute them (Bokhari).

1615. Ibn Mas'ud relates: We were with the Holy Prophet in the course of a journey when he drew apart and in his absence we saw a red bird which had two little ones with it. We caught them and the mother bird came and started beating the earth with its wings. By that time the Holy Prophet returned and exclaimed: Who has distressed this bird on account of its young? Return them to her. He also noticed a mound of ants to which we had set fire. He inquired: Who has set fire to this? We answered: We have. He observed: It does not behove any to torment with fire except the Lord of the fire (Abu Daud).

282.

On the Undesirability of a Person of Means postponing Fulfilment of his Obligations

Allah, the Exalted, has said:

387. Allah commands you to make over the trusts to those best fitted to discharge them (4.57).

388. Let him who is entrusted render back his trust when he is called upon to do so (2.84).

1616. Abu Hurairah relates that the Holy Prophet said: It is wrong on the part of a person of means to shilly shally in fulfilling his obligations; and if the repayment of a debt due to any of you is undertaken by a person of means you should agree to the substitution (Bokhari and Muslim).

283.

On Prohibition of Retracting a Gift

1617. Ibn Abbas relates that the Holy Prophet said: He who retracts a gift is like the dog that devours its vomit (Bokhari and Muslim).

1618. Umar ibn Khattab relates: I had dedicated a horse in the cause of Allah but the person to whom I gave it was neglecting it and I was thinking of buying it from him believing that he would sell it cheap. So I inquired about it from the Holy Prophet who said: Do not buy it even if he should be willing to sell it for a *dirhem*, for this would be retracting your gift and he who does that is like one who devours his vomit (Bokhari and Muslim).

284.

On the Sanctity of the Property of an Orphan

Allah, the Exalted, has said:

389. Those who eat up the property of orphans unjustly, only swallow fire into their bellies and shall enter a blazing fire (4. 11).

390. Approach not the property of the orphan during his minority, except for the most beneficent purpose (6. 153).

391. They ask thee concerning orphans. Tell them: The promotion of their welfare is very meritorious. There is no harm in your living together with them, for they are your brethren, and Allah will know him who seeks to promote their welfare and also him who seeks to do them harm (2. 221).

1619. Abu Hurairah relates that the Holy Prophet said: Eschew the seven fatalities. He was asked: Messenger of Allah, what are they? He answered: Associating anything with Allah; sorcery; slaying unjustly a life declared sacred by Allah; devouring interest; devouring the property of the orphan; running away from the enemy in battle and calumniating chaste, unwary believing women (Bokhari and Muslim).

285.

On Prohibition of Taking Interest

Allah, the Exalted, has said:

392. Those who devour interest stand like one whom Satan has smitten with insanity. That is so because they keep saying: The business of buying and selling is also like lending money on interest: whereas Allah has made buying and selling lawful and has made the taking of interest unlawful. Remember, therefore, that he who desists because of the admonition that has come to him from his Lord may retain what he has gained in the past and his affair is committed to Allah, but those who revert to the practice are the inmates of the Fire; therein shall they abide. Allah will wipe out interest and will foster charity. Allah loves not confirmed disbelievers and arch sinners. O ye who believe, be mindful of your duty to Allah and relinquish your claim to what remains of interest, if you are truly believers (2. 276-279).

1620. Ibn Mas'ud relates that the Holy Prophet cursed him who takes and him who pays interest (Muslim). Tirmidhi adds: And those who witness and transcribe a transaction involving the taking and paying of interest.

286.
On Prohibition of Showing Off

Allah, the Exalted, has said:

393. They had only been commanded to worship Allah, devoting themselves wholly to Him in full sincerity (98. 6).

394. Render not vain your alms with reproaches or injury, like one who spends his wealth to be seen of people and believes not in Allah and the Last Day (2. 265).

395. They join the Prayer only for show, and thus remember Allah but little (4. 143).

1621. Abu Hurairah relates that he heard the Holy Prophet say: Allah, the Exalted, says: I am far above the association of associators. If any one associates another with Me in anything he does, I reject him and his act of associating anything with Me (Muslim).

1622. Abu Hurairah relates that he heard the Holy Prophet say: One of the first men to be judged on the Day of Judgment will be one who will have been martyred. He will be summoned and will be shown all the bounties that had been bestowed upon him. He will recognise them and will be asked: How did you employ them? He will say: I fought in Thy cause and was martyred. He will be told: You lie; you fought so that you might be called a champion; and so you were known. Judgment will be passed on him and he will be dragged on his face and thrown into the Fire. A man will be brought who had acquired knowledge and had studied the Quran. He will be shown the bounties bestowed on him and will recognise them and will be asked: How did you employ them? He will say: I acquired knowledge and taught it and studied the Quran to win Thy pleasure. He will be told: You lie. You acquired knowledge so that you might be called a savant and you recited the Quran so that you might be called a *qari;* and so you were called. Judgment will be passed on him and he will be dragged on his face and thrown into the Fire. A man will be brought on whom Allah will have bestowed plenty and every kind of wealth. He will be shown the bounties bestowed on him and will recognise them and will be asked: How did you employ them? He will say: I spent in every one of the causes that Thou dost approve and did not leave out one, so as to win Thy pleasure. He will be told: You lie; you did all that so that you might be called bountiful; and so were you called. Judgment will be passed on him and he will be dragged on his face and thrown into the Fire (Muslim).

1623. This *hadith* is the same as No. 1546.

1624. Jundub ibn Abdullah ibn Sufyan relates that the Holy Prophet said: He who acts so as to boast among people will have his defaults noised about, and he whose motive is to show off will be recompensed accordingly (Bokhari and Muslim).

1625. This *hadith* is the same as No. 1396.

287.

On that which is not Showing Off

1626. Abu Dharr relates that the Holy Prophet was asked: What about a person who does some good deed and people praise him for it? He answered: This is an immediate appreciation of a believer's good deed (Muslim).

288.

On the Prohibition of Looking at Strange Women

Allah, the Exalted, has said:

396. Direct the believing men to restrain their looks (24.31).

397. The ear and the eye and the heart shall all be called to account (17.57).

398. He knows the treachery of the eyes and that which the mind conceals (40.19).

399. Surely thy Lord is on the watch (89.15).

1627. Abu Hurairah relates that the Holy Prophet said: A part of adultery is man's portion which he achieves anyhow. The adultery of the eyes is looking at that which is forbidden; the adultery of the ears is listening to that which is forbidden; the adultery of the tongue is uttering that which is forbidden; the adultery of the hand is grasping that which is forbidden; the adultery of the feet is walking to that which is forbidden; and the heart yearns and desires and the genitals confirm it or give it the lie (Bokhari and Muslim).

1628. This *hadith* is the same as No. 192.

1629. Abu Talha Zaid ibn Sahl relates: We were sitting talking on a platform in front of our house when the Holy Prophet came and stopped by us and said: Why do you sit along the streets? We replied: We do no harm, we only sit and converse. He said: If you must, then discharge your obligation; namely, guard your eyes, respond to salutation and converse decently (Muslim).

1630. Jarir relates: I asked the Holy Prophet about a sudden involuntary glance. He said: Avert your eyes (Muslim).

1631. Umm Salamah relates that she was with the Holy Prophet and Maimuna was there also when Ibn Umm Maktum came. This was after we had been commanded to veil ourselves. The Holy Prophet said: Veil yourselves from him. We said: Messenger of Allah, he is blind, he cannot see us and does not recognise us; whereupon the Holy Prophet said: But are you blind and cannot see him (Abu Daud and Tirmidhi)?

1632. Abu Sa'id relates that the Holy Prophet said: A man must not look at another man's genitals, nor must a woman look at another woman's genitals; nor should two naked men lie under one cover, nor two naked women under the same cover (Muslim).

289.

On Prohibition of being alone with a Strange Woman

Allah, the Exalted, has said:

400. When you ask them for something, ask from behind a curtain (33.54).

1633. Uqbah ibn 'Amir relates that the Holy Prophet said: Do not visit women outside the prohibited degrees. A man from among the Ansar asked: What about in-laws? He answered: They are fatal (Bokhari and Muslim).

1634. Ibn Abbas relates that the Holy Prophet said: No one of you should meet a woman apart unless she is accompanied by a relative within the prohibited degrees (Bokhari and Muslim).

1635. Buraidah relates that the Holy Prophet said: The sanctity of the women of those who go forth in the cause of Allah for those who remain at home is the same as the sanctity of their own mothers. One who remains at home and plays false in the matter of his women one who has gone forth will on the Day of Judgment find the latter stand up and take away as much of his good works as he pleases till he is satisfied. Then the Holy Prophet turned to us and said: Now what do you think (Muslim)?

290.

On Prohibition of Men and Women Apeing One Another

1636. Ibn Abbas relates that the Holy Prophet cursed effeminate men and masculine women. Another version is: The Holy Prophet cursed men who ape women and cursed women who ape men (Bokhari).

1637.   Abu Hurairah relates that the Holy Prophet cursed men who dress like women and cursed women who dress like men (Abu Daud).

1638.   Abu Hurairah relates that the Holy Prophet said: There are two types of the dwellers of the Fire whom I have not seen: One, men holding whips like the tails of cows with which they will chastise people; and second, women who will be clad but will appear naked, and who will twist their shoulders delicately and walk undulatingly. Their heads will appear like the humps of Bukhti camels. They will not enter Paradise nor perceive its fragrance though its fragrance is perceptible from such and such a distance (Muslim).

291.
On Prohibition of Apeing Satan and Disbelievers

1639.   Jabir relates that the Holy Prophet said: Do not eat with the left hand for Satan eats with the left hand (Muslim).

1640.   Ibn Umar relates that the Holy Prophet said: Do not eat with the left hand nor drink with it, for Satan eats with his left hand and drinks with it (Muslim).

1641.   Abu Hurairah relates that the Holy Prophet said: The Jews and Christians do not dye their hair, do you do the opposite (Bokhari and Muslim).

292.
On Prohibition of Dyeing Hair Black

1642.   Jabir relates that Abu Qahafah, father of Abu Bakr, was presented to the Holy Prophet on the day of the fall of Mecca, and his head and beard were snow white. The Holy Prophet said: Change this, but avoid black (Muslim).

293.
On Prohibition of Shaving Part of Head

1643.   Ibn Umar relates that the Holy Prophet forbade shaving part of the head (Bokhari and Muslim).

1644.   Ibn Umar relates that the Holy Prophet saw a boy with his head part shaven. He forbade this, saying: Shave the whole of it or leave the whole (Abu Daud).

1645. Abdullah ibn Ja'far relates that the Holy Prophet permitted the family of Ja'far to mourn for him for three days. Then he came to them and said: Do not weep for my brother after today. Then he said: Bring my brother's sons to me. We were brought to him feeling like bereft chicks. He then asked: Call me a barber; and when he came he directed him to shave our heads, which he did (Abu Daud).

1646. Ali relates that the Holy Prophet forbade a woman shaving her head (Nisai).

294.

On Prohibition of Wigs, Tattooing and Filing of Teeth

Allah, the Exalted, has said:

401. They invoke beside Him none but lifeless objects; and they invoke none but Satan, the rebellious one, whom Allah has cast away. He said to Allah: I will assuredly beguile a fixed portion from Thy servants, and will lead them astray, and will excite in them vain desires, and will incite them to cut off the ears of cattle to alter Allah's creation (4.118-121).

1647. Asma' relates that a woman asked the Holy Prophet: Messenger of Allah, my daughter suffered from smallpox and her hair fell off. Now I have celebrated her marriage. Can I get her a wig? He answered: Allah has cursed the maker and the wearer of a wig (Bokhari and Muslim). Another version is: The maker of a wig and she who desires a wig.

1648. Ayesha relates about the same (Bokhari and Muslim).

1649. Humaid ibn Abdur Rahman relates that he heard Mu'awiah say from the pulpit the year he was on Pilgrimage, taking hold of a bunch of hair from the hands of a guard: O people of Medina, where are your divines? I heard the Holy Prophet forbid this and say: The Bani Israel were ruined when their women took to this kind of thing (Bokhari and Muslim).

1650. Ibn Umar relates that the Holy Prophet cursed the maker and wearer of a wig and the tattooer and the one who is tattooed (Bokhari and Muslim).

1651. Ibn Mas'ud said: Allah has cursed tattooers and those who are tattooed, and those women who have their teeth filed for beauty and those who have their hair plucked and thus alter Allah's creation. A woman asked him: What is all this? He answered: Why should I not curse those whom the Holy Prophet cursed? Allah, the Exalted, has said in His Book: Whatever the Messenger gives you that take, and whatsoever he forbids you from that abstain (59.8) (Bokhari and Muslim).

295.
On Prohibition of Plucking away White Hair

1652. Amr ibn Shu'aib relates on the authority of his father and grandfather that the Holy Prophet said: Do not pluck away white hair for they are the light of the countenance of a Muslim on the Day of Judgment (Abu Daud and Tirmidhi).

1653. Ayesha relates that the Holy Prophet said: He who does that which has not our approval is rejected (Muslim).

296.
On Prohibition of Employing the Right Hand for Cleaning

1654. Abu Qatadah relates that the Holy Prophet said: Do not use your right hand while passing water, nor for washing or cleaning, and do not breathe into the vessel from which you drink (Bokhari and Muslim).

297.
On the Undesirability of Wearing only one Shoe or Sock

1655. Abu Hurairah relates that the Holy Prophet said: You should not walk about wearing only one shoe; you should wear both or discard both (Bokhari and Muslim).

1656. Abu Hurairah relates that he heard the Holy Prophet say: When the lace of one of your shoes snaps do not walk about in the other till you have had the first one repaired (Muslim).

1657. Jabir relates that the Holy Prophet forbade a person tying up his shoe while standing (Abu Daud).

298.
On Prohibition of leaving an Open Fire Burning at Night

1658. Ibn Umar relates that the Holy Prophet said: Do not leave a fire burning in your homes when you go to sleep (Bokhari and Muslim).

1659. This *hadith* is the same as No. 162.

1660. Jabir relates that the Holy Prophet said: Cover up the opening of vessels, tie up the mouth of the water-skin, lock up the doors and put out the lamps, for Satan does not lift up the covering of a vessel, nor unloosen the mouth of a water-skin, nor open a locked door. If one of you can cover the opening of a vessel only by placing a piece of wood across it, let him do it, or at least pronounce the name of Allah on it. A mouse sometimes burns down a house on top of its dwellers (Muslim).

299.
On Prohibition of Affectation

Allah, the Exalted, has said:

402.   Say to the people, O Prophet: I ask not of you any recompense for conveying Allah's message to you, nor am I one given to affectation (38.87).

1661.   Ibn Umar relates: We have been forbidden affectation (Bokhari).

1662.   Masruq relates: We visited Abdullah ibn Mas'ud and he said to us: He who has knowledge of a matter may talk of it, and he who has not knowledge of it should say: Allah knows best. It is part of knowledge that a person who has not knowledge of a matter should say: Allah knows best. Allah said to His Prophet: Say to the people: I ask not of you any recompense for conveying Allah's message to you, nor am I one given to affectation (38.87) (Bokhari).

300.
On Prohibition of Bewailing the Dead

1663.   Umar ibn Khattab relates that the Holy Prophet said: A corpse is tormented in its grave on account of the bewailing over it (Bokhari and Muslim).

1664.   Ibn Mas'ud relates that the Holy Prophet said: He who beats his face and tears his clothes and bewails his fate over a misfortune as was done in pre-Islamic days is not of us (Bokhari and Muslim).

1665.   Abu Burdah relates that Abu Musa fell ill and became unconscious. His head was in the lap of one of the women of the family. She cried out in a loud voice. When Abu Musa recovered consciousness he said: I detest what the Holy Prophet detested. He detested a woman who cried out aloud, or shaved her head, or tore her clothes (Bokhari and Muslim).

1666.   Mughirah ibn Shu'bah relates that he heard the Holy Prophet say: A person who is bewailed will be chastised for it on the Day of Judgment (Bokhari and Muslim).

1667.   Umm Atiyyah Nusaibah relates: The Holy Prophet made us promise as part of the covenant that we would not bewail the dead (Bokhari and Muslim).

1668. Nu'man ibn Bashir relates that when Abdullah ibn Rawahal became unconscious in his illness his sister started bewailing him: O thou mountain among men, and such and such! He recovered consciousness and said: Whatever you said I was asked: Are you like this (Bokhari)?

1669. This *hadith* is the same as No. 929.

1670. Abu Malik Ash'ari relates that the Holy Prophet said: If a woman who is given to bewailing does not repent before her death, she will be raised on the Day of Judgment wearing a coat of pitch and a scarf of rust (Muslim).

1671. Usaid ibn Abi Usaid relates that a woman who had made the covenant at the hands of the Holy Prophet said: Among the matters in respect of which the Holy Prophet took from us a promise that we would not disobey him were the pinching of our faces, bewailing, tearing our garments and unloosening our hair (Abu Daud).

1672. Abu Musa relates that the Holy Prophet said: When a person dies and a mourner bewails him saying: O mountain among men, O chieftain, and such like, Allah appoints two angels who pommel him with their fists and ask: Were you like this (Tirmidhi)?

1673. This *hadith* is the same as No. 1583.

301.
On Eschewing Soothsayers and the Like

1674. Ayesha relates: Some people asked the Holy Prophet about soothsayers. He said: They do not amount to anything. He was told: Messenger of Allah, they sometimes make predictions which come true. Upon this the Holy Prophet said: That is something true which Satan hears by chance from the angels and which he whispers into the ears of his friends and they mix a hundred falsehoolds with it (Bokhari and Muslim). Bokhari's version is: Ayesha relates that she heard the Holy Prophet say: The angels descend into the atmosphere talking of something that has been decreed in heaven and Satan stealthily hears part of it and communicates it to the soothsayers and they mix a hundred falsehoods with it from themselves.

1675. Safiyyah bint Abu Ubaid relates on the authority of some of the wives of the Holy Prophet that he said: He who goes to one who claims to tell him where he will find his lost property and affirms the righteousness of such a pretender will lose the benefit of his Prayers during forty days (Muslim).

1676. Qubaisah ibn Mukhariq relates that he heard the Holy Prophet say: Oracles and drawing lines and observing the direction of the flight of birds to deduce omens from them are all satanic practices (Abu Daud).

1677. Ibn Abbas relates that the Holy Prophet said: He who dabbles in divination learns a portion of magic, the more he knows the more of a magician he becomes (Abu Daud).

1678. This *hadith* is comprehended in No. 704.

1679. Abu Mas'ud Badri relates that the Holy Prophet forbade the utilisation of the price of a dog, the earning of an adulteress and the fees of a soothsayer (Bokhari and Muslim).

302.
On Prohibition of Believing in Ill Omens

1680. Anas relates that the Holy Prophet said: There is no infection and no bad omen, but I am pleased with good augury. He was asked: What is good augury? He answered: A good word (Bokhari and Muslim).

1681. Ibn Umar relates that the Holy Prophet said: There is no infection and no ill omen. Had there been any ill luck it would have been in a house and a woman and a horse (Bokhari and Muslim).

1682. Buraidah relates that the Holy Prophet never took ill augury (Abu Daud).

1683. Urwah ibn 'Amir relates: The art of divination was mentioned to the Holy Prophet. He said: The best of it is a good omen, but even that does not turn a Muslim away from that which he has determined. If any of you should see something which he dislikes he should supplicate: Allah, from Thee alone proceeds good and Thou alone canst repel evil. There is no strength to resist evil nor power to do good except through Thee (Abu Daud).

303.
On Prohibition of Portraits and Likenesses

1684. Ibn Umar relates that the Holy Prophet said: Those who make pictures will be chastised on the Day of Judgment and it will be said of them: Now put life into that which you made (Bokhari and Muslim).

1685. Ayesha relates: The Holy Prophet returned from a journey and in his absence I had screened a platform in front of my house with a curtain on which there were pictures. When the Holy Prophet saw it, he changed colour and said: Ayesha, the worst chastised by Allah on the Day of Judgment will be those who copy Allah's creation. So I cut it up and made one or two pillow covers from it (Bokhari and Muslim).

1686. Ibn Abbas relates that he heard the Holy Prophet say: For every painter there will be a person appointed in respect of every one of his paintings who will chastise him for it in hell (Bokhari and Muslim).

1687. This *hadith* is comprehended in No. 1549.

1688. Ibn Mas'ud relates that he heard the Holy Prophet say: Allah, the Exalted, says: Who commits a greater wrong than one who is after creating the like of My creation? Let them make an ant, or a grain of corn or a grain of barley (Bokhari and Muslim).

1689. Abu Hurairah relates that he heard the Holy Prophet say: The worst chastised on the Day of Judgment will be the portrait painters (Bokhari and Muslim).

1690. Abu Talha relates that the Holy Prophet said: Angels will not enter a house in which there is a dog or a portrait (Bokhari and Muslim).

1691. Ibn Umar relates that Gabriel promised to visit the Holy Prophet but delayed and the waiting sat heavy on the Holy Prophet. When he emerged from his house he encountered Gabriel and complained to him of the delay. He answered: We do not enter a house in which there is a dog or a portrait (Bokhari).

1692. Ayesha relates: Gabriel had promised to visit the Holy Prophet at a certain hour. The hour came and no Gabriel. The Holy Prophet had a stick in his hand. He threw it away saying: Allah goes not against His promise, nor His messenger. Then he noticed a dog under his sofa and asked: When did this dog come in? I said: I did not perceive it come in. He directed it to be put out and it was expelled. Then Gabriel came and the Holy Prophet said to him: You had promised to visit me and I sat waiting for you but you did not come. He said: I was hindered by the dog in your house. We do not enter a house in which there is a dog or a portrait (Muslim).

1693. Hayyan ibn Husain relates: Ali ibn Abi Talib said to me: Shall I assign you a task that the Holy Prophet had assigned to me? Leave not a portrait unwiped out, and leave not a high grave unlevelled (Muslim).

304.
On Prohibition of Keeping a Dog

1694. Ibn Umar relates that he heard the Holy Prophet say: He who keeps a dog except for hunting or guarding cattle shall be deprived of two *qirats* of his merit every day (Bokhari and Muslim).

1695. Abu Hurairah relates that the Holy Prophet said: He who keeps a dog loses a *qirat* of his good deeds every day, unless it is a watch dog for his fields or cattle (Bokhari and Muslim). Muslim's version is: He who keeps a dog except for hunting or guarding crops or cattle shall lose two *qirats* of his merit every day.

305.
On the Undesirability of Bells etc.

1696. Abu Hurairah relates that the Holy Prophet said: Angels do not accompany a caravan that includes a dog or a bell (Muslim).

1697. Abu Hurairah relates that the bell is an instrument of Satan (Abu Daud).

306.
On Aversion towards Riding a Camel that eats Refuse

1698. Ibn Umar relates that the Holy Prophet forbade riding a camel that eats refuse (Abu Daud).

307.
On Prohibition of Spitting in a Mosque etc.

1699. Anas relates that the Holy Prophet said: Spitting in a mosque is a sin and its expiation is to bury it (Bokhari and Muslim).

1700. Ayesha relates: If the Holy Prophet saw spittal or running from the nose or matter from a cough on the wall of a mosque he would scrape it away (Bokhari and Muslim).

1701. Anas relates that the Holy Prohet said: It is not right to use the mosques for passing water or easing oneself. They are built for the remembrance of Allah and the recitation of the Quran and whatever the Messenger of Allah might direct (Muslim).

308.
On the Undesirability of Raising Voices in a Mosque

1702. Abu Hurairah relates that he heard the Holy Prophet say: Anyone who hears another seeking his lost property in the mosque should retort: May Allah restore it not to thee; for mosques are not built for such a purpose (Muslim).

1703. Abu Hurairah relates that the Holy Prophet said: If you should see a person buying or selling in a mosque, say to him: May Allah make thy bargain not profitable; and if you should see one seeking his lost property say: May He not restore it to you (Tirmidhi).

1704. Buraidah relates that a man inquired in the mosque: Who called away the red camel? Whereupon the Holy Prophet said: May you not find it. Mosques are built for the purpose for which they are built (Muslim).

1705. Amr ibn Shu'aib relates on the authority of his father and grandfather that the Holy Prophet forbade buying and selling and seeking lost property and reciting poetry in the mosque (Abu Daud and Tirmidhi).

1706. Saib ibn Yazid relates: I was in the mosque when someone hit me with a pebble. I looked up and saw it was Umar ibn Khattab. He said to me: Go and fetch those two to me. When I brought them up he asked them: Where are you from? They said: We are from Taif. He said: Had you belonged to the town I would have punished you for raising your voices in the mosque of the Holy Prophet (Bokhari).

309.

On Prohibition of entering a Mosque after eating Raw Onions, Garlic etc.

1707. Ibn Umar relates that the Holy Prophet said: He who has eaten garlic should not approach our mosque (or our mosques) (Bokhari and Muslim).

1708. Anas relates that the Holy Prophet said: He who has eaten garlic should not approach us or join us in Prayer (Bokhari and Muslim).

1709. Jabir relates that the Holy Prophet said: He who has eaten garlic or onions should keep away from us (or should keep away from our mosque) (Bokhari and Muslim). Muslim's version is: He who has eaten garlic or onions or any other malodorous herb should not approach our mosque for angels also suffer from that which causes suffering to humans.

1710. Umar ibn Khattab said in his Friday service: Then you eat of two malodorous herbs, garlic and onions. I have known the Holy Prophet direct that a person who smelt of them be expelled from the mosque as far as *baqisah*. He who must eat of them should rid them of their odour by cooking them (Muslim).

310.

On the Undesirability of Sitting with Legs Drawn up During Sermon

1711. Mu'az ibn Anas Juhni relates that the Holy Prophet forbade a person sitting with his legs drawn up to his belly during the Friday sermon (Abu Daud and Tirmidhi).

311.

On Prohibition of having a Haircut etc. by one intending to offer a Sacrifice on Festival

1712. Umm Salamah relates that the Holy Prophet said: One who intends to offer a sacrifice on the occasion of the Festival of Sacrifices should not have his hair cut or his nails pared during the first days of the month till he has offered his sacrifice (Muslim).

312.

On Prohibition of taking an Oath on Anything beside Allah

1713. Ibn Umar relates that the Holy Prophet said: Allah forbids you taking an oath by your fathers. He who must take an oath should swear by Allah or keep silent (Bokhari and Muslim).

1714. Abdur Rahman ibn Samurah relates that the Holy Prophet said: Do not swear by idols or by your fathers (Muslim).

1715. Buraidah relates that the Holy Prophet said: He who swears by his integrity is not of us (Abu Daud).

1716. Buraidah relates that the Holy Prophet said: If a person takes an oath that in such and such case he would be rid of Islam, then if he should turn out to be a liar he will be as he swore and if he should turn out to have spoken the truth he will not revert to Islam entire (Abu Daud).

1717. Ibn Umar heard a man say: No, by the Ka'aba; and admonished him: Do not swear by anything beside Allah, for I have heard the Holy Prophet say: He who swears by anything beside Allah is guilty of an act of disbelief (or of associating something with Allah) (Tirmidhi).

313.

On Prohibition of Taking a False Oath

1718. Ibn Mas'ud relates that the Holy Prophet said: He who swears a false oath to obtain the property of a Muslim unjustly shall meet Allah when He is incensed against him; and he cited from the Book of Allah in support of his affirmation: Those who take a paltry price in exchange for their covenant with Allah and their oaths, shall have no portion in the life to come. Allah will not speak to them nor cast a look upon them on the Day of Judgment, nor will He purify them. For them shall be a grievous punishment (3.78) (Bokhari and Muslim).

1719. Abu Umamah relates that the Holy Prophet said: He who takes away the right of a Muslim by swearing falsely will be condemned by Allah to

the Fire and will be excluded by Him from Paradise. A man asked him: Even
if it is a small thing, Messenger of Allah? He answered: Even if it is the twig of
a berry bush (Muslim).

1720. Abdullah ibn Amr ibn 'As relates that the Holy Prophet said: Of
the major sins are: Associating anything with Allah, disobedience of parents,
murder and a false oath (Bokhari). Another version is: A rustic came to the
Holy Prophet and asked: Messenger of Allah, what are the major sins? He
answered: Associating anything with Allah. The man asked: And after that?
The Holy Prophet replied: A false oath which deprives a Muslim of his
property.

314.
On the Desirability of Expiation of Oaths

1721. This *hadith* is the same as No. 72, with the addition: He should
expiate his oath.

1722. This *hadith* is the same as the preceding one.

1723. Abu Musa relates that the Holy Prophet said: I am hoping that, if
Allah wills, I would not swear to do something, but that if a better alternative
presented itself I would adopt it and expiate my oath (Bokhari and Muslim).

1724. Abu Hurairah relates that the Holy Prophet said: That one of you
should persist in adhering to his oath in the matter of his family is more sinful
for him in the estimation of Allah than that he should expiate his oath as
prescribed by Allah (Bokhari and Muslim).

315.
On Expiation of Oaths

Allah, the Exalted, has said:

*403. Allah will not call you to account for your meaning-
less oaths but will call you to account for breaking your
oaths by which you bind yourselves; the expiation of such
breach is the feeding of ten poor persons with such average
food as you eat yourselves, or providing clothing for them,
or procuring the freedom of one held in bondage. Whoso
lacks the means shall fast for three days. That is the
expiation of your breaking the oaths that you have sworn.
Do observe your oaths (5.90).*

1725. Ayesha relates that the verse 5.90 was revealed concerning people
who are in the habit of repeating: No, by Allah; and: Yes, by Allah (Bokhari).

316.
On the Undesirability of Swearing in Buying and Selling

1726. Abu Hurairah relates that he heard the Holy Prophet say: An oath forwards a transaction but wipes out the profit (Bokhari and Muslim).

1727. Abu Qatadah relates that he heard the Holy Prophet say: Beware of much swearing in matters of buying and selling for it promotes trade and then wipes it out (Muslim).

317.
On Prohibition of Asking in the Name of Allah

1728. Jabir relates that the Holy Prophet said: No one should ask in the name of Allah anything except Paradise (Abu Daud).

1729. Ibn Umar relates that the Holy Prophet said: Grant asylum to him who begs for it in the name of Allah, and give to him who asks in the name of Allah, and respond to him who invites you, and compensate him who is benevolent towards you, but if you cannot afford it go on praying for him till you are satisfied that you have compensated him adequately (Abu Daud and Nisai).

318.
On Prohibition of Title of King of Kings

1730. Abu Hurairah relates that the Holy Prophet said: The most humiliating title in the estimation of Allah is for a person to be called King of Kings (Bokhari and Muslim).

319.
On Prohibition of Employing Title of Honour for a Hypocrite

1731. Buraidah relates that the Holy Prophet said: Do not address a hypocrite by an honorific title, for even if he should be entitled to it, you would arouse Allah's wrath by using it for him.

320.
On Prohibition of Abusing a Disease

1732. Jabir relates that the Holy Prophet visited Umm Saib and asked her: What ails you, Umm Saib, you are shivering! She answered: It is a fever, may Allah not bless it. He said to her: Do not abuse fever, for it cleans out sins as a furnace cleans out the dirt of iron (Muslim).

321.
On Prohibition of Condemning the Weather

1733. Ubayy ibn Ka'ab relates that the Holy Prophet said: Do not abuse the wind. Should your experience of it be disagreeable supplicate: Allah, we beg of Thee the good of this wind, and the good of that which it contains and the good of that which it has been commanded; and we week Thy protection against the evil of this wind and the evil of that which it contains and the evil of that which it has been commanded (Tirmidhi).

1734. Abu Hurairah relates that he heard the Holy Prophet say: The wind is of the mercy of Allah, it bears His mercy and His chastisement. When you experience it do not abuse it, but beg of Allah its good and seek Allah's protection against its evil (Abu Daud).

1735. Ayesha relates that when the wind blew the Holy Prophet would say: Allah, I beg of Thee its good and the good of that which it contains and the good of the purpose for which it has been sent; and seek Thy protection against its evil and the evil of that which it contains and the evil of the purpose for which it has been sent (Muslim).

322.
On Prohibition of Speaking Ill of a Rooster

1736. Zaid ibn Khalid Juhni relates that the Holy Prophet said: Do not abuse a rooster for it wakes you up for Prayer (Abu Daud).

323.
On Prohibition of Attributing Rain to the Direction of a Planet

1737. Zaid ibn Khalid relates: The Holy Prophet led the dawn Prayer at Hudaibiyyah. It had rained during the night. After concluding the Prayer he turned to the congregation and said: Do you know what your Lord has said?

He was answered: Allah and His Messenger know best. He told us: He has said: This morning My servants have got up some believing in Me and others denying Me. He who said: We have been granted rain by the grace and mercy of Allah; believes in Me, and he who said: We have been granted rain by such and such a planet; he denied Me and believed in the planets (Bokhari and Muslim).

324.

On Prohibition of Calling a Muslim a Disbeliever

1738. Ibn Umar relates that the Holy Prophet said: When a man addresses his brother with: O disbeliever; one of them will certainly deserve the title; the one addressed if he is such, else it will revert to him who uttered it (Bokhari and Muslim).

1739. Abu Dharr relates that he heard the Holy Prophet say: If one of you should call another a disbeliever or an enemy of Allah and he should in fact not be such, the title will revert to the one who uttered it (Bokhari and Muslim).

325.

On Prohibition of Loose Talk

1740. Ibn Mas'ud relates that the Holy Prophet said: A believer does not taunt or curse or abuse or talk indecently (Tirmidhi).

1741. Anas relates that the Holy Prophet said: Indecency disfigures everything and modesty enhances the charm of everything (Tirmidhi).

326.

On the Undesirability of Employing Exaggerated Terms

1742. Ibn Mas'ud relates that the Holy Prophet said: Ruined are those who exaggerate. He repeated it three times (Muslim).

1743. Abdullah ibn Amr ibn 'As relates that the Holy Prophet said: He who rolls his tongue as does a bullock in eating grass offends Allah (Abu Daud and Tirmidhi).

1744. Jabir ibn Abdullah relates that the Holy Prophet said: The dearest of you to me and the closest of you to me on the Day of Judgment will be those who are the best behaved, and the most offensive to me and the farthest from me on the Day of Judgment will be the most voluble, the most boring and the most rhetorical (Tirmidhi).

327.

On the Undesirability of Self Condemnation

1745. Ayesha relates that the Holy Prophet said: Let no one of you say: My soul is corrupted *(Khabusat)*. But if he must, he might say: My soul is in bad shape *(Laqasat)* (Bokhari and Muslim).

328.

On the Undesirability of Calling Grapes Karm

1746. Abu Hurairah relates that the Holy Prophet said: Do not call grapes *Karm*, for a Muslim is *Karm* (Bokhari and Muslim). Another version is: *Karm* is the heart of a believer.

1747. This *hadith* is a repetition of part of the immediately preceding *hadith*.

329.

On the Prohibition of Describing the Beauty of a Woman

1748. Ibn Mas'ud relates that the Holy Prophet said: Let not a woman embrace another woman and then describe her to her husband in such detail as if he was looking at her (Bokhari and Muslim).

330.

On the Desirability of Supplication in Full Confidence

1749. Abu Hurairah relates that the Holy prophet said: Let not any of you supplicate: Allah, forgive me if Thou will; Allah, have mercy on me if Thou will. A supplication should be made in full confidence for no one has the power to compel the Divine (Muslim). Another version is: A supplicant should supplicate in full confidence and should magnify his desire for acceptance of his supplication for no bounty is too great for Allah.

1750. Anas relates that the Holy Prophet said: When one of you supplicates he should ask in full confidence and should not say: Allah, bestow on me if Thou will; for there is no forcing Him (Bokhari and Muslim).

331.

On the Undesirability of Combining what Allah wills and So and So wills

1751. Huzaifah relates that the Holy Prophet said: Say not: What Allah wills and So and So wills, but say: What Allah wills, and then separately what So and So wills (Abu Daud).

332.
On the Undesirability of Conversation after Evening Prayer

1752. Abu Barzah relates that the Holy Prophet disapproved of a person sleeping immediately before evening Prayer and conversing after it (Bokhari and Muslim).

1753. Ibn Umar relates that towards the end of his life the Holy Prophet when he finished the evening Prayer said: Note this night of yours for at the end of one hundred years from now no one who is on the earth today will have survived (Bokhari and Muslim).

1754. This *hadith* is the same as No. 1067.

333.
On Prohibition of a Woman Refusing herself to Her Husband when He calls Her

1755. This *hadith* is the same as No 283.

334.
On Prohibition of a Woman Observing a Voluntary Fast without her Husband's Permission

1756. This *hadith* is the same as No. 284.

335.
On Prohibition of Going Ahead of the Imam in Prayer

1757. Abu Hurairah relates that the Holy Prophet said: Are you not afraid that if any of you raises his head from his prostration before the Imam does so, Allah will make his head that of a donkey or will make his shape that of a donkey (Bokhari and Muslim)?

336.
On Prohibition of Placing One's Hand on One's Side during Prayer

1758. Abu Hurairah relates that the Holy Prophet forbade putting one's hand on one's side during Prayer (Bokhari and Muslim).

337.

On the Undesirability of Joining Prayer when Food has been Served

1759. Ayesha relates that she heard the Holy Prophet say: Prayer is not permissible when food has been served nor at a time when a person is in need of relieving himself either way (Muslim).

338.

On Prohibition of Raising one's Eyes aloft during Prayer

1760. Anas relates that the Holy Prophet said: How is it that people raise their eyes towards the sky during Prayer? He emphasised this and added: Let them refrain, else they will lose their sight (Bokhari).

339.

On the Undesirability of Eyes Straying during Prayer

1761. Ayesha relates: I asked the Holy Prophet about glancing to the right or left during Prayer. He said: This is a swoop of Satan which he practises upon a worshipper during his Prayer (Bokhari).

1762. Anas relates that the Holy Prophet said: Beware of glancing in one direction or the other during Prayer for this is ruinous. If there should be no help for it, it might be permissible during voluntary Prayer but not during prescribed Prayers (Tirmidhi).

340.

On Prohibition of Facing towards Graves during Prayer

1763. Abu Marthad Kannaz ibn Husain relates that he heard the Holy Prophet say: Do not face graves during Prayer nor sit on them (Muslim).

341.

On Prohibition of Passing in front of a Worshipper engaged in Prayer

1764. Abdullah ibn Harith ibn Simnah relates that the Holy Prophet said: If a person who passes in front of one engaged in Prayer realised the enormity of it he would wait for forty (?) rather than pass in front. The narrator was not sure whether the Holy Prophet said forty days or months or years (Bokhari and Muslim).

342.

On the Undesirability of Continuing in Voluntary Prayer after Iqamah

1765. Abu Hurairah relates that the Holy Prophet said: Once the *Iqamah* is called no Prayer is permissible except the obligatory Prayer (Muslim).

343.

On the Undesirability of specially selecting Friday for Observing a Fast etc.

1766. Abu Hurairah relates that the Holy Prophet said: Do not select the night previous to Friday specially for voluntary Prayer nor select Friday specially for observing a fast unless it should happen to be one of the days on which a person normally observes a fast (Muslim).

1767. Abu Hurairah relates that he heard the Holy Prophet say: No one of you should fast on Friday by itself unless he observes a fast on the preceding day or the succeeding day (Bokhari and Muslim).

1768. Muhammad ibn Abbad relates: I asked Jabir: Did the Holy Prophet forbid fasting on Friday? He said: Yes (Bokhari and Muslim).

1769. Juwairiah bint Harith relates that the Holy Prophet visited her on Friday and she was fasting. He asked her: Did you observe the fast yesterday? She said: No. He asked: Do you intend to observe the fast tomorrow? She said: No. He said: In that case give up your fast today (Bokhari).

344.

On Prohibition of Extending a Fast beyond One Day

1770. Abu Hurairah and Ayesha relate that the Holy Prophet forbade the continuation of a fast beyond one day (Bokhari and Muslim).

1771. Ibn Umar relates that the Holy Prophet forbade the continuation of a fast beyond one day. It was said to him: But you do it. He answered: I am not like you. I am given to eat and to drink (Bokhari and Muslim).

345.

On Prohibition of Sitting on a Grave

1772. Abu Hurairah relates that the Holy Prophet said: That one of you should sit on a brand of fire by which his clothes should burn and the heat should mark his skin would be better for him then that he should sit on a grave (Muslim).

346.
On Prohibition of Building over a Grave

1773. Jabir relates that the Holy Prophet forbade that a grave should be bricked over or should be sat upon or should have a building erected over it (Muslim).

347.
On Prohibition of a Slave Running away from his Master

1774. Jabir relates that the Holy Prophet said: If a slave runs away from his master the guarantee of Islam in his favour is cancelled (Muslim).

1775. Jabir relates that the Holy Prophet said: If a slave runs away from his master his Prayer is not accepted (Muslim). Another version is: He is guilty of disbelief.

348.
On the Undesirability of Intercession in the Matter of Prescribed Penalties

Allah, the Exalted, has said:

404. Flog the adulteress and the adulterer, each one of them, with a hundred stripes, and let not pity for them restrain you from executing the judgment of Allah, if you believe in Allah and the Last Day (24:3).

1776. This *hadith* is the same as No. 654.

349.
On Prohibition of Pollution

Allah, the Exalted, has said:

405. Those who malign believing men and believing women for that which they have not done shall bear the guilt of a calumny and a manifest sin (33.59).

1777. Abu Hurairah relates that the Holy Prophet said: Avoid two accursed practices. He was asked: What are the two accursed practices? He answered: A person relieving himself in a pathway frequented by people or in a shaded place used by them (Muslim).

350.
On Prohibition of Passing Water into a Pond or Reservoir

1778. Jabir relates that the Holy Prophet forbade anyone passing water into a pond or reservoir (Muslim).

351.
On Prohibition of Preferring one Child over another in the Matter of Gifts

1779. Nu'man ibn Bashir relates that his father took him to the Holy Prophet and said: I have gifted one of my slaves to this son of mine. The Holy Prophet inquired: Have you made a similar gift to everyone of your children? He said: No; whereupon the Holy Prophet said: Then take this gift back. One version is: The Holy Prophet asked: Have you done this for all your children? He answered: No. The Holy Prophet then said: Be mindful of your obligation to Allah and do justice between your children. My father then returned and revoked his gift. Another version is that the Holy Prophet asked: Bashir, have you other children beside this one? He answered: Yes. The Holy Prophet asked: Have you made a gift like this to all of them? He said: No. The Holy Prophet said: Then do not make me a witness for I will not be a witness to a wrong; and he asked: Would you desire that they should behave equally well towards you? He said: Certainly. The Holy Prophet said: Then why don't you? (Bokhari and Muslim).

352.
On the Period of Mourning to be observed by a Widow

1780. Zainab bint Abu Salamah relates: I visited Umm Habibah, wife of the Holy Prophet when her father Abu Sufyan had died. She sent for a yellow perfume and rubbed it on one of her maids and then rubbed it on both her own cheeks and said: I had no desire for a perfume except that I heard the Holy Prophet say from the pulpit: It is not permissible for a woman who believes in Allah and the Last Day that she should mourn a dead person for more than three days except in the case of her husband when the period of mourning is four months and ten days. Zainab then continued: I then visited Zainab bint Jahsh when her brother died and she sent for perfume and rubbed some of it on herself and said: I have no need for perfume except that I heard the Holy Prophet say from the pulpit: It is not permissible for a woman who believes in Allah and the Last Day that she should mourn a dead person for more than three days except in the case of her husband when the period is four months and ten days (Bokhari and Muslim).

353.

On Prohibition of Undesirable Commercial Practices

1781. Anas relates that the Holy Prophet forbade that a person in the city should sell to a villager on commission even if it should be his brother or father or mother (Bokhari and Muslim).

1782. Ibn Umar relates that the Holy Prophet said: Do not purchase goods from a caravan till they arrive in the market (Bokhari and Muslim).

1783. Ibn Abbas relates that the Holy Prophet said: Do not go out to meet caravans to buy from them nor should one in the city sell for one in the country. Ta'us asked him: What is the meaning of a man in the city selling the goods of one in the country? The Holy Prophet answered: He should not be his commision agent (Bokhari and Muslim).

1784. Abu Hurairah relates that the Holy Prophet forbade that a man in the city should be the commission agent of a man in the country and forbade fictitious bids and that a man should make an offer while the offer of his brother is pending or that he should make a proposal of marriage while the proposal of his brother is pending or that a woman should try that a sister of hers might be divorced so that she might take her place. Another version is: The Holy Prophet forbade meeting caravans in advance or that a city dweller should act as a commission agent for a rustic or that a woman should make it a condition of marriage that a sister of hers should be divorced or that a person should make a fictitious bid on the bid of a brother and forbade the accumulation of milk in the udder of an animal (Bokhari and Muslim).

1785. Ibn Umar relates that the Holy Prophet said: None of you should make an offer to buy when the offer of another is pending, nor make a proposal of marriage when a proposal of a brother is pending, except with the permission of the latter (Bokhari and Muslim).

1786. Uqbah ibn 'Amir relates that the Holy Prophet said: A believer is the brother of a believer and it is not permissible for a believer to make an offer of purchase while an offer of a brother is pending nor that one should make a proposal of marriage while a proposal of his brother is pending until the latter gives up (Muslim).

354.

On Prohibition of Extravagance

1787. Abu Hurairah relates that the Holy Prophet said: Three things are pleasing to Allah and three are displeasing to Him. It pleases Him that you should worship Him and should not associate anything with Him and that you should hold fast to the rope of Allah all together without being divided and it is displeasing to Him that you should indulge in much talk and much asking and in wasting money (Muslim).

1788. Warrad, the clerk of Mughirah, relates: Mughirah ibn Shu'bah dictated a letter to me addressed to Mu'awiah that the Holy Prophet used to supplicate at the end of each prescribed Prayer: There is none worthy of worship save Allah, the One who has no associate, His is the Kingdom and His is the praise and He has power to do all that He wills. Allah, no one can stop that which Thou dost bestow and no one can bestow that which Thou dost hold back, nor does the high status of any avail against Thee; and wrote further that the Holy Prophet forbade idle talk, waste of wealth and too much asking. He also forbade disobedience of parents, infanticide of female children and wrongful acquisition (Bokhari and Muslim).

355.
On Prohibition of Pointing at Another with a Weapon

1789. Abu Hurairah relates that the Holy Prophet said: No one of you should point at his brother with a weapon for he does not know lest Satan should make him let it loose from his hand and he may in consequence fall into a pit of fire (Bokhari and Muslim). Muslim's version is: The Holy Prophet said: He who points at a brother with a sharp edged weapon is cursed by the angels till he throws away the weapon even if the other person should be his real brother.

1790. Jabir relates: The Holy Prophet forbade that anyone should present a drawn sword to another (Abu Daud and Tirmidhi).

356.
On the Undesirability of Leaving a Mosque after Azan before Conclusion of Prayer

1791. Abu Sha'tha relates: We were sitting with Abu Hurairah in the mosque when the *muezzin* called the *Azan*. A man stood up in the mosque and started walking out. Abu Hurairah continued to stare at him till he went out of the mosque. Abu Hurairah then said: This one has disobeyed the Holy Prophet (Muslim).

357.
On the Undesirability of Refusing Perfume

1792. Abu Hurairah relates that the Holy Prophet said: A person should not refuse a gift of perfume for it is light in weight and has a good smell (Muslim).

1793. Anas relates that the Holy Prophet never refused perfume (Bokhari).

358.

On the Undesirability of Praising a Person to his Face

1794. Abu Musa relates that the Holy Prophet heard a man praising another one extravagantly, whereupon he said: You have ruined (or you have broken the back of) this man (Bokhari and Muslim).

1795. Abu Bakr relates that mention of a man was made to the Holy Prophet and someone praised him. The Holy Prophet said to the latter: Fie on you, you have cut the throat of your companion. He repeated this several times and then added: If you must praise somebody, you should say: I reckon So and So is such and such if you consider him such; and you will be accountable to Allah and no one can be declared pure before Allah (Bokhari and Muslim).

1796. Hamam ibn Harith relates on the authority of Miqdad that a man started praising Uthman and Miqdad sat down on his haunches and began to thrust pebbles into the mouth of the speaker. Uthman asked him: What is the matter? He answered: The Holy Prophet has said: When you see such as praise others fill their mouths with dust (Muslim).

359.

On the Undesirability of Leaving or Coming to a Plague-Stricken Town

Allah, the Exalted, has said:

406. Wheresoever you may be death will overtake you, even if you be in strongly built towers (4:79).

407. Do not push yourselves into ruin with your own hands (2:196).

1797. Ibn Abbas relates that Umar ibn Khattab started towards Syria and when he arrived at Sargh he was met by Abu Ubaidah ibn Jarrah, the commander of the Muslim forces, and his officers who told him that an epidemic had broken out in Syria. Ibn Abbas relates: Umar said to me: Call in the earlier Emigrants. I called them and he told them that an epidemic had broken out in Syria and took counsel with them but they differed among themselves. Some of them said: You started on an errand and we do not see why you should back away from it. Others said: You have the companions of the Holy Prophet and many other people with you and we do not see why you should expose them to this epidemic. He asked them to withdraw and asked me to call the Helpers. So I called them and he took counsel with them and they followed the Emigrants and differed among themselves as they had differed. So he asked them to withdraw and asked me to call the prominent among the Quraish out of those emigrants who were present at the fall of Mecca. So I called them and not any two of them differed in their view. They told him: We think that you should go back and not lead the people into the epidemic. So Umar had it announced that he would start back the next morning. When all was ready the next morning, Abu Ubaidah ibn Jarrah said to Umar: Do your propose to run away from the decree of Allah? Umar replied: Abu Ubaidah, I wish someone else had said this (Umar did not like to be opposed by him). Umar continued: Yes, we are running away from the decree of Allah to the decree of Allah and added: Now tell me if you had a herd of camels in the valley and the valley had two sides; one fertile and green and the other dry and barren then if you graze them in the green part would not that be by the decree of Allah, or if you were to graze them in the dry part, would not that be by the decree of Allah? Then Abdur Rahman ibn Auf who had been absent on some errand of his own came up and said: I have some knowledge about this matter. I heard the Holy Prophet say: If you hear of an epidemic in a land then do not enter it, and if you happen to be in a land where an epidemic appears, do not run away from it. On this Umar praised Allah and returned (Bokhari and Muslim).

1798. Usama ibn Zaid relates that the Holy Prophet said: If you hear of the plague in a land, do not enter it and if it appears in a land in which you happen to be do not travel out of it (Bokhari and Muslim).

360.

On Prohibition of Sorcery

Allah, the Exalted, has said:

408. It was not Solomon who disbelieved, it was the rebellious ones who disbelieved teaching people sorcery (2: 103).

1799. This *hadith* is the same as No. 1619.

361.

On Prohibition of Carrying the Quran into Enemy Territory

1800. Ibn Umar relates that the Holy Prophet forbade anyone carrying with him the Quran into enemy territory (Bokhari and Muslim).

362.

On Prohibition of the Use of Gold and Silver Vessels

1801. This *hadith* is the same as No. 781.
1802. This *hadith* is the same as No. 780.
1803. Anas ibn Sirin relates: I was with Anas ibn Malik in the

company of some Zoroastrians when a sweet was brought in a silver vessel and
Anas would not eat off it. The man who had brought it was told: Change the
vessel. He changed the vessel and when he brought it Anas ate off it (Baihiqi).

363.

On Prohibition of Saffron-coloured Garments

1804. Anas relates that the Holy Prophet forbade a person wearing
saffron-coloured garments (Bokhari and Muslim).

1805. Abdullah ibn Amr ibn 'As relates: The Holy Prophet saw me
wearing two saffron-coloured garments and inquired: Has your mother
ordered you to wear these? I asked: Shall I wash them out? He answered: You
had better burn them. Another version is that he added: These are garments
of the unbelievers so do not wear them (Muslim).

364.

On Prohibition of Vowing Silence

1806. Ali relates: I have guarded in my memory the saying of the Holy
Prophet: No one is an orphan after coming of age. There is no value in silence
from morning till night (Abu Daud).

1807. Qais ibn Abu Hazim relates that Abu Bakr came upon a woman
of Ahas whose name was Zainab and he saw that she did not speak. He
inquired: Why does she not speak? He was answered: She has sworn to silence.
He said to her: Speak and converse, such silence is not permissible. It is a non-
Islamic practice. Thereupon she started speaking (Bokhari).

365.

On Prohibition of Attributing Wrong Fatherhood

1808. Sa'ad ibn Abi Waqqas relates that the Holy Prophet said: He who
attributes his fatherhood to someone other than his father knowing that he is
not his father will be excluded from Paradise (Bokhari and Muslim).

1809. Abu Hurairah relates that the Holy Prophet said: Do not turn
away from your fathers. He who turns away from his father is guilty of
disbelief (Bokhari and Muslim).

1810. Omitted.

1811. Abu Dharr relates that he heard the Holy Prophet say: He who deliberately lets himself be called the son of another than his father is guilty of disbelief, and he who claims as his that which does not belong to him is not one of us. Let him prepare his seat in hell. If a person calls another an unbeliever or an enemy of Allah and he is not such he will find that his charge will revert on himself (Bokhari and Muslim).

366.
On Prohibition of that which Allah and His Messenger have Forbidden

Allah, the Exalted, has said:

409.   Let those who oppose the command of the Messenger beware lest a trial afflict them or a grievous punishment overtake them (24.64).

410.   Allah warns you against His Chastisement (3.31).

411.   Surely, the vengeance of Thy Lord is severe (95.13).

412.   Such is the chastisement of Thy Lord which He inflicts upon corrupt cities. Surely, His chastisement is grievously painful (11.103).

1812. Abu Hurairah relates that the Holy Prophet said: Allah, the Exalted, is jealous and His jealousy is incited by a person doing that which Allah has forbidden (Bokhari and Muslim).

367.
On Expiation of Involuntary Infringement of Divine Command

Allah, the Exalted, has said:

413.   Should a tribulation on the part of Satan assail thee, do thou seek refuge with Allah (41.17).

414.   When a suggestion from Satan assails those who are righteous, they are instantly alerted and become watchful (7.202).

415.   Those who, when they commit an indecency or wrong themselves, call Allah to mind and implore forgiveness for their sins (and who can forgive sins except Allah?) and do not persist knowingly in that of which they have been guilty. It is these whose reward is forgiveness from their Lord and gardens beneath which rivers flow, wherein they shall abide.

Excellent is the reward of those who work righteousness (3.136-137).

416.　Turn ye to Allah all together, O believers, that you prosper (24.32).

1813.　Abu Hurairah relates that the Holy Prophet said: He who swears an oath and involuntarily says: By Lat and Uzzah; should at once affirm: There is none worthy of worship save Allah. And he who should say to his companion: Come, I shall gamble with you; should expiate by giving alms (Bokhari and Muslim).

368.

On Signs of the Last Day etc.

1814.　Nawas ibn Sam'an relates that the Holy Prophet mentioned the Anti-Christ one morning and represented him as so little and also as so great that we thought that he might be already present in some date-palm garden close by. When we returned to him he might have perceived our perplexity and asked us: What are you worried about? We said: Messenger of Allah, you talked about the Anti-Christ this morning and belittled him and also represented him as great till we believed that he might be present in one of the date-palm gardens. He said: It was something besides the Anti-Christ that makes me afraid with regard to you. I am not afraid for you in respect of the Anti-Christ. Should he appear while I am among you I would be your defender against him, but should he appear when I am not among you then everyone of you must look after himself. Allah will be the guardian over every Muslim in my place. He will be a rough haired youth and one of his eyes will lack sight. I find that he might resemble Uzza ibn Qatan. He who encounters him from among you should recite to him the opening verses of *sura* Al-Kahf (Chapter 18). He will emerge from the road between Syria and Iraq and will carry sword and blood right and left. Then remain steadfast, ye servants of Allah. We asked him: Messenger of Allah, how long will be his stay in the earth? He answered: Forty days. One of his days will be like a year, one will be like a month, one will be like a week and the rest of his days will be like your average days. We asked: Messenger of Allah, on this day which will be like a year will it suffice for us to observe the five Prayers in one day? He answered: No. You should make an estimate of the passage of time. We asked: Messenger of Allah, what will be the speed of his movement in the earth? He answered: Like a cloud which is being driven by the wind. He will arrive among a people and will call them to his obedience and they will respond to him and believe in him. He will command the sky and it will send down rain on the people. He will command the earth and it will produce pasture for them and their cattle will come back to them in the evening with high humps and full udders and fat sides. Then he will arrive among a people and will call them to his obedience but they will reject his call and he will turn away from them. They will be afflicted with drought and famine and will become destitute. He will pass through desert places and will call on them to put forth their treasures and their treasures will follow him like bees. He will then call a man in the glow of youth and will strike him with his sword and cut him into two pieces which will be separated from each other the length of an arrow. He will then call him and he will obey with a cheerful and smiling face.

While he is in the middle of all this, Allah, the Exalted, will raise the Messiah, son of Mary, who will arrive close to the white minaret in the East of Damascus, wearing two saffron-coloured garments, his hands resting on the wings of two angels. When he bends his head drops of water shining like silver will fall from it and when he raises it there will be drops like pearls falling from it. A non-believer who is touched by his breath will expire and his breath will reach as far as his look. He will pursue the Anti-Christ and will encounter him at the gate of Lud and will slaughter him. The Messiah will then come to people whom God had shielded from the Anti-Christ. He will wipe away the dust from their faces and will inform them about their grades in Paradise. While he will be so occupied, Allah, the Exalted, will send revelation to him: I have created some people whom no one will be able to fight and withstand. Therefore lead these, my servants, to Mount Sinai. Allah will then raise Gog and Magog and they will spread out leaping across every barrier of land and sea (21. 97). Their advance groups will pass over Lake Tabariah and drink up all its water and when its rear groups pass near it they will say: At one time there used to be water here. The Prophet of Allah, the Messiah and his companions will be beleaguered till a calf's head will appear better to them than a hundred dinars appear to you today.

Then the Prophet of Allah, the Messiah, and his companions will turn to Allah, the Exalted, and will supplicate Him so that Allah will create a germ in the necks of the people of Gog and Magog in consequence of which they will all die suddenly one day. Thereafter the Prophet of Allah, the Messiah, and his companions will descend from the Mount but will not find a hand's breadth of space free from the corpses of the followers of Gog and Magog and their stink. Then the Prophet of Allah, the Messiah, and his companions will supplicate Allah, the Lord of honour, and He will send birds like the necks of *Bukhti* camels which will carry the corpses and drop them wherever Allah wills. Then Allah will send down rain whereby every dwelling whether made of clay or of hair will be cleansed and become like a mirror. Then the earth will be commanded to produce its fruits and to regain its blessing, so that a whole group of people will be filled by eating of one pomegranate and will be able to take shelter under the shade of its leaves. Milk will be so blest that the milk of one she-camel will suffice for a large company and that of a cow will suffice for a tribe and that of a goat will suffice for a family. While they are in this condition Allah will send a pure breeze which will strike them below their armpits whereby the soul of every believer and Muslim will pass into the custody of Allah and only the worst of the people will be left whose men will consort openly with women like donkeys and the Judgment will be held (Muslim).

1815. Ribi' ibn Hirash relates: I went with Abu Mas'ud to Huzaifah and Abu Mas'ud said to him: Tell us what you heard from the Holy Prophet about the Anti-Christ. He said: The Anti-Christ will appear and with him shall be water and fire. That which the people see as water will be fire that burns and that which the people see as fire will be cool and sweet water. He who, from among you, encounters him should jump into that which he sees as fire for that will be sweet and wholesome. Abu Mas'ud said: I have also heard this from the Holy Prophet (Bokhari and Muslim).

1816. Abdullah ibn Amr ibn 'As relates that the Holy Prophet said: Anti-Christ will appear among my people and will remain for forty, I do not know, forty days or forty months or forty years. Then Allah will raise Jesus, son of Mary, who will pursue him and will slaughter him. Thereafter people will survive for seven years and there will be no enmity between any two. Then Allah, the Lord of honour and glory, will send a cool breeze from the direction of Syria and there will not remain on the face of the earth a single one in whose heart there will be the smallest particle of good or of faith but that his soul will be taken into custody, so much so that if any of you entered into the heart of a mountain the breeze will follow him and enter therein and take his soul into custody. And there will remain only the worst people who will be promiscuous like the birds and like wild beasts in their behaviour. They will not know any good and will not refrain from any evil. Then Satan will appear among them in the garb of a man and will ask them: Will you not obey me? They will inquire from him: What do you command us to do? He will command them to worship idols. In this condition their provision will be plenty and their life will be comfortable, then the trumpet will be blown and everyone who hears it will turn his neck towards it and will raise it. The first to hear it will be a man who will be occupied with repairing the basin for his camels. He will become unconscious and everyone around him will become unconscious, then Allah will send rain which will be like the dew and people's bodies will thereby grow. Then the trumpet will be blown once more and the people will be seen standing. It will then be said: O people, come forward to your Lord. Then there will be a command: Make them stand, they will be called to account. Then it will be said: Separate from them the share of the Fire. It will be asked: How much? It will be said: Nine hundred and ninety nine out of a thousand. That will be the day which will turn children grey-headed and the day when the calamity will overtake the guilty (Muslim).

1817. Anas relates that the Holy Prophet said: There will be no city which the Anti-Christ will not trample under his feet except Mecca and Medina and there will not be a dome of these two cities but that angels will stand in rows on it guarding it. The Anti-Christ will arrive at Sabakhah and Medina will be shaken three times whereby Allah will expel from it every disbeliever and hypocrite (Muslim).

1818. Anas relates that the Holy Prophet said: Anti-Christ will be followed by seventy thousand Jews of Isfahan who will be clad in robes of satin (Muslim).

1819. Umm Shariq relates that she heard the Holy Prophet say: People will fly into the mountains for shelter against the Anti-Christ (Muslim).

1820. Imran ibn Husain relates that he heard the Holy Prophet say: Between the creation of Adam and the Judgment Day there is no affair greater than the mischief of the Anti-Christ (Muslim).

1821. Abu Sa'id Khudri relates that the Holy Prophet said: The Anti-Christ will appear and a believer will set out towards him and will encounter his guards. They will ask him: Whither are you bent? He will say: I am proceeding to this one who has appeared. They will ask him: Do you not believe in our Lord? He will answer: Our Lord has no secrecy. Some of them will say: Let us kill him. Others will say: Has not your master forbidden you killing anybody without his orders? So they will take him to the Anti-Christ. When the believer will see him he will call out: O ye people, this is the Anti-Christ who was mentioned by the Holy Prophet. The Anti-Christ will then direct that he should be laid out and should be beaten on his belly and on his back. After such beating he will ask the man: Do you not believe in me? He will say: You are the Anti-Christ. The Anti-Christ will then order that he should be sawn through from the top of his head to the joining between his legs. The Anti-Christ will then pass between the two parts of his body and addressing them will say: Rise up. Thereupon the man will become whole and stand up. The Anti-Christ will say to him: Do you believe in me? And he will answer: I have only increased in my intelligence concerning you; and will say to the people: He will not be able to do anything now to anyone. The Anti-Christ will then seize him that he might slaughter him but Allah will make his neck from its base upwards as if it was made of brass and the Anti-Christ will not find any space in which to insert a weapon to cut off his neck. He will then take hold of his arms and legs and throw him away. People will think that the Anti-Christ has thrown him into the fire and he will in fact be thrown into Paradise. The Holy Prophet added: This man will have the highest grade of martyrdom in the estimation of the Lord of the worlds (Muslim).

1822. Mughirah ibn Shu'bah relates: No one inquired from the Holy Prophet about the Anti-Christ more than I did, and he said to me: He will not harm you. I said to him: It is said that there will be a mountain of bread and a stream of water with the Anti-Christ. The Holy Prophet said: The affair is easier for Allah than that (Bokhari and Muslim).

1823. Anas relates that the Holy Prophet said: Every Prophet has warned his people against the one-eyed liar. Hearken, he is one-eyed and your

Lord is not one-eyed. Between the eyes of the Anti-Christ will be the impress of the letters KFR (Bokhari and Muslim).

1824. Abu Hurairah relates that the Holy Prophet said: I shall tell you something about the Anti-Christ which no Prophet has told his people and that is that he is one-eyed and that he will have with him what will appear like paradise and fire. But that which he will call paradise will be the Fire (Bokhari and Muslim).

1825. Ibn Umar relates that the Holy Prophet mentioned the Anti-Christ to the people and said: Allah is not one-eyed but hearken, the Anti-Christ is blind of his right eye which will appear like a swollen grape (Bokhari and Muslim).

1826. Abu Hurairah relates that the Holy Prophet said: The Judgment will not be set up till the Muslims fight the Jews and a Jew will seek to hide himself behind a rock or a tree and the rock or the tree will call out: O Muslim, here is a Jew hiding behind me. Come and kill him. But the thorny *gharqad* will not call out like this for it is one of the trees of the Jews (Bokhari and Muslim).

1827. Abu Hurairah relates that the Holy Prophet said: By Him in Whose hands is my life, this world will not end till a man passing a grave will revert to it and say: How I wish I was in the place of the one in this grave. He will not say this out of faith but only out of misfortune (Bokhari and Muslim).

1828. Abu Hurairah relates that the Holy Prophet said: The Judgment will not be set up till a mountain of gold appears in the Euphrates on which people will be killed in large numbers, as many as ninety nine out of a hundred, every one of them saying: Maybe I will be the one to be lucky. Another version is: Soon there will appear a treasure of gold from the Euphrates. He who should see it should take nothing from it (Bokhari and Muslim).

1829. Abu Hurairah relates that he heard the Holy Prophet say: People will leave Medina in good condition except for wild beasts and birds. Last of all will come two shepherds of the Muzainah tribe intending to enter Medina with their goats but will find it full of wild beasts and turn away. When they arrive at Seniyyah-til-Wada'a they will fall on their faces (Bokhari and Muslim).

1830. Abu Sa'id Khudri relates that the Holy Prophet said: From your Khalifas there will be one in the latter days who will distribute wealth without counting (Muslim).

1831. Abu Musa relates that the Holy Prophet said: A time will come when a man will go about with alms out of his gold and will not find anyone who would take it from him. One man will be seen being followed by forty women dependent upon him on account of the paucity of men and the excess of women (Muslim).

1832. Abu Hurairah relates that the Holy Prophet said: A man purchased a piece of land from another and found in it a vessel filled with gold. So he said to the seller of the land: Take your gold, I purchased the land from you and did not purchase the gold. The seller said to him: I sold you the land with all that it contained. So they took their dispute to a third one and he asked them: Have you any children? One of them said: I have a boy; and the other said: I have a girl. So the man decided: Marry the boy to the girl and spend the money on them (Bokhari and Muslim).

1833. Abu Hurairah relates that he heard the Holy Prophet say: Two women had each her child with her when a wolf came and made away with the child of one of them. She said to her companion: The wolf has taken away your child; and the other retorted: Indeed, the wolf took away your child. They took their dispute to David and he decided in favour of the older woman. When they left him they passed by Solomon, son of David, and told him what had happened. He said: Bring me a knife, I shall cut the child in two and divide it between you; whereupon the younger one cried out: Allah have mercy on you do not do this, the child belongs to the other one. So Solomon decided in favour of the younger one (Bokhari and Muslim).

1834. Mirdas Aslam relates that the Holy Prophet said: The righteous will depart one by one and the useless ones will remain like the husk of barley or dates for whom Allah will have no care (Bokhari).

1835. Rifa'a ibn Rafi' Zarqi relates that Gabriel came to the Holy Prophet and asked: How do·you estimate among you those who fought at Badr? He answered: As the best of Muslims (or words to that effect). Gabriel said: The same applies to the angels who were present at Badr (Bokhari).

1836. Ibn Umar relates that the Holy Prophet said: When Allah afflicts a people with His chastisement it envelops all of them but then they are raised up according to their conduct in life (Bokhari and Muslim).

1837. Jabir relates: There was a trunk of a date-palm tree on which the Holy Prophet would lean when delivering his sermon. When a pulpit was placed in the mosque we heard the trunk cry out like the cry of a pregnant she-camel. The Holy Prophet descended from the pulpit and put his hand on the trunk and it became quiet. Another version is: When the Friday arrived the Holy Prophet sat on the pulpit and the trunk of the date-palm tree on which he used to lean cried out as if it would splinter asunder. A third version is: It cried like the crying of a child and the Holy Prophet came down and took hold of it and drew it to himself and it began to sob like a child that is being comforted till it stopped, satisfied. The Holy Prophet said: It cried remembering what it used to hear of the Reminder (Bokhari).

1838. Jurthum ibn Nashir relates that the Holy Prophet said: Allah, the Exalted, has laid down certain obligations which do not neglect, and has set certain limits which do not transgress, and has forbidden certain things which do not commit, and has kept silent about other things out of mercy for you and not out of forgetfulness. So do not seek to discover them (Dar Qutni).

1839. Abdullah ibn Abi Aufa relates: We accompanied the Holy

Prophet in seven expeditions and we ate locusts. One version is: We ate locusts with him (Bokhari and Muslim).

1840. Abu Hurairah relates that the Holy Prophet said: A believer is not stung twice from the same hole (Bokhari and Muslim).

1841. Abu Hurairah relates that the Holy Prophet said: Allah will not talk to those on the Day of Judgment, nor look at them, nor purify them, and for them will be a painful chastisement: One, a man, who has with him spare water in the desert which he holds back from a traveller; two, a man who sells something to another after the afternoon Prayer swearing by Allah that he had paid so much for it and the other believes in him and pays him accordingly though in reality it was not true; and three, a man, who makes the covenant of obedience with an Imam to gain some wordly purpose and then if he achieves the purpose through him he fulfils the covenant and if he does not achieve the purpose he does not fulfil the covenant (Bokhari and Muslim).

1842. Abu Hurairah relates that the Holy Prophet said: Between the blowing of two trumpets there are forty. Someone asked Abu Hurairah: Forty days? He said: I am not sure. He was asked: Forty months? He said: I am not sure. The Holy Prophet added: Everything of the human body disappears except the little bone at the end of the spine from which its second creation is compounded. Then Allah will send down rain from heaven and people will be grown like vegetables (Bokhari and Muslim).

1843. Abu Hurairah relates: While the Holy Prophet was sitting talking to people a rustic came and asked: When will the Judgment be? The Holy Prophet continued his talk. Some of those present thought that the Holy Prophet had heard him but did not like the interruption and the others said he did not hear him. When the Holy Prophet finished what he was saying, he asked: Where is the one who inquired about the Judgment. The man said: Here am I, Messenger of Allah. The Holy Prophet said: When the trust is betrayed expect the Judgment. The man inquired: What is the betrayal? The Holy Prophet answered: When authority is committed to those not fit to administer it, then expect the Judgment (Bokhari).

1844. Abu Hurairah relates that the Holy Prophet said: Your leaders will lead you in Prayer, then if they go right this will be meritorious for you and for them. But if they go wrong, you will have the merit but they will bear the responsibility for the wrong (Bokhari).

1845. Abu Hurairah relates with reference to the verse: You are the best of people for you have been raised for the benefit of mankind (3. 111); that the Holy Prophet said: The best people for mankind are those who pull people with chains round their necks till they enter Islam (Bokhari).

1846. Abu Hurairah relates that the Holy Prophet said: Allah is much pleased with people who enter Paradise in chains (Bokhari).

1847. Abu Hurairah relates that the Holy Prophet said that the dearest parts of the cities to Allah are its mosques and the most offensive parts are its markets (Muslim).

1848. Salman Farisi said: Do not be, if you can help it, the first to enter a market or the last to emerge therefrom for that is the arena of Satan and that is where he unfurls his standard (Muslim). Barqani's version is: The Holy Prophet said: Do not be the first to enter the market and the last to emerge therefrom inasmuch as Satan lays his eggs and hatches them there.

1849. 'Asim Ahwal relates on the authority of Abdullah ibn Sarijas that he said to the Holy Prophet: Messenger of Allah, Allah has forgiven all your shortcomings; and he said: And yours also. 'Asim says: I said to Abdullah: Did the Holy Prophet ask for forgiveness for you? and he answered: Yes, and for you also; and recited the verse: Seek forgiveness for thy frailties and for the believing men and the believing women (47. 20). (Muslim).

1850. Abu Mas'ud Ansari relates that the Holy Prophet said that one of the admonitions of previous Prophets which has reached people is: If you discard modesty then you can do what you wish (Bokhari).

1851. Ibn Mas'ud relates that the Holy Prophet said that the first matter concerning which people will be judged on the Day of Judgment will be the matter of shedding blood (Bokhari and Muslim).

1852. Ayesha relates that the Holy Prophet said: Angels were created from light and *jinns* from blazing fire, and Adam was created from that which you have been told (Muslim).

1853. Ayesha relates that the conduct of the Holy Prophet was all in accordance with the Quran (Muslim).

1854. Ayesha relates that the Holy Prophet said: He who desires meeting with Allah, Allah is pleased with meeting him and he who dislikes meeting with Allah, Allah dislikes meeting him. I asked: Messenger of Allah, does this mean dislike of death, for, if so, we all dislike death. He answered: I did not mean that. What I meant was that a believer when he is told of Allah's mercy His pleasure and His Paradise is pleased with the prospect of meeting Allah and Allah is pleased with meeting him. But a disbeliever when he is told of the chastisement of Allah and His wrath dislikes meeting with Allah and Allah dislikes meeting with him (Muslim).

1855. Safayyah bint Huyyi (wife of the Holy Prophet) relates: The Holy Prophet was in retreat in the mosque and I went there to see him one evening and after having talked to him he stood up to accompany me a part of the way. Two men passed us and when they saw the Holy Prophet they quickened their pace. The Holy Prophet called out to them: Stop a moment. This is Safayyah bint Huyyi. They expostulated: Holy is Allah, Messenger of Allah. The Holy Prophet observed: Satan courses through a man's mind like the circulation of the blood and I apprehended lest he might drop some evil thought in your minds (Bokhari and Muslim).

1856. Abbas ibn Abdul Muttalib relates: I was with the Holy Prophet on the day of Hunain. Abu Sufyan and I kept close to the Holy Prophet throughout. He was riding his white mule and at the first encounter between the Muslims and the pagans the Muslims turned back and ran. The Holy

Prophet urged his mule towards the pagans. I was holding the bridle of his mule trying to restrain it from proceeding too fast and Abu Sufyan was holding the Holy Prophet's stirrup. The Holy Prophet said to me: Abbas, call out to those who had made the covenant at Samurah and I called out in my loudest voice: Where are those of the covenant of Samurah? My voice is naturally far reaching and as soon as they heard my voice they turned towards the Holy Prophet, like a cow turning towards her calf, shouting: Here we are, here we are; and they started fighting the pagans. People were shouting: O company of Helpers, O company of Helpers, and then calling: Bani Harith ibn Khazraj! The Holy Prophet raised his head from his seat on his mule and observed the fighting and said: The battle is heating up. Then the Holy Prophet threw some pebbles at the pagans and said: By the Lord of Muhammad they will be defeated. I noticed that as soon as the Holy Prophet threw the pebbles all the fierceness of the enemy was subdued and they started running away (Muslim).

1857.   Abu Hurairah relates that the Holy Prophet said: O ye people, Allah is pure and only accepts purity. Allah has commanded the believers in the same terms in which He commanded His Messengers. Allah has said: O ye Messengers, eat of the things that are pure and act righteously (23. 52) and has said: Eat of the good things we have provided for you (7. 161). Then he mentioned the case of a man who sets out on a long journey, his hair becomes ruffled and his face is covered with dust and he raises his hands towards heaven and supplicates: Lord, Lord: while his food is unlawful and his drink is unlawful and his sustenance is unlawful. How would the supplication of such a one find acceptance (Muslim)?

1858.   This *hadith* is the same as No. 620.

1859.   Abu Hurairah relates that the Holy Prophet said: Jaxartes, Oxus, Euphrates and the Nile are all from the rivers of Paradise (Muslim).

1860.   Abu Hurairah relates: The Holy Prophet took hold of my hand and said: Allah created the earth on Saturday and made in it mountains on Sunday and created trees on Monday and created disagreeable things on Tuesday and created light on Wednesday and spread out animals in the earth on Thursday and created Adam in the afternoon on Friday in the wake of His creation in the last hour of the day before evening (Muslim).

1861.   Khalid ibn Walid relates: In the Battle of Muta seven swords broke in my hand and all that remained in my hands was a small Yemeni sword (Bokhari).

1862.   Amr ibn 'As relates that he heard the Holy Prophet say: When a judge uses his judgment and comes to a right decision he has a double reward. When he uses his judgment and makes a mistake he has a single reward (Bokhari and Muslim).

1863.   Ayesha relates that the Holy Prophet said: Fever is a demonstration of the heat of hell. Try to cool it down with water (Bokhari and Muslim).

1864. Ayesha relates that the Holy Prophet said: If a person dies under the obligation of having to make up a deficiency of fasts his heir should observe the number of fasts on his behalf (Bokhari and Muslim).

1865. Auf ibn Malik ibn Tufail relates that Ayesha was told that Abdullah ibn Zubair had said in respect of a sale or a gift that she had made: If Ayesha does not stop this kind of thing I shall declare her incapable of adminstering her property. She asked: Has he really said this? and was told that he had. Thereupon she declared: I vow it before Allah that I shall never speak to Ibn Zubair. When this period became long Ibn Zubair had someone intercede on his behalf with her. She said: I shall accept no intercession on his behalf and will not go back on my vow. After the lapse of another long period Ibn Zubair approached Miswar ibn Makhramah and Abdur Rahman ibn Aswad ibn Abd Yaghuth and said to them: I request you in the name of Allah that you take me to Ayesha for it is not lawful for her that she should have vowed to cut off my relationship with her. These two took him with them and went to Ayesha and called out: Peace be on you and the mercy of Allah and His blessings. Have we your permission to enter? She said: You may enter. They asked: All of us? She answered: Yes, all of you; not knowing that Ibn Zubair was with them. When they entered, Ibn Zubair went behind the screen and holding on to Ayesha, his aunt, began to plead with her and to weep and his two companions also pleaded that she should talk to him and accept his apology. They said: You are aware that the Holy Prophet has forbidden cutting off communication and has said that it is not lawful for a Muslim to keep away from a brother Muslim for more than three days. When they persisted in urging her she also reminded them of the rights of kinship and started weeping. She said: I have made a vow which is very severe but they continued their pleading till she relented and spoke to Ibn Zubair. As expiation of her vow she freed forty slaves but even so whenever she mentioned her vow thereafter she would take to weeping till her scarf became wet with her tears (Bokhari).

1866. Uqbah ibn 'Amir relates that the Holy Prophet went over to the graves of the martyrs of the Battle of Uhud and prayed over them eight years after the battle as if he was saying goodbye to the living and to the dead. Then he ascended the pulpit and said: I am going ahead of you and I am a witness over you and our meeting shall be at the Reservoir and I am looking at it just now. I am not afraid on your account that you will become guilty of associating anything with Allah but I am afraid that you might become fond of this world. Uqbah says this was my last opportunity of looking at the Holy Prophet (Bokhari and Muslim).

Another version is: I am afraid that you might become fond of the world and start fighting among yourselves and be ruined as those were ruined who were before you. Uqbah says: This was the last time that I saw the Holy Prophet on the pulpit. Another version is: I am your forerunner and am a witness against you and I am looking at the Reservoir at this moment and I have been given the keys of the treasures of the earth (or the keys of the earth) and I am not afraid that after I am gone you will associate anything with Allah but I am afraid that you might become fond of the world.

1867. Abu Zaid Amr ibn Akhtab relates: The Holy Prophet led the dawn Prayer and thereafter mounted the pulpit and addressed us till the time of the noon Prayer. He then came down from the pulpit and led the Prayer and again ascended the pulpit and addressed us till the time of the afternoon Prayer when he came down and led the Prayer and again mounted the pulpit and addressed us till the sun went down. In the course of his address he talked to us of that which had happened and that which was to happen. The most knowledgeable among us have preserved it in their memories (Muslim).

1868. Ayesha relates that the Holy Prophet said: He who vows that he would obey Allah, should obey Him. But he who vows that he would disobey Allah, should not do so (Bokhari).

1869. Umm Shariq relates that the Holy Prophet told her to kill lizards saying: It blew on the fire which was kindled for Abraham (Bokhari and Muslim).

1870. Abu Hurairah relates that the Holy Prophet said: He who kills a lizard at the first stroke will have so many good deeds to his credit. He who kills it at the second stroke will have so many (less than the first) and he who kills it at the third stroke will have so many. Another version is: He who kills a lizard at the first stroke will be credited with a hundred good deeds and at the second stroke less than that and at the third less than the second (Muslim).

1871. Abu Hurairah relates that the Holy Prophet said: A man made up his mind to give alms. He set out with his alms and put them in the hands of a thief. Next day people began to say: Last night a thief was bestowed alms. The man supplicated: Allah, to Thee belongs all Praise. I shall now give alms again. He went out with his alms and put them in the hands of an adulteress. Next day the people talked: Last night alms were bestowed on an adulteress. The man supplicated: Allah, I praise Thee for enabling me to bestow alms even on an adulteress and I shall give alms once more. He went out with his alms and put them in the hands of a rich man. Next day the people talked: Last night alms were bestowed upon a rich man. The man supplicated: Allah, all praise is Thine, in respect of the thief and the adulteress and the rich man. He was told in his dream: Your alms to the thief might persuade the thief to stop stealing, and in consequence of your alms the adulteress might give up her misconduct and the rich man might draw a lesson from your alms and might start spending out of that which Allah has bestowed upon him (Bokhari).

1872. Abu Hurairah relates: We were with the Holy Prophet when he had been invited to a meal and he was offered a chop. He liked chops and while eating it he addressed us: I will be the leader of mankind on the Day of Judgment. Do you know how? It will be that Allah will assemble all mankind, the first and the last in a wide plain so that they will all be visible and would all be able to hear any call. The sun will be low on that day and the people will undergo unbelievable suffering and grief. Then they will say to one another: Do you realize at what pass you have arrived? Can you find someone who might intercede for you with your Lord? Some will say to others: Adam is your father; and they will go to him and say: Adam, you are the father of man, Allah created you out of His own power and breathed into you of His spirit and commanded the angels to bow down to you and made you dwell in the garden. Then will you not intercede for us with your Lord? Do you not see our condition and the suffering that has overtaken us? Adam will say: The wrath of my Lord has been kindled this day as it has never been kindled before nor will it be kindled like it again. He had forbidden me eating of a particular tree and I disobeyed Him. I am afraid for myself, for myself, for myself. Go to someone else. Go to Noah. They will go to Noah and say: Noah, you were the first Messenger to the people of the earth and Allah called you a grateful servant. Do you not see our condition and how we suffer? Will you not then intercede for us with your Lord? He will say: The wrath of my Lord is kindled today as it had never been kindled before and will not be kindled hereafter. I had an opportunity of supplication which I used on behalf of my people. I am afraid for myself, for myself, for myself. Go to someone else, go to Abraham. They will say: Abraham, you are Allah's Prophet and His Friend from among the denizens of the earth. Do intercede for us with your Lord. Do you see what condition we are in? He will say to them: The wrath of my Lord is kindled today as it has never been kindled before and will not be kindled hereafter. Three falsehoods are attributed to me. I am afraid for myself, for myself, for myself. Go to someone else, go to Moses. They will go to Moses and say: Moses, you are a Messenger of Allah, Allah honoured you with His words and His messages to people. Do intercede for us with your Lord. Do you not see what condition we are in? He will say: The wrath of my Lord has been kindled this day as it has never been kindled before nor will it be kindled hereafter. I killed a person whom I had not been commanded to kill. I am afraid for myself, for myself, for myself. Go to someone else, go to Jesus. They will go to Jesus and will say to him: Jesus, you are the Messenger of Allah and His word which He conveyed to Mary and a spirit from Him and you talked to people in your childhood. Do intercede for us with your Lord. Do you not see what condition we are in? Jesus will say: The wrath of my Lord is kindled today as it had never been kindled before and will not be kindled again. He did not mention any of his faults but said: I am afraid for myself, for myself, for myself. Go to someone else, go to Muhammad. Another version is: They will come to me and will say: Muhammad, you are the Messenger of Allah and the Seal of the Prophets and Allah has forgiven you all your shortcomings, the first and the last, do you intercede for us with your Lord. Do you not see what condition we are in? Then I will proceed under the Throne and shall fall down in prostration before my Lord, then Allah will bestow upon me knowledge of His Praise and Glorification such as He will not have bestowed upon anyone before me. Then He will say to me: Muhammad, raise your head and supplicate, you will be given, and intercede, your intercession will be accepted. I shall raise my head and will supplicate. My people, O Lord, my people. O Lord, my people, O Lord. Allah will say: Muhammad, admit into Paradise through its gate on the right such of thy people who are not subject to accounting and for the rest they will be admitted along with the rest of mankind through the various gates of Paradise. The Holy Prophet added: By Him in Whose hands is my life the distance between two gates of Paradise will be as wide as between Mecca and Hijr or between Mecca and Busra (Bokhari and Muslim).

1873. Ibn Abbas relates: Abraham brought Ismael and his mother while she was giving him suck and placed them near the site of the house under a big tree above where Zam Zam is in the higher part of the mosque. At that time there was no one in Mecca nor was there any water. He put both of them there and placed with them a bag of dates and a water-skin full of water. He then turned away and Ishmael's mother followed him and said: Abraham, where are you going, leaving us in this valley where there is no friend nor anything? She repeated this several times but Abraham paid no attention to her. Then she asked him: Has Allah commanded you to do this? He answered: Yes. She said: Then He will not let us perish; and she turned back. Abraham went forward till he arrived at Semiyah where he was not visible to them. He faced towards the side of the House and raising his hands supplicated: Our Lord, I have settled some of my progeny in a barren valley near Thy Sacred House, that they may perform Prayer with due observance, our Lord. So make people's hearts incline towards them and provide them with fruits of all kinds that they may be grateful (14. 18).

Ishmael's mother would give suck to Ishmael and would herself drink of the water till the water-skin became empty. She then felt thirsty and her boy felt thirsty and she saw him rolling about. She walked away in one direction being unable to witness his agony. The nearest elevation to her was Safa. She stood on top of it and looked to see whether she could spot anyone but she saw no one and descended from Safa and when she was in the valley she raised a portion of her garment and began to run like a person distracted till she arrived at the top of Marwah and stood there to see if she could spot anyone. But she did not see anyone. This she did seven times. Ibn Abbas relates that the Holy Prophet said: That is why people run between the two.

When she arrived on Marwah the seventh time she heard a voice and she ejaculated: Sshs! (silencing herself) and she lent ear and heard a sound again and said: You have made yourself heard; if you have any succour for us then hear my supplication. Then she saw an angel at the spot where Zam Zam is. He struck the earth with his heel (or with his wings) till the water appeared. She dug a sort of cistern for it and began to fill her water-skin from it with her hands. While she was doing it the water continued to increase in quantity equal to that which she took of it. (Ibn Abbas relates that the Holy Prophet said: May Allah have mercy on Ishmael's mother, if she had left the Zam Zam alone (or if she had not filled her water-skin with it) Zam Zam would have become a running spring for us). So she drank of it and gave suck to the child. The angel said to her: Be not afraid of perishing for here is the site on which this boy and his father shall build a House for Allah and Allah will not let those around it perish. The site of the House was a little higher than the surrounding earth like a dome. When rainwater came it passed on its right or on its left.

Ishmael and his mother continued thus till a group of the tribe Jurhum coming by way of Kada'a encamped below the site of Mecca. They observed a bird circling round and round and said: This bird is circling over water. We have been passing through this valley over a period and there was no water in it. So they sent one or two men to investigate and they came upon the water and returned and told them of it. They all went and found Ishmael's mother near the water. They said to her: Will you permit us to make our camp near you? She said: Yes, but you will have no right over the water. They agreed. (Ibn Abbas relates that the Holy Prophet said: Ishmael's mother got her wish, for she had wanted company). So they made camp there and sent for their families who joined them and they were quite a number of households. Ishmael grew up and learnt Arabic from them. He was handsome and was everybody's favourite. When he came of age they gave him one of their own daughters in marriage. Ishmael's mother died and Abraham came after Ishmael's marriage and was looking for something which he had left behind but not finding Ishmael he inquired from his wife about him. She said: He has gone out to get (or hunt) provision for us. Then he asked her about their life and condition and she told him: We are in evil case. We live a life of straitness and privation; and she made other complaints. He said to her: When your husband comes home, convey my greetings to him and tell him that he should change the sill of his door. When Ishmael returned he perceived something in the atmosphere and asked his wife: Did anyone come to see you? She said: Yes, such and such an old man came and asked me about you and I told him, and he asked me how we were carrying on and I told him we were hard up. He asked: Did he leave a message? She answered: Yes. He told me to convey his greetings to you and to tell you to change your door-sill. Ishmael said: This was my father, and he has directed me that I should part with you. So go back to your people. Then he divorced her and married another woman from among them.

Abraham kept away from them for a while and then visited them. But again he did not find Ishmael at home and asked his wife about him. She told him: He has gone out to find provision for us. He asked her how they were carrying on and inquired about their condition and circumstances. She said: We are well off; and praised Allah. He asked: What is your food? She said: Meat. He asked: What is your drink? She answered: Water. He supplicated: Allah bless their meat and their water. (The Holy Prophet observed: They had no grain at the time, for if they had grain he would have blessed that also. That is why no one except the people of Mecca can live on meat and water alone and it does not suit others).

Another version is: Abraham came and inquired: Where is Ishmael? His wife said: He has gone out hunting and asked Abraham: Will you not stay and eat and drink? He asked: What is your food and drink? She answered: Our food is meat and our drink is water. He supplicated: Allah bless their food and their drink (the Holy Prophet observed: This is the blessing of the prayer of Abraham). Abraham said: When your husband returns, convey my greetings to him and tell him to strengthen his door-sill. When Ishmael returned he inquired: Did anyone come? She said: Yes, a handsome old gentleman came and she praised him. She continued: He asked me about you and I told him. He asked me: How we were living and I told him: Well. Ishmael asked: Did he leave any message with you? She answered: Yes, he left his greetings for you and his direction that you should strengthen your door-sill. Ishmael said: This was my father, and you are the door-sill which he ordered me to hold to.

Abraham kept away from them for some time and when he came again Ishmael was sitting under a big tree near Zam Zam repairing his arrows. When he perceived Abraham, he stood up and they greeted each other like father and son. Abraham told Ishmael: Allah has laid upon me a commandment. Ishmael said: Then do what your Lord has commanded you to do. He said: Will you help me? Ishmael said: I shall help you. Abraham said: Allah has commanded me to build a House here and he pointed towards the dome and its surrounding area. Then they started raising the foundations.

Ishmael fetched the stones and Abraham laid them on and when the foundation had been raised Ishmael brought a stone and placed it for Abraham so that he stood on it and continued to build while Ishmael handed the stones to him. And both of them prayed: Our Lord, accept this offering from us, indeed Thou art the All-Hearing, the All-Knowing (2.128).

Another version is: Abraham took Ishmael and his mother with him and they had a water-skin full of water. Ishmael's mother drank of the water and gave suck to her child till they came to Mecca and Abraham put his wife under a big tree. Abraham then turned away and Ishmael's mother followed him till when they arrived at Kada'a she called to him from behind and said: Abraham, with whom are you leaving us? He answered: With Allah. She said: I am happy with Allah and she returned keeping on drinking from the water-skin and giving suck to her child. When the water gave out, she thought, I had better go and have a look and see if I can spot anyone. She ascended to the top of Safa and looked but did not see anyone. She descended to the valley and ran to Marwah and did it several times and then thought that she should go and look at the child. So she went and saw that he was in the same condition as if he was approaching death. She found it difficult to control herself and hoping to find someone again went and ascended Safa and looked and looked but did not see anyone. She ran between Safa and Marwah seven times altogether. She then thought of going again and looking at the child when she heard a sound and she supplicated: If you can do anything to help, come to my aid. Suddenly, Gabriel appeared and struck the earth with his heel and water began to flow. Ishmael's mother was greatly struck and she started digging a pit (Bokhari).

1874. Sa'id ibn Zaid relates that he heard the Holy Prophet say: Mushrooms are a species of *manna* and their water is healing for the eye (Bokhari and Muslim).

369.
On Seeking Forgiveness

Allah, the Exalted, has said:

417.   Ask forgiveness for thy frailties (47. 20).

418.   Ask forgiveness of Allah, surely, Allah is Most Forgiving, Ever Merciful (4. 107).

419.   Glorify Thy Lord with His Praise and seek forgiveness of Him. Surely He is Oft-Returning with compassion (110. 4).

420.   For those who are constantly mindful of their duty to Allah, there are Gardens with their Lord beneath which rivers flow, wherein they shall abide, and pure spouses. They shall also enjoy the pleasure of Allah. Allah is mindful of His servants who supplicate: Lord, surely we have believed; forgive us, therefore, our sins and shield us from the torment of the Fire. They are the steadfast, the faithful, the humble, those who spend in the cause of Allah and those who seek forgiveness in the small hours of the morning (3. 16-17).

421.   Whoso does evil or wrongs his soul, and then asks forgiveness of Allah will find Allah Most Forgiving, Ever Merciful (4. 111).

422.   Allah would not chastise them while thou wast among them nor would Allah chastise them if they supplicated for forgiveness (8. 34).

423.   Those who, when they commit an indecency or wrong themselves, call Allah to mind and implore forgiveness for their sins (and who can forgive sins except Allah?) and do not persist knowingly in that of which they have been guilty (3. 136).

1875.   Aghirr Muzani relates that the Holy Prophet said: Sometimes I perceive a veil over my heart and I supplicate Allah for forgiveness a hundred times in a day (Muslim).

1876. Abu Hurairah relates that he heard the Holy Prophet say: I supplicate Allah and turn to Him more than seventy times a day (Bokhari).

1877. This *hadith* is the same as No. 425.

1878. Ibn Umar relates: We could count in one sitting the Holy Prophet supplicating a hundred times: Lord, forgive me and turn to me for Thou art Oft-Returning with compassion, Ever-Merciful (Abu Daud and Tirmidhi).

1879. Ibn Abbas relates that the Holy Prophet said: For him who is constant in supplicating Allah for forgiveness He provides deliverance from every straitness and relief from every suffering and endows him whence he knows not (Abu Daud).

1880. Ibn Mas‘ud relates that the Holy Prophet said: He who supplicates: I seek the forgiveness of Allah, there is none worthy of worship save Him, the Ever-Living, the Self-Subsisting, and turn to Him in repentance; will be forgiven his sins, even if he should have deserted in the face of the enemy (Abu Daud, Tirmidhi and Hakim).

1881. Shaddad ibn Aus relates that the Holy Prophet said: The highest *istighfar* (seeking forgiveness) is that a servant should say: Allah, Thou art my Lord, there is none worthy of worship save Thee. Thou didst create me and I am Thy servant, and I try to comport myself according to my promise to Thee and my covenant with Thee as far as it is within my power. I seek Thy protection from the evil of that which I have done. I acknowledge the bounties that Thou has bestowed upon me and confess my sins; do Thou, then, forgive me my sins, for verily none has the power to forgive save Thee alone. He who supplicates in these terms during the day, believing in them, and should die before evening will be of the dwellers of Paradise; and he who supplicates in these terms during the night and should die before morning will be of the dwellers of Paradise (Bokhari).

1882. Thauban relates that when the Holy Prophet concluded his Prayer, he would seek forgiveness three times and would add: Allah, Thou art the Bestower of Peace and from Thee is peace. Blessed art Thou, Lord of glory and honour. Auza‘i, one of the narrators was asked: In what terms did the Holy Prophet seek forgiveness? He answered: He would say: I beg Allah for forgiveness; I beg Allah for forgiveness (Muslim).

1883. Ayesha relates that before his death the Holy Prophet often repeated: Holy is Allah and to Him belongs all praise. I beg forgiveness of Allah and turn to Him in repentance (Bokhari and Muslim).

1884. This *hadith* is the same as No. 445.

1885. Ibn Umar relates that the Holy Prophet said: O ye party of women, give alms and be diligent in seeking forgiveness for I have seen you forming the majority among the dwellers of the Fire. One of the women asked him: What is the cause of our being the majority among the dwellers of the Fire? He answered: You are too ready to condemn and you are ungrateful to your husbands and despite your deficiency in intelligence and matters of faith you are the greatest cause of destroying the intelligence of a man. The women asked him: What is the deficiency in intelligence and matters of faith that we suffer from? He answered: The evidence of two women is equal to that of one man and a woman cannot partake in Prayer during her monthly days (Muslim).

370.

On the Bounties of Paradise

Allah, the Exalted, has said:

424. The righteous will surely be amid gardens and fountains; they will be told: Enter therein, in peace and security. We shall cleanse their hearts of all traces of ill-will; they will be as brethren seated on couches facing one another. They shall never be weary nor shall they be ejected therefrom (15. 46-49).

425. O My servants, there is no fear for you this day, nor shall you grieve. Enter the Garden, you and your companions, delighted and joyful. Dishes and cups of gold will be passed round to them and in them will be all the heart desires and in which the eyes delight. Therein will you abide. This is the Garden to which you have been made heirs, because of that which you practised. Therein for you is fruit in abundance of which you will eat (43. 69-74).

426. Verily, the righteous will be in a place of security, among gardens and springs attired in fine silk and heavy brocade, facing one another, Thus will it be. We shall give them as companions fair maidens having wide lustrous eyes. They will call therein for every kind of fruit, dwelling in security. They will not suffer any death therein after the first death, and Allah will safeguard them against the torment of the Fire as an act of grace from thy Lord. That is the supreme triumph (44. 52-58).

427. The virtuous will be in bliss, seated on couches, viewing everything. Thou wilt discern in their faces the freshness of bliss. They will be given to drink of a pure sealed beverage, sealed with musk, and tempered with the water of Tasnim, a spring of which the chosen ones will drink. After this should the aspirants aspire (83. 23-29).

1886. Jabir relates that the Holy Prophet said that the dwellers of Paradise will eat and drink but will not have to answer the call of nature or to blow their noses or to pass water. Their food will be digested resulting only in a belch smelling of musk. They will be taught glorification of Allah and proclaiming His Greatness as you are taught breathing (Muslim).

1887. Abu Hurairah relates that the Holy Prophet said: Allah, the Exalted, says: I have prepared for my righteous servants that which the eye has not seen and the ear has not heard and the mind of man has not conceived. If you wish you might recall: No one knows what bliss is kept hidden from them (32. 18). (Bokhari and Muslim).

1888. Abu Hurairah relates that the Holy Prophet said: The first group that enters Paradise will be like the full moon and those who follow them will be like a very bright planet in the sky. They will not be in need of passing water or of answering the call of nature or of spitting or of blowing their noses. Their combs will be of gold and their perspiration will be like musk. Their fireplaces will send forth the fragrance of aloes. Their consorts will be beautiful large-eyed maidens. They will all be equally well behaved, their features like their father Adam and in height like him rising sixty arms length towards the sky (Bokhari and Muslim). Another version is: Their vessels will be of gold, their perspiration will be like musk, every one of them will have two consorts whose beauty will be such that their marrow will be visible through their flesh, there will be no differences or ill-will between them, they will all be single-minded glorifying Allah, morn and eve.

1889. Mughirah ibn Shu'bah relates that the Holy Prophet said: Moses asked his Lord: Who will be of the lowest rank in Paradise? He was told: It will be a man who will arrive when the dwellers of Paradise have all entered Paradise. He will be told: Enter into Paradise. But he will say: How shall I enter, Lord, when everyone has settled in his place and has appropriated whatever has been allotted to him? He will be asked: Will you be satisfied if you have a kingdom like the kingdoms of the monarchs of the world? He will say: I will be content, Lord. He will be told: You have such and its like, and its like, and its like. At the mention of the fifth he will say: Lord, I am content; and will be told: That is for you and ten times more. You will have whatever your soul desires and the delight of your eyes. He will say: Lord, I am satisfied. Moses said: Who will be of the highest rank in Paradise? Allah will say: Those will be the ones whom I shall have exalted with my own hands and whose rank I shall attest with my seal. No eye has seen, no ear has heard and the mind of no man has conceived of their status (Muslim).

1890. Ibn Mas'ud relates that the Holy Prophet said: I know of the coming out of the Fire of its last dweller or the last one to enter Paradise. It will be a man who will emerge from the Fire crawling on all fours. Allah, the Lord of honour and glory, will say to him: Go and enter Paradise. He will go to Paradise and it will seem to him that it is full. So he will turn back and will say: Lord, I have found it full. Allah will say: Go and enter Paradise. He will again go and will imagine that it is full. He will go back and say: Lord, I have found it full. Allah will say: Go and enter Paradise. You have the equal of the whole world and ten times more like it (or: you have ten times the like of the world). He will say: Dost Thou mock me and laugh at me and Thou art the King? Ibn Mas'ud relates: At this I saw the Holy Prophet laugh till his back teeth could be seen and he was saying: Such will be the last of the dwellers of Paradise (Bokhari and Muslim).

1891. Abu Musa relates that the Holy Prophet said: A believer will have a tent in Paradise hollowed out of a single pearl of which the length will be seventy miles in heaven. The believer will have his family with him, he will go about in it and one of them will not be able to see another (Bokhari and Muslim).

1892. Abu Sa'id Khudri relates that the Holy Prophet said: There is a tree in Paradise under which a rider of a fast pony will not be able to traverse the distance between one end and the other in a hundred years (Bokhari and Muslim).

1893. Abu Sa'id Khudri relates that the Holy Prophet said: The dwellers of Paradise will look at the mansions of those above them as you look at the bright distant planets in the eastern and western horizon. Such will be the differences in their ranks. He was asked: Messenger of Allah, will these be the mansions of the Prophets which no one else will be able to reach? He said: Yes indeed, but by Him in Whose hands is my soul there will also be those who had faith in Allah and affirmed the righteousness of the Prophets (Bokhari and Muslim).

1894. Abu Hurairah relates that the Holy Prophet said: A space in Paradise equal to the distance between the two ends of a bow would be better than all that upon which the sun rises and sets (Bokhari and Muslim).

1895. Anas relates that the Holy Prophet said: In Paradise there is a market place where people will gather every week and the northern breeze will scatter perfume over their faces and clothes whereby they will increase in their good looks, then they will return to their families who will also have increased in their good looks and beauty. The members of their families will say to them: You have become more handsome and more beautiful. And they will answer: You too have become more handsome and beautiful during our absence (Muslim).

1896. Sahl ibn Sa'ad relates that the Holy Prophet said: The dwellers of Paradise will look at each other from their mansions as you look at the planets in the sky (Bokhari and Muslim).

1897. Sahl ibn Sa'ad relates: I was present in the company of the Holy Prophet in which he described the conditions of Paradise and said in the end: In it there is that which no eye has seen, no ear has heard nor has the mind of man conceived it. Then he recited: They withdraw themselves from their beds in the latter part of the night for Prayer, and they call on their Lord in fear and hope, and spend out of that which We have bestowed on them. No one knows what bliss is kept hidden from them as a reward for what they used to do (32. 17-18). (Bokhari and Muslim).

1898. Abu Sa'id and Abu Hurairah relate that the Holy Prophet said: When the dwellers of Paradise enter Paradise a crier will announce: You will live for ever and will not die, you will be in health and will not fall ill, you will be young and will not grow old and you will be in comfort and will not encounter any trouble whatever (Muslim).

1899. Abu Hurairah relates that the Holy Prophet said: The best of you in Paradise will be asked: Wish whatever you desire. He will wish and wish and will be asked: Have you wished? He will answer: Yes. He will be told: You have whatever you wished and the like of it over again (Muslim).

1900. Abu Sa'id Khudri relates that the Holy Prophet said: Allah, the Lord of honour and glory, will call the dwellers of Paradise and they will respond: Here we are, our Lord, and all good is in Thy hands. He will ask them: Are you happy? They will answer: Why should we not be happy, our Lord, when You have bestowed upon us that which You have not bestowed on any of Your other creation. He will say to them: Shall I bestow upon you even better than that? They will inquire: What could be better than that? He will say: I bestow upon you My Pleasure and I shall never hereafter be wroth with you (Bokhari and Muslim).

1901. This *hadith* is the same as No. 1055.

1902. Suhaib relates that the Holy Prophet said: When the dwellers of Paradise will have entered Paradise, Allah, the Blessed and the Exalted, will ask them: Do you desire anything more that I should give you? They will answer: Have you not made our countenances bright? Have you not admitted us to Paradise and delivered us from the Fire? Thereupon, Allah will lift the veil from His countenance and the dwellers of Paradise will not have known anything dearer to them than looking at their Lord (Muslim).

SUBJECT INDEX

The following subject matters refer to the relevant chapter numbers. Special attention should be given to the subjects listed under *PROHIBITIONS* and *UNDESIRABLE MATTERS* since in many cases these are the sole index entries.

325

FOOD
Dislike of eating while leaning against a pillow. 108.
Drinking. 111, 112, 113, 114, 115, 116.
Eating. 104, 105, 106, 107, 109.
Not finding fault with —. 101.
Prayer when — has been served. 337.
Saving —. 110.
Table manners. 100.

FORBEARANCE
Forgiveness and —. 75.
Gentleness and —. 74.

FORGIVENESS
— and forbearance. 75.
Seeking —. 369.

FUNERAL PRAYERS (see under *BURIAL*)

GENEROSITY (see under *SPENDING*)

GENTLENESS
— and forbearance. 74.

GIFTS, GIVING
Hastening towards —. 59.
Prohibitions concerning —. 276, 283, 351.

GIRLS
Kind treatment of —. 33.

GOOD
Consultation and paying for —. 97.
Doing — to friends of parents. 42.
Enjoining —. 23, 24.
Increasing — in later life. 12.
New ways of doing —. 19.
Pointing out the way of —. 19.
Variety of —. 13.
Vying to do —. 10.

GOODWILL (see under *BENEVOLENCE*)

GRAVES (see also under *BURIAL*)
Admonition in a graveyard. 159.
Permission for men to visit —. 66.
Prohibitions concerning —. 345.

GREAT, THE
Honouring —. 44

GREETING
— children. 135.

— non-Muslims. 137.
— when arriving and departing. 138.
— when entering a house. 134.
— women. 138.
Manner of —. 131.
Multiplying the — of peace. 130.
Order of —. 132.
Repetition of —. 133.
Shaking hands. 142.

GRIEF
Shedding of tears in —. 152.

GUEST
Honouring —. 94.

HANDS
Right —. 99, 296.
Shaking —. 142.

HOPE
Combining — and fear. 53.
Exaltation of —. 52.
— and good expectation. 51.

HUMILITY
Courtesy and —. 71.

HUNGER
Excellence of —. 56.

HURT
Endurance of —. 76.

HUSBAND AND WIFE
Husband's right concerning wife. 35.
Woman refusing herself to her husband. 333.

HYPOCRISY (see under *FALSEHOOD*)

INJUNCTIONS
Violation of —. 77.

INTERCESSION
—. 30.

INVESTIGATION
Need of —. 260.

INVITATION
Person who is invited being accompanied by another. 103.

JOURNEYING (see under *TRAVEL*)

SNEEZING
— and yawning. 141.

SPEECH (see under *DISCOURSE*)

SPENDING
Moderation in —. 57.
— for family and children. 36.
— in a good cause. 60.
— out of that which is good. 37.

STEADFASTNESS
—. 3.

STRIVING
—. 11.

SUFFERING (see under *THE SICK*)

SUPPLICATION
Miscellaneous matters concerning —. 251.
—. 249.
— against apprehended mischief. 172.
— for absent ones. 250.
— in full confidence. 330.
— on journeying. 169, 171, 173.
— on observing the new moon. 219.
— on retiring and rising. 245. 248.
— on wearing new articles. 124.

TEETH
Brushing of —. 214.
Filing of —. 294.

TRAVEL
Glorification on returning home. 176.
Glorification while climbing and descending. 170.
Helping a companion. 168.
Proceeding to the mosque on return. 177.
Returning home by day. 175.
Rules of journeying. 167.
Setting out on a journey. 165.
Speedy return from a journey. 174.
Supplication of a traveller. 171.
Supplication on arrival. 173.
Supplication when starting a journey. 169.
— in company under a leader. 166.
Woman being prohibited from travelling alone. 178.
Varying the route of return. 98.

TRUST
—. 7.

TRUSTS
Discharging —. 25.

TRUTHFULNESS
—. 4.

UNDESIRABLE MATTERS
Bells. 305.
Camels that eat refuse. 306.
Clothes. 297.
Combinations, wrong. 331.
Dead, praying for the. 67.
Exaggeration. 326.
Fasting on Friday. 343.
Grapes being called karm. 328.
Mosque, conduct in. 308, 310, 356.
Obligations, postponement of. 282.
Penalties, intercession for. 348.
Perfume, refusing. 357.
Plague-stricken town, visiting a. 359.
Praising a person. 358.
Prayer, conduct at. 332, 337, 339, 342.
Self-condemnation. 327.
Swearing. 316.

WATER (see under *FOOD*)

WEAK, THE
Kind treatment of —. 33.
Superiority of — among Muslims. 32.

WEEPING
Shedding of tears in grief. 152.
— and trembling over the remains of wrong-doers. 164.
— for fear of Allah. 54.

WIDOWS AND WIVES (see under *WOMEN*)

WOMEN
Greeting —. 136.
Husband's right concerning wife. 35.
Kindness towards —. 34.
Period of mourning to be observed by a widow. 352.
Prohibitions concerning —. 178, 288, 289, 290, 329, 333, 334.

WORSHIP
Moderation in —. 14.
— during disturbances. 238.